Language, Logic and Epistemology

Recent publications by Christopher Norris

DECONSTRUCTION: THEORY AND PRACTICE 3rd Edn

HILARY PUTNAM: REALISM, REASON, AND THE USES OF UNCERTAINTY

TRUTH MATTERS: REALISM, ANTI-REALISM AND RESPONSE-DEPENDENCE

DECONSTRUCTION AND THE UNFINISHED PROJECT OF MODERNITY

MINDING THE GAP: EPISTEMOLOGY AND PHILOSOPHY OF SCIENCE IN THE TWO TRADITIONS

QUANTUM THEORY AND THE FLIGHT FROM REALISM; PHILOSOPHICAL RESPONSES TO QUANTUM MECHANICS

AGAINST RELATIVISM: PHILOSOPHY OF SCIENCE, DECONSTRUCTION AND CRITICAL THEORY

NEW IDOLS OF THE CAVE: ON THE LIMITS OF ANTI-REALISM

RESOURCES OF REALISM: PROSPECTS FOR 'POST-ANALYTIC' PHILOSOPHY

Edited with David Roden

JACQUES DERRIDA

Edited with Christa Knellwolf

THE CAMBRIDGE HISTORY OF LITERARY CRITICISM, Vol 9: TWENTIETH CENTURY HISTORICAL, PHILOSOPHICAL AND PSYCHOLOGICAL PERSPECTIVES

Language, Logic and Epistemology: A Modal-Realist Approach

Christopher Norris

Distinguished Research Professor in Philosophy, Cardiff University, UK

First published 2004 by
PALGRAVE MACMILLAN
Houndmills, Basingstoke, Hampshire RG21 6XS and
175 Fifth Avenue, New York, N.Y. 10010
Companies and representatives throughout the world

PALGRAVE MACMILLAN is the global academic imprint of the Palgrave
Macmillan division of St. Martin's Press, LLC and of Palgrave Macmillan Ltd.
Macmillan® is a registered trademark in the United States, United Kingdom
and other countries. Palgrave is a registered trademark in the European
Union and other countries.

ISBN 1–4039–2165–2 hardback

This book is printed on paper suitable for recycling and made from fully
managed and sustained forest sources.

A catalogue record for this book is available from the British Library.

Library of Congress Cataloging-in-Publication Data
Norris, Christopher, 1947–
    Language, logic and epistemology : a modal-realist approach / Christopher Norris.
        p.   cm.
    Includes bibliographical references and index.
    ISBN 1–4039–2165–2
    1. Philosophy, Modern—20th century.   2. Deconstruction.
    3. Poststructuralism.   4. Language—Philosophy.   5. Knowledge,
    Theory of.   6. Logic.   I. Title.

    B804.N67 2004
    190'.9'04—dc22   2003060853

10   9   8   7   6   5   4   3   2   1
13   12   11   10   09   08   07   06   05   04

Printed and bound in Great Britain by
Antony Rowe Ltd, Chippenham and Eastbourne

For Alison, Clare and Jenny

Contents

Acknowledgements

As usual my work on this book has been helped, stimulated, jogged along, and generally made more enjoyable by regular discussion with my colleagues in the Philosophy Section at Cardiff. It is a tribute to their spirit of shared intellectual commitment – as well as their resilience and good humour – that such discussion continues to flourish despite what appears a concerted effort to prevent it on the part of government policy-makers and tame bureaucrats. I should like to thank Barry Wilkins in particular for his friendship and encouragement over the years; also Robin Attfield for much good advice and constructive commentary on work in progress. Alex Miller left Cardiff for a post in Australia when the book was just beginning to shape up but I expect he will recognise how much of it (especially the sections on rule-following and response-dependence) grew out of our various exchanges and productive disagreements. My post-graduate students – among them (most recently) Jason Barker, Gideon Calder, Paul Gorton, Theo Grammenos, Carol Jones, Laurence Peddle, and Rea Walldén – have helped a great deal in enabling me to see where some point needed clarification or some line of argument strengthening. The chapter on deconstructive musicology was in large part inspired (or provoked) by discussions with Ken Gloag, my colleague in the Music Department at Cardiff and convenor of our jointly taught MA course in Music and Cultural Politics. He will probably not find much to agree with here but the chapter owes a lot to his shrewd comments in and out of the seminar room.

David Roden cast an expert eye over sections of Chapter 2 where I venture a formalised (modal-logical) rendition of Derrida's arguments concerning the thematics of 'supplementarity' in Rousseau and of 'iterability' in the discourse of Austinian speech-act theory. You can teach an old dog one or two new tricks but it helps no end to have a young dog around to gnaw at these technical bones. Recasting the passages from Derrida in symbolic notation was a tough exercise but (I trust) well worth the effort if it helps to convince at least a few anti-Derridean 'analytic' diehards that they have missed something important. Anyway I am grateful to David for this, as likewise for the huge amount of reading and the powers of acute critical scholarship which he brought to our recently coedited four-volume anthology of writings on Derrida. Special mention also to Janos Barcsak, David Edwards, Dan Latimer, Peter Murray, Daniele Procida, Alison Scott-Baumann, David Skilton, Christine Southwell, Manuel Barbeito Varela, Alison Venables, and Robin Wood for reasons too many and varied to recount. My copy-editor Selvin Vedamanickam and the production contact Jophcy Joseph, at Integra Software Services in Pondicherry, were helpful, friendly and patient far beyond the call of duty and also provided my first experience of how these things are done in an age of global electronic communications. My debts nearer home – to Alison, Clare, and Jenny – should go without saying by now but I shall say them once again with undiminished gratitude and affection.

Meanwhile it would be wrong to let this occasion pass without expressing my unreserved support for those millions of people worldwide who have come out in opposition to the unjust and illegal war against Iraq that is currently being waged 'in our name' by the US and British governments. If there is any hope to be had in these bad times then it rests with the collective courage and resistance – along with the sense of implacable moral outrage – that have brought the protestors together across otherwise large political differences of view. I should especially like to thank my comrades in Cor Cochion Caerdydd for their untiring dedication to the anti-war cause; also those others in and around Cardiff who have devoted vast amounts of time and energy to organising local meetings and events. Ten years ago I published a book about the first (1991) Gulf War which, among other things, took postmodernists to task for adopting an extreme anti-realist, relativist, or linguistic-constructivist position and thereby effectively depriving themselves of any factual or moral ground upon which to mount such resistance. This present volume is for the most part pitched at a philosophic level far removed from the context of current world-political events. All the same there are some continuities worth remarking, in particular as concerns my discussion (Chapter 3) of Noam Chomsky's work in theoretical linguistics and cognitive psychology. I trust that my taking issue with Chomsky on certain relatively technical points will not obscure my immense admiration for his brave and uniquely authoritative stand against this and other recent shameful episodes in the history of man's inhumanity to man.

Cardiff, Wales   April 2003

Note

Several chapters or versions thereof have appeared previously in journals or edited volumes. I am grateful for permission to reprint this material in revised form to Sage Publishers and to the editors and publishers of *Metaphilosophy*, *Philosophy at Yeditepe*, and *Pretexts*.

Introduction

This volume brings together a number of chapters which I should happily describe as 'inter-disciplinary' if that term had not acquired – to my mind at least – certain negative or worrisome connotations. These have to do with the currently widespread idea that the boundaries between disciplines are so many artificial constructs of comparatively recent date whose chief function (so the argument goes) is to shore up standard academic divisions of labour. Such thinking derives from a wide range of sources, among them post-structuralism, postmodernism, cultural studies, the 'strong' programme in sociology of science, Kuhnian paradigm-relativism, the 'linguistic turn' (after late Wittgenstein) in various fields of thought, and Richard Rorty's neopragmatist notion of 'truth' as just the compliment we pay to this or that currently favoured style of talk. It has also taken heart from developments in post-empiricist epistemology which – following Quine – emphasise the 'underdetermination' of theory by evidence and the 'theory-laden' character of observation-statements. In Chapter 6 I discuss the way that analytic philosophy has tended very often to swing back and forth between a 'normal', constructive or problem-solving discourse and a whole range of (by its own lights) untypically extreme reactive proposals. If this account suggests an analogy with Kuhn on the cyclic alternation of 'normal' and 'revolutionary' periods in the history of science then it does so more with a view to locating the sources of such chronic instability within the analytic enterprise.

Not that Quine would have taken at all kindly to finding himself lumped among the cultural relativists or the purveyors of a wholesale postmodern scepticism with regard to standards of scientific method and truth. All the same his attack on the two last 'dogmas' of logical empiricism – the analytic/synthetic distinction and the idea of scientific statements or hypotheses as individually testable against the evidence – is often thought to have opened the way (*via* Kuhn) to a full-scale doctrine of paradigm-incommensurability and hence to the claim that there exist no objective (i.e., non-paradigm-internal) criteria of rational theory-choice. Thus, according to Quine, we can always conserve some anomalous empirical result by redistributing predicates or truth-values across the entire existing 'fabric' of belief. This might involve renouncing a hitherto cherished item of physical theory, or even – at the limit – suspending an axiom of classical logic, such as bivalence or excluded middle. And, conversely, we can always 'save' some cherished theoretical belief by putting the empirical anomaly down to defects in our measuring apparatus, the limits of precise observation, or – again at the limit – perceptual hallucination. From here it is arguably no great distance to the kind of cultural-relativist thinking that would challenge the very idea of scientific method as possessing certain distinctive standards – of empirical warrant, replicability, and respect for the ground-rules of evidential reasoning – which set it apart from other, less rigorous (e.g., sociological) modes of enquiry. What this amounts to, in effect, is a wholesale inversion of the old 'unity of science' programme which proposed a hard-to-soft scale of priority with physics at the top, then chemistry, biology, economics, certain (empirically grounded) branches of psychology, sociology, and anthropology, and then – very much at the bottom of the scale – such manifestly unscientific 'disciplines' as ethics, aesthetics, and literary criticism.

To be sure, this was a crudely simplified model and one whose fortunes were closely tied to the rise and fall of old-style logical positivism. Few philosophers of science would nowadays subscribe to such a doctrine, especially in the wake of Quine's 'Two Dogmas' and after so much work that has emphasised the problems with any appeal to the empirical evidence which fails to take account of its theoretically mediated character, not to mention those various historical or socio-cultural factors that might have played a role in the scientific 'context of discovery'. On the other hand thinking has sometimes swung so far in the opposite direction – toward a 'sociology-first' perspective – that it seems to herald the emergence of a new orthodoxy with its own, equally partial or distorting methodological bias. What very often seems to motivate such work is a covert desire, on its practitioners' part, to occupy the high ground of explanatory method while appearing to operate on a principle of parity that grants the physical sciences their place in a strictly egalitarian or non-hierarchical range of discourses. However this claim must look highly dubious if one considers how the principle of parity works out in practice. For it is a chief tenet of the strong-sociological approach that its method applies to *all* scientific theories, whether those (like the phlogiston theory of combustion) that we now think of as totally discredited, or those (like Newton's theories of space-time and gravity) that have now been superseded while retaining a certain limited field of application, or again, those – like Special Relativity or the DNA model of genetic inheritance – which presently count among the best established scientific truths. For, according to the strong sociologists, there is no question of confining this approach to cases where scientists got things wrong and where explanations should therefore take account of historical, cultural, ideological, or other such 'extraneous' factors. On the contrary: the approach is equally valid when applied to (what we think of as) 'good' science since here also we have to take account of that whole range of motivating interests and incentives that might have played a role in persuading scientists to pursue some particular line of enquiry.

Yet of course this puts the ball very firmly in the sociologists' court since it gives them the last explanatory word as to what constitutes the crucial difference between theories that have retained 'scientific' credibility and those that have since fallen by the wayside or else been subject to continuing refinement and modification. That difference lies not so much in the fact that some theories can be shown to manifest a greater degree of theoretical, empirical, or predictive warrant but rather in the fact that they have gained acceptance amongst a wide enough section of the scientific community to count as valid for all practical (i.e., socially relevant) purposes. Thus the principle of parity works out in effect as a kind of all-purpose device for demoting scientific truth-claims – along with those arguments typically advanced by mainstream philosophers and historians of science – and for boosting the interests of sociology as a discipline inherently less prone to delusions of epistemological grandeur. The usual response to any such charge of academic empire-building is to invoke a self-reflexive principle whereby the strong sociologists of knowledge take their own claims as like-wise subject to sociological analysis and explanation. However that argument cuts both ways, on the one hand seeking to disown the idea of privileged self-exemption, while on the other reinforcing the general claim that sociology alone has the resources to handle such a wholesale critique of epistemic authority, its own authority included.

The same can be said of those cultural-relativist and 'strong' descriptivist approaches that cheerfully acknowledge the standard counter-argument brought against them by realist philosophers of science, that is, that by treating *all* truth-claims as 'relative' to some given discourse, paradigm, or language-game they deprive themselves of any epistemic ground upon which to mount their case. Here again their response – like that of the soci-ologists – is a version of the self-reflexivity thesis which denies that they want or need such a ground since theirs is a discourse with no further aim than to challenge existing conceptions of truth and thereby open the cultural conversation to as many different voices as possible. This is also a main plank in Paul Feyerabend's case for 'epistemological anarchism', or the idea that science gets along best when it takes a lesson from John Stuart Mill and advocates the maximum diversity of opinions and beliefs, rather than seeking vainly after some uniform method that would place strict limits on the range of valid (scientifically admissible) options. It is a notion carried furthest by those – like Richard Rorty – who press right through with the strong-descriptivist or paradigm-relativist case for a levelling of the standards that 'conventionally' apply in different areas of discourse (see Chapter 6). For Rorty, there is nothing that prevents us from switching vocabularies once in a while so as to jazz up the conversation and redescribe the objects of one discipline (maybe subatomic physics or molecular biology) in the language of another (maybe cultural anthropology or literary theory). After all, if one takes the Rortian nominalist line and denies that there exist any natural kinds or any language that would somehow 'cut nature at the joints', then it follows that these are just so many optional language-games that can only be assessed by their capacity to throw up novel or challenging descriptions, rather than their merely notional power to advance the interests of scientific knowledge. Indeed, those interests are much better served if we strive to keep science in a perpetual state of Kuhnian 'revolutionary' ferment by constantly junking habitual modes of talk – those that have entered its 'normal' or literal vocabulary – and drawing on the widest possible range of metaphors from other fields. In which case the very idea of a 'discipline' – whether in the natural or the social and human sciences – is one that we can well do without since it imposes needless restrictions on our freedom to produce ever more inventive or creative modes of metaphorical redescription.

As should be evident by now I am (to say the least) unpersuaded by this currently fashionable turn toward various forms of paradigm-relativist or socio-linguistic-constructivist thinking. Still I should not wish to give the impression – one much exploited by Rorty and his fellow anti-disciplinarians – that realism stands or falls on the attempt to enforce a rigorous policing of academic bounds. After all, the move toward a more 'interdisciplinary' approach must be a good thing if it helps to loosen up the standard, overly professionalised division of labour and encourages people to talk to each other across otherwise non-communicating fields of interest. Indeed it is a notable feature of advanced work in the natural and the human sciences alike that cutting-edge research or increasing specialisation very often involves a good working knowledge of developments in other areas. Thus molecular biologists can scarcely get by without a well-informed grasp of present-day thinking in subatomic physics, while philosophers of language will be ill-advised to ignore what is going on in disciplines like cognitive psychology or neuro-science (see Chapters 3 and 5). One could continue listing the various ways in which specialisation leads, paradoxically, to an ever-increasing degree of reliance on interdisciplinary channels of exchange and on the willingness to keep those channels open despite the various countervailing pressures exerted by the need to secure recognition among members of this or that academic peer-group. Just recently this whole debate has been bedevilled by a renewed outbreak of the so-called 'science wars' with scientists lining up to denounce people in the broadly 'humanities' sector for their luddite rejection of science and all its works while sociologists, cultural theorists, and others attack the scientists for their arrogant presumption of possessing some uniquely privileged claim to truth. This latter reaction has no doubt

been fuelled by popular fears about the harmful, indeed potentially cata-
strophic, results of applied scientific research in fields from nuclear physics
to genetic engineering. At the same time scientists – physicists especially – have
tended to interpret *any* such challenge as issuing from downright ignorance,
prejudice, or science-envy among those with no such impressive record of
well-documented progress. Yet it is clear that sociologists and cultural historians do have something of interest to contribute to our better understanding
of how science actually gets done, even if they are sometimes apt to push
this claim too far and mistake the socio-cultural 'context of discovery' for the
scientific 'context of justification'.

Of course there are those – among them the 'strong' sociologists of knowledge – who would reject this distinction and, along with it, the whole idea
of science as an enterprise aimed toward truth at the end of enquiry. Others
of a somewhat less sceptical mind would all the same question whether
scientific theories can really sustain any such truth-based (however qualified
or fallibilist) construal. These latter include anti-realists like Michael Dummett
who advance metaphysical and logical arguments against the existence of
objective (recognition-transcendent) truths, and 'constructive empiricists'
like Bas van Fraassen who urge that empirical adequacy, rather than truth, is
the best that science should hope to achieve in the way of observational or
predictive warrant. I shall say no more on this topic now since it involves
some fine discriminations of argument and receives its share of detailed
attention in the following chapters. For the moment my point is simply
that these, more nuanced or technical varieties of anti-realist thinking can
readily be taken as lending support to the kinds of wholesale social-
constructivist or cultural-relativist doctrine outlined above. This in turn
goes along with the desire to subvert established disciplinary distinctions –
like that between the physical and the human or social sciences – and
moreover, in many cases, to grant the latter a privileged status when it comes
to 'explaining' the processes of scientific knowledge-acquisition.

My case – in brief – is that this is very much to put the cart before the
horse, or to treat certain highly contestable theories in sociology, linguistics,
or even philosophical semantics as somehow a better, more reliable source
of knowledge than the well-tried methods and procedures of the physical
sciences. Also it falls in with a certain mode of thought – most evident in
Rorty's writings – which carries the 'linguistic turn' to a point where truth is
conceived as *nothing more* than a projection of our various language-games,
vocabularies, or preferential modes of talk. For this opens the door to various
kinds of irrationalist doctrine or pseudo-science (including the more dubious
forms of 'alternative' medicine) which draw sustenance from the misplaced
belief that wishing can somehow make it so. After all, if we are free to
'redescribe' reality in any way we choose, subject only to certain loose
constraints on the range of available descriptions, then there is nothing –
no objective truth about (say) the genetic structure of the AIDS virus or its

capacity to mutate in response to different sorts of vaccine – that can or should prevent us from interpreting the evidence in ways more conducive to our peace of mind. One can see why such ideas should exert a strong appeal among those predisposed toward a general suspicion of 'conventional' science and hence eager to invest their faith elsewhere. Still they amount to no more than a false source of comfort and – at worst – a callous exploitation of the human propensity to accept whatever suits our psychological needs and desires.

It is now more than a hundred years since this issue first arose between William James with his pragmatist notion of the 'will to believe' and those opponents of James – like Bertrand Russell and W.K. Clifford – who argued, firstly, that belief was in no sense volitional (since arrived at through a process beyond our deliberative control) and, secondly, that truth was an objective matter and not to be confused (on pain of gross self-deception) with what is 'good in the way of belief'. It seems to me that this debate is still very much alive and that Rorty's neopragmatism is best seen as an update on the basic Jamesian doctrine which also incorporates a range of ideas from post-Wittgensteinian philosophy of language, post-Kuhnian philosophy of science, and other sources of the currently widespread linguistic or descriptivist turn. I should also want to claim – more generally – that a realist approach to these issues can provide a better, more adequate understanding of science not only in epistemological terms (i.e., as regards our knowledge of the growth of scientific knowledge) but also from an ethical or socio-political standpoint. Quite simply, there is no purpose to be served by criticising science, its practical applications or its wider social consequences unless such criticism is firmly based on a realist assessment of its powers and capacities in that regard. And it is hard to see how this might square with an outlook that treats all talk of (supposed) physical realia – from atoms, molecules, and viruses to stars and galaxies – as nothing more than nominal entities which just happen to play a prominent role in some currently favoured language-game or process of socio-cultural negotiation.

II

However this is to anticipate large tracts of argument which I hope that the reader will wish to pursue in more detail. What I have offered so far is a brief explanation of why these chapters can fairly be described as 'interdisciplinary' but *not* as 'anti-disciplinary' in any sense of that term. My point is that we can easily go wrong in assessing the work of some particular thinker if we fail to apply the appropriate kinds of generic criteria or standards of evaluation. One striking example is the prevalent idea among many analytic philosophers that Jacques Derrida's writings offer no semblance of logical argumentation but should rather be seen as so many exercises in 'textualist' sophistry and gamesmanship. On the contrary, I argue: what we find in

Derrida – especially in early texts such as *Of Grammatology* – is a careful and meticulous working-through of certain fundamental issues in philosophy of logic, among them issues concerning the status of 'deviant' (many-valued) and modal logics (Chapter 1). Thus when Derrida discusses the 'logic of supplementarity' in certain texts of Rousseau his commentary elicits some extreme complexities of modal implication that cannot be accounted for in terms of any classical or bivalent (truth-functional) logic but are none the less pursued with the utmost analytic rigour. Indeed they emerge all the more sharply for his showing how Rousseau's discourse is constrained to manifest those complicating features *despite and against* its overt expressions of authorial intent. Yet Derrida is insistent that this 'supplementary' logic is one whose operations have to be revealed through a reading that presses as far as possible toward a classically consistent (bivalent) construal of Rousseau's various claims. It is only at the limit – where this attempt breaks down against the evidence of logical anomalies in Rousseau's text – that Derrida perforce switches over to a deviant, 'supplementary' logic that is able to accommodate these problems. Thus he shows nothing like the strong inclination of a thinker such as Michael Dummett to suspend bivalence whenever it is a question of some statement that happens to exceed our best means of empirical verification or – in the case of mathematics – our best available proof procedures. Philosophers have often shied away from any adequate engagement with Derrida's work through their fixed idea (mostly picked up at second hand) that his writings fall lamentably short of the analytic rigour that distinguishes philosophy of language or logic from textual commentary in a 'literary' mode.

So this is one case in which false generic expectations have resulted in a widespread failure to grasp the significance of a mode of thinking which just happens not to accord with the norms of a prevalent academic discourse. Another such instance – discussed in Chapter 5 – is that of the 'New Musicology' where deconstructionist ideas have been taken up and deployed in a manner that shows less than adequate regard for their specific (primarily language-oriented) context of valid application. Here I argue that this wholesale transference of ideas from one discipline to another is apt to produce a theoretical discourse which ignores the difference between music as a mode of perceptual (albeit conceptually informed) experience and verbal language as a mode of signification where perceptual qualities play (at most) a strictly subordinate role. Hence the notion that concepts like 'organic form' can have no reference to the music itself, to its intrinsic structures, or our perceptual responses to them. Rather – these theorists maintain – such concepts are solely and exclusively the product of a certain 'aesthetic ideology', one that music analysts naively project onto any work whose canonical status is taken as sufficient guarantee that it merits their devoted attention. The same goes for other presumptive criteria of musical worth such as structural unity, thematic integration, or long-range tonal development, all of them denounced as belonging to a certain hegemonic discourse (that of mainstream academic musicology) which unfailingly finds its own values reflected and confirmed by just those canonical works.

What's more, so it is argued, this discourse takes a further, decidedly sinister turn when it is applied not only to particular works but to entire musical cultures or national traditions, such as the Austro-German line of descent which has always figured as a touchstone of aesthetic worth for critics from Schenker down. Thus the analyst's taken-for-granted values of organic form, thematic development, motivic growth, and so forth, are complicit with a 'national-aestheticist' conception of great works as authentically expressing the spirit of a great musical culture. To resist that dangerous conception – it follows – is also to reject (or to deconstruct) the very notion of music as possessing those qualities most prized by the exponents of mainstream music analysis. In which case it is just another symptom of 'aesthetic ideology' if critics (or listeners) mistakenly suppose that our experience of music might benefit – or our musical perceptions be sharpened and refined – through the kinds of improved structural grasp that analysis purports to provide. However there is something perverse and doctrinaire about a theory with extra-musical sources, that is, with its origins in 'literary' deconstruction, which none the less presumes to reject or invalidate a large body of musical analysis that at best can do much to extend and enhance our powers of musical appreciation. If the reception-history of Derrida's work among most philosophers bears witness to one form of misunderstanding brought about by skewed generic expectations then the emergence of 'deconstructive musicology' offers another, just as striking example of the way that over-zealous cross-disciplinary initiatives can sometimes go drastically awry. With respect to the latter, I suggest that this 'linguisticist' bias can best be offset by some knowledge of developments in another discipline – cognitive psychology – which allows for the fact that musical perceptions are always to some extent conceptually informed, while none the less treating perceptual experience with due regard for its relative autonomy, or (in the current jargon) its relatively 'encapsulated' character. An approach along these lines does more to explain how the resistance to 'aesthetic ideology' might come about through a better, more perceptive or intelligent grasp of just those salient structural features that challenge orthodox conceptions of organic form. At least it has the decided advantage of *not* deconstructing our perceptual responses – or our modes of analytically informed musical experience – to the point where they count for nothing as compared with the power of ideological demystification vested in certain discourses of music theory.

I have perhaps said enough to give the reader some idea of what to expect in the following chapters. They are not all of them directly or explicitly concerned with the topic of interdisciplinarity, though they all do have a bearing on that topic, most often (as suggested above) by way of sounding a certain cautionary note. Chapter 4 focuses on the topic of response-dependence, that is, the extent to which veridical judgements in certain areas of discourse (prototypically those involving Lockean 'secondary qualities' like colour, taste, or tactile sensation) have to be construed with reference to normalised or optimal modes of human perceptual response. Thus, for instance, the appropriate standard of correctness for statements such as 'this object is red' would be spelled out as a quantified biconditional of the form: 'x is red iff (i.e., if and only if) x appears red to a normally sighted or visually unimpaired subject who views x under normal lighting conditions and in the absence of any proximate light-source that might create interference effects or distorted colour-perceptions'. Response-dependence (RD) theory has lately been proposed as the means of establishing a third way between objectivist or 'metaphysical' realism on the one hand and various anti-realist or verificationist (e.g., Dummettian) positions on the other. In its basic form the theory holds that as concerns any given area of discourse we can specify certain conditions of epistemic or assertoric warrant which decide what shall count as a valid judgement or an instance of correct, that is, normal, competent, or epistemically adequate response. This claim has been advanced across a range of disciplines, among them epistemology, cognitive psychology, philosophy of science and mathematics, moral and political theory, and the social sciences. Thus in each case it seeks to defuse the issue between realists and anti-realists by spelling out just those criteria that have to be met in order for a judgement to pass the test of warranted assertibility. However – I argue – the RD approach is one that inclines very strongly toward an anti-realist standpoint and which otherwise amounts to a trivial thesis equating truth with 'best opinion' (or optimal response) and defining 'best judgement' in terms of idealised perceptual, epistemic, or rational warrant. What the theory cannot accommodate is any substantive (that is, non-circular) version of the realist case for the existence of objective truth-values that might always exceed our recognitional capacities or means of finding them out.

Here I concentrate chiefly on the implications of this debate for philosophy of mathematics and the natural sciences, as well as its bearing on issues in moral and political theory. A constant point of reference is Plato's dialogue *Euthyphro* where Socrates propounds an objectivist view (that the gods approve pious acts *just because* those acts are pious and they [the gods] by very definition possess an infallible virtue-tracking capacity) while Euthryphro puts the opposite case (that those acts must be counted pious *just because* they are approved by the gods and there exists no higher tribunal). When transposed to the context of present-day ethical philosophy this works out as the difference of views between those who espouse a realist conception of moral values – so that even the best qualified respondents might just be wrong – and those who take it that there is simply no appeal to standards of moral virtue or political justice that might (conceivably) transcend any given consensus of best opinion. Elsewhere the same question arises with respect to mathematical statements or theorems, that is, the issue as to whether they possess an objective (recognition-transcendent) truth-value or whether such values must be taken to obtain only in so far as there exists an adequate proof-procedure in any given case. Some philosophers – including Crispin Wright – have put the case for response-dependence as a useful means of addressing this issue since it allows for a duly flexible approach whereby different areas of discourse can be ranked on a scale that runs all the way from those where perceptual or judgemental responses play a strictly ineliminable role to those where standards of objectivity seem to exert a more compelling claim. Thus Wright introduces additional terms – such as 'superassertibility' or 'cognitive command' – which are meant to capture these intuitive distinctions and provide a more adequate, fine-tuned basis for comparison. However – I argue – this approach still runs into the circularity problem and/or the realist's objection that it ultimately makes truth dependent on the scope and limits of human knowledge. I conclude that an RD approach does nothing to resolve these long-standing problems but that it does serve a useful purpose by throwing them into sharper relief.

Chapter 2, on Wittgenstein, is likely to provoke the sharpest reactions since it examines a range of Wittgensteinian arguments – some of which occupy a prominent role in the thinking of Wright and other RD theorists – and finds them plainly inadequate on various grounds. In particular I take issue with Wittgenstein's treatment of mathematics and his idea that there are no standards of correctness or truth in mathematical and other kinds of rule-following activity save those supplied by an appeal to some existing language-game or cultural 'form of life'. Whence Saul Kripke's famous exegesis in which he does little more than repeat Wittgenstein's 'sceptical paradox' – that is, that there exist as many ways of continuing the series 'n + 2' as there exist different possible (albeit 'deviant') understandings of it – and then propose a 'sceptical solution' which again takes communal 'agreement in judgement' as the sole standard of correctness. There is, I should acknowledge, a polemical edge to some of my remarks in this chapter, especially as concerns Wittgenstein's therapeutic claim to have coaxed philosophers down from their needless 'metaphysical' anxieties, or – in his well-known metaphor – to have shown the fly the way out of the fly-bottle. On the contrary: no thinker has done more to raise hypercultivated doubts and misgivings with regard to mathematics, the physical sciences, and (not least) the idea that moral values may be held to transcend any given context of communal judgement or belief. Indeed, the extent of Wittgenstein's influence can be seen most clearly in those forms of cultural-relativist thinking that have resulted from the linguistic turn across various disciplines. It also emerges to striking effect when thinkers of a basically different persuasion feel themselves obliged to take a lengthy detour *via* Wittgenstein before proposing some qualified defence of a realist (or quasi-realist) construal of the subject-area concerned.

III

Thus I have quite a lot to say about the way that certain kinds of mediating approach – such as the appeal to response-dependence as an answer to problems from Wittgenstein – can well end up (despite their professed intent) by blurring crucial distinctions. For there is a constant tendency in work of this kind to suggest that, for instance, mathematical knowledge can usefully be thought of by analogy with colour-perception, or moral judgements by analogy with more or less reliable modes of sensory response. And this despite the fact – as their proponents readily concede – that such comparisons should serve only as the starting point for further, more discriminate or contrastive treatment. Yet the tendency still comes through in various RD claims to the effect that (for instance) mathematical realists can have all the 'objectivity' they need if they will only acknowledge the role of human judgement – even at the limit of idealised rational acceptability – as determining the truth-value of mathematical statements. Or again, moral realists can maintain their position – and head off any attack from the subjectivist, projectivist, or cultural-relativist quarter – just so long as they temper their claims for the 'objectivity' of moral values with a due recognition that all such values must be indexed to a standard of optimised human response. However it is clear that in both cases the realist will scarcely be satisfied with this compromise solution. That is to say, she will regard it either as trivially circular – on a reading that equates truth *tout court* with idealised epistemic warrant – or else as yielding crucial ground to the anti-realist through its allowance that truth is always subject to the scope and limits of human judgement, no matter how expert or well-qualified.

Such debates have become pretty much the hallmark of recent analytic philosophy and may therefore seem strikingly remote from the kinds of topic pursued in my chapters on Derrida and the New Musicology. However it is a main purpose of this book to point up connections between them and to argue that they all raise important issues with regard to the wider question of just how far philosophers and theorists can properly or usefully go in the effort to break down existing disciplinary boundaries. Thus the chief problem with RD theory is the way that it tends to start out from a certain (Lockean) construal of secondary qualities, that is, one rooted in the theory of sensory perception, and then extend that approach – with whatever detailed reservations – to areas of discourse such as mathematics and morals. In the case of deconstruction as applied to music theory the upshot is most often an opposite tendency to devalue the role of perceptual responses – even (or especially) those informed by analytic concepts and categories – and hence to lose touch with anything germane to our actual experience of music. This results from a failure to grasp the pertinence of deconstruction as a mode of textual close-reading which involves the exposure of logical anomalies specific to verbal discourse and which therefore cannot be transposed directly to a realm where phenomenal cognition plays a primary (albeit conceptually mediated) role.

My chapter on Derrida is likewise intended to clear away certain prevalent sources of confusion. Of course I am not denying that his work has implications for disciplines other than philosophy of logic and language. To make such a claim would clearly be absurd, given the extraordinary range of topics that Derrida has engaged over the past four decades. Rather I suggest that we will not get far toward grasping the specific pertinence of Derrida's later (more thematically varied) work unless we read it with a mind alert to those particular modes of deviant or 'supplementary' logic that receive their fullest, most rigorous exposition in writings like *Of Grammatology* and 'Signature Event Context'. Thus it is wrong to suppose that deconstruction can be readily enlisted in support of the claims put forward by 'strong' sociologists of knowledge or by those who take a lead from Quine and Kuhn in treating scientific theories as always 'underdetermined' by the evidence and hence as ultimately subject to negotiation on non-scientific, that is, socio-cultural or ideological terms. Here (to repeat) I concur with defenders of the realist position in finding it frankly preposterous that sociological theories whose status is at best highly contestable should be accorded a superior explanatory power as compared with the manifest record of achievement in the physical or natural sciences.

Of course this argument will not impress the strong sociologists or those sceptical philosophers of science who are adept at producing counter-examples to the idea of scientific knowledge as converging on truth at the end of enquiry. Nor will it carry much weight with anti-realists like Dummett who deny that we can possibly conceive of truths which transcend our best methods of proof, ascertainment, or empirical verification, or again, with 'constructive empiricists' such as Bas van Fraassen who decree that science should advance no claims for the existence of entities too small, too large, or too fast-moving to show up by means of technologically unassisted human observation (see Chapter 6). Here again it seems to me that such arguments only get a hold through the kinds of confusion that inevitably result when philosophers fail to distinguish with sufficient clarity between perceptual, theoretical, logical, and other (e.g., abductive or causal-explanatory) grounds for rational assent. Thus Dummett's case for the non-existence of recognition-transcendent truths goes along with his strong metaphysical commitment to a verificationist position and his use of logico-semantic arguments to support that position despite its inherently problematic character when applied to our knowledge of the growth of knowledge in mathematics and the physical sciences. And van Fraassen's constructive-empiricist programme ends up by endorsing a curiously anthropocentric conception of scientific knowledge, one that restricts its range of putative realia to just those objects that happen to fall within the scope of human perceptual capacities.

However this is to ignore the fact that a great many crucial advances in scientific knowledge have come about precisely through the break with such naive ideas of perceptual self-evidence, or through a willingness to set such evidence aside in the interests of attaining a heightened power of theoretical or causal-explanatory grasp. Indeed van Fraassen's argument must appear yet more arbitrary or rationally under-motivated when he offers a concession to the effect that objects perceived through optical microscopes or telescopes are admissible as falling within the stipulated range whereas those – like atoms, molecules, or remote galaxies – that require the use of electron microscopes or radio telescopes are therefore to be treated as theoretical posits and denied any claim to 'real' (empirically verified) existence. Yet why should we suppose that there is anything inherently less reliable about sophisticated types of apparatus whose working principles are well understood and whose design, development, and construction incorporates a vast amount of acquired scientific and technological know-how? Any theory – like van Fraassen's – that discounts such considerations in favour of 'straightforward' perceptual self-evidence must also disregard the sheer amount of complex cognitive processing that goes on between the stage of passive sensory uptake (or the Quinean 'barrage' of incoming stimuli) and the stage at which observers may be said to perceive objects in their visual field. For this is the other side of Quine's point about the 'theory-laden' character of observation-statements, namely the fact that it need not be construed in wholesale paradigm-relativist terms but rather as supporting a realist case for the progressive refinement and extension of our knowledge through modes of enhanced theoretical as well as applied technological understanding.

Of course that alternative account will not look in the least degree plausible if one accepts Quine's 'naturalised epistemology' at full strength, that is, his behaviourist theory of knowledge according to which such putative 'advances' can only be a matter of pragmatic adjustment between incoming stimuli and the overall 'web' or 'fabric' of beliefs at any given time. On this view there is simply no room for such normative constraints upon the process of rational theory-formation as might be required in order to validate the realist case. However its deficit in this regard – its failure to provide an adequate account of what distinguishes valid (knowledge-conducive) from merely pragmatic or face-saving adjustments – is often adduced by way of objection to Quine's radical-empiricist outlook. All of which brings us back to the issue of just how far perceptual experience is theoretically informed and theoretical understanding advanced or sometimes retarded by various kinds of (supposed) perceptual self-evidence. So there is a sense in which all these chapters can be seen to turn on the various kinds of relationship that exist between theory (or conceptual analysis) and the real or presumptive self-evidence of perceptual warrant. In some cases – as with the New Musicology – my argument tends toward the rehabilitation of perceptual claims against a highly abstract or theoreticist discourse that tilts too far in the former direction. Elsewhere, with regard to epistemology and philosophy of science, I recommend an approach that makes due allowance for the theoretically informed character of all perceptions but also – perfectly consistent with this – the possibility of assessing hypotheses and truth-claims according to criteria that are *not* just those of Quinean pragmatic adjustment across the entire fabric of beliefs-held-true at any given time. This possibility depends on the existence of certain jointly realist and rational constraints on the process of theory-construction that find a good measure of support in the kinds of argument lately advanced by cognitive psychologists.

Hence Chapter 3 on Noam Chomsky's modular (nativist and internalist) approach to issues in philosophy of mind and his objections to the causal (externalist) theory of reference proposed by Kripke and Putnam. Those objections, I argue, are less than persuasive and could well be dropped – or significantly qualified – without compromising Chomsky's rationalist principles or his commitment to the values of human intellectual and moral-political autonomy. More than that: his project might well benefit by accommodating certain features of the causal theory, along with realist arguments from philosophy of mathematics, logic, and the formal sciences. This would make it less crucially dependent on the strong nativist hypothesis – or doctrine of innate ideas – which Chomsky takes to form an indispensable component of his rationalist case. Also it would help to explain how his postulated structures of cognitive-linguistic representation hook up with those real-world objects and events that must otherwise be thought of as playing no role in the truth-value properly assigned to our statements concerning them.

This point relates directly to Chomsky's political writings – where issues of truth and factual warrant are very much in question – as well as to his specialised work in linguistics and cognitive psychology. Moreover, he is committed to a realist position with regard to those various abstract entities – linguistic universals, syntactic structures, logical forms, and propositions – without which his project would lack any adequate theoretical or ontological basis. This commitment is especially clear in Chomsky's computational approach where modular processing is defined in terms of formal operations on syntactically structured mental representations. Indeed it is here that he differs most sharply with behaviourists, empiricists, and others who deny that the mind could have access to truths beyond reach of sensory-perceptual experience. I therefore suggest that Chomsky's project would be better served by an epistemology that made sufficient room *both* for causal realism of the Kripke/Putnam variety *and* for realist arguments in philosophy of mathematics, logic, and the formal sciences. Such arguments in no way compromise his claim for the inherent creativity and rational character of human cognitive-linguistic powers. Rather they furnish that claim with the kind of jointly scientific and philosophical support that cannot be had from an approach strictly premised on nativist/internalist principles. Thus my chapter makes a case for reading Chomsky somewhat against the grain but none the less in keeping with the overall character of his project. In particular it brings out the close relationship between his specialist and non-specialist (i.e., political) writings, a relationship that Chomsky has often downplayed so as not to invite charges of across-the-board ideological bias. What emerges from my alternative (realist) construal is the extent to which his work in theoretical linguistics and cognitive psychology both informs and gains support from the position he has taken on socio-political issues.

So these chapters are indeed 'interdisciplinary' to the extent that they advocate an exchange of ideas across different, relatively specialised areas of discourse. Where they take a more sceptical view of such developments is with regard to the notion that intra-disciplinary standards are *nothing more* than so many artificial barriers erected *just in order* to keep people from straying across from one to another merely academic or professional topic-domain. At any rate my chief hope is that this book will contribute to a furthering of such debates despite its predominantly critical emphasis on the kinds of confusion that sometimes result from any too promiscuous or wholesale version of the anti-disciplinarian case.

Note: I have not thought it necessary to provide bibliographical data for the various thinkers and texts mentioned here since they are all treated more extensively in subsequent chapters and the relevant details can be tracked readily enough through the index and endnotes.

1
Derrida on Rousseau: Deconstruction as Philosophy of Logic

In the lengthy reading of Rousseau which makes up the central portion of Jacques Derrida's *Of Grammatology* there is much that should interest philosophers of logic (Derrida 1976). Just recently some writers – Graham Priest among them – have broken the effective veto on discussion of Derrida's work in the analytic community and ventured to suggest that his proposals concerning the 'logic of supplementarity' might usefully be looked at in relation to current debate about deviant, many-valued, or paraconsistent logics (Priest 1994, 1995; also Norris 2000a: 125–47, 148–71). What I aim to do here is to put the case that Derrida's commentary on Rousseau is not only an exercise in rhetorical deconstruction – or 'literary' close-reading – but also, more to the point, a set-piece example of modal-logical analysis. Before that I shall discuss some salient issues that emerged from the notorious exchange (the 'determined non-encounter', as Derrida ironically described it) between Derrida and John Searle on the topic of Austinian speech-act theory, a debate which has left its protagonists – as well as the rival commentators – deeply divided as to who came off best (Austin 1963; Derrida 1977a,b, 1989; Searle 1977).

Most relevant, from a logical point of view, is Derrida's claim that speech-act theory on the standard construal has to marginalise certain standing possibilities of misinterpretation – or a certain potential for cross-purpose failures of linguistic grasp – in order to maintain its normative credentials. That is to say, such Austinian 'misfires' have to be set aside as mere accidents in no way intrinsic to communicative discourse if the theory is to make good on its more systematic or methodological ambitions. Searle thinks this just a plain example of Derrida's distressing penchant for ignoring what should be self-evident, that is, that such cases are by their very nature deviant, non-typical, and only recognisable as such by contrast with the normative reference-class of successful or 'felicitous' speech-acts (Searle 1977). Yet *by what right*, Derrida asks, can he establish this juridical exclusion-zone and thereby remove any threat they might pose to the normal business of speech-act communication, not to mention the enterprise of speech-act theory? Especially if it can be shown that they constitute a kind of 'necessary possibility', an accident that might always befall any utterance whose intention cannot be known for sure and whose role across a strictly non-delimitable range of contexts, situations, or circumstances lays it open to various (maybe 'deviant' or non-standard) construals?

Here it is worth noting that Derrida's appeal to the idea of 'necessary possibility' is one that finds a place in the thinking of modal logicians and which receives a perspicuous representation in the modal-logical symbolism (Hughes and Cresswell 1996; Loux 1979; White 1975). Thus, informally: 'If it is possible that, for any given speech-act, the utterer's meaning or range of appropriate contexts is indeterminate, then *necessarily* it is possible that this should be the case.' Which can be rendered:

$$(s)\Diamond\{[\exists(c)\ \exists(m)(Qcs \wedge Rms \wedge (Ic \vee Im))] \Rightarrow \Box\Diamond[\exists(c)\ \exists(m)(Qcs \wedge Rms \wedge (Ic \vee Im))]\}$$

where the variable letter 's' ranges over speech-acts, 'c' ranges over contexts, and 'm' over meanings. The predicate 'Ix' can be construed as 'x is indeterminate'. 'Qxy' and 'Rxy' are dummy relation terms that relate speech-acts to their meanings and contexts respectively. We can understand 'Qcs' as 'c is a member of the set of all contexts of s' and 'Rms' as 'm is a member of the set of meanings of s'. (I am grateful to my colleague David Roden for his permission to incorporate *verbation* this sharpened formulation of my several earlier attempts to arrive at an adequate and perspicuous symbolism.) Here '$\Rightarrow$' denotes strict implication (so that A$\Rightarrow$B is defined as ~$\Diamond$[A$\wedge$~B]), the diamond is the possibility operator and the box the necessity operator, as in standard modal notation. The formula states, then, that if it is possible that there is a meaning or context of a speech-act that is indeterminate then it is *necessarily* possible that this be so. As it happens there is a well-known formula to just this effect which was first proposed during the 1940s by Ruth Barcan Marcus, a logician widely credited with having brought modal logic up to date from its Aristotelian and medieval sources (see Barcan 1946, 1947; Bradley and Swartz 1979: 236–37; also Lewis 1912; Lewis and Langford 1932; Marcus 1993; Prior 1956; Smullyan 1948). This she did – in brief – by extending the resources of modal propositional logic through introduction of the quantifiers (x), ($\forall$x) and ($\exists$x), along with the standard forms of predicate notation. In fact there were two versions of the Barcan Formula, the second stronger (and more controversial) than the first. The first version holds that if it is *possible* that there exists an item x which has the property F then *necessarily* there exists an item x which possibly has that property. (Thus: $\Diamond[\exists x]Fx \Rightarrow [\exists x]\Diamond Fx$.) According to the second, if every item necessarily has property F then it is necessary that everything has the property F. (Thus: $[x]\Box Fx \Rightarrow \Box[x]Fx$.) (See Marcus 1962, 1993; also Kripke 1963.)

Given time one could work patiently through Derrida's essay on Austin and re-state its leading propositions in terms of the modalised predicate logic captured in these two versions of the Barcan formula. That is to say, the possibility that *any* given speech-act might fail to meet the Austinian conditions for felicitous utterance (i.e., those of serious intent and contextual propriety) necessarily entails that *all* speech-acts are subject to the same sorts of 'misfire', cross-purpose understanding, failure of communicative uptake, and so forth. Moreover, as we shall see in connection with his reading of Rousseau, modal considerations play a central role in Derrida's treatment of the 'supplementary' logic – a logic strictly inconceivable in non-modalised 'classsical' or truth-functional terms – which he finds everywhere at work in Rousseau's texts. This raises the question as to which kind of logic should properly take priority, since on the standard view it is the truth-functional calculus that provides the indispensable groundwork for logical reasoning while modal considerations enter – if at all – as refinements or special-case adjustments brought in to supplement the standard account. (For a deeply informed critical-historical survey, see Kneale and Kneale 1962.) However that assumption is open to doubt if one takes the point of modal logicians who claim that truth-functional logic is itself dependent on modal concepts in the absence of which it would lack any kind of demonstrative force (Hintikka 1963; Kripke 1980; Lewis 1918). Thus:

> [g]iven that logic is concerned . . . with formulating principles of *valid* inference and determining which propositions *imply* which, and given that the concepts of validity and implication are themselves modal concepts, it is modal logic rather than truth-functional logic which deserves to be seen as central to the science of logic itself. . . . From a philosophical point of view, it is much sounder to view modal logic as the indispensable core of logic, to view truth-functional logic as one of its fragments, and to view 'other' logics – epistemic, deontic, temporal, and the like – as accretions either upon modal logic (a fairly standard view, as it happens) or upon its truth-functional component. (Bradley and Swartz 1979: 219)

When we come to examine Derrida's reading of Rousseau we shall see that it gives reason to doubt whether those 'other' (deontic and temporal) components can be held within any such clearly assigned order of priority. That is to say, the 'supplementary' logic of Rousseau's texts is one that involves all manner of intractable problems not only with regard to classical values of determinate truth and falsehood but also with regard to deontological issues (what *ought to have been* as opposed to what *has been* the case) and issues of temporal precedence (such as that of *nature* over *culture* or *speech* over *writing*) (Derrida 1976). And those problems cannot be resolved either on the standard truth-functional view or on the view – as stated by Bradley and Swartz – that such considerations are best treated as dependent upon (or secondary to) the standard modal distinction between necessary and possible truths.

All the same it is clear that Derrida is in agreement with Ruth Barcan Marcus as concerns (1) the indispensability of modal concepts in philosophy of logic, and (2) the principle according to which if it is *possible* that some item has (or lacks) a certain property then *necessarily* the item must be thought of as possessing (or lacking) that same property. Thus – for instance – if for some given speech-act it might be the case that neither utterer's meaning nor contextual criteria were sufficient to determine its felicity-conditions then this is the case (necessarily so) for any speech-act that runs such a risk of performative infelicity (Derrida 1977a, 1989). As it stands, this argument follows directly from the earlier, less contentious version of Barcan's formula ($\Diamond[\exists x]Fx \Rightarrow [\exists x]\Diamond Fx$) but might also be construed – to more powerful if controversial effect – as involving the later version ($[x]\Box Fx \Rightarrow \Box[x]Fx$). And again: if the Rousseauist order of priority between 'nature' and 'culture' might always be subject to a supplementary logic which inverts or complicates that order then *necessarily* it follows that in any given instance the nature/culture opposition (along with its range of associated predicates) will manifest the workings of just such a 'classically' deviant or anomalous logic (Derrida 1976; also Norris 2000a: 125–47, 148–71). David Roden has pointed out (in correspondence) that both Barcan formulae appear to involve a modal operator shift which finds no place in my formal rendition of Derrida's argument three paragraphs above. Whatever the problems here from a logical standpoint it is worth remarking that Derrida's arguments about speech-act iterability and the Rousseauist logic of supplementarity involve a comparable shift. That is to say, they exhibit a regular pattern of modal transition from (1) the *actual occurrence* of such logico-linguistic and pragmatic complications, *via* (2) their *standing possibility* in various contexts, to (3) the *structural necessity* that this should be the case. I should perhaps note that Derrida's usage of the term 'structural', here and elsewhere, derives in large part from his reading of Husserl and has to do with the conditions of possibility – among them logical conditions – for thought, knowledge, and experience in general (Derrida 1973, 1978b). At any rate it is wrong to conclude that his not having offered any formalised rendition of these arguments must indicate some failure of conceptual grasp or downright indifference to standards of logical accountability.

In what follows I shall seek to justify this claim through a detailed analysis of Derrida's texts on Austin and Rousseau. Meanwhile it is worth noting that Ruth Barcan Marcus has been among the fiercest opponents of Derrida and has lent her name to a number of campaigns designed to discredit what she and others see as the pernicious influence of 'deconstruction' on literary theorists – and even some philosophers – who lack the required degree of logical training or acumen (for documentation, see Derrida 1989: 158–9;

also Norris 1996). This episode is of more than anecdotal interest for the light it sheds on those fixed preconceptions which have so far prevented most analytic philosophers from taking anything like full measure of Derrida's contributions to philosophy of logic and language. Of course the fact that his proposals can be expressed in symbolic, that is, quantified modal predicate form is in itself no guarantee of their actually holding for all or any samples of speech-act utterance. Still I should say that Derrida makes good his case *contra* Searle through a reading of Austin that demonstrates the extent to which every performative locution can in principle be subject to doubt as concerns both its intended force and its capacity to function across an open-ended range of possible contexts while none the less counting as a token of the self-same speech-act type (see also Wheeler 2000).

My own view is that Derrida's is the more perceptive, philosophically acute, and indeed *logically* compelling account, even if it poses some sizeable problems for any speech-act theory premised on Austin's more confident statements of intent (see for instance Searle 1969). In this case, as with Derrida on Rousseau, what emerges is a strictly unignorable counter-logic – a logic of logical anomalies – which cannot be dismissed as a product of perverse ingenuity merely on the grounds that it goes against certain common sense habits of thought. For if speech-act theory is primarily concerned with the question 'how to do things with words' – how speakers successfully secure communicative uptake for various kinds of performative utterance – then it is also (as in Austin) *necessarily* concerned with those various sorts of 'misfire' which result when words fail to do what speakers require of them or when recipients fail to grasp the intended gist. And moreover, if such misfires are always possible – if they make up the necessary contrast-class by which to specify the normative criteria for genuine ('felicitous') speech-acts – then it is by no means a straightforward matter, as Searle thinks, to determine the order of priority here. That is to say, Derrida is deploying a 'supplementary' logic (Derrida 1976) which may go against certain classical axioms – like that which holds 'deviant' cases to count as such only by reference to a given (pre-established) norm – but the effect of which is to raise doubt as to whether those axioms can fully account for the range of linguistic phenomena involved. And this argument is put forward not only on the basis of some shrewdly chosen problematical examples from Austin's text but also as a matter of logical inference from the conditions of possibility for *any* kind of speech-act – 'normal' or 'deviant' – in whatever context of utterance. Thus although it is the case (as Derrida nowhere denies) that for most practical purposes we can be taken to mean what we say and say what we mean, still we have to account for those other, necessarily possible cases where communicative uptake fails to occur for whatever reason.

Such a claim, I am aware, will meet with resistance among a good many readers whose impression of Derrida from various sources is that of a 'brilliant' but wayward thinker with absolutely no regard for the protocols of logical consistency, rigour, and truth. Thus opponents like Searle revile him for flouting such elementary standards while admirers – such as Richard Rorty – count this among Derrida's most signal contributions to a postmodern-pragmatist culture where philosophy should henceforth take its place as just one 'kind of writing' among others (Rorty 1978). So where Rorty thinks that Derrida is at his best when adopting all manner of 'literary' tricks in order to deflate the grandiose pretensions of philosophy – and at his worst when trying to play the philosophers at their own earnest game – Searle takes the view that his work merely shows a failure to grasp the most basic principles of rational or common sense argument. In other words they are pretty much agreed in supposing that Derrida is a kind of anti-philosopher whose greatest merit (on Rorty's account) or whose besetting vice (as Searle sees it) is his lack of respect for the ground rules of logic and his 'textualist' desire to run rings around anyone – Searle in particular – who seeks to uphold those rules.

II

In what follows I shall put the case that both parties are wrong and that Derrida is – among other things – a keenly perceptive logician whose work has a direct relevance to issues that have mostly concerned thinkers in the 'other', that is, mainstream-analytic tradition. More than that, he has raised those issues through a mode of textual close-reading that is none the less acute – and logically accountable – for its attentiveness to details of rhetorical structure that are often ignored by philosophers of language, or thought to be of interest only (if at all) to literary critics and theorists. Hence Searle's attitude of frank exasperation when confronted with Derrida's claim to the effect that there is no clear line to be drawn between on the one hand 'genuine', 'serious', or 'authentic' speech-acts which carry the right kind of illocutionary force and, on the other, such 'deviant', 'parasitic', or otherwise 'etiolated' speech-acts as those that are cited, taken out of context, uttered by an actor on the stage, or by characters in novels. For Derrida this lack of adequate criteria by which to maintain the distinction is a consequence of the fact that *all* speech-acts involve the rehearsal in certain contexts of certain endlessly reiterable forms of words, that is to say, phrases which possess such a force only in so far as they are capable of being 'grafted' from one situation to another. So to utter a performative is always to cite a verbal formula whose iterability – or whose capacity to function across a vast range of unpredictable contexts – is enough to raise the question of just what *counts* as an authentic, serious, or good-faith sample of the kind.

Moreover this question is there to be read in passages of Austin's own text, despite his insistence (like Searle's after him) that such problems can arise only in cases which *must* – on common sense-normative grounds – be safely confined to the deviant margins of straightforward communicative language (Austin 1963). Thus, for Derrida, the most remarkable feature of Austin's discourse consists in his acknowledging

> that the possibility of the negative (in this case, of infelicities) is in fact a structural possibility, that failure is an essential risk of the operation under consideration; then, in a move which is almost *immediately simultaneous*, in the name of a kind of ideal regulation, it excludes that risk as accidental, exterior, one which teaches us nothing about the linguistic phenomenon being considered. (Derrida 1977a: 15)

Searle sees this as yet further evidence of Derrida's hopeless failure to grasp the basic principles of speech-act theory, or perhaps – more likely – his determination to trip Austin up on pseudo-problems of his own (Derrida's) perverse devising. That is to say, deconstruction can only get a hold by adopting impossibly rigorous standards of clear-cut conceptual definition, standards which require a decisive procedure (an 'all-or-nothing' logic) whereby to distinguish genuine speech-acts from those merely cited, taken 'out of context', uttered in jest, and so forth. So when it transpires that the theory fails to meet those standards – that it leaves room for borderline cases, contextual underdetermination, or equivocal instances of utterer's intent – this gives Derrida his cue to proclaim that there is *no such thing* as a genuine speech-act or no adequate conceptual basis for Austin's approach. Thus – according to Searle – Derrida's essay exploits the well-worn sophistical technique of creating a false dilemma, one that seeks to outflank the opponent by imposing wholly inappropriate criteria or validity-conditions. For it should otherwise be clear – to any reader not hoodwinked by Derrida's rhetorical gamesmanship – that we *just do* possess the ability to distinguish genuine from non-genuine instances of performative utterance since the latter *just are* 'parasitically' dependent on the former for whatever misleading capacity they have to pass themselves off as good-faith samples of the kind. In short, Derrida is craftily deploying the 'all-or-nothing' terms of classical (deductive) logic in order to impale the speech-act theorist on dilemmas that simply don't arise if one accepts that the criteria for speech-act propriety have to be conceived in a more pragmatic and context-sensitive fashion.

Derrida's first-round response to Searle – 'Limited Inc. a b c' – has been viewed by many analytic philosophers as a striking confirmation of Searle's diagnosis (Derrida 1977b). Thus it affords further proof, if any were needed, that Derrida is not in the business of providing serious (genuine) philosophical arguments but will use all manner of 'literary' tricks in order to play his earnest opponents clean off the field. Certainly he has a good deal of textualist fun at Searle's expense, as for instance by quoting many passages from Searle 'out of context' so as to demonstrate their capacity for saying something totally at odds with his avowed intent, or again, by citing those 'authoritative' statements about Austin's purposes and intentions which show Searle to be staking a proprietary claim in the corporate enterprise of Speech-Act Theory Ltd. Inc. On the other hand – as I have argued elsewhere – this parodic element clearly goes along with a principled commitment to the view that any adequate speech-act theory will need to take account of its own performative aspects, that is to say, the extent to which the theorist's metalanguage is always inextricably involved with those various kinds of speech-act that make up the repertoire of first-order 'natural' linguistic performance. For if the theorist is to talk about 'ordinary language' in what purports, after all, to be *itself* 'ordinary language' (albeit – as Derrida notes elsewhere – a distinctly Oxonian variety in Austin's case) then he had better not claim to address these issues from a vantage point somehow outside and above the vicissitudes of everyday usage (Derrida 1987a).

What chiefly distinguishes Austin's from Searle's approach – on Derrida's account – is the former's extreme sensitivity to just such complicating factors, as for instance in the well-known passage from *How to Do Things With Words* where Austin quite suddenly switches theoretical tack, that is, from a two-term (constative/performative) distinction to a three-term classi-fication involving the locutionary, illocutionary, and perlocutionary aspects of speech-act utterance. This change is brought about by Austin's late-dawning recognition that in fact all constatives have a certain performative aspect ('I hereby declare that $2+2=4$') and all performatives a certain constative component ('It is the case that I hereby promise . . .'). Thus for Austin, as for Derrida, there is always the possibility – a 'necessary possibility', moreover – that theoretical discourse will find itself derailed or its conceptual distinctions subject to challenge by problematic cases which cannot be adequately dealt with by the best methods, concepts, or categories to hand. Hence Derrida's professed admiration for Austin as a thinker always on the look-out for interesting samples of 'ordinary' talk even where these threaten to complicate his argument to the point of requiring such a drastic conceptual overhaul. In other words Austin manifests an uncommon willingness to risk his theoretical commitments by allowing such samples – whether anecdotes from talk or cases thrown up in the course of his own discussion – to exert a constant destabilising pressure on the categories of speech-act theory. So when Austin himself 'deconstructs' the constative/performative distinction it is a move which unsettles any project, like Searle's, that would erect the insights of performative analysis into a full-scale metalinguistic theory based on essentially *constative* criteria, that is, standards of conceptual warrant whose applicability in this context is at any rate open to doubt (Searle 1969). In short, as Derrida ironically notes, his reading of Austin is far more faithful to the spirit (as well as the letter) of Austin's text than is Searle's confidently orthodox claim to know – with presumptive Austinian authority – just what constitutes or fails to constitute an instance of 'genuine' or 'serious' speech-act usage.

All the same this should *not* be taken to imply that Derrida is content simply to relax certain standards of logical truth, rigour, and consistency when the focus switches from constative to performative modes of utterance. Indeed, he takes Searle roundly to task for suggesting that he (Derrida) has skewed the issue by applying a strictly bivalent, 'all-or-nothing' logic to Austin's categories, and has hence typically failed to grasp that those categories need not be perfectly precise or logically exclusive in order to do the work required of them. At this point Derrida comes back with some passages of argument that no doubt manifest a certain mischievous relish but which also indicate a genuine sense of shock that Searle should take refuge in the notion of fuzzy, ill-defined, or approximative concepts. Thus:

> From the moment that Searle entrusts himself to an oppositional logic, to the 'distinction' of concepts by 'contrast' or 'opposition' (a legitimate demand that I share with him, even if I do not at all elicit the same consequences from it), I have difficulty seeing how he is nevertheless able to write [that] phrase...in which he credits me with the 'assumption', 'oddly enough derived from logical positivism', 'that unless a distinction can be made rigorous and precise, it is not really a distinction at all'. (Derrida 1989: 123)

That is to say, this is very much a case of the pot calling the kettle black, with Searle accusing Derrida of lax argumentation while himself adopting a vaguely pragmatic line of least resistance which counts the demand for conceptual precision just a relic of the logical-positivist edict that meaningful discourse be subject to values of determinate (strictly bivalent) truth and falsehood. On the contrary, Derrida responds: '[n]ot only do I find this logic strong, and, in conceptual language and analysis, *an absolute must (il la faut)*, it must...be sustained against all empirical confusion, to the point where the same demand of rigour requires the structure of that logic to be transformed or complicated' (Derrida 1989: 122–23).

What he means by this last, somewhat cryptic phrase will, I trust, become clearer in Section III when I discuss the 'logic of supplementarity' as it emerges from Derrida's reading of Rousseau in *Of Grammatology*. Meanwhile let me cite two further passages from the response to Searle where Derrida specifies just why he finds Searle's position so baffling (or downright evasive) and why he rejects the resort to a notion of indeterminate concepts – or a nonbivalent logic – in order to accommodate anomalous or problematic instances of speech-act usage. They are worth quoting at length because many readers (especially if they have read Searle on Derrida) will no doubt be harbouring grave doubts as to the accuracy of my characterisation so far. 'When a concept is to be treated as a concept', he declares, one has to accept the logic of all or nothing... at any rate, in a theoretical or philosophical discussion of concepts or of things conceptualizable. Whenever one feels obliged to stop doing this (as happens to me when I speak of *différance*, of mark, of supplement, of iterability and of all they entail), it is better to make explicit in the most conceptual, rigorous, formalizing, and pedagogical manner possible the reasons one has for doing so, for thus changing the rules and the context of discourse. (Derrida 1989: 117)

Of course such statements would carry little weight if not borne out by Derrida's practice in the close-reading but also – as this passage clearly requires – in the conceptual analysis and logical exegesis of certain exemplary texts. For it is just his point, as against Searle, that these criteria cannot be disjoined and that any adequate reading of Austin on the topic of performatives has to go by way of a detailed textual engagement which respects and yet, *at the limit of analysis*, may well turn out to complicate the precepts of classical (bivalent) logic. 'To this oppositional logic', Derrida writes,

which is necessarily, legitimately, a logic of 'all or nothing' and without which the distinction and the limits of a concept would have no chance, I oppose nothing, least of all a logic of *approximation* [*à peu près*], a simple empiricism of difference in degree; rather I add a supplementary complication that calls for other concepts... or rather another discourse, another 'logic' that accounts for the impossibility of concluding such a 'general theory'. (Derrida 1989: 117)

I have suggested something of the form that this 'other logic' must take if it is to meet the requirements that Derrida here places upon it. That is to say, it is a logic that nowhere adopts the pragmatic expedient of adjusting its criteria – its standards of logical accountability – to this or that particular case in hand, or of treating any borderline (problematic) case as evaluable only in 'approximative' terms, that is, as involving some 'difference in degree' rather than a clear-cut conceptual distinction.

When Derrida talks of 'empiricism' in this context the word is not deployed as an all-purpose term of abuse for anything that smacks of the Anglophone common sense aversion to grand-style continental theorising. Rather it evokes that strain of radical-empiricist thought, exemplified by Quine, which allows that even the ground rules of classical logic – such as bivalence or excluded middle – might always in principle be open to revision should it be required by some 'recalcitrant' finding in the physical sciences (Quine 1961). Thus, according to Quine, this might after all be the best, most rational course to adopt in response to certain quantum phenomena like wave/particle dualism which would otherwise – on a classical (bivalent) reckoning – pose large problems for a straightforward empiricist account.

As concerns Austinian speech-act theory this attitude equates to Searle's idea that appearances can always be saved – or the theory maintained against Derrida-type objections – by adopting a 'logic of approximation' or a 'simple empiricism of difference in degree'. Hence his main line of counter-argument: that such an 'all-or-nothing' logic is wholly out of place in this area of discourse since concepts need only be as rigorous, exact, or precise as the context of argument requires.

It seems to me that Derrida is very much in earnest as regards the inadequacy of Searle's response, despite his (Derrida's) deconstructive questioning of the serious/non-serious distinction as it figures in Austin's text and whatever his mischievous desire to run rings around Searle's ultra-'serious' attempt to uphold that same distinction. Here it might be useful to ask once again what Derrida means by 'empiricism' and why his usage of the term should not always be taken to conjure pejorative associations. There is a passage from *Of Grammatology* that helps to clarify this issue and that will also provide a convenient point of transition to Derrida's treatment of the 'logic of supplementarity'. 'It may be said', he writes,

> that this style [that of deconstruction] is empiricist and in a certain way that would be correct. The *departure* is radically empiricist. It proceeds like a wandering thought on the possibility of itinerary and of method. It is affected by nonknowledge as by its future and it *ventures out* deliberately . . . But here the very concept of empiricism destroys itself. To *exceed* the metaphysical orb is an attempt to get out of the orbit, to think the entirety of the classical conceptual oppositions, particularly the one within which the value of empiricism is held: the opposition of philosophy and nonphilosophy, another name for empiricism, for this incapacity to sustain on one's own and to the limit the coherence of one's discourse. (Derrida 1976: 162)

What chiefly merits attention here is the fact that 'empiricism' signifies, for Derrida, a moment of 'nonphilosophy' but one which *for just that reason* cannot be dismissed out of hand as merely a regressive or naive retreat from rigorous standards of conceptual accountability. After all, it is precisely his point that 'philosophy' has sustained its claim to adjudicate in matters of truth and falsehood through a constant appeal to such intra-philosophical standards, that is to say, criteria that take for granted the impertinence of any proposition which fails to respect those classical exigencies.

Thus 'empiricism' is one (albeit inadequate) name for that which exceeds the conceptual closure imposed by a certain logocentric order of truths supposedly self-evident to reason. To this extent it signifies the possibility that thinking might exceed those limits and question the pertinence of various distinctions – among them 'philosophy'/'nonphilosophy' – that have always determined (from a philosophic standpoint) what shall count as an instance of truly philosophical discourse as opposed to a naive contentment with common sense appearances. On the other hand 'empiricism' is also the name for that which has resort – like Searle in his reading of Austin – to a vaguely 'approximative' logic, or an ill-defined notion of 'difference in degree' which relaxes the requirements of logical rigour so as to pre-empt any challenge to its own uncritical presuppositions. It is in just this latter (pejorative) sense that Derrida defines it as 'the incapacity to sustain on one's own and to the limit the coherence of one's discourse'. That is to say, the ground rules of classical logic must indeed be applied *to the limit* if one is to test their applicability to problem cases and – where they encounter resistance – to establish precisely what else is required by way of an alternative (deviant, non-standard, or 'supplementary') logic.

So it may be the case that 'a certain' empiricism exerts its claim at precisely the point where this curious logic of logical anomalies turns out to capture certain salient features of the world and our experience/knowledge of it which cannot be captured through the application of standard (classical or bivalent) truth-values. However, this 'logic of supplementarity' is something that emerges only by dint of much careful analysis and, moreover, that nowhere abandons – even though it works to delimit and to complicate – such classical axioms as bivalence or excluded middle. Thus it tells us something of the first importance with regard not only to technical issues in philosophy of logic but also to the question of precisely how far – and under what precise empirical conditions – we might be justified in following Quine and counting logic revisable should the evidence demand it. What sets Derrida's discussion most strikingly apart from Quine's is his treatment of these issues as and when they arise in the reading of certain exemplary texts, texts that are sometimes (infrequently) concerned with questions of an overt logico-philosophic import, but which more often can be seen to raise such questions only at a certain oblique or diagnostic remove. Nevertheless, I shall argue, Derrida's treatment is among the most intelligent, resourceful, and sophisticated studies we have of the way that bivalent logic 'goes over' – in the process of detailed textual exegesis – into a logic more attuned to the paradoxes of self-reference and the impossibility of conceptual closure under certain problematical conditions.

III

His reading of Rousseau is the *locus classicus* for Derrida's proposals in this regard, proposals that have so far not been examined with anything like an adequate regard for their rigour, subtlety, and scope of application beyond the particular case in hand (Derrida 1976: 141–316). What I shall seek to do here is outline that reading – albeit in highly condensed and schematic form – and then discuss its wider implications for philosophy of language and logic. I had better say first (so as to pre-empt one likely rejoinder) that

Derrida's commentary is *not* – or not only – a piece of interpretative criticism, one that fastens on certain themes – like the term 'supplement' in its
various contexts of occurrence – and then deploys them with a view to
subverting other, more orthodox interpretations. To be sure, he does spend
a great deal of time expounding particular passages in Rousseau's work
which have to do with a large variety of topics, from the origin of language
to the development of civil society, from the history of music to the geneal-
ogy of morals, or from educational psychology to the role of writing as a
'supplement' to speech which (supposedly) infects and corrupts the
sources of authentic spoken discourse. What these all have in common – so
Derrida maintains – is a sharply polarised conceptual structure whereby
Rousseau equates everything that is good (spontaneous, genuine, passionate,
sincere, and so on) with the approbative term *nature* and everything that is
bad (artificial, civilised, decadent, corrupt, merely conventional, and so
on) with the derogatory term *culture*. And the same goes for those cryptic
passages in the *Confessions* where Rousseau obliquely acknowledges his
'solitary vice' and reflects on the perversity of supplementing nature (the
good of heterosexual intercourse) with a practice that substitutes imaginary
pleasures and the 'conjuring up of absent beauties' (Derrida 1976: 149–57).
So to this extent, granted, the Derridean reading has to do with certain
distinctive (not to say obsessional) *topoi* that can be seen to exercise a
powerful hold on Rousseau's memory, intellect, and imagination, and which
lend themselves to treatment in something like the traditional expository mode.

   Still, as I have said, this should not be construed by philosophers as evidence
that Derrida is here practising a mode of thematic or literary commentary,
one that makes play with certain 'philosophical' themes – like the logic (or
pseudo-logic) of supplementarity – so as to disguise that fact. Rather, what
chiefly interests Derrida in the reading of Rousseau's texts is '[the] difference
between implication, nominal presence, and thematic application' (ibid.:
135). In other words it is the kind of difference that emerges – unnoticed by
most commentators – when one strives to read Rousseau in accordance with
his own explicit intentions (his *vouloir-dire*) only to find that those intentions
are 'inscribed' in a supplementary logic beyond his power to fully command
or control. No doubt Rousseau *'declares* what he *wishes to say'*, namely that
'articulation and writing are a post-originary malady of language', introduced
with the passage to a 'civilised' (=corrupt, artificial) state of society when
language would have lost its first (natural) character of spontaneous,
passionate utterance. Yet it is also the case – on a closer reading – that Rousseau 'says or *describes* what he *does not wish to say*: articulation and therefore
the space of writing operates at the origin of language' (ibid.: 229). For as he
well knows – and indeed on occasion quite explicitly states – there *can never
have been* any language that lacked those various articulatory features (phonetic
structures, semantic distinctions, grammatical parts of speech, etc.) which

alone make it possible for language to function as a means of communicative utterance.

Nevertheless, according to Rousseau, these must all be counted 'supplementary' (bad or corrupting) additions to an 'original' language – an authentic speech of the passions – that would surely have had no need for such artificial devices since its purpose was fully served in the face-to-face (or the heart-to-heart) of intimate mutual exchange. Even now, he remarks, there are certain languages – those of Italy and Southern Europe – which continue to manifest something of that natural character since they have remained close to the wellspring of passionate speech and have not (like the 'Northern' tongues) acquired all manner of progressively debilitating structural traits. Yet Rousseau is once again compelled to acknowledge that this can be only a matter of degree, and moreover that everything which by rights *ought* to be considered merely a 'supplement' to language in its first (natural) state must rather be thought of as integral and prerequisite to any language whatsoever. Hence the ambiguity – more precisely, the double and contradictory logic – that Derrida discerns in Rousseau's usage of the term across an otherwise diverse range of argumentative contexts. On the one hand 'supplement' may be taken to signify: that which is added *unnecessarily* – by way of gratuitous embellishment – to something that is (ought to be) complete as it stands and which does not (should not) require – even tolerate – any such otiose addition. In this sense the entire development of language away from its passional origins and toward more complex, articulate, or structured forms of expression must be counted a definite *perversion* of language, that is to say, a melancholy sign of the way that 'supplementary' features or devices can somehow (deplorably) come to *stand in* for the living presence of authentic speech. However there a second sense of the term that obtrudes itself – most often – against Rousseau's express intent and which constantly threatens to make him say just the opposite of what he means. On this alternative construal, 'supplement' signifies: that which is required in order to complete what must otherwise be thought of as lacking or deficient in some crucial regard. Thus the 'original' language of Rousseau's conception would quite simply *not have been* a language – would have lacked some or all of those constitutive features that define what properly counts as such – if indeed (as he thinks) it belonged to a time when human beings managed to communicate through a kind of pre-articulate speech-song wholly devoid of phonetic, semantic, or grammatical structures. In short,

> [articulation] broaches language: it opens speech as an institution born of passion but it threatens song as original speech. It pulls language toward need and reason – accomplices – and therefore lends itself to writing more easily. The more articulated a language is, the less accentuated it is, the more rational it is, the less musical it is, and the less it loses by being written, the better it expresses need. It becomes Nordic. (Derrida 1976: 242)

Hence that curious 'logic of supplementarity' which complicates Rousseau's writing to the point where his explicit statements of authorial intent are called into question by other (less prominent but strictly unignorable) statements to contrary effect.

This example gives substance to Derrida's above-cited cryptic remark that what interests him chiefly in Rousseau's texts is '[the] difference between implication, nominal presence, and thematic application' (ibid.: 135). Moreover it is a characteristic of his writing that emerges in so many different connections – or across such a range of thematic concerns – that it cannot be put down to just a blind spot in his thinking about this particular topic. Thus culture is invariably conceived by Rousseau as a falling-away from that original state of nature wherein human beings would as yet have had no need for those various 'civilised' accoutrements like writing as a bad supplement to speech, harmony as a bad supplement to melody, or civic institutions, delegated powers, and representative assemblies as a bad supplement to that which once transpired in the face-to-face of oral community. That this fall should ever have occurred – that nature should have taken this perverse, accidental, yet fateful swerve from its first state of natural innocence – is the chief sign or diagnostic mark of those various 'supplementary' evils that have come to exert their corrupting effect on individual and social mores. In each case, however, it is Derrida's claim that Rousseau's overt (intentional) meaning is contradicted by certain other, strikingly discrepant formulations whose logic runs athwart the manifest sense of his argument. Thus on the one hand, there to be read plainly enough, is what Rousseau *wants to say* – and does quite explicitly say – with respect to the intrinsic and self-evident superiority of nature over culture, speech over writing, melody over harmony, passion over reason, the law of the heart over laws of state, and small-scale 'organic' communities over large-scale, anomic and overly complex societal aggregates. Yet on the other hand, there to be read in certain passages – often in parentheses or *obiter dicta* where their disruptive effect may be least felt – is a series of concessions, qualifying clauses, and seeming *nonsequiturs* that exert a constant destabilising pressure on Rousseau's more explicit avowals of intent. So in reading Rousseau it is not so much a matter of discounting or routinely disregarding his intentions but rather one of aiming, in Derrida's carefully chosen words, at 'a certain relationship, unperceived by the writer, between what he commands and what he does not command of the patterns of the language that he uses' (Derrida 1976: 158).

This point is worth emphasis since hostile commentators – Searle among them – have often charged Derrida with showing no respect for authorial intentions or with riding roughshod over passages which make it quite plain what the author wanted to say (Searle 1977; also Ellis 1989). So I had better now cite the well-known paragraph from *Of Grammatology* where Derrida specifies (again very carefully) the principles that he takes to govern a deconstructive reading and which set it firmly apart from any such free-for-all or 'anything goes' attitude of hermeneutic licence. 'To produce this signifying structure', he writes,

> obviously cannot consist of reproducing, by the effaced and respectful doubling of commentary, the conscious, voluntary, intentional relationship that the writer institutes in his exchanges with the history to which he belongs thanks to the element of language. This moment of doubling commentary should no doubt have its place in a critical reading. To recognize and respect all its classical exigencies is not easy and requires all the instruments of traditional criticism. Without this recognition and this respect, critical production would risk developing in any direction at all and authorize itself to say almost anything. But this indispensable guardrail has always only *protected*, it has never *opened*, a reading. (Derrida 1976: 158)

We should not be too quick to conclude, with the hostile commentators, that this is just a pious expression of respect for principles – those of 'traditional' exegesis or commentary – that Derrida is perfectly willing to flout whenever it suits his convenience. For it is a statement that is fully borne out by the detailed reading of Rousseau which forms its immediate context and also by those other readings – of philosophers from Plato to Kant, Husserl, and Austin – where Derrida likewise combines a due regard for the author's professed intent with a *principled* (not merely opportunist) allowance that authorial intention cannot have the last word (Derrida 1973, 1977a, 1981, 1987b). After all, 'the writer writes *in* a language and *in* a logic whose proper system, laws, and life his discourse by definition cannot dominate absolutely' (ibid.: 158). And again: '[h]e uses them only by letting himself, after a fashion and up to a point, be governed by the system' (ibid.).

None of this should be taken to suggest – let me emphasise again – that authorial intentions are wholly irrelevant or even subject to a large discount when it comes to the business of deconstructing this or that text. Rather, it is a question – in the more familiar analytic parlance – of distinguishing 'utterer's meaning' from 'linguistic meaning', or what a speaker intends to convey by some particular form of words in some particular context of utterance from those background norms (semantic, syntactic, pragmatic, etc.) which determine what their utterance standardly means according to shared linguistic criteria (Davidson 1984; Grice 1989). What is distinctive about Derrida's approach is the fact that he reverses the usual order of priority whereby it is assumed that utterer's meaning can always trump linguistic meaning if the speaker must be taken to intend something different from the standard or default interpretation. (For an extreme version of this argument, see Davidson 1986; also my discussion in Norris 1997.) On the contrary, Derrida maintains: although it is always possible for speakers (or writers) to express more than could ever be grasped on a purely 'linguistic' construal, still there is a need to remark on those counter-instances where logic countermands any straightforward ascription of utterer's intent, or where analysis reveals a certain non-coincidence of authorial meaning and linguistic (logico-semantic) sense. Such is the case with Rousseau's usage of the term 'supplement', a usage that cannot be reduced to the order of univocal meaning or intent and which thus holds out against any attempt to close or to reconcile this conflict of interpretations. That is to say, it has to function *both* in a privative, derogatory sense ('supplement'=that which subtracts and corrupts under the guise of adding and improving) but also – despite Rousseau's intention – in the positive sense: 'supplement'=that which fills a lack or makes good an existing defect. And this is a matter, Derrida writes, 'of Rousseau's situation within the language and the logic that assures to this word or this concept sufficiently *surprising* resources so that the presumed subject of the sentence might always say, through using the "supplement", more, less, or something other than he *would mean* [*voudrait dire*]' (Derrida 1976: 158).

What is 'surprising' – in the etymological sense – about this logic of supplementarity is the way that it *overtakes* authorial intentions and twists them around, so to speak, through a kind of involuntary reversal that leaves Rousseau strictly incapable of meaning what he says or saying what he means. No doubt it is the case that 'Rousseau would like to separate originarity from supplementarity', and indeed that 'all the rights constituted by our logos are on his side', since surely 'it is unthinkable and intolerable that what has the name *origin* should be no more than a point situated within the system of supplementarity' (ibid.: 243). Yet this system (or logic) cannot be ignored if one is to take account of the objections that rise against Rousseau's thesis *by his own admission elsewhere* and which constitute a standing refutation of his claims with respect to the order of priorities between nature and culture, speech and writing, and origin and supplement. For in each case the latter term can be seen to 'wrench language from its condition of origin, from its conditional or its future of origin, from that which it must (ought to) have been and what it has never been; it could only have been born by suspending its relation to all origin' (ibid.: 243). Which is also to say – if one reads Rousseau with sufficient logical care – that '[i]ts history is that of the supplement of (from) origin: of the originary substitute and the substitute of the origin' (ibid.). And this is not just a kind of wilful paradox-mongering on Derrida's part but a conclusion arrived at (as I seek to show here) through textual exegesis and logical analysis of the highest, most rigorous order.

IV

At any rate Derrida's main thesis with regard to the conditions of possibility for language is one that would most likely be endorsed by many analytic philosophers. What it amounts to is a version of the argument advanced by (among others) Donald Davidson: that in order for anything to *count* as a 'language' it must possess certain minimal features that permit it to function in a range of basic expressive-communicative roles (Davidson 1984). Of course there are significant differences between Derrida and Davidson when it comes to specifying just what those features are or just what constitutes the threshold point beyond which language – as opposed to some proto-'language' of the passions – may properly be said to exist. For Derrida, this issue is posed very much against the background of mainly French debates, from Rousseau to Saussure, about the relative priority of *langue* and *parole*, or language-as-system (the object of study for structuralist linguistics) and language as produced by individual speakers in particular contexts of utterance (Saussure 1983). This in turn gives rise to the paradox – or the chicken-and-egg conundrum – that language (*la langue*) must already have existed in order for those individual speech-acts to possess any proper, linguistically communicable sense while it is hard to conceive how *langue* could ever have developed except through the gradual codification of individual speech-acts or items of *parole*. Thus Derrida's interest is chiefly in the way that a thinker like Rousseau attempts to resolve the paradox in favour of a speech-based account even though this involves the projection of a mythic 'original language' which must *either* have been no language at all *or else* have been marked by those very same traits (articulation, structure, difference, and hierarchy) which supposedly belong only to language in its 'civilised' (decadent) state. As a result, when Derrida specifies the minimal conditions for what counts as a language, he does so in broadly Saussurean terms which depict Rousseau as a kind of proto-structuralist *malgré lui*, one whose intermittent grasp of those conditions compelled him to question the very possibility that language might once have existed in any such natural, innocent, or prelapsarian state. From which it follows – on Derrida's account – that the structures concerned are primarily those which form the basis of Saussurean linguistic theory, that is to say, structures having to do with the various systemic and contrastive relationships that constitute *la langue* at the phonetic and semantic level.

For Davidson, conversely, the prerequisite features of language are those various logico-syntactic attributes – negation, conjunction, and disjunction along with the quantifiers and sentential connectives – which can plausibly be argued to provide a common basis for inter-lingual translation (Davidson 1984). This reflects his primary concern to explain how such translation (or mutual understanding) can indeed take place despite the arguments for radical incommensurability mounted by paradigm-relativists of sundry persuasion such as Quine (1961), Kuhn (1970), Feyerabend (1975), and Whorf (1956). Where these thinkers go wrong – Davidson argues – is in being decidedly over-impressed by the evidence that different languages (or language communities) operate with different *semantic* fields and under-impressed by the extent of those shared structural features that languages must possess if they are to function effectively as a means of communication.

This is why, as he puts it, syntax is so much more 'sociable' than semantics, namely through its offering grounds for the assurance that reliable translation *can* indeed occur despite and across those divergences of 'conceptual scheme' that would otherwise render it impossible. So it is natural enough – given this agenda – that Davidson should place maximum stress on the logical connectives and allied functions rather than the structural-semantic aspects of language that tend to predominate in Derrida's approach.

All the same – as I have said – their thinking has more in common than might appear from this face-value characterisation. For with Derrida also the main point of interest is not so much the ambiguity (or semantic over-determination) of a word like 'supplement' in isolated instances of usage but rather the *logic* of supplementarity as revealed through a mode of conceptual exegesis that scarcely conforms to accepted models of textual or thematic exegesis. Indeed there is a somewhat comical footnote in *Of Grammatology* (243n) where he cites Rousseau on the supposed fact that 'the Arabs have more than a thousand words for *camel* and more than a hundred for *sword*, etc.', just as the semantical case for paradigm-relativism makes much of the fact that the language of certain nomadic farmers picks out manifold shades of 'green', or that Eskimo language has many different words for 'white'. All the same, as Davidson sensibly remarks, Whorf makes a pretty good job of describing *in English* what it is like to inhabit the conceptual scheme of cultures very different from ours, just as Kuhn makes a fair shot at describing the worldview of pre-Copernican astronomy or the thinking of physicists before Galileo and chemists before Lavoisier (Davidson 1984: 184). What enables them to do so – despite and against their sceptical-relativist princi-ples – is the existence of certain basic regularities (like the logical constants) which must be at work in any such process of inter-lingual or inter-paradigm translation. So likewise, when Derrida talks of the 'logic proper to Rousseau's discourse' (Derrida 1976: 215) he is not referring only to certain blind spots of logical contradiction in Rousseau's text or to the kind of paradoxical pseudo-logic that literary critics often treat as a hallmark of poetic value. Still less is he suggesting – as Nietzsche and some deconstructionists would have it – that the ground rules of classical logic (such as bivalence or excluded middle) are in truth nothing more than illusory constraints that can always be subverted by a reading that demonstrates their merely persua-sive (i.e., rhetorical) character (see especially de Man 1979). Rather, his point is that Rousseau's discourse exemplifies a form of deviant, 'classically' unthinkable, but none the less rigorous logic which cannot be grasped except on condition – as Derrida declares in his response to Searle – that one attempts *so far as possible* to read his texts in accordance with those strictly indispensable ground rules.

This is why I have put the case that Derrida, like Davidson, rejects any theory that would treat semantics as prior to logic, or issues of meaning as prior to issues concerning the various logical functions that enable speakers to communicate reliably across otherwise large differences of linguistic or cultural context. Of course this goes against the dominant idea – among hostile and friendly commentators alike – that Derrida is out to deny the very possibility of reliable communication, or at least any prospect that it might be based on trans-contextual regularities and constants of the kind that early Davidson seeks to establish. I say 'early Davidson' in order to distinguish the truth-based, logically grounded approach that he once developed with a view to countering Quinean, Kuhnian and other versions of the conceptual scheme-relativist argument from the strikingly different (indeed, flatly incompatible) line of thought pursued in his later essay 'A Nice Derangement of Epitaphs' (1986). Here Davidson famously proposes that 'there is no such thing as a language', if by 'language' we mean something like the notional object of theoretical linguistics, philosophical semantics, transformational-generative grammar, or any such attempt to describe or explain what underlies and makes possible our various kinds of linguistic-interpretive-communicative grasp. Thus, according to Davidson's 'minimalist' view, we most often get along in figuring out people's meanings and intentions through an ad hoc mixture of 'luck, wit and wisdom', that is to say, through a socially acquired knack for responding to various context-specific cues and clues, rather than working on a 'prior theory' that would somehow provide an advance specification of what it takes to interpret them correctly. This goes along with a generalised version of the Davidsonian 'principle of charity' which requires nothing more than our predisposed willingness to 'bring them out right' – or interpret them as saying something relevant and meaningful – even where they mis-speak themselves, use the wrong expression, or utter some piece of (apparent) nonsense. Since we do this all the time – and manifest a striking degree of tolerance for verbal aberrations of just that kind – then surely it must indicate something important about what goes on in the everyday business of understanding others and getting them to understand us.

Davidson's main example here is that of malapropism, as in the title of his essay which is taken from Sheridan's play 'The Rivals' and alludes to Mrs Malaprop's comical penchant for mixing up her words, for example, saying 'a nice derangement of epitaphs' when what she *means* – and what the audience knows she means – is 'a nice arrangement of epithets'. However this optimising strategy is by no means confined to such extreme (pathological) cases or to speech-acts, like hers, where there is simply no connection between utterer's meaning and the sense of their utterance as given by a dictionary or survey of standard lexico-grammatical usage. For – as Davidson argues – it is a strategy everywhere involved in our capacity to interpret novel utterances, fresh turns of phrase, metaphors, ironies, oblique implications, and even the most familiar items of language when these occur (as they always do) in new or at any rate slightly unfamiliar contexts. So linguistic competence is much more a matter of pragmatic adjustment, intuitive guesswork, and localised (context-sensitive) uptake than of applying a set of interpretative rules that would somehow – impossibly – determine *in advance* what should or should not be counted a meaningful, well-formed, or relevant usage. Hence Davidson's idea that 'prior theories', though playing some minimal role in this process, are largely irrelevant when it comes to interpreting particular speech-acts in particular contexts of utterance. What we chiefly rely on here is the kind of 'passing theory' – or informed guess as to what the speaker most likely intends to convey – that works well enough for such one-off applications but which has to be revised (or abandoned altogether) as soon as we are faced with a different speaker or the same speaker in a different context.

Thus we do not get much help – if any at all – from our generalised competence as language-users, at least if this 'competence' is taken to involve the interpreter's possession of a prior theory (an innate or acquired grasp of meanings, structures, grammatical rules, and so forth) which by very definition fails to provide the relevant sorts of guidance. For there are, according to Davidson, 'no rules for arriving at passing theories, no rules in any strict sense, as opposed to rough maxims' (Davidson 1986: 173). On his view 'the asymptote of agreement and understanding is where passing theories coincide', and if we want to explain this in terms of two people 'having the same language', then we shall need to qualify the claim by saying 'that they tend to converge on passing theories' (ibid.: 173). In which case it follows that 'degree or relative frequency of convergence [is] a measure of similarity of language' (ibid.). So in the end there is no difference – or none that really counts in philosophical or linguistic-theoretical terms – between 'knowing a language' and 'knowing our way around in the world generally'. Both come down to our practical savvy, our 'wit, luck and wisdom' in judging situations, and – what amounts to the same thing – our readiness to junk any prior theory that does not fit the case in hand. By the same token, linguists and philosophers are getting things back-to-front when they try to produce some generalised (non-context-specific) account of the rules, regularities, semantic structures, generative mechanisms, or whatever, that supposedly subtend and explain our powers of everyday linguistic-communicative grasp. Such theories miss the point when it comes to describing how people *actually* manage to do things with words just as those people would themselves miss the point – fail to get their meanings across or understand what was said to them – if indeed they were wholly or largely reliant on the kinds of linguistic competence the theories purport to describe. So any project of this sort must inevitably fail 'for the same reasons the more complete and specific prior theories fail: none of them satisfies the demand for a description of the ability that speaker and interpreter share and that is adequate to interpretation' (Davidson 1986: 171).

I have taken this rather lengthy detour *via* Davidson's 'A Nice Derangement' because it has struck some exegetes as adopting an approach to issues of language, meaning, and interpretation which invites comparison with Derrida's work, in particular his deconstructive reading of Austin in 'Signature Event Context' (see for instance Pradhan 1986; Wheeler 1986). What these thinkers have in common, so the argument goes, is (1) an emphasis on the capacity of speech-acts to function across a vast (unpredictable and unspecifiable) range of communicative contexts, (2) the rejection of any theory that would claim to establish normative criteria for deciding in advance just which kinds of speech-act are meaningful, valid, or appropriate in just which kinds of context, and resulting from this (3) a 'minimalist-semantic' conception of meaning which strives so far as possible to avoid all dependence on prior theories of whatever type. Thus, according to one of these commentators,

> [i]f a sentence can be put to any use, and if its meaning does not restrict its use in any way, and it retains the same meaning in the context of those multiple uses; or if a sign can always be removed from its context and grafted into another context and its identity as a sign does not hamper its functioning as that sign in those new contexts; then we had better posit only the minimum required semantically to constitute that sentence or that sign as that unit of language. (Pradhan 1986: 75)

For Derrida this involves the notion of 'iterability' as that which enables speech-acts, written marks, or other such linguistic tokens to be cited ('grafted') from one context to the next while avoiding any more specific appeal to identity-conditions or criteria for deciding what shall count as an appropriate or relevantly similar context (Derrida 1977a). For Davidson, as we have seen, it takes the form of a basically pragmatist approach according to which 'passing theories' (or ad hoc adjustments) are the best we can reasonably hope for since they alone offer any prospect of achieving some measure of convergence between utterer's intent and communicative uptake. Hence the idea that Davidson and Derrida are likewise converging – albeit from different angles – on a kind of interpretative theory to end all theories, or a minimalist conception that finds no room for more substantive specifications of meaning or context.

It seems to me – for reasons that I have set out above – that this proposal gets Derrida wrong on certain crucial points and that his readings of Austin and Rousseau (among others) have more in common with the 'early' Davidson position than with that advanced in 'A Nice Derangement of Epitaphs' (see also Norris 1997). That is to say, what Derrida shares with early Davidson is the belief that interpretation cannot even make a start except on the premise that linguistic understanding is primarily a matter of the logical resources that alone make it possible for speech-acts or texts to communicate across otherwise unbridgeable differences of language, culture, social context, background presupposition, and so forth. Early Davidson sets these conditions out in the form of a Tarskian (truth-based) formal semantics which – as he argues – can then be extended to natural languages by way of those various logical constants in the absence of which they would fail to qualify as 'languages', properly speaking. In which case there is no making sense of the Quinean, Kuhnian, or Whorfian claim that since 'conceptual schemes' (semantically construed) vary so widely across different languages or cultures therefore translation from one to another is strictly impossible, or at best a matter of approximate convergence for practical purposes. After all, as Davidson pointedly remarks, 'Whorf, wanting to demonstrate that Hopi incorporates a metaphysics so alien to ours that Hopi and English cannot, as he puts it "be calibrated", uses English to convey the contents of sample Hopi sentences' (Davidson 1984: 184). The same goes for Quine's across-the-board talk of 'ontological relativity' and Kuhn's idea that scientific revolutions bring about such a wholesale paradigm-shift that there is simply no room for comparing different theories in point of truth, explanatory power, or predictive warrant. Where the error comes in, so Davidson maintains, is through these thinkers' shared tendency to promote issues of semantics – the fact that various languages differ in their range of lexical or descriptive resources – over issues concerning the elements of logical structure that all languages must have in common in order to qualify as such. Thus 'what forms the skeleton of what we call a language is the pattern of inference and structure created by the logical constants: the sentential connectives, quantifiers, and devices for cross-reference' (Davidson 1984: 182).

All of this seems to go pretty much by the board when later Davidson advances his claim that 'there is no such thing as a language' and puts the case for regarding 'prior theories' – among them (presumably) truth-based logico-semantic theories of just this type – as more or less redundant when it comes to the business of figuring out what speakers mean in particular contexts of utterance. One way of bringing this lesson home – he suggests – 'is to reflect on the fact that an interpreter must be expected to have different prior theories for different speakers – not as different, usually, as his passing theories; but these are matters that depend on how well the interpreter knows his speaker' (Davidson 1986: 171). In which case clearly the role of prior theories must be thought of as 'vanishingly small', or as subject to revision – or outright abandonment – whenever we encounter some speech-act that fails to make sense (or which yields an aberrant interpretation) on our currently accepted prior theory. What this amounts to is a massive extension of the early-Davidson 'principle of charity' which now requires not that we maximise the truth-content of sample utterances by construing their sense in accordance with shared (presumptively rational) standards of accountability but rather that we simply ignore or discount the linguistic meaning of any utterance that does not make sense by our best interpretative lights. For if indeed there is 'no word or construction that cannot be converted to a new use by an ingenious or ignorant speaker' (*vide* Mrs Malaprop), and if linguistic uptake can amount to no more than 'the ability to converge on a passing theory from time to time', then surely it follows that 'we have abandoned . . . the ordinary notion of a language' (Davidson 1986: 170). But this is no great loss, Davidson thinks, since we can get along perfectly well by applying the extended principle of charity plus those elements of 'luck, wit and wisdom' that always play a part in our everyday dealings with language and the world.

So one can see why some theorists (or anti-theorists) have perceived a striking resemblance between late Davidson's 'minimalist-semantic' approach and Derrida's idea of 'iterability' as the best – least semantically burdened – account of how speech-acts or textual inscriptions can function across an open-ended range of possible contexts while somehow retaining just sufficient in the way of identity criteria from one such context to the next. However, as I have said, this resemblance turns out to have sharp limits if one looks in more detail at Derrida's readings of Austin, Rousseau, and others. For it then becomes apparent that he, like early Davidson, places more emphasis on the logical components of linguistic understanding – the connectives, quantifiers, devices for cross-reference, and so forth – as opposed to the kinds of primarily semantic consideration that lead thinkers like Quine, Kuhn, and Whorf to raise large problems about inter-lingual translation or cross-paradigm understanding. To be sure, Derrida's 'logic of supplementarity' is one that might itself be thought to raise similar problems for any attempt – like early Davidson's – to resist the force of such sceptical arguments. Thus it does, undeniably, complicate our sense of the relationship between what Rousseau expressly intended to say and what – on a closer, more critical reading – turns out to be the counter-logic at work in various passages of his text. Yet this is *not* to say either that Rousseau's intentions must henceforth be counted irrelevant for the purposes of any such reading, nor again that the 'logic of supplementarity' precludes our ever grasping the operative concepts that organise Rousseau's discourse. Rather, it is to say that we can best understand what Rousseau gives us to read through the kind of close-focused textual exegesis that registers precisely those logical tensions and moments of aporia which mark the presence of incompatible themes and motifs. And such a reading could not even make a start were it not for the imperative – as Derrida conceives it – of applying the ground-rules of classical (bivalent) logic right up to the point where those principles encounter some obstacle or check to their consistent application.

V

I must now give substance to these general claims by examining a number of extended passages from *Of Grammatology* where Derrida spells out exactly what is involved in this logic of supplementarity. One has to do with the origins, nature, and historical development of music, a subject that greatly preoccupied Rousseau and which called forth some typically complex sequences of assertion and counter-assertion. What Rousseau explicitly *says* about music is very much what one might expect him to say, given his general view that the 'progress' of civilisation has been everywhere marked by a falling-away from the innocence of origins and a decadent resort to the kinds of 'supplementary' device that typify latter-day European culture and language. So the story that Rousseau chooses to tell is one in which music at first took rise from a spontaneous expression of the feelings which as yet had no need for merely decorous conventions or for supplements – such as harmony or counterpoint – whose advent signalled a thenceforth inevitable process of long-term decline. 'If music awakens in song, if it is initially uttered, *vociferated*, it is because, like all speech, it is born in passion; that is to say, in the transgression of need by desire and the awakening of pity by imagination' (Derrida 1976: 195). Indeed music and spoken language have their shared point of origin in a kind of pre-articulate speech-song that would have served to communicate all those genuine emotions – prototypically, that of 'pity', or compassion – which set human beings apart from the other animals and must therefore be taken to have marked the emergence of human society from a pre-social state of nature. Moreover, just as spoken language began to degenerate with the development of grammar, articulation, and other such gratuitous 'supplements', so music acquired those disfiguring features that Rousseau identifies with the predominant French styles and conventions of his time. Here again, he makes a partial exception of the Italian and other Southern-European musical cultures where melody has retained at least something of its primacy as an authentic language of the passions, and where music has not yet gone so far down the path toward harmonic-contrapuntal decadence. But in general the process has been one of progressive corruption which reflects – for Rousseau – the wider predicament of a culture whose ever more complex forms of social and political organisation are likewise to be seen as so many symptoms of the same chronic malaise.

What is more, this unnatural degenerative process finds an analogue in the way that writing – or the graphic 'supplement' to speech – comes to exercise an altogether bad and corrupting influence on the development of language in general, and especially those languages that count themselves the most 'advanced' or 'civilised'. For 'if supplementarity is a necessarily indefinite process', then

> writing is the supplement par excellence since it marks the place where the supplement proposes itself as supplement of supplement, sign of sign, *taking the place of* a speech already significant; it displaces the *proper place* of the sentence, the unique time of the sentence pronounced *hic et nunc* by an irreplaceable subject, and in turn innervates the voice. It marks the place of the initial doubling. (Derrida 1976: 281)

Thus writing takes on for Rousseau the full range of pejorative associations – artifice, conventionality, and removal from the sphere of authentic (face-to-face) communication – which Derrida brings out in a great many texts of the Western logocentric tradition from Plato to Husserl, Saussure, and Lévi-Strauss (Derrida 1973, 1976, 1978a, 1981). At its most straightforward the link between harmony (or counterpoint) and writing is simply the fact that whereas melodies can be learned – or got 'by heart' – without any need for graphic notation in the form of a musical score, this becomes more difficult – and finally impossible – as music acquires harmonic complications beyond the unaided mnemonic capacity of even the best-trained musicians. However the connection goes deeper than this and involves all those above-mentioned negative attributes or predicates which mark the term 'writing' as it figures in Rousseau's discourse. So it is, in Derrida's words, that

> [t]he growth of music, the desolating separation of song and speech, has the form of writing as 'dangerous supplement': calculation and grammaticality, *loss of energy and substitution*. The history of music is parallel to the history of language, its evil is in essence graphic. When he undertakes to explain *how music has degenerated*, Rousseau recalls the unhappy history of the language and its disastrous 'perfecting': 'To the degree that the language improved, melody, being governed by new rules, imperceptibly *lost its previous energy*, and the *calculus of intervals was substituted for nicety of inflection'*. (Derrida's italics; cited in Derrida 1976: 199)

Thus, according to Rousseau, it was once the case – and would still be the case had language and music not taken this 'disastrous' wrong turn – that the human passions were fully expressed in a kind of emotionally heightened speech-song that communicated straight from heart to heart and which had no need for such supplementary adjuncts as articulation, grammatical structure, writing, harmony, musical notation, or the 'calculus of intervals'. These latter he thinks of as having somehow *befallen* language and music through an accident of 'progress' that need not – should not – have happened yet which also (by a certain perverse compulsion) marked their development from the outset. This is why, as Derrida shows, Rousseau's language is itself subject to extreme complexities of modal and temporal articulation whenever it broaches the issue of priority between nature and culture, speech and writing, melody and harmony, or origin and supplement. In each case what should by all rights have been a self-sufficient entity requiring (or admitting) no such addition turns out – by the logic of Rousseau's argument – to have harboured a certain incompleteness *at source* which belies that claim and thus complicates his argument despite and against its manifest intent.

This complication first enters at the point where Rousseau attempts to define what it is about passional utterance – speech or song – in its earliest (i.e., most natural, spontaneous) character that none the less sets it decisively apart from the expression of animal need. 'Everything proceeds from this inaugural distinction: "It seems then that need dictated the first gestures, while the passions wrung forth the first words"' (Derrida 1976: 195). By the same token music could only have arisen when speech had advanced to the stage of expressing passions – distinctively human passions – as opposed to mere snarls of 'anger', grunts of 'contentment', or other such non-human animal noises. Thus '[t]here is no music before language. Music is born of voice and not of sound. No prelinguistic sonority can, according to Rousseau, open the time of music. In the beginning is song' (ibid.: 195). 'Song', that is, in a sense of the term that would include those instances of passional language (or emotionally heightened speech) which had not yet become 'music', properly so called, but would exclude – as Rousseau firmly declares – any animal sound (such as birdsong) which lacks the distinctively linguistic attributes of meaning and articulation. 'That is why there is no animal music', as Derrida writes, closely paraphrasing Rousseau. 'One speaks of animal music only by looseness of vocabulary and by anthropomorphic projection' (ibid.: 195–96). Yet in that case one is surely entitled to ask what has now become of Rousseau's claim that language and music both took rise from a 'natural' expression of feelings, emotions, or sentiments which would somehow have remained as yet untouched by the corrupting ('sup-plementary') effects of culture or civilised artifice. For there is simply no way that Rousseau can put this case while maintaining the distinction – equally crucial to his argument – between that which belongs to the realm of merely animal pseudo- or proto-'expression' and that which belongs to the human realm of articulate and meaningful language. Thus if the stage of transition from 'sounds' or 'noises' to language, in the proper usage of that term, is the point at which culture supervenes upon nature – or the point at which intersubjective feeling takes over from the dictates of animal need – then clearly *by the logic of Rousseau's argument* one has to conclude that language could never have existed in any such 'natural' (pre-linguistic) state. And if the song is indeed, as Rousseau declares, 'a kind of modification of the human voice', then just as clearly 'it is difficult to assign it an absolutely characteristic (*propre*) modality' (ibid.: 196). For it is just those defining or 'characteristic' features – of melody, cadence, emotional expressiveness, and empathetic power – which Rousseau takes to distinguish song (authentically *human* song) from the kinds of song-like animal 'expression' which possess no genuine claim to that title.

The same complication emerges when Rousseau attempts to make good his argument for the 'natural' priority of melody over harmony, or the straightforward expression of human sentiments through an unadorned singing line over the various false and artificial embellishments introduced by later composers, among them – pre-eminently – Rameau and the fash-ionable French figures of his day. (That Rousseau's own compositions in a more 'natural' Italianate style enjoyed no comparable measure of success is doubtless a fact of some psychological or socio-cultural significance but philosophically beside the point.) 'Melody being *forgotten*', Rousseau laments,

> and the attention of musicians being completely turned toward harmony, everything gradually came to be governed according to this *new object*. The genres, the modes, the scale, all received new faces. Harmonic successions came to dictate the sequence of parts. This sequence having *usurped the name* of melody, it was, in effect, impossible to recognize the *traits of its mother* in this new melody. And our musical system having thus *gradually* become purely harmonic, it is not surprising that its *oral tone [accent]* has *suffered*, and that our music has lost almost all its *energy*. Thus we see how singing *gradually* became an art entirely *separate* from speech, from which it takes its origin; how the harmonics of sounds resulted in the *forgetting* of vocal inflections; and finally, how music, restricted to purely physical concurrences of vibrations, found itself *deprived* of the moral power it had yielded when it was the *twofold voice of nature*. (cited by Derrida, 1976: 199–200)

This passage brings out very clearly the logical strains that emerge within Rousseau's discourse when he attempts to theorise the origins of music and the causes of its subsequent decline. For how can it be thought – and consistently maintained – that the fateful swerve from melody to harmony (or nature to culture) was something that befell music only by an accident of cultural change and not through its inherent propensity to develop and extend its resources in just that way? After all, on Rousseau's own submission, the earliest (most natural) stage of musical expression was one *already marked* by certain characteristics – 'the genres, the modes, and the scale' – which could only have belonged to that post-originary (decadent) phase when melody had acquired a range of conventional forms and devices, along with the 'supplementary' traits of harmony and counterpoint. Thus, far from having wrongfully 'usurped the name' of melody, harmony must rather be conceived as an integral component and defining feature of all melodious utterance, even at the outset – the mythic point of origin – when by rights it should have found absolutely no place in the authentic speech-song of passional language. For has not Rousseau quite explicitly acknowledged that song is in itself and by its very nature 'a kind of modification of the human voice'? In which case the 'twofold voice of nature' – originary speech and song – would not so much have 'suffered' a gradual decline and a process of increasing 'separation' that deprived it of its 'moral power' but would rather have taken the course that it did through a *natural* development of harmonic resources that were *always already* present at the earliest stage of melodic expression.

Again, how could it have been that 'the harmonics of sounds resulted in the *forgetting* of vocal inflections'? For, according to Rousseau, those inflections *originally* came about through a certain harmonic modification of the human voice that marked the transition from a realm of animal noises (such as birdsong) provoked by nothing more than physical need to a realm of humanly significant passional utterance. To the extent that 'music pre-supposes voice, it comes into being at the same time as human society. As speech, it requires that the other be present to me as other through compassion. Animals, whose pity is not awakened by the imagination, have no affinity with the other as such' (Derrida 1976: 195). Such feelings should have characterised the earliest stage of musical development, a stage (more properly) when 'development' had not yet occurred and when there was – as yet – no room for the 'desolating' split between nature and culture (or melody and harmony) which wrenched music from its otherwise preordained natural path. Yet it is impossible to ignore the counter-logic that runs athwart Rousseau's professed statements of intent and compels him to acknowledge – not without 'embarrassment' – the fact that this split must *already* have occurred by the time that music was able to express even the most basic of human feelings and emotions.

Rousseau strives to avoid this self-contradictory upshot by specifying just how the accident befell and by means of what alien, parasitic device harmony managed to substitute itself for the melody of living song. It is the musical *interval*, he thinks, that must be blamed for having thus opened the way to all manner of subsequent abuses. For the interval brings with it an element of 'spacing', a *differential* relationship between tones which disrupts the otherwise self-sufficient character of melody by introducing an unwanted harmonic dimension that breaches the original (natural) unity of speech and song. Such is at any rate what Rousseau wishes to say: that the interval obtrudes as a bad supplement, an accidental perversion of music, or a source of harmonic conflicts and tensions that should never have befallen the development of music had it only remained true to its original (purely melodic) vocation. And he does indeed say just that in a number of passages – cited by Derrida – where the emphasis falls on this unnatural, perverse, and above all *accidental* character of harmony as that which can only have impinged upon melody as a threat from *outside* its original (proper) domain.

Yet there are other, symptomatically revealing passages where Rousseau is constrained to say just the opposite, namely that harmony is and was *always* implicit in melody, since the interval – or the differential 'spacing' of tones – is something which enters into all conceivable forms of musical expression, even those (such as monody, folk-song, or 'primitive' chant) that *on the face of it* have not yet arrived at the stage of multivocal harmony or counterpoint. For in these cases also it is a fact of acoustics as well as a subjectively verifiable truth about the phenomenology of musical perception that we don't hear only the bare, unaccompanied melodic line. Rather that line is perceived as carrying along with it an additional range of harmonic overtones and relationships in the absence of which we should simply not perceive it as possessing the distinctive melodic traits of contour, cadence, modal inflection, intervallic structure, and so forth. Thus, in Derrida's words,

> [t]his fissure [i.e., the interval] is not one among others. It is *the* fissure: the necessity of interval, the harsh law of spacing. It could not endanger song except by being inscribed in it from its birth and in its essence. Spacing is not the accident of song. Or rather, as accident and accessory, fall and supplement, it is that also without which, strictly speaking, the song would not have come into being.... [T]he interval is part of the definition of song. It is therefore, so to speak, an originary accessory and an essential accident. Like writing. (Derrida 1976: 200)

Hence – to repeat – that curious 'logic of supplementarity' which brings it about that what *should* have been original, self-sufficient, and exempt from addition turns out to harbour a certain lack that can only be supplied by conceding its dependence on some 'accident' of culture or history which should *never have occurred* in the natural course of things. However this logic is none the less rigorous – and Derrida's reading likewise – for the fact that Rousseau is compelled to articulate some 'classically' unthinkable conjunctions of claim and counter-claim with regard to these strictly undecidable issues of priority between nature and culture, speech and writing, melody and harmony, and so forth.

To be sure, when his commentary comes closest to a *paraphrase* of Rousseau's arguments then this requires some highly complex – at times even tortuous – deviations from classical logic, deviations that typically involve recourse to modal or tensed constructions which strain the limits of intelligibility and often lean over into downright paradox. Thus for instance (to repeat): the 'supplementary' character of articulation is that which 'wrenches language from its condition of origin, from its conditional or future of origin, from that which it must (ought to) have been and what it has never been; it could only have been born by suspending its relation to all origin' (Derrida 1976: 243). In such passages Derrida is no doubt pressing beyond any order of statement that might be acceptable in terms of those various modal or tense-logics that philosophers have lately proposed by way of extending and refining the resources of the first-order propositional and predicate calculus (see especially Hintikka 1969; Hughes and Cresswell 1996; Loux [ed.] 1979; Prior 1957). However it should also be clear that he does so precisely in order to reveal the kinds of paradox and *illogicality* that result when Rousseau attempts to make good his case for there once having existed a proto-language devoid of those necessary (language-constitutive) features which *must* have been already in place for the transition to occur from the realm of pre-articulate (merely 'animal') sounds. Granted, Rousseau 'wants us to think of this movement as an accident' (Derrida 1976: 242), just as Austin wants us to think of performative 'infelicities' as somehow befalling the communicative process through an accident or mischance that in no way affects the normative conditions of speech-act utterance. Yet despite his intentions Rousseau 'describes it...in its originary necessity', that is to say, as a 'natural progress' which 'does not come unexpectedly' in the wake of spontaneous, passionate speech-song but which *must be there* from the very first moment when language arrives on the scene.

The following passage brings out very clearly the way that Derrida's commentary pursues the twists and turns of Rousseau's argument by citing passages that directly contradict his thesis and which hence expose the 'supplementary' logic that structures his entire discourse on the origins of language and music.

> Before articulation...there is no speech, no song, and thus no music. Passion could not be expressed or imitated without articulation. The 'cry of nature', the 'simple sounds [that] emerge naturally from the throat', do not make a language because articulation has not yet played there. 'Natural sounds are inarticulate.' Convention has its hold only upon articulation, which pulls language out of the cry, and increases itself with consonants, tenses, and quantity. *Thus language is born out of the process of its own degeneration*. That is why, in order to convey Rousseau's *descriptive* procedure, which does not wish to restore the facts but merely to measure a deviation, it is perhaps imprudent to call by the name of zero degree or simple origin that out of which the deviation is measured or the structure outlined. Zero degree or origin implies that the commencement be simple, that it not be at the same time the beginning of a degeneration, that it be possible to think of it in the form of presence in general, whether it be a modified presence or not, whether it be past event or permanent essence. To speak of simple origin, it must also be possible to measure deviation according to a simple axis and in a single direction. Is it still necessary to recall that nothing in Rousseau's description authorizes us to do so? (Derrida 1976: 242)

As direct quotation gives way to paraphrase and paraphrase, in turn, to a detailed analysis of Rousseau's discourse and its various complexities of tense, logic, and modal implication so Derrida's reasoning can be seen to maintain a clearly marked distance from the text in hand, or from anything like a straightforward proposal that the exegete endorse this logic of supplementarity as a substitute for 'classical' concepts. Indeed the whole passage is a striking example of the way that Derrida deploys those concepts as providing the sole legitimate means by which to 'measure a deviation', that is, to expose the extent to which Rousseau's discourse is compelled to undergo such 'supplementary' twists and turns in order to preserve some semblance of articulate sense or intelligible argument. So commentators like Priest (1995) are right to find something of interest here for theorists of deviant, many-valued, or paraconsistent logic but wrong to suppose that Derrida's exposition of Rousseau should be taken as a straightforward recommendation that we adopt the logic of supplementarity as another such alternative to classical norms. Rather – as emerges most emphatically from the passage cited above – it is a mode of paradoxical pseudo-logic that is forced upon Rousseau by those false premises which cannot but generate aporias or contradictions once subject to a reading that calls them to account in rigorous (bivalent or classically consistent) terms. Thus where Rousseau claims to measure the degree of 'deviation' that separates civilised (articulate) language and music from their presumed 'natural' origin, Derrida estimates the 'deviant' character of Rousseau's discourse precisely by its ultimate failure to redeem that claim and its need to adopt such exiguous logical (or quasi-logical) resources in the effort to sustain its *strictly unthinkable* thesis. At any rate it is clear from a careful reading of the above passage that Derrida is applying standards of consistency and truth which place his commentary decidedly at odds with the manifest purport of Rousseau's argument and which construe that argument in deconstructive (i.e., critical-diagnostic) rather than purely exegetical terms.

What I wish to emphasise again is the fact that Derrida nowhere takes refuge in an approximative logic or one that would abandon principles such as bivalence or excluded middle in response to any anomalies discovered in the course of empirical – or textual – investigation. We have seen already how Derrida rejects this face-saving proposal when Searle accuses him of holding Austinian speech-act theory accountable to standards of clear-cut conceptual definition which cannot be met – so Searle protests – when it comes to our normal, everyday linguistic practices. On this point he is wholly in agreement with a logician like Frege and totally at odds with Searle: that 'unless a distinction can be made rigorous and precise, it is not really a distinction at all' (Derrida 1989: 123; Frege 1952; Searle 1977). But we should also bear in mind his further claim – again in the context of speech-act philosophy – that this 'demand of rigour' may finally require 'the structure of that logic to be transformed or complicated' (Derrida 1989: 123). That is to say, the close-reading of texts such as those of Austin and Rousseau may give rise to aporias that cannot be subsumed under any 'classical' logic, but that would simply escape notice if those standards were relaxed to the point of abandoning the bivalent truth/falsehood distinction.

VI

Thus Derrida's approach to philosophy of logic is in this respect more conservative – or classical – than that of empirically minded logical revisionists like Quine or those, like Dummett, who would renounce bivalence or excluded middle whenever it is a question of statements that lack any determinate proof-procedure or means of verification (Dummett 1978; Quine 1961). In their case the willingness to revise logic is more a matter of foregone philosophical commitment, even if Quine takes it as something that might be forced upon us by certain empirical discoveries in physics (such as wave/particle dualism) and Dummett is led to suspend bivalence chiefly on account of his intuitionist, that is, non-classical and anti-realist approach to issues in the philosophy of mathematics (Dummett 1977). Still both thinkers may fairly be said to incline very strongly in this direction and to do so for reasons which – although different – involve an ultimate readiness to revise or qualify the principles of classical logic. For Derrida, those principles hold as a matter of strict necessity *right up to the point* where it can actually be shown – on the textual evidence to hand – that they encounter some obstacle which leaves no alternative except to 'transform' or 'complicate' the logic that assigns truth-values to a given statement. Indeed I would claim that Derrida's exposition of the 'logic of supplementarity' as it emerges through his reading of Rousseau is in this respect more rigorously argued and more responsive to the demonstrable need for such analysis than either Quine's somewhat speculative arguments based on just one possible interpretation of the quantum phenomena or Dummett's highly contentious understanding of the scope and limits of mathematical knowledge. (For further discussion, see Norris 2000a, 2002a.) Thus it has to do not only with certain curious blind spots or logical anomalies in Rousseau's text but also with the plain *impossibility* that things could ever have been as Rousseau describes them, for example, as concerns the absolute priority of melody over harmony in music or of a natural 'language of the passions' over all those mere 'supplementary' devices – articulation, grammar, structural traits of whatever kind – that supposedly signalled the onset of linguistic and cultural decline. For there is simply no conceiving that idyllic phase when speech would have lacked those same *language-constitutive* features but would yet have been a 'language' in the sense of that term which Rousseau elsewhere (in his more theoretical, even proto-structuralist moments) considers to mark the stage of transition from animal noise to human speech.

That this impossibility is found to emerge through a meticulously argued reading of Rousseau should lead us to conclude that the aporias in question are not so much products of 'textualist' ingenuity on Derrida's part but rather have to do with certain empirically warranted and theoretically ascertainable truths about language. Thus, as I have said, his approach falls square with an argument like 'early' Davidson's concerning the minimal range of necessary attributes – quantifiers, devices for negation, conjunction, disjunction, anaphora, cross-reference, and so forth – that any language surely *must* possess if it is to function effectively *as* a language, rather than a means of vaguely emotive pseudo-communication (Davidson 1984). So the Derridean 'logic of supplementarity' has this much in common with other, more 'classical' modes of logic: that whilst laying claim to its own kind of formal rigour and validity-conditions it must also correspond to the way things stand with respect to some given subject-domain or specific area of discourse. That is to say, when Derrida finds Rousseau obliquely conceding (despite his declarations elsewhere) that 'harmony is the originary supplement of melody', or that melody could never have existed in a state of pure pre-harmonic grace, this has implications not only for philosophy of logic but also for our thinking about music and the history of music. For indeed it is the case – empirically so, as a matter of acoustics and the overtone-series, and phenomenologically speaking, as concerns the ubiquitous role of harmony in our perceptions of melodic contour – that what *ought* (for Rousseau) to figure as a mere 'supplement' turns out to be the very *condition of possibility* for music and musical experience in general.

There is a sense in which Rousseau acknowledges this – recognises it to follow from the basic principles of acoustics and music-theory – but also a sense in which he constantly endeavours to deny or repress that knowledge. For 'Rousseau never makes explicit the originarity of the lack that makes necessary the addition of the supplement – the quantity and the differences of quantity that always already shape melody. He does not make it explicit, or rather he says it without saying it, in an oblique and clandestine manner' (Derrida 1976: 214). And again: 'Rousseau wishes to restore a natural degree of art within which chromatics, harmonics, and interval would be unknown. He wishes to efface what he had...already recognised, that there is harmony within melody, etc. But the *origin must (should) have been* (such is, here and elsewhere, the grammar and the lexicon of the relationship to origin) *pure* melody' (ibid.). That Rousseau is unable to sustain this thesis against certain powerful objections that arise from the logic of his own discourse is a fact that should interest logicians as much as musicologists and cultural historians. For it offers a striking example of the way that complications which develop in the course of arguing from (apparently) self-evident premises to (apparently) sound conclusions can introduce doubt as to whether those premises are indeed self-evident or those conclusions warranted by anything more than strength of doctrinal attachment. This emerges very clearly from certain passages in Rousseau's writing on the theory of music where he effectively concedes as much through a curious reversal of the very terms – or the order of priority between them – which bear the whole weight of his argument. Thus: 'harmony would be very difficult to distinguish from melody, unless one adds to the latter the ideas of rhythm and measure, without which, in effect, no melody can have a determined character; whereas harmony has its own by itself, independent of every other quality' (cited by Derrida, 1976: 210). But in that case – as Austin might have said – it is harmony that 'wears the trousers' with respect to this conceptual opposition and melody that lacks the self-sufficient expressive resources which would enable it to manage perfectly well without the 'supplement' of harmony.

This I take to be the single most distinctive feature of the 'logic of supplementarity' as Derrida expounds it through his reading of Rousseau. That is to say, it is an exception to the general rule which requires that we distinguish logical *validity* from argumentative *soundness*, or the question what counts as a case of formally valid inference from any question concerning the truth of premises or of conclusions drawn from them. In this respect the logic of supplementarity has more in common with certain kinds of abductive reasoning – or inference to the best explanation – than with classical (e.g., deductive) schemas of truth-preservation (Harman 1965; Lipton 1993; Peirce 1992). Abduction is essentially a mode of inference that reasons backwards (so to speak) from whatever we possess in the way of empirical evidence to whatever best explains or accounts for that same evidence. In so doing it allows for the standing possibility that premises may be confirmed, infirmed, strengthened, or indeed *discovered* through just such well-tried methods of reasoning, especially in the physical sciences. It is therefore a process of rational conjecture which involves the application of standard principles – such as bivalence and excluded middle – but which deploys them in a non-standard way so as to extend the resources of logic beyond its classical limits.

Among other things this provides an answer to the 'paradox of analysis', or the claim that, since deductive logic comes down to a matter of purely definitional (analytic) truth, its conclusions must always be contained in its premises and hence be incapable of making any new or substantive contribution to knowledge (see also Mackie 1973: 1–16; Moore 1968). The paradox received its classic statement in the following passage from C.H. Langford's essay 'The Notion of Analysis in Moore's Philosophy'.

> Let us call what is to be analyzed the analysandum, and let us call that which does the analysing the analysans. The analysis then states an appropriate relation of equivalence between the analysandum and the analysans. And the paradox of analysis is to the effect that, if the verbal expression representing the analysandum has the same meaning as the verbal expression representing the analysans, the analysis states a bare identity and is trivial; but if the two verbal expressions do not have the same meaning, the analysis is incorrect. (Langford 1968: 323)

The approach *via* inference to the best explanation gets around this seeming paradox by maintaining (1) that abductive logic *can* provide grounds for a non-tautological (ampliative) process of knowledge-acquisition, and (2) that this process is none the less consistent with an application of classical precepts such as bivalence and excluded middle. That is to say, it rejects any Quinean empiricist recourse to across-the-board logical revisability – or any Dummett-type anti-realist proposal to suspend those classical precepts – while none the less extending the scope of valid inference well beyond the highly restrictive terms laid down by a hardline deductive-nomological conception of valid reasoning. It may well be objected that arguments of this sort have their place in philosophy of science and other empirically oriented disciplines but not – surely – in the business of textual interpretation where the only 'data' are words on the page and where these are subject to entirely different (by which it is implied, less exacting or rigorous) standards of accountability. However this objection misses the mark if applied to Derrida's commentary on Rousseau since the operative standards here – as I have argued – are simply not those of 'interpretation' in the usual (literary-critical) sense of that term. Rather, they have to do with the evidence of certain logical anomalies that *cannot be ignored* by a sufficiently attentive reading and which therefore require an abductive revision of various 'self-evident' premises – such as the absolute priority of nature over culture, speech over writing, or melody over harmony – whose claim is countermanded by the logic of Rousseau's discourse.

Take for instance the passage where Rousseau strives to separate two conceptions of 'melody', the one marked already by a kind of creeping harmonic corruption, while the other preserves its spontaneity and naturalness by appealing to the passional origins of primitive song. '*Melody* has reference to two different principles', he writes, 'according to the manner in which we consider it'.

> Taken in the connection of sounds, and by the rules of the mode, it has its principle in harmony; since it is an harmonic analysis which gives the degrees of the gamut [scale], the chords of the mode, and the laws of the modulation, the only elements of singing. According to this principle, the whole force of melody is bounded to flattering the ear by agreeable sounds, as one flatters the eye by agreeable concords of colours; but when taken as an art of imitation, by which the mind may be affected by different images, the heart moved by different sentiments, the passions excited or calmed, in a word, moral effect be operated, which surpass the immediate empire of the sense, another principle must be sought for it, for we see no hold, by which the harmony alone, and whatever comes from it, can affect us thus. (cited by Derrida, 1976: 212)

Yet this second (presumptively more natural and genuine) 'principle' of melody is one whose appeal to the 'art of imitation' must be seen to complicate Rousseau's argument – to skew it against his avowed intent – by introducing elements of cultural differentiation which should properly have no place in any such account. After all, as Derrida pointedly asks, 'what is it within melody that imitates and expresses?' (ibid.: 212–13). To which Rousseau provides a ready answer: '[i]t is the *accent* of language that determines the melody in each nation; it is the *accent* which makes us speak while singing, and speak with *more or less energy*, according as the language has more or less accent' (ibid.: 213). But one may then ask what constitutes the 'accent' peculiar to this or that 'natural' language, or just what can serve as the objective criterion for making such otherwise culturally loaded evaluative contrasts and distinctions. For they must have to do with those differential features – of prosody, tonality, the 'chords of the mode', 'laws of modulation', and so forth – which *should* by all rights pertain only to 'melody' when construed on the first (harmonically compromised) principle and not to melody truly conceived as a natural, spontaneous utterance of human passions. However it is precisely Rousseau's point that 'accent' is the sole distinguishing mark by which to judge authentic as opposed to artificial or degenerate languages.

Thus, according to Rousseau, there once was (must have been) a time when speech and song had not yet gone their separate ways and when '[a]ccents constituted singing, quantity constituted measure, and one spoke as much by sounds and rhythm as by articulations and words' (cited by Derrida, 1976: 214). Yet here already – as Rousseau is constrained to acknowledge – there is simply no conceiving how 'accent' is produced (or how languages might be compared in point of their accentual features) unless with regard to differential structures like 'quantity', 'measure', and 'articulation'. That is to say, it is impossible for Rousseau to maintain his position concerning the natural priority of melody over harmony without *either* ignoring these various items of counter-evidence *or* allowing them to twist the logic of his argument against its own avowed or manifest intent. The same applies to Rousseau's concept of *imitation*, referring as it does to that which defines the very nature of human sociality – whatever lifts music and language beyond the realm of mere animal need – yet also to that which supposedly inhabits a realm of spontaneous (natural) human passion as yet untouched by the disfiguring marks of cultural progress. 'Rousseau has need of imitation', Derrida writes:

> he advances it as the possibility of song and the emergence out of animality, but he exalts it only as a reproduction adding itself to the represented though it *adds nothing*, simply supplements it. In that sense he praises art or *mimesis* as a supplement. But by the same token praise may instantly turn to criticism. Since the supplementary mimesis adds *nothing*, is it not useless? And if, nevertheless, adding itself to the represented, it is not nothing, is that imitative supplement not dangerous to the integrity of what is represented and to the original purity of nature? (Derrida 1976: 203)

Thus 'imitation', like 'supplement', is a term whose logical grammar – whose 'syncategorematic' status, to adopt the analytic parlance – is such as to induce an unsettling effect in any context of argument where it purports to establish that certain concepts (like 'nature', 'speech', and 'melody') must take priority over certain others (like 'culture', 'writing', and 'harmony').

In Rousseau's case what emerges is a sequence of contradictory propositions which cannot be reconciled according to the terms of a classical (bivalent) logic and which therefore require *either* that this logic be abandoned *or* that Rousseau abandon his cardinal premise with respect to that supposedly self-evident order of priority. As I read him Derrida regards the first option as philosopically a non-starter since it would licence any number of revisionist proposals – like the suspension of bivalence or excluded middle – whose effect would be to render thinking altogether devoid of conceptual clarity and precision. This is why, to repeat, he insists against Searle that there is strictly no place in discussions of this sort for a 'logic of approximation' or 'a simple empiricism of difference in degree'. Rather what is required is a rigorous application of bivalent logic – 'a logic of "all or nothing" without which the distinction and the limits of a concept would have no chance' (Derrida 1989: 117) – but one that goes on to reason abductively from certain contradictions in Rousseau's discourse to the necessity of revising or abandoning Rousseau's premises. Thus the Derridean 'logic of supplementarity' differs from other revisionist programmes in its insistence that any change in our thinking can only be warranted – logically justified – when arrived at through a strict application of bivalent ('all or nothing') criteria. Otherwise it could offer no adequate grounds for drawing the kinds of conclusion that Derrida draws, that is, that *as a matter of logical necessity as well as a matter of empirical fact* there cannot be melody without harmony or a language of the passions that is not already marked by those differential features – of accent, tonality, 'laws of modulation', and so forth – that belong to a given (however 'primitive') stage of cultural development. 'It is a question', he writes, 'of a supplement at the origin of languages. This supplement lays bare an additive substitution, a supplement of speech. It is inserted at the point where language begins to be articulated, is born, that is, from falling short of itself, when its accent or intonation, marking origin or passion within it, is effaced under that *other* mark of origin which is articulation' (Derrida 1976: 270). And this not merely as an odd, unlooked-for consequence of Rousseau's obsessional desire to prove just the opposite but rather as a matter of linguistic, historical, and *logical* necessity.

VII

My point is that Derrida arrives at these claims through a reading of Rousseau that undoubtedly places considerable strain on the precepts of classical (bivalent) logic but which is none the less obliged to respect those precepts – to follow them so far as possible – since it would otherwise be able to establish nothing concerning the self-contradictory nature of Rousseau's thematic premises. Thus when Derrida notes the emergence of a different, that is, non-classical or 'supplementary' logic in Rousseau's text it is only on the basis – as the logical outcome – of applying the axioms of bivalence and excluded middle to certain problematical passages which must then be seen to cast doubt on the coherence of Rousseau's project.

This is why Derrida's commentary goes out of its way to insist on the strictly unresolvable tensions and logical strains that characterise not only Rousseau's writings about language, music, history, and social development but also its own best efforts to produce a consistent (non-contradictory) reading of Rousseau. These complications arise at precisely the stage where commentary is obliged – logically compelled – to register the presence of a deep-laid conflict between 'implication, nominal presence, and thematic exposition'. They typically take the form of an attempt, on Rousseau's part, to establish a clear-cut conceptual distinction which *should* be sufficient to resolve the problem but which then turns out to require yet another distinction, and so on to the point where his argument displays that repeated pattern of substitutive swerves from origin which Derrida terms the 'logic of supplementarity'. Thus:

> Just as there is a good musical form (melody) and a bad musical form (harmony), there is a good and a bad melodic form. By a dichotomous operation that one must ever begin anew and carry further, Rousseau exhausts himself in trying to separate, as two exterior and heterogeneous forces, a positive and a negative principle. Of course, the malign element in melody communicates with the malign element in music in general, that is to say with harmony. This second dissociation between good and bad melodic form puts the first exteriority into question: there is harmony already within melody. (Derrida 1976: 212)

However, once again, this case would lack any semblance of demonstrative force – of philosophical cogency and rigour – were it not for Derrida's applying the precepts of classical logic in his own exposition of Rousseau's text and also his holding that text accountable to standards which *cannot be other* than those of bivalence and excluded middle. For it is crucial to Derrida's argument, here as in the exchange with Searle, that any relaxation of those classical criteria will produce a merely 'approximative' logic and a blurring of conceptual distinctions whose effect is to render thought incapable of reflecting critically on its own premises or presuppositions.

I have argued a similar case elsewhere with regard to the proposal – by Quine, Putnam, and others – that the best way around certain long-standing conceptual problems in the philosophy of quantum mechanics (e.g., those of wave/particle dualism or quantum superposition) is to adopt an alternative, non-bivalent logic which thereby resolves those problems at a stroke while conserving the full range of empirical predictions and measurement data (see Norris 2000b, 2002b; also Putnam 1983; Quine 1961). However the trouble with this approach – especially when applied, in Quinean fashion, as a matter of straightforward 'pragmatic convenience' – is that it leaves no room for the kind of abductive reasoning that would question the premises of the orthodox quantum theory precisely on account of the logical anomalies (or conceptual paradoxes) to which that theory is inescapably prone unless granted such special-case exemption from the requirements of classical logic. Thus the orthodox theory has often been maintained in the face of realist challenges – such as that mounted by David Bohm – through its advocates' claim that quantum phenomena just *do not* conform to the rule of distributed (bivalent) truth- and falsehood values and hence that the theory simply *cannot* be criticised on terms which apply only to the realm of macrophysical objects and events (see especially Bohm 1957; also Cushing 1994 and Holland 1993). However this argument will appear less attractive – and more like a face-saving strategy of last resort – if one asks what in that case could possibly *count* as good reason for revising or renouncing some given scientific theory (whether in the micro or the macro domain) as a result of recalcitrant empirical findings. For such revision entails that those findings be construed – in bivalent terms – according to a logic that requires *one or other* of two possible responses, that is, that the theory be retained and the data subject to reinterpretation or the data conserved and the theory revised or abandoned. So there is an obvious problem with the Quinean proposal for across-the-board logical revisability or the Putnam-type argument for a three-valued 'quantum logic' when these suggestions are held accountable to standards of consistency or reflexive self-application. And this problem is yet more acute – as I have said – if any room is to be found for a process of abductive reasoning that requires the application of bivalent logic in order to confirm, disconfirm, or revise certain premises as the result of continuing empirical investigation. At any rate there seems rather little to be said for a logical-revisionist approach whose upshot – if consistently applied – would be to render such premises altogether proof against any possible objection on grounds of their leading to paradoxical or self-contradictory results.

Let me take one further example from Derrida by way of bringing out this requirement that bivalence retain its place even – or especially – where it encounters obstacles such as those thrown up by Rousseau's discourse on the origins of language and culture. Thus, according to Rousseau, the first societies exhibited a state of natural, harmonious human co-existence that was as yet unmarked by those various differential structures – rank, class, social privilege, delegated power, representative assemblies, and so forth – which only later came to exert their artificial and corrupting social effect. However it is clear as a matter of conceptual necessity as well as of historical, anthropological, or socio-cultural reflection that such structures – in some form or another – must be taken to constitute the *very precondition* of societal existence. This is why, as Derrida remarks, all attempts to draw a line between 'nature' and 'culture' while counting some cultures more 'natural' than others must at length give rise to the kinds of logical complication that characterise Rousseau's text. In short, 'language is born out of the process of its own degeneration' (Derrida 1976: 242), a statement that may seem wilfully paradoxical but which captures both the curious double-logic of Rousseau's discourse and the straightforward (conceptually self-evident) truth that there cannot ever have been any language – or any state of social existence – that would meet the requirement of transparent communion in the face-to-face of unmediated mutual understanding. Just as language depends on a system of differential structures, contrasts, and relationships so society depends on – cannot be conceived in the absence of – those structures which articulate social or cultural distinctions of various kinds. And this applies just as much to that Rousseauist conception of 'nature' – a nature supposedly untouched by the ravages of cultural decline – which is yet paradoxically required to do service as a description of how human beings once lived in a state of (what else?) social co-existence under certain distinctively *cultural* rules and constraints. 'All the contradictions of the discourse are *regulated*, rendered necessary yet unresolved, by this structure of the concept of nature. *Before all determinations of a natural law, there is, effectively constraining the discourse, a law of the concept of nature'* (Derrida 1976: 233; author's italics).

Hence the difference that Derrida constantly remarks between that which Rousseau *expressly wishes to say* and that which he is none the less *compelled to describe* by a logic that resists, contradicts, or countermands his avowed meaning. Thus 'Rousseau's discourse lets itself be constrained by a complexity which always has the form of a supplement of or from the origin. His declared intention is not annulled by this but rather *inscribed* within a system which it no longer dominates' (ibid.: 243). Moreover this demonstrable non-coincidence of meaning and intent has implications beyond what it tells us concerning Rousseau's problematic ideas about the origins of human society. Nor are those implications by any means exhausted when Derrida extends his analysis to other texts – notably by Saussure and Lévi-Strauss – where a range of kindred binary oppositions (nature/culture, speech/writing, authentic passion *versus* civilised artifice) are likewise subject to a deconstructive reading (see Derrida 1976: 27–73, 101–40). Rather his case is that Rousseau's predicament is one that will inevitably mark any discourse on these or related themes beyond a certain stage of conceptual or logico-semantic complexity. That is to say, this particular form of deviant ('supplementary') logic is certain to emerge whenever it is a question of fixing – or attempting to fix – some notional point of origin for language or society that would *not yet* partake of the defining traits (articulation, difference, structure, hierarchical relationship, etc.) in the absence of which no language or society could possibly have come into being. Indeed, Derrida remarks,

> [t]he expression 'primitive times', and all the evidence which will be used to describe them, refer to no date, no event, no chronology. One can vary the facts without modifying the structural invariant. In every possible

historical structure, there seemingly would be a prehistoric, presocial, and also prelinguistic stratum, that one ought always to be able to lay bare. (Derrida 1976: 252)

However it is precisely Derrida's point – borne out by the meticulous analysis of passages in Rousseau's text – that this zero-point of history, society, and language is one that cannot be described or evoked without giving rise to that counter-logic (or logic of logical anomalies) which marks the emergence of supplementarity and hence the non-existence of anything that answers to Rousseau's wishful description.

So it is wrong – a very definite misreading of Derrida's work – to suggest that deconstruction is really nothing more than a rhetorical technique for generating textual aporias which has long been the stock-in-trade of literary critics professionally skilled in finding out instances of paradox, ambiguity, or multiple meaning (Brooks 1947; Wimsatt 1954). Indeed Derrida is at pains – in *Of Grammatology* and other texts – to insist that his readings are not so much concerned with localised examples of semantic over-determination but rather with the logical syntax of terms (such as 'supplement', 'différance', 'pharmakon', and 'parergon') whose contradictory meanings cannot be contained by any such familiar model of literary interpretation (Derrida 1973, 1981, 1987b). To be sure, Derrida makes this case through a critical-expository reading of Rousseau which promotes textual fidelity to a high point of principle and which even insists – in one notorious passage – that 'there is nothing outside the text' (*il n'y a pas de hors-texte*; more accurately: 'no "outside" to the text') (Derrida 1976: 158). However this should *not* be taken to suggest that he is concerned only with the sacrosanct 'words on the page' or that he must subscribe to some kind of far-gone transcendental-idealist doctrine according to which textual inscriptions are the only items that should figure in this drastically pared-down ontology. What he is claiming, rather, is that deconstruction is able to bring out certain logical complications which also have much to tell us concerning the *real* (as distinct from the mythic or idealised) conditions of emergence for language and society.

This is why, as I have said, Derrida's reading of Rousseau has less to do with thematic commentary in the literary-critical mode and more to do with issues in philosophy of logic and philosophical semantics. Chief among them are (1) the status of 'deviant' *vis-à-vis* classical logics, and (2) the question – at the heart of much philosophical debate from Aristotle to Kant and beyond – as to how logic can be *both* a matter of formal (or transcendental) warrant *and* a mode of reasoning that, in some cases, permits the extension or refinement of our knowledge concerning matters of substantive import. Given time one could pursue these topics back to Derrida's early, in many ways formative studies of Husserl and his detailed account of the latter's attempt to reconcile those seemingly discrepant claims (Derrida 1973, 1978b). One could also instance the numerous passages in *Of Grammatology* where Derrida takes up this theme from Husserl – the opposition between logical 'structure' and empirical 'genesis' – and finds it prefigured in the texts of Rousseau at just those points where Rousseau's argument manifests the kinds of conceptual strain imposed by his attempt to theorise the natural (pre-cultural) origins of culture. Thus, according to Rousseau, there *should* or by rights *must have been* at one time a mode of social existence – a 'perpetual spring', a 'happy and durable epoch' – when humankind enjoyed all the benefits of society without its subsequent corrupting effects. 'The more we reflect on it', he writes, 'the more we shall find that this state was the least subject to revolutions, and altogether the very best man could experience; so that he can have departed from it only through some fatal accident, which, for the public good, should never have happened' (cited by Derrida, 1976: 259). Yet this idea is called into question by the counter-logic that regularly surfaces to undermine Rousseau's wishful professions of belief and to demonstrate the sheer impossibility that any such state could once have existed, let alone have formed 'the most happy and *durable*' epoch of human history. In Derrida's words, '[t]he passage from the state of nature to the state of language and society, the advent of supplementarity, remains then outside the grasp of the simple alternative of genesis and structure, of fact and principle, of historical and philosophical reason' (ibid.: 259).

VIII

It seems to me that logicians – especially those with an interest in issues of modal and tense-logic – have much to learn from a reading of Derrida which accords his text the kind of detailed attention that he brings to the texts of Rousseau. For it is among the most striking features of his Rousseau commentary that Derrida engages in some highly complex – at times logically and grammatically tortuous – attempts to reconstruct the rationale of Rousseau's argument in a form that would respect the principles of bivalence and excluded middle. That he fails in this endeavour and demonstrates rather the sheer impossibility of carrying it through is a sign not so much of Derrida's fixed intention to subvert those principles as of his fixed determination to apply them right up to the point where they encounter unignorable resistance from Rousseau's text.

Let me cite another extended passage from *Of Grammatology* which exemplifies the kinds of logical complication – the extraordinary twists of tense-logic and modal or hypothetical-subjunctive reasoning – which characterise Rousseau's discourse on the origins of language, music, and society. The passage in question again has to do with his attempt to explain how the 'grammar' of music – its codified conventions and (above all) its structures of harmonic development – might somehow be thought of *both* as having their source in the wellspring of natural melody *and* as having come upon that source from outside through an accident of culture that need not – better not – have happened. Thus:

> instead of concluding from this simultaneity [i.e., their common point of origin] that the song broached itself in grammar, that difference had already begun to corrupt melody, to make both it and its laws possible at the same time, Rousseau prefers to believe that grammar *must (should) have* been comprised... within melody. There *must (should) have* been plenitude and not lack, presence without difference. From then on the dangerous supplement, scale or harmony, *adds itself from the outside as evil and lack* to happy and innocent plenitude. It would come from an outside which would be simply the outside. This conforms to the logic of identity and to the principle of classical ontology (the outside is outside, being is, etc.) but not to the logic of supplementarity, which would have it that the outside be inside, that the other and the lack come to add themselves as a plus that replaces a minus, that what adds itself to something takes the place of a default in the thing, that the default, as the outside of the inside, should be already within the inside, etc. What Rousseau in fact describes is that the lack, adding itself as a plus to a plus, cuts into an energy which *must (should) have* been and remain intact. (Derrida 1976: 215)

There are two main points that I wish to make about this passage – and about Derrida's reading of Rousseau more generally – by way of bringing out its relevance to issues in philosophy of logic. One is that it shows the complex array of tensed and modal constructions ('had already', 'must [should have] been', 'would come from', 'would be simply', 'would have it that', 'should be already', etc.) to which Rousseau typically has recourse in order to maintain the natural – supposedly self-evident – priority of passion over reason, melody over harmony, or spontaneous utterance over grammar and articulation. Thus what Rousseau undoubtedly 'prefers to believe' with regard to these and other, kindred topics is expressed clearly enough in various propositions (or individual statements) concerning those respective orders of priority. However it is far from clear that Rousseau can maintain this position if one looks beyond the presumptive self-evidence of authorial intent to the logical grammar of a term like 'supplement'. For it then turns out that he cannot get around the obstacles to any straightforward (empirically plausible and logically coherent) statement of his views without having recourse to some tortuous locutions which symptomatically betray the stress-points in his argument. Yet of course those stress-points could never emerge – or register as such – were it not for Derrida's applying the precepts of classical (two-valued) logic and his doing so, moreover, in keeping with the strictest requirements of Rousseau's text. That is to say, Rousseau could not possibly advance a single proposition concerning those topics except on the understanding that every such statement is subject to assessment in bivalent (true-or-false) terms. And this condition applies whatever the extent of those modal, counterfactual, or tense-logical complexities that Derrida brings out in his reading of Rousseau.

Hence my second point: that the 'logic of supplementarity' is *not* proposed by Derrida as a substitute, replacement, or alternative to 'classical' logic but rather as a measure of just how far Rousseau is forced to equivocate in the effort to maintain his express position with regard to these various *topoi*. Here again I should wish to emphasise that if Derrida is indeed a logical 'revisionist' then this is not so much – as with Quine or Dummett – a distinctive philosophical *parti pris* but a matter of remarking certain logical *aberrations* that characterise the discourse of certain writers, chief among them Rousseau. That is to say, there is no question of renouncing those classical precepts (such as bivalence or excluded middle) which alone provide Derrida with the necessary means by which to analyse Rousseau's text and to bring out its various tensions, complications, and aporias. On the other hand this is not merely a matter of Rousseau's having fallen prey to conceptual confusions which he might have avoided with a bit more care in framing his arguments or thinking their implications through. For the logic of supplementarity is both indispensable to Rousseau's argument – the only form in which he is able to articulate its various propositions – and also (as Derrida shows) the main point of leverage for a reading that effectively subverts all its governing premises. Thus 'Rousseau cannot utilize it [the "concept of the supplement"] at the same time in all the virtualities of its meaning'. On the contrary:

> [t]he way in which he determines the concept and, in so doing, lets himself be determined by that very thing which he excludes from it, the direction in which he bends it, here as addition, there as substitute, now as the positivity and exteriority of evil, now as a happy auxiliary, all this conveys neither a passivity nor an activity, neither an unconsciousness not a lucidity on the part of the author...The concept of the supplement is a sort of blind spot in Rousseau's text, the not-seen that opens and limits visibility. (Derrida 1976: 163)

This is why Derrida is at pains to insist that deconstruction is in no sense a 'psychoanalysis' of philosophy, or a depth-hermeneutical technique whose chief aim – as might be supposed – is to uncover certain 'repressed' or 'sublimated' themes in Rousseau's discourse. Rather it is concerned with those blind spots of *logical* contradiction where that discourse runs up against the impossibility of straighforwardly saying what it means or meaning what it says.

Nor should this position seem so far removed from a good deal of work in the mainstream analytic line of descent, that is, the Frege–Russell tradition of thinking about issues in philosophy of language and logic. After all, it is taken for granted there that analysis can quite legitimately challenge the presumed self-evidence of utterer's intent – or the normative authority of 'ordinary language' – and concern itself with logico-semantic structures that need not be thought of as playing any role in the consciousness of this or that speaker. Frege's canonical account of the relationship between 'sense' and 'reference' and Russell's broadly similar 'Theory of Descriptions' are of course the paradigm examples of this approach (Frege 1952; Russell 1905). Thus Derrida's 'revisionism' is more like that which separates thinkers in the Frege–Russell camp from thinkers (such as Wittgenstein and Austin) who take it that 'ordinary language' is our best source of guidance in these matters, and hence that any claim to go beyond the deliverance of unaided linguistic intuition – or, worse still, to correct for certain 'blind spots' in our everyday habits of usage – is so much wasted effort (Austin 1963; Wittgenstein 1953). That is to say, Derrida takes the view – upheld by analytic 'revisionists' like Gilbert Ryle – that ordinary language can be systematically misleading and that in such cases we are entitled to press the claims of logical analysis beyond anything acceptable in terms of straightforward (philosophically untutored) linguistic grasp (Ryle 1949, 1954). It is also one reason for his downright refusal to accept Searle's idea that concepts (or logical distinctions) need only be as precise as required by this or that context of usage, so that – for instance – an 'all-or-nothing' logic has no valid application in the context of Austinian speech-act theory. For the point is, surely, that *even if* such a loosening of clear-cut logical criteria has its place in some items of everyday parlance *even so* it should not be thought to carry over – or to licence a similar laxity of conceptual grasp – in the philosophic treatment of those same items.

Whence, to repeat, Derrida's remark that 'the writer writes *in* a language and *in* a logic whose proper system, laws, and life his discourse by definition cannot dominate absolutely' (1976: 158). This comment has a double pertinence as applied to Rousseau since his discourse can be seen to exhibit all the signs of a thinking that is caught between two logics – that of classical (bivalent) truth/falsehood and the logic of supplementarity – whose conflicting claims it has to somehow negotiate from one sentence to the next. But it also applies to any speaker or writer whose language might always be logically constrained to mean something other than what they intend or have it in mind to say. 'This is why', as Derrida writes,

> travelling along the system of supplementarity with a blind infallibility, and the sure foot of the sleepwalker, Rousseau must at once denounce *mimesis* and art as supplements (supplements that are dangerous when they are not useless, superfluous when they are not disastrous, in truth both at the same time) and recognize in them man's good fortune, the expression of passion, the emergence from the inanimate. (Derrida 1976: 205)

Commentators like Priest are right to suggest that the Derridean 'logic of supplementarity' merits recognition as oné among the range of deviant, non-standard, or paraconsistent logics that have lately received a good deal of philosophical attention (Priest 1994, 1995). However it is also important to emphasise that Derrida is not for one moment proposing the overthrow, abandonment, or supersession of classical (bivalent) concepts. For the point about *any* such deviant logic – whether adopted in response to anomalous quantum-physical data or to textual aberrations like those of Rousseau – is that it must be taken to indicate some problem or unresolved dilemma with respect to the topic in hand (Gibbins 1987; Haack 1974). Thus it requires not so much an outlook of unqualified endorsement – such as commentators often ascribe to Derrida concerning the logic of supplementarity – but rather a process of diagnostic reasoning that questions the premises (the 'unthought axiomatics') which can be shown to have produced that dilemma.

At any rate there is no justification for the idea that Derrida seeks to subvert the most basic principles of truth, logic and reason. How this idea took hold in so many quarters is perhaps more a question for sociologists and chroniclers of academic culture than for philosophers who might instead take the time actually to read Derrida's work rather than endorse the standard dismissive estimate. Then they will find, I suggest, that his Rousseau commentary makes a highly original contribution to philosophy of logic and language, not least for its being cast in the form – one more familiar to literary critics – of a critical exegesis finely responsive to verbal details and nuances. What distinguishes Derrida's work is the way that he raises such issues through a mode of analysis that combines textual explication with the utmost rigour of logico-semantic grasp. Beyond that, he draws out some extreme complexities of modal, subjunctive, or counterfactual reasoning – like those cited above – whose gist can be paraphrased (albeit very often at tortuous length) and whose logical form can sometimes be captured in a suitably refined symbolic notation but which serve above all to indicate the aberrant (logically anomalous) character of Rousseau's discourse. Thus Derrida implicitly rejects any approach that would assign the 'logic of supplementarity' to its rightful (albeit 'deviant') place within the range of alternative, that is, non-classical logics which might always be invoked so as to accommodate some awkward or recalcitrant case. Quite simply, bivalence is the *sine qua non* for a reasoned and philosophically accountable treatment of these topics that would not rest content with an 'approximative' logic, and thereby forego any claim to conceptual rigour. At the same time, *contra* theorists like Searle, Derrida insists on the absolute impossibility that philosophy of language should somehow attain a methodological perspective outside and above the kinds of problematic instance that provide its most challenging material. Hence – to repeat – his attraction to Austin as a thinker who remained keenly aware of the problems thrown up for his own theory by cases which failed to fit in with some existing categorical scheme. Yet it is also very clearly the case that Derrida never goes so far as his post-structuralist disciples would wish in renouncing the distinction between object-language and metalanguage, that is to say, the necessity that reading should aim 'at a certain relationship, unperceived by the author, between what he commands and what he does not command of the language that he uses' (Derrida 1976: 158). In keeping with these principles – as I have argued here – his work offers some of the best, most searching and perceptive commentary anywhere to be found in the recent literature on philosophical semantics and philosophy of logic.

References

Austin, J.L. (1963). *How to Do Things With Words*. Oxford: Oxford University Press.

Barcan, Ruth C. (Ruth Barcan Marcus) (1946). 'A functional calculus of first order based on strict implication', *Journal of Symbolic Logic* 11: 1–16.

——(1947). 'The identity of individuals in a strict functional calculus of second order', *Journal of Symbolic Logic* 12: 12–15.

Bohm, David (1957). *Causality and Chance in Modern Physics*. London: Routledge & Kegan Paul.

Bradley, Raymond and Norman Swartz (1979). *Possible Worlds: An Introduction to Logic and its Philosophy*. Oxford: Blackwell.

Brooks, Cleanth (1947). *The Well-Wrought Urn: Studies in the Structure of Poetry*. New York: Harcourt, Brace.

Cushing, James T. (1994). *Quantum Mechanics: Historical Contingency and the Copenhagen Hegemony*. Chicago, Ill.: University of Chicago Press.

Davidson, Donald (1984). *Inquiries into Truth and Interpretation*. Oxford: Oxford University Press.

——(1986). 'A nice derangement of epitaphs', in Ernest LePore (ed.), *Truth and Interpretation: Perspectives on the Philosophy of Donald Davidson*. Oxford: Blackwell. pp. 433–46.

de Man, Paul (1979). *Allegories of Reading: Figural Language in Rousseau, Nietzsche, Rilke, and Proust*. New Haven: Yale University Press.

Derrida, Jacques (1973). *'Speech and Phenomena' and Other Essays on Husserl's Theory of Signs*, trans. David B. Allison. Evanston, Ill.: Northwestern University Press.

——(1976). *Of Grammatology*, trans. Gayatri C. Spivak. Baltimore: Johns Hopkins University Press.

——(1977a). 'Signature event context', *Glyph*, I. Baltimore: Johns Hopkins University Press. pp. 172–97.

——(1977b). 'Limited Inc. a b c', *Glyph*, II. Baltimore: Johns Hopkins University Press. pp. 162–254.

——(1978a). 'Structure, sign and play in the discourse of the human sciences', in *Writing and Difference*, trans. Alan Bass. London: Routledge & Kegan Paul. pp. 278–93.

——(1978b). *Edmund Husserl's 'Origin of Geometry': An Introduction*, trans. John P. Leavey. Pittsburgh: Duquesne University Press.

——(1981). 'Plato's pharmacy', in *Dissemination*, trans. Barbara Johnson. London: Athlone Press. pp. 61–171.

——(1987a). *The Post Card: from Socrates to Freud and beyond*, trans. Alan Bass. Chicago: University of Chicago Press.

——(1987b). 'The parergon', in *The Truth in Painting*, trans. Geoff Bennington and Ian McLeod. Chicago, Ill.: University of Chicago Press. pp. 15–147.

——(1989). 'Afterword: toward an ethic of conversation', in *Limited Inc* (ed.) Gerald Graff. Evanston, Ill.: Northwestern University Press. pp. 111–60.

Dummett, Michael (1977). *Elements of Intuitionism*. Oxford: Oxford University Press.

——(1978). *Truth and Other Enigmas*. London: Duckworth.

Ellis, John M. (1989). *Against Deconstruction*. Princeton, N.J.: Princeton University Press.

Feyerabend, Paul K. (1975). *Against Method*. London: New Left Books.

Frege, Gottlob (1952). 'On sense and reference', in P. Geach and M. Black (eds), *Selections from the Philosophical Writings of Gottlob Frege*. Oxford: Blackwell. pp. 56–78.

Gibbins, Peter (1987). *Particles and Paradoxes: The Limits of Quantum Logic*. Cambridge: Cambridge University Press.

Grice, H.P. (1989). *Studies in the Ways of Words*. Cambridge, Mass.: Harvard University Press.

Haack, Susan (1974). *Deviant Logic: Some Philosophical Issues*. Cambridge: Cambridge University Press.

Harman, Gilbert (1965). 'Inference to the best explanation', *Philosophical Review* **74**(1): 88–95.

Hintikka, Jaakko (1963). 'The modes of modality', *Acta Philosophica Fennica* **16**: 65–81.

——(1969). *Models for Modalities*. Dordrecht: D. Reidel.

Holland, Peter (1993). *The Quantum Theory of Motion: An Account of the de Broglie-Bohm Causal Interpretation of Quantum Mechanics*. Cambridge: Cambridge University Press.

Hughes, G.E. and Cresswell, M.J. (1996). *A New Introduction to Modal Logic*. London: Routledge.

Kneale, W. and Kneale, M. (1962). *The Development of Logic*. Oxford: Clarendon Press.

Kripke, Saul (1963). 'Semantical considerations in modal logic', *Acta Philosophica Fennica* **16**: 57–90.

——(1980). *Naming and Necessity*. Oxford: Blackwell.

Kuhn, Thomas S. (1970). *The Structure of Scientific Revolutions*, 2nd edn. Chicago, Ill.: University of Chicago Press.

Langford, C.H. (1968). 'The notion of analysis in Moore's philosophy', in P.A. Schilpp (ed.), *The Philosophy of G.E. Moore*. La Salle: Open Court. pp. 321–41.

Lewis, C.I. (1912). 'Implication and the algebra of logic', *Mind* **21**: 522–31.

——(1918). *A Survey of Symbolic Logic*. Berkeley: University of California Press.

Lewis, C.I. and Langford, C.H. (1932). *Symbolic Logic*, 2nd edn. New York: Dover.

Lipton, Peter (1993). *Inference to the Best Explanation*. London: Routledge.

Loux, Michael J. (ed.) (1979). *The Possible and the Actual: Readings in the Metaphysics of Modality*. Ithaca, N.Y.: Cornell University Press.

Mackie, J.L. (1973). *Truth, Probability and Paradox*. Oxford: Clarendon Press.

Marcus, Ruth Barcan (Ruth C. Barcan) (1962). 'Interpreting Quantification', *Inquiry* **5**: 252–59.

Marcus, Ruth Barcan (1993). *Modalities*. New York: Oxford University Press.

Moore, G.E. (1968). 'A reply to my critics', in P.A. Schilpp (ed.), *The Philosophy of G.E. Moore*. La Salle: Open Court. pp. 535–687.

Norris, Christopher (1996). 'Of an apoplectic tone recently adopted in philosophy', in *Reclaiming Truth: Contribution to a Critique of Cultural Relativism*. London: Lawrence & Wishart. pp. 222–53.

——(1997). *Resources of Realism: Prospects for 'Post-analytic' Philosophy*. London: Macmillan.

——(2000a). *Minding the Gap: Epistemology and Philosophy of Science in the Two Traditions*. Amherst, Mass.: University of Massachusetts Press.

——(2000b). *Quantum Theory and the Flight from Realism: Philosophical Responses to Quantum Mechanics*. London: Routledge.

——(2002a). *Truth Matters: Realism, Anti-realism and Response-Dependence*. Edinburgh: Edinburgh University Press.

——(2002b). *Hilary Putnam: Realism, Reason, and the Uses of Uncertainty*. Manchester: Manchester University Press.

Peirce, Charles S. (1992). *Reasoning and the Logic of Things*. Cambridge, Mass.: Harvard University Press.

Pradhan, Shekar (1986). 'Minimalist semantics: Davidson and Derrida on meaning, use, and convention', *Diacritics* **16**(1): 66–77.

Priest, Graham (1994). 'Derrida and self-reference', *Australasian Journal of Philosophy* **72**(1): 103–111.

——(1995). *The Limits of Thought*. Cambridge: Cambridge University Press.

Prior, A.N. (1956). 'Modality and quantification in S5', *Journal of Symbolic Logic* **21**: 60–62.

——(1957). *Time and Modality*. Oxford: Clarendon Press.

Putnam, Hilary (1983). *Realism and Reason (Philosophical Papers* Vol. 3). Cambridge: Cambridge University Press.

Quine, W.V. (1961). 'Two dogmas of empiricism', in *From a Logical Point of View*, 2nd edn. Cambridge, Mass.: Harvard University Press. pp. 20–46.

Rorty, Richard (1978). 'Philosophy as a kind of writing: an essay on Jacques Derrida', in *Consequences of Pragmatism*. Brighton: Harvester Press. pp. 89–109.

Russell, Bertrand (1905). 'On denoting', *Mind* **14**: 479–93.

Ryle, Gilbert (1949). *The Concept of Mind*. London: Hutchinson.

——(1954). *Dilemmas*. Cambridge: Cambridge University Press.

Saussure, Ferdinand de (1983). *Course in General Linguistics*, trans. Roy Harris. London: Duckworth.

Searle, John R. (1969). *Speech Acts*. Cambridge: Cambridge University Press.

——(1977). 'Reiterating the differences', *Glyph*, I. Baltimore: Johns Hopkins University Press. pp. 198–208.

Smullyan, A.E. (1948). 'Modality and description', *Journal of Symbolic Logic* **13**: 31–37.

Wheeler, Samuel C. (1986). 'Indeterminacy of French translation: Derrida and Davidson', in Ernest LePore (ed.), *Truth and Interpretation: Perspectives on the Philosophy of Donald Davidson*. Oxford: Blackwell. pp. 477–94.

——(2000). *Deconstruction as Analytic Philosophy*. Stanford, CA.: Stanford University Press.

White, Alan R. (1975). *Modal Thinking*. Oxford: Blackwell.

Whorf, Benjamin L. (1956). *Language, Thought and Reality: Selected Writings* (ed.) J.B. Carroll. Cambridge, Mass.: MIT Press.

Wimsatt, William K. (1954). *The Verbal Icon: Studies in the Meaning of Poetry*. Lexington, Ky.: University of Kentucky Press.

Wittgenstein, Ludwig (1953). *Philosophical Investigations*, trans. G.E.M. Anscombe. Oxford: Blackwell.

2
The Limits of *Whose* Language?: Wittgenstein on Logic, Mathematics, and Science

I

I think that most likely in a century's time – if humanity survives that long and still goes in for philosophical debate – there will be a great deal of head-scratching among philosophers as to why one of their number, Ludwig Wittgenstein, exerted such a massive influence on so many thinkers of an earlier generation. Also I would hazard a guess that much of this discussion will be carried on in cultural, historical, and psycho-biographical terms rather than through the kinds of 'purely' conceptual exegesis that have characterised most treatments of his work up to now. (For a notable exception – a shrewdly perceptive study in the 'life-and-times' mode – see Janik and Toulmin 1973.) The recent Cambridge *Companion to Wittgenstein* (Sluga and Stern [eds] 1996) is very much a state-of-the-art anthology that all the same shows a few signs of this incipient trend. For there are few things more remarkable about the period from 1960 to the present than the way in which Wittgenstein has routinely figured as a major – unignorable – point of reference for anyone who wants to venture some new line of argument or defend some established philosophical position against challenge from whatever quarter. Moreover, this compulsion has exercised a hold not only on true believers – Wittgenstein's heirs, disciples, and devoted exegetes – but also on those who register dissent yet still feel bound to run their case through the standard Wittgensteinian hoops. (See Norris 2000, for further discussion of some recent and particularly striking cases.) In what follows I shall try to explain this puzzling cultural phenomenon in a fairly objective or non-partisan manner.

No doubt it will be said – by the true believers and perhaps a good few of the dutiful dissenters – that my approach is no such thing but rather an expression of anti-Wittgensteinian prejudice. To which I would respond (somewhat grumpily no doubt) that the Wittgenstein cult is so massive and pervasive a feature of the current philosophical scene that anyone who takes the view from outside is apt to be treated as adopting something more like a plainly nonsensical 'view from nowhere'. For if there is one line of argument that always comes up in this context it is the idea that any given statement must be thought of as making good sense just so long as it plays a role in some existing language-game or cultural 'form of life' (Wittgenstein 1953, 1969; also Williams 1999; Winch 1987). In which case philosophers must be badly off the track or in the grip of some grandiose delusion if they think to correct or to criticise beliefs that do indeed play such a role. Among its further consequences are (1) the idea that philosophy 'leaves everything as it is', that is, cannot rightfully aspire to steer our thinking onto different tracks, (2) the notion that 'everything is in order' with any given language-game or life-form since each possesses its own criteria or standards of justification, and (3) the doctrine of 'meaning as use', i.e., the veto on theories of meaning, propositional content, or logico-semantic structure that would presume to clarify – even to rectify – the kinds of everyday usage that are perfectly intelligible by our own or some other set of communal lights (see for instance Frege 1952; Russell 1905). So philosophers are simply deluded if they imagine that theirs is a special sort of discipline which calls language to order and which could lay down guidelines – or logical rules – for the better conduct of rational enquiry in this or that branch of the natural, social, or human sciences (Winch 1958).

Such was the position that Wittgenstein adopted when he came back to philosophy after the famous mid-life break which resulted from his disenchantment with the kinds of thinking represented by Frege, Russell, and (not least) his own early work. In the *Tractatus Logico-Philosophicus* Wittgenstein had taken just the opposite view, namely, that we needed to get clear about the various confusions that thinking was heir to if it went along with habitual or 'common sense' modes of linguistic usage (Wittgenstein 1961). On this Tractarian account the only meaningful propositions are those whose logical structure corresponds to factual (real-world) states of affairs. At the time Wittgenstein was much influenced by Russellian logical atomism, that is, the idea that analysis should proceed by isolating certain atomic (undecomposable) elements of any such given proposition and then showing how these can be conjoined in a more complex (logically articulated) form (see Russell 1986, 1993, 1994; also Griffin 1964; Reck [ed.] 2002; Tait [ed.] 1997). Thus, according to early Wittgenstein, the world is made up of facts – not objects – and propositions are assigned a truth-value depending on whether or not they correspond to the way things stand in reality. So the only propositions that are apt for assessment in terms of objective truth or falsehood are those that can be verified (or falsified) through the methods of empirical enquiry or those whose truth is self-evident in virtue of their logical form. These latter – the propositions of logic – are strictly tautologous since they hold as a matter of formal (or definitional) necessity and are hence utterly devoid of empirical content. Any proposition which falls into neither class – which involves some claim that cannot be empirically verified nor shown to be purely a product of logical definition – must therefore count as meaningless by these criteria. That is to say, it should be treated as a pseudo-statement that has no specifiable truth-conditions and which merely mimics the form of genuine, *bona fide* propositions in logic, mathematics, or the natural sciences (Ayer [ed.] 1959).

However – as is well known – the *Tractatus* lent itself to another reading, one that went strongly against this logical-positivist construal and looked forward to Wittgenstein's later ideas. Hence the last few cryptic passages where Wittgenstein suggests that the entire foregoing argument was intended only as a ground-clearing exercise, a needful propaedeutic whose sole purpose was to demonstrate the limits of any such narrowly verificationist approach. What should now be understood by any well-attuned reader is that this approach left aside all the most important issues, among them questions having to do with ethics, aesthetics, and religious faith. Such questions might not be susceptible to treatment – might even appear non-sensical – from the viewpoint that Wittgenstein had adopted (or appeared to adopt) throughout the main body of his work. However, in his famous metaphor, this had been merely a kind of disposable ladder whose steps were the various numbered propositions that gave the *Tractatus* its impressive appearance of logical consistency and rigour. Having reached this vantage point atop all the arguments laid out so far we should now be able to kick the ladder away and grasp the real import of Wittgenstein's text, that is, his conviction that truth is not exhausted by the formal propositions of logic and the methods of empirical science. To be sure, these place a strict limit on the range of meaningful statements whose truth-conditions can be specified in adequate (logically accountable or empirically verifiable) terms. However there are truths which can be *shown* – not stated – through a mode of oblique or suggestive presentation that exceeds the grasp of any narrowly verificationist account. Moreover these truths are of primary concern for anyone who has come, like Wittgenstein, to regard that account as the merest of techniques for evading the central problems of human existence (Malcolm 1975, 1977).

Such is at any rate the received view, one that would have us read the *Tractatus* as a kind of self-consuming artefact, a text that deploys all the elaborate devices of its own logical scaffolding in order to expose the weakness of the structure and the need to cast aside those delusory supports (Crary and Read [eds] 2000). This was not, of course, a view that commended itself to Wittgenstein's earliest admirers – including Russell and members of the Vienna Circle – who took the *Tractatus* as a striking, if at times somewhat cryptic and elusive rendition of arguments that were then being developed in the name of Logical Positivism. (See Baker 1988; Waismann 1979.) For them, the most significant portions of the text were those that expounded the verificationist doctrine and which insisted on a rigorous beating of the bounds between meaningful (i.e., empirically warranted or logically self-evident) propositions and others whose failure to meet this standard required that they be treated as pseudo-statements or instances of empty 'metaphysics' (Carnap 1959). It is clear enough from his various recorded remarks and his subsequent history of troubled dealings with Russell that Wittgenstein himself rejected this reading and considered the *Tractatus* to have been ill-served – misconstrued in a damaging, even morally offensive way – by its first generation of English translators and exegetes (McGuiness 1988; Wittgenstein 1973). So the passages that mattered were those which the Logical Positivists had been apt to pass over in tactful silence or to regard as unfortunate lapses into nonsense brought about by Wittgenstein's lingering penchant for just such metaphysical excesses. In short, they had to do with the cardinal distinction between *stating* and *showing*, the idea that logic in its formal or crystalline perfection amounted to just a series of empty tautologies, and above all the claim – central to Wittgenstein's later thinking – that there existed other (more humanly significant) ways of making sense that could not be captured by any such verificationist approach.

So it is hardly surprising, given the evidence of Wittgenstein's views, that Russell and his like-minded associates are now widely thought to have misread the *Tractatus* by ignoring any passage that stood in the way of their own preferred interpretation. Also, as I have said, there is the fact that when Wittgenstein eventually 'returned' to philosophy after his self-imposed period of academic exile he did so with the fixed purpose of attacking those ideas about language, truth, and logic that had once – whatever his ultimate purpose – played such a major role in the *Tractatus* and its early reception-history. That return was marked by a massive outpouring of work, unpublished in his lifetime, which has since been edited by his literary executors and given at least some semblance of order by assemblage into various texts on a range of loosely related themes. More recently there has appeared an electronic edition of the *Nachlass* (Wittgenstein 2000) which will no doubt give rise to much further debate concerning editorial and interpretative issues. Along with this immense concentration of scholarly labour has gone an equally determined effort to confirm the view of Wittgenstein's progress as one that started out from his rapid disenchantment with Russell-style logical atomism and which then achieved its consummate expression in the writings of his 'late' period (Baker and Hacker 1983, 1984, 1985; Hacker 1996a,b). Thus the standard narrative is one that endorses not only Wittgenstein's preferred view of his own philosophical development but also the manifest superiority of a late-Wittgensteinian perspective as compared with other (e.g. Russellian) conceptions of language, logic, and truth. That is to say, it is a strongly fideist approach which takes Wittgenstein very much at his word in all matters concerning the proper interpretation of his texts and the correct (i.e., Wittgenstein-approved) view of what counts as a meaningful statement. In which case Russell must surely have failed to take the point of those cryptic concluding passages from the *Tractatus* – and failed, moreover, to grasp the significance of Wittgenstein's later work – on account of his adherence to a now discredited conception of philosophical enquiry. (For a large-scale example of this way of treating them, mostly to Wittgenstein's advantage, see Ray Monk's recent biographies of the two thinkers [Monk 1990, 1996, 2000].) And this despite the plentiful evidence that, so far from being out of his depth, Russell saw very clearly what Wittgenstein was driving at and did not like what he saw. That is to say, he perceived all the signs of retreat into a kind of high-toned verbal obscurantism and a vague appeal to linguistic custom which must indeed 'leave everything as it is', including those confusions implicit in our forms of everyday talk which logicians might reasonably hope to diagnose and clarify (Russell 1959).

II

Indeed it is among the most notable features of recent work in the broadly analytic tradition that as Wittgenstein's reputation has soared to the point where no philosopher can address those issues without the obligatory detour *via* Wittgenstein so Russell's has been subject to a marked downgrading, very often – one suspects – on account of his presumed failure to grasp the true significance of Wittgenstein's thought. (For a spirited against-the-stream effort to reverse this consensus, see Ayer 1985.) To Russell it was clear that in certain areas – philosophy of logic, mathematics, and science – there is a need for the kind of analytic approach that is *not* content to 'leave everything as it is' with regard to our everyday forms of linguistic usage. Thus philosophers are fully justified – not overstepping the mark – when they seek to correct certain errors or confusions whose source is to be found in the various shortcomings (failures of reference, ambiguities of scope, misleading grammatical expressions, and so forth) which characterise 'ordinary' language (Russell 1905, 1994). For Wittgenstein, conversely, philosophers can only go wrong – betray delusions of epistemological grandeur – if they purport to see further or deeper than the kinds of insight to be had from within our various communal language-games or forms of life. As he puts it:

> 'A proposition is a queer thing!' Here we have in germ the subliming of our whole account of logic. The tendency to assume a pure intermediary between the propositional *signs* and the facts. Or even to try to purify, to sublime, the signs themselves. – For our forms of expression prevent us in all sorts of ways from seeing that nothing out of the ordinary is involved, by sending us off in pursuit of chimeras... Thought, language, now appear to us as the unique correlate, picture, of the world. These concepts: proposition, language, thought, world, stand in line one behind the other, each equivalent to each. (But what are these words to be used for now? The language-game in which they are to be applied is missing.) (1953, I, Section 94)

So we are mistaken if we conceive of philosophy as a kind of 'foundational' discipline, one that is most properly (constructively) engaged in providing principles, ground rules, or justificatory arguments which can then be applied to disciplines such as mathematics or the physical sciences (Wittgenstein 1953, 1956, 1969, 1976). And we are likewise mistaken – so Wittgenstein maintains – if we suppose that philosophy has any warrant to challenge the working practices of scientists, mathematicians or others through claiming to reveal some conceptual problem or (by them) unnoticed logical complication that renders those practices philosophically suspect. For this is once again to grant philosophy an adjudicative power above and beyond the various practice-specific criteria that properly decide what shall count as a valid or acceptable statement in this or that context of enquiry.

The literary theorist Stanley Fish – himself much influenced by Wittgenstein – has expressed this position more colourfully in terms of what he calls 'positive foundationalist theory hope' and 'negative anti-foundationalist theory hope' (Fish 1989). The former deludedly seeks to provide philosophical support for its interpretative claims through recourse to theories, principles, or grounds which purport to transcend any particular context of utterance while the latter just as deludedly seeks to undermine orthodox beliefs and values by adopting a generalised sceptical stance which is meant to reveal their lack of any such absolute foundational warrant. Both approaches are examples of misplaced 'theory-hope', so Fish contends, since both betray an exaggerated confidence in the power of theory to support or subvert the various norms and conventions that prevail within some given 'interpretive community'. Thus persuasion – or rhetorical effect – goes 'all the way down' and theories depend for their persuasive force on whatever they can muster in the way of assent among like-minded readers or interpreters. The positive hopers typically go wrong by adducing all kinds of heavyweight philosophical argument to back their case while the negative hopers typically go wrong by supposing that minds could ever be changed by a theory that did not in the end gain credence by appealing to some other set of in-place (even if relatively heterodox) norms and conventions.

For Wittgenstein also it is an error to think that philosophical reflection – or analysis – could bring about a change in those various language-games or life-forms that constitute our very horizons of intelligibility. Thus his falling out with Russell marked the point of divergence between two very different conceptions of philosophical enquiry, or two quite distinct branches of the 'analytic' enterprise. Since then there has grown up a veritable industry of textual exegesis whose chief concern is to vindicate Wittgenstein against the counter-arguments standardly advanced by upholders of the Frege–Russell tradition. Some of these commentaries adopt a tone of prosecuting zeal toward any philosopher who presumes to question the standard Wittgensteinian wisdom (see especially Baker and Hacker 1984). Elsewhere it is more a matter of making sure that any case one puts forward has already been tested against the full range of predictable objections – does it fall prey to the 'private language' argument? does it involve the problematical idea of 'following a rule'? does it bank on an appeal to standards of veridical warrant beyond those endorsed by some existing language-game? – and can therefore be proposed without fear of reprisals. (For discussion of some recent, especially striking examples, see Norris 2000.) At any rate Wittgenstein's commanding presence – or presumed authority in all such matters – is a fact that can scarcely have escaped anyone who has kept up with recent debates within the broadly analytic tradition.

Then again, this compulsion sometimes takes the form of an imperative to redeem Wittgenstein's (on the face of it) strongly anti-realist and cultural-relativist arguments by maintaining that in fact they are no such thing since – to repeat – philosophy on his account 'leaves everything as it is' (Diamond 1991). So it is wrong to think that he adopts a position – a *philosophical* position – with respect to the issue between realism and anti-realism as debated by those who have not sufficiently absorbed the implications of Wittgenstein's thought. Rather we should take him at his word (as always) and see that everything is perfectly in order with our various communally sanctioned practices, among them those particular disciplines – such as the physical sciences – where realism has a fair claim to represent the outlook of most practitioners, along with the idea that truth-values objectively transcend any localised (culture-specific) context of belief. In short, we have grievously misread Wittgenstein if we suppose that the 'linguistic turn' entails a relativisation of truth to language and of language to the various beliefs, values, socio-cultural priorities, and so forth, which characterise some given 'form of life'. For one can still be as 'realist' as one likes with respect to (say) subatomic particles, remote galaxies, or even mathematical entities such as numbers, sets, and classes just so long as one acknowledges the fact of their belonging to a certain distinctive language-game with its place in a certain cultural tradition.

So the question naturally arises: just what are the realists worrying about when they profess to find this whole line of argument unconvincing and suggest that it is merely a strategy adopted to head off awkward objections from defenders of scientific realism? After all, does it make any difference whether we are committed to some range of statements such as 'atoms exist', 'the charge on every electron is negative', and 'the number created by 311 successive iterations of the digit 1 is a prime number' or whether – in Wittgensteinian fashion – we assert those statements in identical form but along with the implicit rider: 'according to the language-games of present-day particle physics and mathematics'? For Wittgenstein this is a pointless distinction – a difference that makes no difference – since we just cannot conceive of any statement, theory, or hypothesis that would not have its meaning or truth-conditions set by its playing a role in some shared discourse which alone provides the standards for correct usage of the various concepts and expressions involved (Wittgenstein 1953, 1969, 1974). That is to say, such statements presuppose the existence of certain communal norms which enable speakers – members of the relevant community – to acquire and manifest the kinds of competence that are needed in order to assert them with adequate warrant (see also Dummett 1978, 1991). Otherwise we should be driven to adopt some version of the hopeless Cartesian appeal to a realm of apodictic truths that are somehow self-evident to reason, or whose warrant amounts to no more than their striking the solitary thinker as beyond all possibility of rational doubt. Such is Wittgenstein's 'private language' argument, intended to show that we simply cannot make sense of this idea since language is of its very nature a shared activity, and any 'language' known only to a single speaker would be strictly unintelligible – that is, fail to meet the conditions for being a language – even to the individual concerned (1953, I, Sections 246–339 *passim*; also Johnston 1993; Stern 1995; Stroud 2000). As for the notion that mathematical truth might be arrived at by apodictic means, that is, through the solitary thinker's running a proof-procedure 'in his head' and achieving the correct result, we can best see what's wrong with this – so Wittgenstein suggests – by considering the case of a man who buys several copies of the morning paper just to make sure that what it says is true (1953, I, Section 265).

Besides, the whole idea of checking mathematical proofs with reference to some range of results obtained through a process of purely 'mental' cogitation is one that lies open to the obvious charge of vicious regress, since those results would likewise require checking through some further such proof-procedure, and so on *ad infinitum*. Either that, or it entails a vicious circularity whereby the purported justification turns out to presuppose the truth or validity of just that statement, theorem, or procedure whose veridical warrant is presently subject to review. Hence Wittgenstein's claim that community-wide agreement is the furthest we can possibly get in seeking for standards of 'objective' truth and falsehood which are taken to transcend any localised consensus or sampling of best opinion. Still the realist need not be worried, he thinks, since certain propositions (such as those of truth-functional logic and elementary arithmetic) are so deeply entrenched in our various scientific and other practices that we cannot entertain any serious doubt with regard to their holding good for all practical, that is, humanly relevant purposes. These are 'hinge propositions' – Wittgenstein's phrase – upon which there turn such a vast range of (to us) indispensable reckoning procedures, deductive reasonings, methods of inference, standards of proof, and so forth, that they must be thought sufficiently firm against sceptical doubt (Wittgenstein 1969). Or again: such propositions are like the bed of a river that follows an unvarying course despite all the seasonal shifts of current above it and despite the various surface swirls and eddies (ibid.: Sections 95–99). The point of these analogies is to coax us down from the false idea that realism with respect to logic, mathematics, and the formal sciences can be sustained only by espousing an objectivist conception of truth and must therefore be compromised – or totally undermined – by any notion of truth as 'internal' to our various languages, practices, or forms of life. In short, the realists are creating no problem for Wittgenstein – but a lot of unnecessary problems for themselves – when they take this line against Wittgenstein's (supposed) anti-realism and its (supposed) cultural-relativist consequences. For their alternative proposal, that is, that such truths are 'objective' in the sense 'recognition-transcendent' or 'true quite apart from our best means of proof or ascertainment' is one that would make it impossible to explain how we could ever acquire knowledge of them or be in a position to manifest that knowledge (Dummett 1991).

Hence the most usual way, since Wittgenstein, of framing the sceptic's perennial challenge and offering what purports to be an adequate answer in Wittgensteinian terms. Where scepticism mostly gets a hold is through the realist's ill-advised claim that the truth-value of any well-formed statement – whether in logic, mathematics, the natural sciences, history, or other areas of discourse – is fixed by the way things stand (or once stood) as a matter of objective reality, and not at all by conditions having to do with the scope and limits of our knowledge (Williams 1996). This applies both to cases where we do possess some adequate proof-procedure or means of verification and to cases where we do not but can all the same venture a well-formed hypothesis – such as 'Goldbach's Conjecture is true' or 'the Higgs Boson exists' – and be sure that our statement is rendered true or false (albeit unbeknownst to ourselves) by an objectively existing state of affairs in mathematical or subatomic reality (Alston 1996; Devitt 1986; Katz 1998; Soames 1999). In both instances truth must be construed as verification-transcendent, whether or not we just happen to have hit on a method or procedure for finding it out. What the realist will not concede is that the truth of such statements might have anything to do with the compass of existing human knowledge or even – at the limit – such knowledge as we might attain under ideal epistemic conditions when all the evidence was in. To which the sceptic standardly responds that this creates a hopeless dilemma for the realist since she has placed truth absolutely and forever beyond the reach of human knowledge. That is to say, the upshot of hard-line realism is an objectivist doctrine which totally defeats the realist's purpose since it opens the way to an outlook of wholesale scepticism such that the truth-value of *any* statement must be thought of as something that intrinsically eludes the best powers of human cognitive, epistemic, or rational grasp (Williams 1996).

This case has been put in its sharpest form by thinkers like Paul Benacerraf and Hilary Putnam who contend that, quite simply, 'nothing works' in philosophy of mathematics since one can *either* have objectivist (platonist) truth, *or* humanly attainable knowledge, but surely not both (Benacerraf 1983; Putnam 1983). Hence Wittgenstein's alternative proposal: that we abandon the delusory 'view from nowhere' that engendered these problems in the first place and instead take the far more sensible view that mathematical procedures have their well-defined role – along with the criteria for their correct application – in and through the practices which decide what shall count as an instance of valid mathematical reasoning (Wittgenstein 1956, 1976; also Shanker [ed.] 1996; Wright 1980). This gives us (supposedly) the best of both worlds, or at any rate the worst of neither: a conception of truth that can claim to avoid both the objectivist upshot of in-principle unknowability and the threat of cultural relativism, that is to say, the surely unacceptable notion that mathematical 'truths' are nothing more than constructions devised in response to some particular range of localised interests, practical needs, or social incentives (see for instance Bloor 1976, 1983). However the realist is likely to think it a typical example of the Wittgensteinian compromise formula which says, in effect: 'by all means carry on talking that way – *as if* it were a matter of objective, recognition-transcendent mathematical truths – just so long as you acknowledge that they would lie beyond our utmost epistemic reach were it not for their intrinsically practice-dependent character'. Moreover the realist will be apt to remark that there exists a vast (indeed infinite) range of mathematical truths that we do not yet know, that cannot be known by any method that is a part of our existing mathematical practice, and which might lie forever beyond the reach of even the most sophisticated proof-procedures devisable by human intelligence (Dales and Oliveri [eds] 1998). Indeed there are formal proofs to just that effect, having to do with the fact that the number of valid mathematical and logical propositions necessarily exceeds the number of sentences available to express or articulate those same propositions (Soames 1999). Also there is Gödel's incompleteness-theorem, the gist of which – contrary to widespread report – is that we are capable of knowing certain necessary truths about the scope and limits of computability beyond whatever can be proved as a matter of formal (axiomatic-deductive) proof (Gödel 1962; also Penrose 1996). However such arguments count for nothing from a Wittgensteinian viewpoint since they involve a conception of mathematical truth which goes clean against any practice-based or communally warranted approach. Thus, for Wittgenstein, the 'limits of my language' are indeed 'the limits of my world' in so far as that world cannot possibly contain any truths that might in principle outrun the range of statements which happen to lie within the reach of our capacity to prove or ascertain them.

III

So it seems that the realist may indeed have cause to worry about any proposed solution or negotiated settlement on Wittgensteinian terms. After all – to revert to his favoured metaphor – if the furthest we can get toward truth *sans phrase* is the idea that certain truths (such as those of logic or elementary arithmetic) are deeply entrenched like the bed of a river then it also needs saying that river beds *do* change their course, albeit most often over long periods and not so swiftly or chaotically as the surface swirls and eddies (Wittgenstein 1969, Sections 95–99). Thus the metaphor must be read as implying that these truths *are* indeed culture-relative – dependent on their role within a given practice or life-form – even though they seem to us as 'objective' as can be on account of their longevity, widespread acceptance, and entwinement with a great range of activities (whether everyday or scientific) that would otherwise make no sense. So Wittgensteinian 'realism' is not quite what it appears, or what its advocates would have us believe when they cite his innocuous-sounding claim that philosophy should 'leave everything as it is', including the 'reality' of all those objects that figure in the specialised language-games of subatomic physics or molecular biology. Some would even extend this accommodating licence to mathematical talk about abstract entities like numbers, sets, and classes, or logical talk of propositions as having a distinct mode of existence apart from sentences and statements, or linguists' talk about types of syntactic or semantic structure beyond the particular (token) utterance in hand. So there is room as it seems – on this liberal construal – for a marked relaxation of Wittgenstein's nominalist strictures and a welcome to language-games that posit the reality of these and other universals. After all, it would scarcely be accordant with his thinking to declare them philosophically off-bounds, given his insistence on the need for philosophy to respect the variety of language-games and the range of differing criteria involved.

However this seeming ontological largesse turns out to have a price attached, namely the allowance that such talk is in order *just so long* as we acknowledge its role in some particular (more or less specialised) discourse, and don't fall into the trap of believing that it picks out entities – whether concrete or abstract – that exist quite apart from the discourse in question. And of course the realist will be strongly inclined to reject this settlement since it is just her point that, if true, then statements such as 'water has the molecular structure H_2O', or 'the charge on every electron is negative', or 'every even number is the sum of two primes' are true by virtue of the way things stand in physical or mathematical reality, and not by virtue of their playing a role in some communally sanctioned language-game. That is to say, she will not wish to endorse such a reading of her own position if it involves reconstruing statements like these as 'true' only in so far as they accord with the criteria for truth that happen to prevail within this or that belief-community. For if there is one principle that the realist cannot afford to give up without yielding crucial ground to the sceptic it is that which makes a firm distinction between consensus belief and veridical knowledge, or whatever passes for truth among those (supposedly) best qualified to judge and whatever is the case quite aside from such appeals to the currency of authorised belief. (For further discussion, see Alston 1996; Armstrong 1978; Devitt 1986; Marsonet [ed.] 2002.)

Quite conceivably science has surprises in store that will force us to abandon or modify the claim that 'water is H_2O' or that 'the charge on every electron is negative'. But in that case the revision – if justified – will be a consequence of our actually finding out more about the molecular structure of water or the charge characteristics of subatomic particles. What it *will not* amount to – again if justified – is a switch in our preferential language-game or a result of our adopting some new mode of talk wherein the terms 'water' or 'electron' come be to be deployed with a different range of associated predicates. In the case of Goldbach's Conjecture (that every even number is the sum of two primes) there is as yet no formalised proof-procedure and hence no means of assigning the statement a determinate truth-value. So for those, like Dummett, who adopt an anti-realist approach this statement must belong to the 'disputed class', that is, the class of statements that cannot be proved (or verified) and which therefore possess no truth-value since we are unable to recognise their truth-conditions or manifest a working grasp of any method that would demonstrate their truth or falsity (Dummett 1978). To which the mathematical realist will respond that their truth-value has *nothing to do* with the scope and limits of our present-best or even our future best-possible means of ascertainment. Rather it is a question of whether or not those statements accord with the way things stand as a matter of objective (recognition-transcendent) mathematical truth.

This is why realists had better think twice before accepting the Wittgensteinian settlement. On these terms 'realism' with respect to any given area of discourse entails no more than a readiness to grant that it is one kind of talk among others, a language-game perfectly intelligible by its own lights and unlikely to cause much harm *unless* overtaken by delusions of ontological grandeur. However the realist will want to protest that this lets the whole argument go by default since it fails to acknowledge her basic point, that is, that truth-values are ultimately fixed by the relationship that holds between truth-bearers (in this case mathematical statements) and truth-makers (in this case numbers, sets, classes, and functions along with their various objective properties and the range of valid propositions concerning them). There is clearly no room for interpreting Wittgenstein as ready to accept such a view, whatever the well-known problems that arise when attempting to decide which passages are intended *in propria persona*, that is, as statements attributable to Wittgenstein himself, and which should be regarded as expressing the beliefs of a naive or misguided collocutor. For if one thing emerges with constant emphasis from his various scattered discussions of logic, mathematics, and 'following a rule' it is Wittgenstein's refusal to grant the existence of objective (recognition-transcendent) truths that would somehow decide the truth-value of our statements – or the correctness of our rule-following procedures – quite apart from any reference to the kinds of practice wherein those statements and procedures have their place (see Wittgenstein 1953, I, Sections 201–92 *passim*; also Miller and Wright [eds] 2002).

Thus for Wittgenstein, as likewise for Dummett, it simply cannot make sense to claim with regard to some well-formed mathematical theorem that it *must* be either true or false – objectively so – even though its proof turns out to exceed our furthest computational capacities or our utmost powers of formal demonstration. For this would be to grant the (non-Wittgensteinian) realist's case that truth in such matters has ultimately nothing to do with the practices and communal standards of enquiry which effectively decide what shall count – for us – as a true, valid, or meaningful statement. In other words it would fall into the platonist trap of positing a realm of absolute ideal objectivities that by very definition must lie beyond our cognitive or epistemic reach yet concerning which we can gain knowledge through some kind of quasi-perceptual acquaintance. Hence, as I have said, the pyrrhic conclusion that 'nothing works' in philosophy of mathematics since we can *either* have objective mathematical truth *or* mathematical knowledge but certainly not both unless at the cost of embracing a downright contradictory epistemological creed (Benacerraf 1983).

There is a typically oblique and elusive passage from the *Philosophical Investigations* where Wittgenstein starts out by propounding (or rehearsing) the realist position and then goes off at a thought-experimental tangent which leaves one in doubt as to just what the passage is intended to convey. Thus surely it is the case, his imaginary collocutor protests, that 'mathematical truth is independent of whether human beings know it or not?'. To which he responds:

> Certainly, the propositions 'Human beings believe that twice two is four' and 'Twice two is four' do not mean the same. The latter is a mathematical proposition: the other, if it makes sense at all, may perhaps mean: human beings have *arrived* at the mathematical proposition. The two propositions have entirely different *uses*. – But what would *this* mean: 'Even though everybody believed that twice two was five it would still be four'? – For what would it be like for everybody to believe that? – Well, I could imagine, for instance, that people had a different calculus, or a technique which we should not call 'calculating'. But would it be *wrong*? (Is a coronation *wrong*? To beings different from ourselves it might look extremely odd.) (Wittgenstein 1953, II, pp. 226–5e)

What typifies Wittgenstein's rhetorical strategy here is the way that he moves from a statement of the realist (objectivist) position, *via* a counterfactual hypothesis (that we can at least imagine other people who deployed entirely different calculating methods), to the question: could we then be justified in counting them *wrong* – objectively so – if they came up with some (to us) arithmetically erroneous statement such as 'twice two is five'? And the gist of his remarks becomes yet more obscure when Wittgenstein compares the issue of what it means to be 'right' or 'wrong' in mathematical judgements with the issue of how such standards might apply in the case of a ritual event – a coronation – if viewed by some observer with a whole different set of cultural or socio-political values and beliefs.

This analogy has the effect – like so many of Wittgenstein's offbeat comparisons – of deflecting attention from the case in hand and making it extremely hard to know just what he is driving at. Thus when he asks: 'But would it be *wrong?*' one is left uncertain whether this applies to the wrongness of the statement 'twice two is five' (and the correctness of 'twice two is four') even though all members of a given community subscribed to the former claim, or whether it applies to the wrongness (i.e., the ethnocentric prejudice) of thinking that we must be correct in counting them wrong, given that they used a different calculus, or different computational techniques. This latter construal perhaps finds support from Wittgenstein's idea that such questions can usefully be treated by analogy with cases – like that of the coronation – where it is crucially a matter of how different people observe, interpret, or evaluate events from their own cultural perspective. But in that case clearly what is *wrong*, according to Wittgenstein, is the objectivist presumption that truth-values are fixed by the way things stand in mathematical reality, and hence that 'twice two is four' has the objective value 'true' and 'twice two is five' the objective value 'false' even though the latter proposition is conceived to enjoy universal credence among members of some (to us) weirdly deviant mathematical community. In short, this passage can most plausibly be read as attempting to coax us down from a realist conception of mathematical truth to a practice-based or communitarian conception.

It would be hard to exaggerate the impact of Wittgenstein's thinking on the subsequent course of philosophical discussion with regard to the status of truth-claims in mathematics, logic, and the formal as well as the natural sciences (Klenk 1976; Shanker [ed.] 1996). I have written at length elsewhere about the complex, often tortuous attempts of thinkers like John McDowell and Thomas Nagel to produce a viable conception of mathematics that would conserve what they take to be our basic realist intuitions while not falling prey to Wittgenstein's various scepticism-inducing moves (McDowell 1994; Nagel 1997; Norris 2000). Others again – Michael Dummett and Crispin Wright among them – have sought to remove the sceptical sting and avoid any taint of cultural relativism by proposing a kind of philosophical research-programme designed to test different areas of discourse (logic, mathematics, the physical sciences, history, ethics, and aesthetics) in point of their aptness (or otherwise) for ascriptions of bivalent truth or falsehood (see Dummett 1991; Norris 2002; Wright 1992). What is required, on this account, is a context-sensitive adjustment to the differing criteria that competent reasoners bring to bear when assessing various kinds of statement.

Thus, for Dummett, in the paradigm case of mathematics we can best avoid the problems thrown up by a full-fledged Wittgensteinian or communitarian approach if we restrict the class of bivalent (determinately true or false) statements to those for which we can or could in principle produce some adequate formal proof. These will then be counted among the class of truth-apt statements, or – in Dummett's preferred idiom – the class of those that are *bona fide* candidates for 'warranted assertibility'. However, once again, this can scarcely satisfy the realist about mathematics since it means that a well-formed statement in the Dummettian 'disputed class' – such as 'Goldbach's Conjecture is true' – must be treated as neither true nor false since no computer program, however powerful, could run through the infinite series of even numbers to check that they are all the sum of two primes, and we do not possess a formal proof-procedure that would do the job more economically. Besides, Dummett's proposal has the further awkward consequence that the statement 'Fermat's Last Theorem is true' must be thought of as having been neither true nor false right up until the time when Andrew Wiles produced the clinching stages of argument in his celebrated proof. Such cases can best be viewed as a *reductio as absurdum* of the anti-realist position. That is to say, they serve to show not so much that 'nothing works' in philosophy of mathematics but rather that anti-realism fails to work when confronted with instances that only make sense on the premise that mathematical truths have a timeless, universal, objective existence quite apart from our best methods and procedures for finding them out.

Crispin Wright is another thinker much influenced by Wittgenstein but increasingly anxious to distance himself from the more sceptical or relativist implications of Wittgenstein's thought. I shall not here present any detailed discussion of his various proposals in this regard (for further discussion, see Norris 2002). Sufficient to say that Wright follows Dummett in offering a kind of discourse taxonomy wherein different areas are rated or ranked with respect to their aptness for ascriptions of bivalent truth/falsehood, along with certain other epistemic criteria – such as 'superassertibility' and 'cognitive command' – which are likewise intended as a measure of their fitness for judgements of the relevant kind (Wright 1992). Thus if a statement is to count properly as 'superassertible' then it must be one whose 'pedigree would survive arbitrarily close scrutiny', that is to say, whose truth would still be maintained by rational investigators when all the evidence was in, or at the ideal limit-point of epistemic enquiry (ibid.: 48). 'Cognitive Command' is a stronger requirement in most ways since it shifts the focus from an epistemic (no matter how idealised) context to one where the specified admission criteria have more to do with objective – or at any rate objective-sounding – terms of reference. 'When a discourse exhibits Cognitive Command', Wright explains, 'any difference of opinion will be such that there are considerations quite independent of the conflict which, if known about, would mandate withdrawal of one (or both) of the contending views' (ibid.: 103). However this conception still leaves room for a reading that would stress the phrase 'considerations...if known about', the effect of which depends very largely on whether one takes 'considerations' in the sense of 'objective factors properly requiring consideration' or 'appropriate reasonings and judgements in response to those same considerations'. At any rate – as I have argued elsewhere – Wright's approach to the issue of mathematical truth is a complex, at times contradictory mixture of Wittgensteinian scepticism (induced chiefly by the rule-following 'paradox') and his attempt to work out a kind of scaled-down, practice-internal (quasi-)objectivism that would thereby meet the Wittgensteinian challenge while also bidding fair to assuage the realist's worries (Norris 2002).

Thus, for instance: 'in shifting to a broadly intuitionistic conception of, say, number theory, we do not immediately foreclose on the idea that the series of natural numbers constitutes a real object of mathematical investigation, which it is harmless and correct to think of the number theoretician as explaining' (Wright 1992: 5). What he can possibly mean by describing this idea as 'harmless and correct' is a nice question in semantics as well as in philosophy of logic and mathematics. However it is evident – from this and other passages – that Wright's 'realism' stops well short of conceding the objectivist case for mathematical truth as *in no way* internal to (or dependent upon) those various practices, proof-procedures, or methods of verification which constitute the scope and limits of our knowledge at any given time. His unwillingness to go that far in a realist direction despite his qualms with regard to the full-fledged Wittgensteinian position can best be explained, I think, by the fact that Wright – like so many others – has been over-impressed by the force of those passages where Wittgenstein offers reasons to doubt that we possess any clear or definite concept of what it means to 'follow a rule'. These passages have since given rise to a huge volume of secondary literature, much of it largely exegetical in character and premised (as so often) on the fideist belief that philosophy must come to grips with the problem *on Wittgenstein's terms* – or something very like them – since any other approach would be beside the point or evading the issue. (See Wittgenstein 1953, I, Sections 201–92 *passim*; also Baker and Hacker 1984; Kripke 1982; Miller and Wright [eds] 2002.)

I started out with some slightly acerbic comments on the way in which philosophers of otherwise diverse persuasion had fallen under his spell and felt themselves compelled to run their arguments through the Wittgensteinian mill so as to head off likely objections. Nowhere is this more apparent than in the rule-following debate, prompted by Saul Kripke's strangely non-committal but immensely influential book where he puts the case for reading these passages in conjunction with Wittgenstein's thoughts about 'private languages' (Kripke 1982). I shall not here add any more to the weight of commentary beyond what is required by way of explaining why this whole debate seems to me so completely off-the-track. But it is worth attention if only to show the extent to which Wittgenstein's influence has dictated the recent (post-1970) agenda in various fields of philosophical enquiry.

IV

The problem – if such it is – has to do with the kind of elementary rule-following procedure that consists in obeying an instruction like: 'continue this numerical sequence in increments of 2'. Wittgenstein asks us to imagine a pupil who goes on in the standard (arithmetically and pedagogically approved) way until he reaches a certain number and then the sequence appears to go wild. So he counts, say, from 4 to 1000 adding 2 at each stage and we think this evidence enough that he has grasped the rule for 'n + 2' along with the fact that such recursive operations extend to any arbitrary point in the numerical series. But when prompted to carry on for a while – just to make sure – he writes down the numbers 1004, 1008, 1012, and so forth. So we indicate his error ('You were meant to add *two*: look how you began the series!') and he answers 'Yes, isn't that right? I thought that was how I was *meant* to do it' (Wittgenstein 1953, I, Section 185). Or suppose, Wittgenstein invites us, that 'he pointed to the series and said: "But I went on in the same way." – It would now be no use to say: "But can't you see . . . ?" – and repeat the old examples and explanations. – In such a case we might say, perhaps: It comes natural [*sic*] to this person to understand our order with our explanations as *we* should understand the order: "Add 2 up to 1000, 4 up to 2000, 6 up to 3000 and so on" ' (ibid.). Thus the dialogue soon reaches a stage where our attempted explanations simply run out and we despair of getting the pupil see that he has either misunderstood the rule or failed to apply it consistently. Or rather, we shall soon reach that stage if – like Wittgenstein – we ourselves find it hard to see how there *could* be any standard of correctness in arithmetical rule-following that would not come down to what we (or the pupil) *meant* by some particular form of words, such as 'n + 2' or 'go on in the same way'.

Such is the rule-following 'paradox' taken up by Kripke from Wittgenstein's scattered remarks: that if different people might indeed, quite conceivably, mean different things when they utter or interpret any such form of words then there is nothing – no fact of the matter – that could possibly decide the issue. Moreover there is no way to be sure that *the same person* must have *meant the same thing* from one instance to the next. For if 'meaning-by' can vary so drastically between individuals then how are we to know *even in our own case* that what we mean now by 'n + 2' is what we meant on any number of past occasions? After all, our situation in this regard is equivalent to our situation *vis-à-vis* the pupil who just cannot be brought to understand that his rule-following has gone off the rails when assessed by (what else?) our own standards of rule-following correctness. That is to say, if there is no deep further fact about meaning that fixes the operative standard from one to another individual then, just as surely, there is no deep further fact about *my* having meant this or that when I issued some instruction or applied some rule in the past. Of course I might declare – and be thoroughly convinced – that

I learned the rule for 'n + 2' way back in primary school and have since then applied it in just the same way and with similar results on any number of subsequent occasions. But the question remains: did the rule which I applied (or which *I now think that I recall* having applied) really have this power to reach forward, so to speak, and determine the standard of correctness for every future application? Wittgenstein has two sceptical objections to any such line of counter-argument. First: it ignores the possibility that memory might just be playing me false and leading me to foist my present understanding of the rule onto all those past understandings. And second: it ignores his point about the pupil's always being able to say – in answer to the charge of inconsistency – that, on the contrary, he has applied the rule for 'n + 2' in a manner perfectly consistent with his own understanding of that rule, that is, '+2 up to 1000', '+4 up to 2000', '+8 up to 3000', and so forth. Neither in his case nor in mine can there be any ultimate (practice-transcendent) standard of consistency or truth which could somehow guarantee that past and present usages accorded with a common rule. For this would require the existence of a higher-level rule for the application of first-order rules, and beyond that an infinite (vicious) regress of rules which could never – at any point – come to rest in a moment of apodictic certainty.

Thus my situation is really no different from that of the pupil when it comes to judging what is or is not an instance of carrying on in accord with previous applications of the rule. We are each convinced – and with equal warrant – that we are doing just that and that the other party has for some strange reason departed from the rule at an arbitrary stage in the proceedings. In which case perhaps I shall find it hard to convince even myself – let alone the recalcitrant pupil – that there *do* exist standards of correctness and consistency in rule-following and that I have adhered to those standards while he has unaccountably ignored them. For of course, in Wittgenstein's conjectural scenario, the student will be just as baffled by my strange persistence in failing to grasp that 'n + 2' strictly requires that the series be continued in accordance with his (not my) understanding of the rule. Nor can I be sure that this *really was* my understanding when I issued my instruction in the first place. Of course I might say: 'But I already knew, at the time when I gave the order, that he ought to write 1002 after 1000'. Certainly, Wittgenstein replies, 'and you can also say you *meant* it then; only you should not let yourself be misled by the grammar of the words "know" and "mean". For you don't want to say that you thought of the step from 1000 to 1002 at that time – and even if you did think of this step, still you did not think of other ones' (1953, I, Section 187). That is, it can scarcely be supposed that anyone who grasps the rule for 'n + 2' must some-how have in mind – know in advance – the entire series of numbers to which that formula provides the key. So, again, there is no deciding *in point of consistency* between my firm belief that I acted in accordance with the rule by continuing '1002, 1004, and so forth', and his (the pupil's) firm belief that he obeyed it by writing down a different, to my mind weirdly inconsistent sequence of numerals. What we have is a stand-off where each party is convinced that the other has gone wrong but where both are stuck for any argument that could adjudicate the issue between them.

At this point Wittgenstein gently intervenes with some remarks in a 'therapeutic' vein which might just succeed in talking them down from the impasse that they have so far managed to create. Thus: 'your idea was that that act of meaning the order had in its own way already traversed all those steps: that when you meant it your mind as it were flew ahead and took all the steps before you physically arrived at this or that one' (1953, I, Section 188). But of course this idea has already been demolished through Wittgenstein's various arguments against the appeal to correctness in rule-following as a matter of conformity between past and present or present and future applications. For if indeed the only possible ground of that appeal is some deep further fact about the *meaning* of the rule for this or that individual on this or that occasion then the absence of any such putative 'fact' makes the argument a non-starter. All the same – he concedes – it is an idea that goes so deep into our normal or habitual ways of thinking that it cannot be dislodged except through further therapy. 'You were inclined', he suggests, 'to use such expressions as: "the steps are *really* already taken, even before I take them in writing or orally or in thought". And it seemed as if they were in some *unique* way predetermined, anticipated – as only the act of meaning can anticipate reality.' (1953, I, Section 188.) So what needs to be exorcised in order to give us philosophical peace is the idea of meanings and intentions as somehow fixing the rules in advance or determining the right answer in any given case. We shall then come to see that this whole confusion took rise from a certain 'bewitchment of our intelligence by language', namely that exerted by a word like 'determine', with its tendency to suggest that rules function like super-rigid tracks laid down by an initial (determinative) act of thought and thereafter stretching out beyond any finite range of applications so as to decide the correct response for whatever value of an algebraic formula such as $y = x^2$. If we can just throw off this mistaken conception – so Wittgenstein thinks – then we shall come to accept that everything is in order with our standing mathematical or logical procedures and that nothing more is needed by way of justification.

At which point the naive collocutor asks: 'But *are* the steps then *not* determined by the algebraic formula?' (Section 189). However, 'the question contains a mistake' since it shows that the collocutor is still held captive by a false picture, one that carries the same suggestion of rules as a kind of super-rigid machinery which continues – once programmed by our reference-fixing meanings or intentions – to churn out correct answers in every case. Rather we should take Wittgenstein's usual advice on such occasions of deadlocked philosophical dispute and ask not so much 'what does this expression (correctly or properly) mean?' but 'how do we typically *use* this expression in particular contexts of utterance?'. Thus '[w]e may perhaps refer to the fact that people are brought by their education (training) so to use the formula $y=x^2$, that they all work out the same value for y when they substitute the same number for x' (Section 189). Or again, that '[t]hese people are so trained that they all take the same step at the same point when they receive the order "add 3"'. We might even express this notion quite harmlessly by saying something like: 'for these people the order "add 3" completely determines every step from one number to the next'. We should then have the means to distinguish that group of people from others 'who do not know what they are to do on receiving this order, or who react to it with perfect certainty, but each one in a different way' (ibid.).

However what is in question here is a certain usage of the word *determine*, or a certain range of applications which have their place within the language-games of elementary arithmetic, algebra, and so forth. What is clearly *not* in question for Wittgenstein is any idea that truth-values might be 'determined' in the sense 'objectively fixed by the way things stand in mathematical reality', rather than by the way things stand with our usage of various words – such as *determine* – whose operative meaning is wholly a matter of their role in this or that discourse. Thus: 'we *call* formulae of a particular kind (with the appropriate methods of use) "formulae which determine a number y for a given value of x", and formulae of another kind, ones which "do not determine the number y for a given value of x" ($y=x^2$ would be of the first kind, $y \cong x^2$ of the second)' (Section 189). From which it follows that any question concerning the power of a formula to determine a given numerical value will be more a question about the meaning (or accepted usage) of the words 'formula' and 'determine' than one about the truth-conditions that apply to certain algebraic formulae. This is why, according to Wittgenstein, 'it is not clear off-hand what we are to make of the question "Is $y=x^2$ a formula which determines y for a given value of x?"'. After all, '[o]ne might address this question to a pupil in order to test whether he understands the use of the word "to determine"; or it might be a mathematical problem to prove that x has only one square' (Section 189). That is to say, usage alone can decide what is *meant* by any given formula, what power it has to *determine* algebraic functions, and what should count as a correct (or incorrect) application of the formula in this or that particular context.

If I have dwelt at some length on these passages from Wittgenstein it is not because I find his arguments convincing or in any degree plausible. Rather it is because they exert a kind of mesmerising power which is hard to shake off – as a good many other commentators have found – even if one takes the view that Wittgenstein was driven to adopt this position by his failure to grasp the objective (recognition-transcendent) status of math-ematical and logical truths. Of course there are wide divergences between those commentators as concerns the extent to which they have followed Wittgenstein along that path or the degree to which they have resisted his conclusions and explored alternative possibilities. Thus some, like Dummett, have espoused an anti-realist approach in philosophy of mathematics that inclines very markedly toward a Wittgensteinian position even though they register certain doubts with regard to its more extreme sceptical implications (cf. Dummett 1978 and 1991). Others, such as Wright, have sought to establish a typology of discourses wherein the chief question is whether they permit the application of a truth-predicate that would not come down to the criterion of communal acceptability or 'truth' by the lights of currently acknowledged best opinion (Wright 1992). All the same, as I have said, this pluralist approach tends to manifest a strong Wittgensteinian bias when it is a matter of defining the terms and conditions on which any given discourse (like that of mathematics) can be treated as genuinely truth-apt (see Norris 2002). For others again it induces a regular compulsion to test their arguments against the usual range of Wittgensteinian objections just to make sure that they will not be accused of ignoring the kinds of problem thrown up by the rule-following debate or the vicious-regress rejoinder (McDowell 1994). Elsewhere there is a kind of professional etiquette which requires that philosophers make the token gesture of acknowledging Wittgenstein's rule-following 'paradox' – often at considerable length – despite what they see as its utter lack of force when set against the fact that mathematical knowledge is the surest knowledge we have and hence that any argument to contrary effect must itself have gone badly off the rails (Nagel 1997; also Norris 2000: 231–59).

Most extraordinary perhaps is Saul Kripke's response in *Wittgenstein on Rules and Private Language*, a book which purports to do no more than draw out and clarify the gist of those worrisome passages, but which finds them logically and philosophically compelling *despite* his frank acknowledgement that they are also 'absurd', 'bizarre', and even 'intolerable' (Kripke 1982). Thus Kripke constructs a whole series of extravagant variations on Wittgenstein's original scenario where the pupil answers correctly (by our lights) when asked to perform calculations within a certain numerical range but then goes haywire – by our lights again – when one of the numbers involved exceeds that limit. For instance, when asked '68 + 57?' he will always answer '5', despite having seemingly grasped and applied the standard addition-rule for a good range of previous test questions in which neither number exceeded 57. So we tax him with all the familiar points about rules, consistency, recursive application, 'carrying on as before', and so forth, and expect him to suddenly smite his brow and recognise the error of his ways. However these arguments are to no avail since – unbeknownst to us – he had been working all along on the 'quus' rule – or the rule for 'quaddition' – which mandates adding up in the usual (as it happens, teacher-approved) fashion *unless* any number exceeds 57, in which case the correct answer (*pace* teacher) is always '5'.

From here Kripke goes on to develop the 'sceptical paradox' along Wittgensteinian lines but with a more acute sense of its completely undermining all our normal assurances with regard to the epistemological foundations of mathematics, logic, and other such formal (rule-governed) disciplines of thought. For can we ever be sure – he asks – that *our own* present application of a rule is in accord with past applications, or that those past applications did not involve some *quus*-type provision for a change of rule (more precisely: a rule-governed change of calculative method) beyond a given numerical limit? Or again: how can we possibly know that the pupil was wrong and we ourselves right in the claim to have reasoned correctly and consistently from one application to the next? For in the absence of any such deep further fact about our always having had the self-same rule in mind – and applied it always in the same way – we can surely be no better placed than him to assert that *this* is the correct answer and to reject all other (aberrant or off-the-track) responses as manifesting a failure to grasp the relevant rule. All of which amounts – on Kripke's submission – to a sharpened re-statement of earlier sceptical problems, among them problems from Hume, that here take on an even greater force in respect of their capacity to cast doubt on our most basic ideas of truth, correctness, and epistemic warrant.

Kripke starts out in a fairly non-committal fashion by presenting his argument as a piece of textual exegesis, claiming no more than to elucidate certain connections between two aspects of Wittgenstein's thinking in the *Investigations*, that is, his reflections on the rule-following 'paradox' and his thoughts about the topic of 'private languages'. However it soon becomes clear that he is impressed by the force of Wittgenstein's arguments and unable to see any solution to the paradox except the so-called 'sceptical solution', one that follows Wittgenstein in making the case that there is no further ground of appeal beyond those habituated usages, practices, and ways of 'carrying on' that define what *counts* as correct rule-following within some given community. I can find no hint in Kripke's book – much as I should like to – that the whole exercise might be intended as a *reductio ad absurdum* of the Wittgensteinian case, or a roundabout strategy for persuading the reader that if *this* is the best solution available then there must be something wrong with the entire line of argument that has led up to it. Certainly he expresses a sense of unease, mounting on occasion to shocked disbelief, that Wittgenstein's rule-following paradox should have compelled him (Kripke) to draw such extreme and philosophically disastrous conclusions. Thus he sees it as a far more potent threat than other, for example, Humean versions of sceptical doubt since it bids fair to subvert or destroy *every* last principle of consistent reasoning, from the most basic kinds of inductive procedure to arithmetic, algebra, deductive logic, and any formal science that has to presuppose the existence of certain objective constraints upon the range of admissible or valid propositions.

Kripke's proposed 'sceptical solution' – that we can carry on citing those principles just so long as they play an accepted role in our various communal practices – is no doubt consonant with Wittgenstein's thinking and therefore quite adequate in purely exegetical terms. However this is a concession too far for the realist who will wish to maintain that mathematical truths – along with the necessary truths of logic – exist for all time, across all possible worlds, and irrespective of whether they happen to play such a role (Katz 1998; Lewis 1973, 1986). Exegetically speaking, Kripke's construal accords with what Wittgenstein says about the impossibility of a one-off rule application and hence (likewise) the impossibility that there could exist any such thing as a 'private language'. Thus: 'is what we call "obeying a rule" something that it would be possible for only *one* man to do, and to do only *once* in his life?'. On the contrary, Wittgenstein asserts: '[t]o obey a rule, to make a report, to give an order, to play a game of chess, are *customs* (uses, institutions)' (1953, I, Section 199). So the concept of 'following a rule' – and the conditions for following that rule correctly – are as much dependent on a shared understanding of linguistic and practice-relative criteria as are the conditions for making sense within some given language-game or cultural form of life. But in that case the standard of correctness equates with what currently passes as such among members of the given community. So if *this* is indeed what Wittgenstein is saying, the realist will retort, one can only conclude that he has failed to grasp the most significant point about mathematics and logic, that is, the existence of objective (non-practice-relative) truth-values that might always transcend not only our present but even our future-best powers of recognition or verification.

V

It is among the greatest ironies of Wittgenstein's reception that he has managed to induce such widespread perplexity in commentators who – some of them at least – are strongly inclined toward a realist position on these and other matters. I call it ironic because Wittgenstein's claim is that his way of thinking brings the therapeutic benefit of coaxing us down from needless philosophical worries and, in Stanley Cavell's emollient phrase, 'leading us back, *via* the community, home' (Cavell 1969: 94). Yet one main effect of Wittgenstein's writings has been to convince many philosophers that there *must* be something wrong with mathematical, scientific, and other varieties of realism, that is to say, with the idea – the default assumption – that for any well-formed and truth-apt statement the question must arise whether it is true or not *as a matter of objective fact* rather than a matter of whether or not we happen to possess some means of ascertaining its truth-value. Thus the clear aim of those passages about rule-following is to undermine any such objectivist conception by showing that truth-values cannot be fixed through an appeal to putative 'facts' about the meaning or intention of individual rule-followers. One may grant that Wittgenstein succeeds in this part of his programme, that is, that his case against the very possibility of a 'private language' goes through to convincing effect and that any realist unwise enough to make it the linchpin of their argument would be backing a lame horse. But this is not to say – far from it – that the realist must then be stuck for an answer when it comes to explaining what could possibly count as an instance of correct rule-following or a truth of mathematics quite apart from the standard of best opinion or communal warrant.

One result of Wittgenstein's construing the issue in this highly prejudicial way is that the realist is supposedly left without a leg to stand on, having yielded so many hostages to sceptical fortune. Hence Wittgenstein's rejoinder in the form of a sigh: 'You have no model of this superlative fact, but you are seduced into using a super-expression. (It might be called a philosophical superlative.)' (1953, I, Section 192) But the realist will do best to come back at this point and protest that indeed she had no such 'superlative fact' in mind, that is to say, no 'fact' whose 'superlative' status depended on her own (or any reasoner's) capacity to mean the same thing – or intend the same kind of rule-following operation – from one instance to the next. What she will surely wish to say – if allowed to get a word in edgeways – is that the standard of correctness in arithmetical, algebraic, deductive, and other such rule-following procedures has *nothing to do* with any thoughts, meanings, or intentions that might be imputed to the individual reasoner. Nor is it a question as to whether or not they can apply some infallible introspective method for checking the consistency of their own performances past, present, and future. Rather the standard of correctness is fixed by those features of the relevant object-domain – algebraic functions, arithmetical products, logical entailment-relations, and so forth – which determine the truth-value of any well-formed (even if unproved or unprovable) statement concerning it. 'Determine', that is to say, in a sense of the word whose operative meaning is itself determined by the way things stand with regard to that object-domain and *not* by its role in some particular language-game (mathematical, pedagogical, or whatever) where the meaning may vary from one to another context of application.

According to Wittgenstein – and Kripke after him – this debate must always arrive at a point where the *only* solution is a 'sceptical solution' along communitarian lines. Thus '[i]t may now be said: "The way the formula is meant determines which steps are to be taken". What is the criterion for the way the formula is meant? It is, for example, the kind of way we always use it, the way we are taught to use it ... *That* will be how meaning it can determine the steps in advance' (Wittgenstein 1953, I, Section 190). However the realist will again do best to reject the stark choice presented here, one that falls out between a private realm of introspectively checkable meanings or intentions and a public realm wherein the standards are set by existing practices and communal warrant. That is, she will regard it as just the kind of dead-end conceptual fix that Wittgenstein has got himself into – along with Kripke and the fideist exegetes – by imposing a fallacious *tertium non datur*, one which excludes the very possibility of objective mathematical and logical truths that determine the veridical status (or otherwise) of our various statements concerning them. There is evidence enough in his later writings that Wittgenstein was himself much troubled by this issue and unable to make adequate sense of any such alternative realist conception. Thus:

> Someone does a sum in his head. He uses the result, let's say, for building a bridge or a machine. – Are you trying to say that he has not *really* arrived at this number by calculation? That it has, say, just 'come' to him in the manner of a kind of dream? There must surely have been calculation going on, and there was. For he *knows* that, and how, he calculated; and the correct result he got would be inexplicable without calculation. – But what if I said: '*It strikes him as if* he had calculated. And why should the correct result be explicable? Is it not incomprehensible enough, that without saying a word, without making a note, he was able to CALCULATE?' (1953, I, Section 364)

No doubt we are supposed to interpret this last passage as yet another cautionary instance of the kind of metaphysical perplexity that thinking always runs into when it ignores Wittgenstein's advice about the pointlessness of raising philosophic questions where no such questions can sensibly be raised. All the same – as so often – it is a passage that strongly suggests his own deep bafflement and his constant circling back to these problems despite and against his own wise counsel.

Of course the exegete will say straight off: but you are completely missing Wittgenstein's point since, don't you see, he is challenging the realist to explain what it could possibly amount to in practice, this 'super-rigid-rail' conception of objective truth-values that somehow fix the correct answer in advance for any application of '$n+2$', $y=x^2$, or suchlike formulas. At this stage, most likely, they will take Wittgenstein's lead and bring the discussion back around to what different parties (say the teacher and the pupil) might be taken to have *had in mind* when they embarked on some rule-following procedure. I trust that the reader will forgive me if I cite another lengthy passage which brings out the sheer tenacity (not to say obtuseness) of the voice that is undoubtedly meant to dominate at this stage in the proceedings. First the imaginary collocutor:

> 'What you are saying, then, comes to this: a new insight – intuition – is needed at every step to carry out the order '$+n$' correctly' – To carry it out correctly! How is it decided what is the right step to take at any particular stage? – 'The right step is the one that accords with the order – as it was *meant*.' – So when you gave the order+2 you meant that he was to write 1002 after 1000 – and did you also mean that he should write 1868 after 1866, and 100036 after 100034, and so on – an infinite series of such propositions? – 'No: what I meant was, that he should write the next but

one number after *every* number that he wrote; and from this all those propositions follow in turn.' – But that is just what is in question: what, at any stage, does follow from that sentence. Or, again, what, at any stage we are to call 'being in accord' with that sentence (and with the *mean*-ing you then put into the sentence – whatever that may have consisted in). It would almost be more correct to say, not that a new intuition was needed at every stage, but that a new decision was needed at every stage. (Wittgenstein 1953, I, Section 186)

Again, it is hard to know just where to start in unpacking the confusions here. At least it is fairly plain that the passages in quote marks are meant to be ascribed to the hapless collocutor and the unmarked passages to Wittgenstein *ipse*, or at any rate his authorised spokesman at this point in the dialogue. What should strike us again is his sheer refusal to conceive that there might be objective truths which depended not all on our *meanings* and *intentions*, our *mental procedures* in following a rule, or our *knowing in advance* – having *present to our minds* – the infinite range of possible applications for a formula such as 'n + 2'. After all, this is Wittgenstein's usual retort to the collocutor whenever he comes up with some presumptively naive or problematical argument for the existence of objective (i.e., non-practice-dependent) truths in arithmetic, algebra, or logic. That is to say, the collocutor *has* to be saddled with a thoroughly discredited epistemology – an appeal to 'private' (hence strictly unknowable) meanings and intentions – in order for Wittgenstein to press right through with his 'sceptical paradox' and thus clear the way for his (and Kripke's) last-ditch 'sceptical solution'.

However one could just as well turn this strategy around and remark that the collocutor's words are here subject to a cock-eyed interpretation that completely misses their point as construed in realist or objectivist terms. For when he – the collocutor – uses such phrases as 'What I meant was . . . [that the pupil should write the next-but-one number after every preceding number, etc.]' there is no implication that his *meaning* or *intending* the pupil to follow the rule in just that way is *itself what fixes* the conditions of correctness for applying the rule or the truth-value of whatever answers may result. Rather those conditions and truth-values are fixed independently of anything that they – the teacher *or* the pupil – may happen to mean, intend, or understand by some particular form of words. Thus the crucial (reference-fixing and rule-determining) part of teacher's sentence is *not* that which reads: 'No: what I meant was . . . ', but that which specifies: 'he should write the next-but-one number after *every* number that he wrote; and from this all those propositions follow in turn'. For when stated in this form – quite aside from such expressions of first-person meaning or intent – the instruction is both perfectly precise and capable of determining (laying down in advance) its full range of future applications.

There is a similar failure – or flat refusal – to take the point of teacher's argument when Wittgenstein asks 'what, at any stage, we are to call "being in accord" with that sentence (and with the *mean*-ing you then put into the sentence – whatever that may have consisted in'. For here again he is preemptively discounting the claim that such a well-formed, clear arithmetical instruction can indeed lay down conditions in advance for its own correct and consistent application *even if* the person who utters it does not have a thought – or a mental picture – corresponding to every instance of '$n+2$' throughout the entire (infinite) series of integers. To require that he *should* have such a picture – and to suggest that if he does not then he simply has not grasped the rule in question – is not so much an odd view of mathematics as a total failure to understand what mathematics is all about. Hence Wittgenstein's strange idea that any talk of a calculation's 'being in accord' with some foregoing sentence of instruction can only be a matter of 'the *mean*-ing you then put into the sentence – whatever that may have consisted in'. But this is just another wrong-footing ploy whose rhetorical intent, once again, is to leave the collocutor awkwardly saddled with a notion of first-person privileged epistemic access which quickly falls prey to the 'no private language' argument.

The trick is most visible when Wittgenstein's translator pointedly inserts that hyphen in the word '*mean*-ing', a device whose deliberate effect is to stress the idea of the collocutor's intending this or that by his use of the formula, rather than its meaning (or its truth-conditions) conceived as existing or obtaining quite apart from whatever he 'then put into the sentence'. The original German text here has *Meinung*, which likewise carries a marked intentional force: 'und auch mit der *Meinung*, die du damals dem Satz gegeben hast, – worin immer diese bestanden haben mag' (1953, I, Section 186). The passage could scarcely have been given this slant had Wittgenstein availed himself of the Fregean tripartite distinction between 'sense', 'reference', and 'idea', the first two of which (*Sinn* and *Bedeutung*) are construed as objective and truth-functional terms having nothing to do with private goings-on in the mind of this or that thinker, while 'ideas' are merely psychological entities which vary from one individual to another and therefore lack such objective status (Frege 1952; also Beaney 1996). However it is precisely Wittgenstein's purpose in much of his late writings to represent such distinctions as belonging to a false or 'sublimated' picture of the role of logic *vis-à-vis* our everyday linguistic and practical activities (see especially Wittgenstein 1953, I, Sections 81–107 *passim*). So it is clear that Anscombe, his translator, has been faithful to Wittgenstein's intentions and employed a device – '*mean*-ing' – which nicely captures his original gist in the absence of any equivalent English distinction.

However, such issues of textual fidelity aside, there is still the question whether Wittgenstein himself has misrepresented the issue by setting his imaginary collocutor up as spokesman for a notionally 'realist' position which can then be shown to fall apart under the least sceptical pressure. For what distinguishes realism, properly construed, is not the 'being in accord' between meanings (or intentions) and rule-following practices but rather the 'being in accord' between those practices and the objective truth-conditions which determine the right answer in any given case. On Wittgenstein's account, conversely, the truth-conditions – or criteria for warranted assertibility – must be thought of as internal to the practice concerned, and the practice conceived as itself determining what shall count as an instance of correctly or consistently following a rule. Thus the very word 'determine' undergoes a kind of Wittgensteinian semantic sea change from 'determine = decide as a matter of objective truth' to 'determine = decide relative to the kinds of truth-constitutive criteria that count within some given practice, language-game, or shared form of life'.

To be sure, Wittgenstein allows his collocutor a whole series of attempted replies, all of which however soon come to grief through the same well-practised line of counter-argument. Thus:

> 'But I already knew, at the time when I gave the order, that he ought to write 1002 after 1000.' – Certainly; and you can also say you *meant* it then; only you should not let yourself be misled by the grammar of the words 'know' and 'mean'. For you don't want to say that you thought of the step from 1000 to 1002 at that time – and even if you did think of this step, still you did not think of other ones. When you said 'I already knew at the time...' that meant something like: 'If I had been asked what number should be written after 1000, I should have replied "1002"'. And that I don't doubt. This assumption is rather of the same kind as: 'If he had fallen in the water then, I should have jumped in after him'. – Now, what was wrong with your idea? (Wittgenstein 1953, I, Section 187)

Well, one is inclined to say, there is a whole lot wrong with the collocutor's idea as Wittgenstein here represents it, that is, the idea that truth or correctness in such matters has anything to do with what is meant or intended by a certain form of words. Still less does it depend on our fallible powers of memory or our ability to recall – with unerring certitude – what we understood by those same words on any number of previous occasions. But there is just as much wrong with Wittgenstein's idea that the collocutor has here been misled by 'the grammar of the words "know" and "mean"', or by their tendency to conjure up false impressions of epistemological security (see also Wittgenstein 1974). For this suggests – once again – that issues of truth must always come down to issues of knowledge or meaning, and moreover, that these latter can only make sense on the terms laid down by some given language-game or communal form of life.

Thus it seems that Wittgenstein *really cannot* perceive any difference between the kind of subjunctive-conditional reasoning that applies in the case of arithmetic or logic ('if I had been asked what number should be written after 1000, I should have replied "1002"'), and the kind that applies in the case of counterfactual hypotheses concerning contingent events ('if he had fallen in the water then, I should have jumped in after him'). Nor indeed could there be any difference worth remarking if Wittgenstein were right and if the sole criterion of correctness in rule-following was that of accordance with certain behavioural regularities or certain dispositions to carry on in a more or less predictable way. Such is the clear implication when he asks (or prompts his collocutor to ask) 'How am I able to obey a rule?' and replies: '[i]f I have exhausted the justifications I have reached bedrock, and my spade is turned. Then I am inclined to say: "This is simply what I do"' (1953, I, Section 217). And again: 'When I obey a rule, I do not choose. I obey the rule *blindly*' (Section 219).

These passages have struck some commentators as oddly and embarrassingly missing the point about logic, mathematics, and the formal sciences, suggesting as they do that it is just a 'brute fact' about our rule-following behaviour that we are disposed to interpret some given instruction or apply some given rule in one way rather than another (McDowell 1994; Nagel 1997). More often it is assumed – on the principle of charity that features so largely in Wittgenstein scholarship – that they represent either a momentary lapse from his usual perspicacity in treating such matters or a case where the offending remarks are best thought of as spoken from a viewpoint (that of the imaginary collocutor) which lacks authorial warrant. However this strategy simply will not work with the above-cited passages since it relies on Wittgenstein's regular use of quote marks to distinguish direct from indirect speech – or first-person comment from instances of *oratio obliqua* – and here it is apparent that the remarks in question (those about blind rule-following) belong to the former category. Besides, they occur in a context where Wittgenstein has effectively closed every option except this surely desperate appeal to the 'brute fact' of our carrying on in accordance with rules that just *do* have a place in this or that communal practice, and which otherwise lack any justification beyond mere force of habit. Thus the only alternative, he thinks, is the realist conception of super-rigid rules – or rails – that can somehow (we imagine) stretch out to infinity and guide our rule-following behaviour beyond any finite range of applications. But this is just another of those false pictures that held us captive and whose grip should be loosened through our coming to see – with Wittgenstein's help – that it resulted only from our chronic 'bewitchment by language'.

VI

It will be evident by now that I am wholly unpersuaded by this idea of Wittgenstein as having delivered us from all our philosophical doubts and perplexities. Indeed I would argue, on the contrary, that his influence has been responsible for more confusion, linguistic bewitchment, and misplaced philosophical endeavour than that of any other thinker in recent times. To adapt his favoured metaphor: it is not so much a case of Wittgenstein's having shown the fly the way out of the fly-bottle as of his having bottled a whole swarm of flies that have since buzzed around in philosophers' heads with just the opposite result (1953, I, Section 309).

How they buzzed around in his own head can be seen from some of the passages I have cited, along with numerous others in a likewise compulsive and far from 'therapeutic' vein. Hence no doubt the continuing stream of biographies, anecdotes, and personal reminiscences that clearly find a large and receptive readership despite the insistence – at least among Wittgenstein's devoted exegetes – that we not commit any version of the vulgar 'biographical fallacy', that is, the error of thinking to explain certain aspects of the work by certain aspects of the life. At times the effort to keep them apart is carried to truly heroic lengths, as in Ray Monk's standard biography which accords the work an expository treatment very much on its own terms – one that admits no serious question as to Wittgenstein's pre-eminent status among modern philosophers – while none the less offering copious evidence of his lifelong subjection to just the kinds of nagging anxiety for which his late writings purport to offer a cure (Monk 1990). To suggest anything like this in the company of devout Wittgensteinians is to be made to feel like 'The Man Who Said the Tactless Thing', or someone who simply fails to take the point of Wittgenstein's wise counsel. In general, I would agree, it is important to respect the distinction between issues of the kind: 'is this argument valid in strictly philosophical terms?' and issues of the kind: 'what particular motives or psychological compulsions might have led philosopher x to adopt this or that particular approach to problem y?'. But in Wittgenstein's case – so I have argued here – the motives and compulsions play so large a role that any treatment of his work that rules them irrelevant for the purposes of critical exegesis is thereby rendered all the more prone to re-enact his pseudo-problems (and pseudo-solutions) in a spirit of unquestioning fideist acceptance.

Yet even Kripke acknowledges the sheer incredulity that is apt to overtake him when he turns aside from the business of faithfully explicating Wittgenstein and reflects on the absurdity of what he is propounding with presumptive warrant from the master (Kripke 1982). Moreover, as I have noted, there is the strange compulsion among thinkers of a sharply divergent bent – those with well-developed realist instincts – to avoid any suspicion that they have not taken due account of those Wittgensteinian counter-arguments that might always rise against them. Non-philosophers – scientists and mathematicians in particular – have tended to muster more resistance, as we learn from various telling episodes recounted in the biographical literature. Thus Monk has some fascinating pages on Wittgenstein's encounter with Alan Turing and the latter's baffled attempts to comprehend what

Wittgenstein could possibly be driving at when he denied the existence of objective (practice-transcendent) mathematical truths (Monk 1990: 417–22). It seems to me that philosophers are ill-advised if they treat such evidence as merely anecdotal or philosophically beside the point. For by any rational standard we have better grounds for accepting mathematics and the physical sciences as a source of guidance in these matters than for adopting a Kripkensteinian 'sceptical solution' whose result – for all its therapeutic intent – is to leave us entirely bereft of such guidance.

I should like to look at another passage from Wittgenstein which brings out his curious tendency to use analogies and metaphors from the techno-scientific domain with the purpose – very often – of questioning our belief in the existence of objective truth-values in mathematics, logic, and the formal disciplines. Here the analogy has to do with mechanical engineering, a field in which the younger Wittgenstein had acquired a fair degree of theoretical knowledge and hands-on practical experience. It occurs toward the end of his reflections on rule-following and, more specifically, his argument against the idea of a 'superlative fact' about the rule-follower's intentions that would somehow extend – like a super-rigid rail – to fix the truth-conditions for every future application. 'You have no model of this superlative fact', Wittgenstein rejoins, 'but you are seduced into using a super-expression' (1953, I, Section 192). Or again: perhaps it is a certain kind of *symbol* that the collocutor has in mind. Thus,

> [t]he machine as symbolizing its action: the action of a machine – I might say at first – seems to be there in it from the start, What does that mean? – If we know the machine, everything else, that is its movement, seems to be already completely determined.
>
> We talk as if these parts could only move in this way, as if they could not do anything else. How is this – do we forget the possibility of their bending, breaking off, melting, and so on? Yes, in many cases we don't think of that at all. We use a machine, or the drawing of a machine, to symbolize a particular action of the machine. For instance, we give someone such a drawing and assume that he will derive the movement of the parts from it. (Just as we give someone a number by telling him that it is the twenty-fifth in the series 1, 4, 9, 16, . . .) (1953, I, Section 193)

Yes indeed, one wants to reply on behalf of the naive (or not-so-naive) collocutor: we do these things and do them, what's more, with ample justification in so far as there are various laws, regularities, and physical constants which may properly be held to govern the working of machines *even though* any given machine might always suffer mechanical failure through just the sorts of accident that Wittgenstein describes. In such instances we do not conclude that a law of nature has broken down but rather that *this machine* has broken down on account of some physical defect which we then seek to explain and, if possible, rectify.

Thus Wittgenstein's rule-following analogy turns out to have implications that go clean against its intended gist. For just as we can tell that the machine has malfunctioned through its failure to work as predicted or specified in accordance with those laws, likewise we can tell that some particular instance of mathematical or logical reasoning has gone off the rails in so far as it produces anomalous results or an outcome at odds with the necessary truths of mathematics and logic. What Wittgenstein himself conspicuously fails to grasp is the fact that those truths (and their objective status) cannot be called into doubt by any number of possible wrong answers or any amount of evidence concerning the error-prone character of human thought. No more can the laws of mechanics or thermodynamics be called into doubt by any number of observed mechanical breakdowns. (See Gefwert [1998] for some relevant discussion of these and kindred analogies in Wittgenstein's later thought.)

Of course it may be said that laws of nature are never directly manifested in the 'real world' – even under controlled laboratory conditions – since there will always be certain interference effects or other such complicating factors which preclude any perfect match between laws and observational data. Thus, for instance, no experiment could perfectly demonstrate Newton's inverse-square law of gravitational attraction since any two given bodies will always be subject to the forces exerted by other bodies, at no matter how great a distance. And again, the theoretical sciences of solid and fluid mechanics depend on certain idealisations – that is to say, on discounting the influence of factors such as friction, viscosity, or turbulent flow – in order to achieve precise statement in the form of universal laws. This is why some philosophers argue that there exists an inverse relation (or a kind of negotiated trade-off) between the power of theories to bring phenomena under law-like generalisations and their capacity to provide accurate descriptive or phenomenological accounts (Cartwright 1989, 1999). All the same these thinkers mostly resist the extreme sceptical verdict, that is, the idea that any appeal to 'laws of nature' is just a kind of metaphysical delusion imposed by our naively realist habits of thought. Rather they conclude that such laws are valid as *ceteris paribus* statements which necessarily ignore the kinds of disturbance which always show up whenever they are put to the test under real-world experimental conditions. Thus – to recall Wittgenstein's analogy – we shall scarcely be inclined to question or reject the laws of mechanics if they are not borne out (confirmed to the highest degree of mathematical precision) by the performance of even the best adjusted and most smoothly functioning machine. For of course there are always energy losses brought about by friction, vibration, inefficiencies of heat transfer, and so forth. Yet the laws hold good none the less – and serve to advance our practical as well as theoretical understanding – just so long as we acknowledge their idealised character and the impossibility that any *actual* machine (or its performance characteristics) will do more than approximate their limit-point degree of mathematical power and precision.

However this is *not* what Wittgenstein intends to suggest by his analogy between a certain conception of rule-following and a certain conception of the way that machines can be thought to function in accordance with the laws of mechanics. 'When does one have the thought: the possible movements of the machine are already there in it in some mysterious way?' Well, he replies,

> when one is doing philosophy. And what leads us into thinking that? The kind of way in which we talk about machines. We say, for example, that a machine *has* (possesses) such-and-such possibilities of movement; we speak of the ideally rigid machine which *can* only move in such-and-such a way. – What is this *possibility* of movement? It is not the *movement*, but it does not seem to be the mere physical conditions for moving either – as, that there is play between socket and pin, the pin not fitting too tight in the socket. For while this is the empirical condition for movement, one could also imagine it to be otherwise. The possibility of movement is, rather, supposed to be like a shadow of the movement itself. But do you know of such a shadow? And by a shadow I do not mean some picture of the movement – for such a picture would not have to be a picture of just *this* movement. But the possibility of this movement must be the possibility of just this movement. (See how high the seas of language run here!) (1953, I, Section 194)

I can think of no other passage in the *Investigations* which so perfectly captures the bafflement that Wittgenstein engenders through his claim to give philosophy peace – to show the fly the way out of the fly-bottle – while in fact conjuring up all manner of hyperinduced problems and perplexities. Thus it is Wittgenstein *ipse* who contrives to suggest that the 'ideally rigid machine' is a shadowy counterpart of the actual machine, or that its movements take place in a realm of delusory abstraction utterly divorced from the 'mere physical conditions for moving'. And again, it is Wittgenstein who persuades us to imagine 'possibilities of movement' that somehow transcend such merely 'physical' factors as the 'play between socket and pin' or 'the pin not fitting too tight in the socket'.

No doubt there is a sense in which the realist about laws of nature would want to defend this position or something very like it, that is, the principle that such laws should be taken as idealisations whose bearing in this or that particular case requires the introduction of various *ceteris paribus* clauses. However this is *not* to say that they inhabit a shadow-land of mere possibility which can only exist 'in some mysterious way' or at some platonic (quasi-mystical) remove from the domain of real-world operative factors such as friction, heat-loss, or mechanical stress. Nor is it to say that what leads us into thinking like this is just 'the kind of way in which we talk about machines', so that if we could only desist from such talk – or from the notion of laws that somehow govern the workings of an ideal machine quite apart from any physical imperfections in this or that actual machine – then at last we might achieve the wished-for state of philosophical peace. Rather it is the case that those laws represent an abstraction (or idealisation) which cannot be perfectly realised in the working of any given machine but which none the less offers a predictive measure of how the machine could be expected to perform if it were not for these various limiting factors.

One cannot read far into the history of technology – especially those fields (like mechanics and aeronautics) of which Wittgenstein had some practical experience – without being struck by the complex, uneven, but constantly evolving process of exchange between theory and applied expertise (see for instance Anderson 1998; Constant 1981; Norris 1997; Vincenti 1990). Thus it is equally striking when he makes such a mystery of the fact that theoretical laws always involve some degree of idealisation and are never directly manifested or precisely borne out by some particular machine or experimental set-up. What emerges from the above-cited passage is Wittgenstein's incapacity to grasp how this mutual interaction of theory and practice might get along – produce real advances in knowledge – without the kind of direct correspondence (the perfect match between laws and instances, ideal and actual machines) that seems to preoccupy his own thinking despite his professed view of it as the merest of misbegotten 'philosophical' delusions. So when Wittgenstein writes, here and elsewhere, about the way in which our minds are prone to be captured by a certain kind of 'picture' – one with the power to mislead thought into all kinds of dead-end perplexity – this charge might more aptly be turned around and applied to Wittgenstein himself. And the same may be said of his cryptic aside: 'How high the seas of language run here!' For it is not so much the scientific language of laws, theories, 'ideally rigid machines', and so forth that has given rise to such confusion but rather the strange 'bewitchment by language' from which Wittgenstein purports to deliver us but which can yet be seen to cast a powerful spell over passages like this.

Nowhere has the spell been exerted to more potent and bewildering effect than in the debate about rule-following as it bears upon issues in philosophy of logic and mathematics. Here again – as I have argued – the bewilderment results from his failure to distinguish the formal conditions of rule-following correctness from the various ways in which subjects may *in fact* carry on as a matter of behavioural disposition or through sheer force of habit. Thus Wittgenstein has this much in common with recent advocates of a naturalised epistemology: that he believes that distinction to be somehow undermined – or rendered deeply problematic – by the various lapses, inconsistencies, *non sequiturs*, wrong answers, rule-following irregularities, and so forth, which can always occur despite our best efforts to think straight about the problem in hand (see for instance Stich 1990). However such depressing evidence of the frailty of human reason has absolutely no implications with regard to the standards of correctness in rule-following or the objective (practice-transcendent) status of mathematical and logical truths. To suppose that it does is a mistake much like that of supposing that the laws of gravity or thermodynamics break down every time that an experiment fails to produce exactly the right results or every time that a machine fails to operate in accordance with our best theoretical predictions. What is so odd about Wittgenstein's use of such analogies is the way that they regularly work to confuse the issue by treating the formal sciences on a par with empirical investigation-procedures and those procedures, conversely, as something very like what we do when drawing a deductive inference, performing arithmetical calculations, or applying a formal rule.

One source of this confusion is his emphasis on just those basic (conceptually primitive) forms of rule-governed activity – like continuing the numerical series 'n + 2' – which might seem to involve nothing more than a 'mechanical' application of the rule concerned, and which thus give the sceptic room to deploy the same sorts of argument standardly used by philosophers since Hume to challenge the claims of inductive reasoning (Hume 1978; also Goodman 1955). Indeed it is precisely Kripke's claim that the 'paradox' about rule-following is a deeper, more disquieting version of Hume's epistemological scepticism since it threatens to destroy not only our confidence in any item of empirical knowledge or Humean 'matter of fact' but also our certitude with respect to mathematical or logical 'truths of reason' (Kripke 1982). However, I would suggest, this disquiet is not so much forced upon us by the cogency of Wittgenstein's arguments as transmitted through a kind of exegetical compulsion that leaves his interpreters chronically prone to extremities of sceptical doubt. At any rate those arguments must seem less plausible – or fail to exert so powerful a spell – if applied to more complex forms of logico-mathematical reasoning. Thus they will not have anything like that degree of rhetorical persuasiveness if the test-case is not some conceptually primitive sample like 'n + 2' but an elaborately formalised proof-procedure of the kind that practising mathematicians (rather than Wittgenstein-influenced philosophers) consider worthy of their interest (Dales and Oliveri [eds] 1998; Detlefson [ed.] 1992). That is to say, such cases most effectively expose the inbuilt bias and the philosophic weakness of any quasi-inductivist approach that draws far-reaching sceptical conclusions from a narrow and unrepresentative range of examples.

VII

David Lewis makes this point by way of challenging the naturalist assumption that knowledge must involve some kind of causal relation between knower and known and hence that there is a problem about mathematics which cannot be resolved unless by adopting an instrumentalist or fictionalist account. Thus we can *either* have objective mathematical truths which by very definition transcend the limits of human epistemic grasp *or* mathematical knowledge that (again by definition) lies within our powers of proof or ascertainment but which for that very reason cannot be objective in the realist sense (Benacerraf 1983). If we find ourselves reduced to this pseudo-dilemma, Lewis suggests, then it is a sign that something has gone badly wrong with our sense of philosophical priorities. 'It's too bad for epistemologists if mathematics in its present form baffles them, but it would be hubris to take that as any reason to reform mathematics...Our knowledge of mathematics is ever so much more secure than our knowledge of the epistemology that seeks to cast doubt on mathematics' (Lewis 1986: 109). And again: '[c]ausal accounts of knowledge are all very well in their place, but if they are put forward as *general* theories, then mathematics refutes them' (ibid.: 109). Where the naturalistic approach goes wrong – and gives rise to sceptical doubt – is by ignoring the basic modal distinction between necessary truths (like those of logic or mathematics) that hold good objectively come what may in our empirical dealings with the world and truth-claims with respect to contingent matters which might have to be abandoned or revised in the light of anomalous findings. Thus: 'nothing can depend counterfactually on non-contingent matters. For instance, nothing can depend counterfactually on what mathematical objects there are...Nothing sensible can be said about how our opinions would be different if there were no number seventeen' (ibid.: 111). If one accepts this case for the distinctive character of mathematical and logical truths then one is bound to regard Wittgenstein's whole treatment of the issue as a species of massive category-mistake or a failure to grasp that such truths cannot be called into question by any kind of empirical counter-evidence. Of course there is a sense in which the truths of logic, like the laws of theoretical physics, involve a certain idealisation or abstraction from those various complicating factors – ambiguities of scope, referential imprecision, problems with quantifying into modal contexts, and so forth – which the opponent can always exploit by way of inducing just such sceptical doubts. However they will then be in the awkward position of having to abandon our most secure items of knowledge in favour of a theory with no better warrant than the evidence that people sometimes fail to reason correctly, just as machines sometimes fail to operate precisely according to the laws of physics.

At times Wittgenstein does seem to allow that mathematical or logical proof-procedures may possess a character of necessary truth that places them beyond reach of empirical refutation and also beyond any prospect of being thrown into doubt by the kinds of imaginary counter-instance that play such a prominent role in his own later thinking. Thus '[t]he question arises: Can't we be mistaken in thinking that we understand a question? For many mathematical proofs do lead us to say that we *cannot* imagine something which we believed we could imagine (e.g., the construction of the heptagon). They lead us to revise what counts as the domain of the imaginable' (1953, I, Section 517). Here Wittgenstein appears to accept the force of a Lewis-type argument for holding mathematical and logical truths to be unrevisable come what may in the way of empirical evidence. However these are untypical and isolated passages which stand in sharp contrast with his programmatic aim, that is, his desire – clearly announced in the opening pages of the *Investigations* – to make us see what is wrong with the Tractarian idea of logic as a 'crystalline structure' of truth-functional propositions that somehow transcends (and should properly regulate) our everyday linguistic practices. On the contrary, Wittgenstein asserts: 'to say that a proposition is whatever can be true or false amounts to saying: we call something a proposition when *in our language* we apply the calculus of truth-functions to it' (1953, I, Section 136).

No doubt philosophers – the earlier Wittgenstein included – have often been prone to think otherwise, that is, to suppose that 'what fits the concept "true", or what the concept "true" fits, is a proposition'. To this way of thinking, 'it is as if we had a concept of true and false, which we could use to determine what is and what is not a proposition. What *engages* with the concept of truth (as with a cogwheel), is a proposition' (Section 136). However this is a bad picture, Wittgenstein suggests, since it leaves us prey to the familiar philosophical delusion, that is, that we can somehow stand apart from those everyday linguistic and practical involvements and thereby attain a more adequate, objective, or perspicuous understanding of them. Rather we should see that this whole idea of propositional 'fit' results from a *sublimated* conception of logic, one that takes hold whenever we are tempted to set up idealised models – like that of the perfectly functioning machine – and hence to ignore what actually goes on in the course of our dealings with language and the world.

Thus philosophers who think of propositions as 'engaging' with the concept of truth ('as with a cogwheel') are like students of mechanics who mistakenly suppose that machines ought to work – should be expected to work – in accordance with the various laws, principles, and theoretical predictions laid down in their physics textbooks. Or so Wittgenstein would have us believe, determined as he is to break the hold on our thought of a 'picture' that once held him captive and which he now wishes to remove from view by every means at his persuasive disposal. What this involves most crucially is leading us to think that talk of propositions, like talk of numbers, only makes sense within some given language-game, and cannot be conceived – on pain of 'metaphysical' bewitchment – as referring to a realm of abstract entities (truth-values or functions) which depend not at all on their happening to play a role in any such game. Of course it may be asked: 'But haven't we got a concept of what a proposition is, of what we take "proposition" to mean?' Yes indeed, Wittgenstein responds, 'just as we also have a concept of what we mean by "game"' (Section 135). Thus, asked what a proposition is, 'we shall give examples and these will include what one may call inductively defined series of propositions. *This* is the kind of way in which we have such a concept as "proposition". (Compare the concept of a proposition with the concept of number.)' (ibid.)

These passages will serve aptly enough as a recapitulation of all those themes and leading motifs that we have traced through various contexts of argument in Wittgenstein's later philosophy. First there is the strongly marked nominalist bias that leads him to treat any talk of 'numbers' and 'propositions' as intelligible only if construed as dependent on their role within this or that language-game. Second, there is his constant recourse to an inductivist conception of justificatory warrant, even in cases – like those of mathematics and logic – where truth-conditions are properly subject to deductive specification, and where Wittgenstein's approach *cannot but* give rise to the rule-following 'paradox' and other sceptical dilemmas (see Dilman 1973 and 1998 for a more sympathetic exposition of his views on this topic). Third, there is Wittgenstein's belief that these problems can arise only if we remain in the grip of a mistaken metaphysical 'picture' which credits the existence of objective truths concerning such abstract (= nominal) entities as those that figure in the discourse of the formal sciences. And fourth, there is his regular use of analogies from the techno-scientific or mechanical domains – like the cogwheel, the socket-and-pin, or the perfectly functioning machine – in order to cast doubt on the notion that such 'sublimated' concepts could ever have a purchase on our everyday linguistic and practical forms of life (Gefwert 1998).

However, as I have argued, the result of all this is to leave Wittgenstein himself in the grip of a scepticism that runs much deeper than he is willing to acknowledge. Moreover it produces a thoroughly mystified conception of the physical sciences that finds no room for theories, principles, or explanatory laws except in the guise of shadowy 'movements' in thought that vainly mimic the motions of real-world ('empirical') phenomena (1953, I, Section 194). It simply will not do for the fideist exegetes to adduce Wittgenstein's periods of study and hands-on experience in engineering, mechanics, aeronautics, and so forth, as evidence that he *must* have known what he was talking about when deploying these analogies to powerful effect in his later work. For there is also a case – and a stronger one, in my view – for thinking that Wittgenstein was deeply disappointed with his efforts in this direction and that his disappointment shows through when he uses metaphors from the techno-scientific domain to cast doubt on the existence of laws or theoretical principles that might somehow engage (as he would have it, in a cog-like manner) with real-world objects and processes. For in that case there seems no alternative but to conclude that those laws and principles must belong to a realm of 'sublime' pseudo-concepts which float entirely free of our everyday (whether scientific or linguistic) forms of life.

'In what sense is logic something sublime?', he asks. For it seems to possess a 'peculiar depth', to lie 'at the bottom of all the sciences', and to 'explore the nature of all things'. To this extent logic 'is not meant to concern itself whether what actually happens is this or that'. Rather 'it takes its rise, not from an interest in the facts of nature, nor from a need to grasp causal connexions; but from an urge to understand the basis, or the essence, of everything empirical' (1953, I, Section 89). And again:

> Thought is surrounded by a halo. – Its essence, logic, presents an order, in fact the a priori order of the world: that is, the order of *possibilities*, which must be common to both world and thought. But this order, it seems, must be *utterly simple*. It is *prior* to all experience, must run through all experience; no empirical cloudiness or uncertainty can be allowed to affect it – It must rather be of the purest crystal. But this crystal does not appear as an abstraction; but as something concrete, indeed, as the most concrete, as it were, the *hardest* thing there is. (1953, I, Section 97)

Like so many passages in late Wittgenstein this expresses both a genuine (deep) problem about philosophy of logic and a deep (yet compulsive and obscurely motivated) puzzlement about how logic applies to our everyday dealings with the world. No doubt it is philosophically hard to explain why the abstract, *a priori*, or necessary truths of logic should accord so well with our practical reasonings on matters of empirical fact. In the same way there is a genuine puzzle concerning the extraordinary power and productiveness of pure mathematics as the source or inspiration of applied scientific discoveries from Galileo to the present. But we shall scarcely make any advance toward a better understanding of this difficult topic by taking Wittgenstein's therapeutic lead and treating it as merely the 'sublimated' product of our chronic bewitchment by language. Rather we should start out from the well-documented fact that mathematics and logic have played a strictly indispensable role in the progress of the physical sciences. (For relevant discussion from a range of viewpoints, see Beth 1959; Hart [ed.] 1996; Kitcher 1983; Shapiro 2000.) And we shall then be less inclined to accept Wittgenstein's leading idea that the truths of mathematics or logic have no 'reality' – or objective warrant – beyond what is expressible in some given language-game. For it fails to explain how such progress could ever have come about *despite and against* the common sense, acculturated habits of thought that defined what should properly count as truth according to current (linguistically entrenched) best opinion (Munz 1985).

This failure has its chief source, I would argue, in Wittgenstein's extreme reaction against his own earlier (Tractarian) approach to these issues and that of those other first-generation analytic philosophers – like Frege and

Russell – whose influence he was now so anxious to disown. More specifically, it stems from Wittgenstein's ultra-nominalist refusal to accept the *sui generis* reality of abstract entities (such as numbers, concepts, and propositions) or the idea of truth-values that transcend their expression in some given language-game or life-form. Thus the rule-following paradox takes rise very largely from his failure to distinguish *numbers* from *numerals*, or mathematical objects (along with their properties and functions) from the various kinds of spoken or written expression that standardly count as 'adding', 'subtracting', or 'continuing a numerical series'. Hence Wittgenstein's strangely baffled reflections on what it means to 'really read' a written passage – to read it attentively, carefully, with genuine ('inward') understanding, and so forth – as opposed to 'function[ing] as a mere reading-machine' or 'read[ing] aloud and correctly without attending to what [one] is reading' (1953, I, Section 156). Hence also his frequent recourse to inscriptionalist or orthographic metaphors and analogies which describe how our thinking goes wrong if we appeal to some inner (private) state in order to sustain that distinction but the result of which – as so often – is to leave the whole matter more mysterious than ever.

Thus we might seek to explain the difference thought-experimentally by imagining ourselves confronted with a Turing-type situation in which there are two kinds of reading-machine. The one kind we are to think of as 100 per cent efficient in carrying out some process of purely mechanical transcription while the other is a 'living machine' (whether human or non-human) expertly trained to perform that same mindless function yet perhaps – how can we be sure? – showing certain signs of intelligent uptake at a certain stage in the process. Whence Wittgenstein's question: at *what stage* precisely might we be justified in saying 'Now he can read!', rather than 'No, he isn't reading; that was just an accident'? (Section 157). Or again, could we possibly be warranted in saying 'I was wrong, and he *did* read it' or 'He only really began to read later on'? These doubts are beside the point, Wittgenstein thinks, since it makes no sense to suppose that there is a stage – a definite point in the training process – where rote-like, mechanical responses leave off and 'real reading' begins. Thus:

> 'reading' meant reacting to written signs in such-and-such ways. This concept was therefore quite independent of that of a mental or other mechanism. – Nor can the teacher here say of the pupil: 'Perhaps he was already reading when he said that word'. For there is no doubt about what he did. – The change when the pupil began to read was a change in his *behaviour*; and it makes no sense here to speak of 'a first word in his new state'. (Section 158)

However this merely confuses the issue by setting up a borderline case – that of the 'living machine' – which is sure to reproduce all the same problems (about meaning, comprehension, 'inward' understanding, etc.) in a yet sharper and more intractable form. That is to say, if we want to maintain the distinction between 'reading'-by-rote and *real* reading then we are still confronted by the need to explain just what it is – if not some private and inscrutable 'inner state' – that makes all the difference. At this point we may be tempted to say: 'the one real criterion for anybody's *reading* is the conscious act of reading, the act of reading the sounds off from the letters' (Section 159). And we may think to back this claim by an appeal to the fact that 'a man surely knows whether he is reading or only pretending to read ... [in so far as] the latter will have none of the sensations that are characteristic of reading, and will perhaps have a set of sensations characteristic of cheating' (ibid.). But again this won't do since it involves just the kind of introspective (private) discovery-procedure that Wittgenstein has shown to run afoul of the circularity and vicious-regress arguments. So all we are left with at this stage is Wittgenstein's remark that 'the change when the pupil began to read was a change in his *behaviour*', that is, in those manifest dispositions to respond to written marks in a certain way that constitutes our only evidence that 'real reading' (as opposed to its mechanical or deceptive simulation) is now taking place.

It is not hard to see how Wittgenstein is led from this behaviourist 'solution' in the case of reading to those various sceptical problems about rule-following, arithmetical calculation, scientific theory-construction, and so forth, which so preoccupy his later thought. Thus he firmly rejects any claim that there might exist objective (practice-transcendent) criteria of adequate conceptual, logical, or indeed linguistic grasp that do not come down to mere accordance with some given language-game or communally sanctioned way of carrying on. Very often this rejection takes the form of a nominalist refusal to countenance the reality of abstract items – such as numbers, propositions, truth-values, and linguistic types as opposed to linguistic tokens – which might otherwise have offered a better way out of his various philosophical dilemmas. Moreover the problem is frequently compounded by his adopting a range of mechanical or inscriptionalist metaphors whose apparent aim is to release us from the mentalist or 'inner state' trap, but whose effect – not least on his own writing – is to conjure up all manner of lingering ghosts in the analogical machine. 'When we do philosophy', he remarks, 'we are like savages, primitive people, who hear the expressions of civilised men, put a false interpretation on them, and then draw the queerest conclusions from it' (1953, I, Section 194). I often have the sense, when reading Wittgenstein, that passages like this were written not so much in the hope of getting others to see the error of their philosophic ways but more out of a profound disquiet at his own persistence in raising doubts where – as he strove to persuade himself – no such doubts could properly be raised. That they have none the less continued to vex the minds of so many philosophers to the point of dictating the very terms of informed or relevant debate is among the most striking and curious features of recent intellectual history.

References

Alston, William P. (1996). *A Realist Theory of Truth*. Ithaca, N.Y.: Cornell University Press.

Anderson, John David (1998). *A History of Aerodynamics and its Impact on Flying Machines*. Cambridge: Cambridge University Press.

Armstrong, David M. (1978). *Universals and Scientific Realism*, 2 vols. Cambridge: Cambridge University Press.

Ayer, A.J. (1985). *Wittgenstein*. London: Weidenfeld & Nicolson.

——(ed.) (1959). *Logical Positivism*. New York: Free Press.

Baker, Gordon P. (1988). *Wittgenstein, Frege and the Vienna Circle*. Oxford: Blackwell.

Baker, Gordon and Hacker, P.M.S. (1983). *Wittgenstein: Meaning and Understanding*. Oxford: Blackwell.

——(1984). *Language, Sense and Nonsense: A Critical Investigation into Modern Theories of Language*. Oxford: Blackwell.

——(1985). *Wittgenstein: Rules, Grammar and Necessity*. Oxford: Blackwell.

Beaney, Michael (1996). *Frege: Making Sense*. London: Duckworth.

Benacerraf, Paul (1983). 'What numbers could not be', in P. Benacerraf and H. Putnam (eds), *The Philosophy of Mathematics*. Cambridge: Cambridge University Press. pp. 272–94.

Beth, Evert Willem (1959). *The Foundations of Mathematics: A Study in the Philosophy of Science*. Amsterdam: North-Holland.

Bloor, David (1976). *Knowledge and Social Imagery*. London: Routledge & Kegan Paul.

——(1983). *Wittgenstein: A Social Theory of Knowledge*. London: Macmillan Press.

Carnap, Rudolf (1959). 'The elimination of metaphysics through logical analysis of language', in Ayer (ed.) 1959: 60–81.

Cartwright, Nancy (1989). *Nature's Capacities and their Measurement*. Oxford: Clarendon Press.

——(1999). *The Dappled World: A Study of the Boundaries of Science*. Cambridge: Cambridge University Press.

Cavell, Stanley (1969). *Must We Mean What We Say?* New York: Oxford University Press.

Constant, Edward W. (1981). *The Origins of the Turbojet Revolution*. Baltimore: Johns Hopkins University Press.

Crary, Alice and Rupert Read (eds) (2000). *The New Wittgenstein*. London: Routledge.

Dales, Garth and Gianluiji Oliveri (eds) (1998). *Truth in Mathematics*. Oxford: Oxford University Press.

Detlefson, Michael (ed.) (1992). *Proof and Knowledge in Mathematics*. London: Routledge.

Devitt, Michael (1986). *Realism and Truth*, 2nd edn. Oxford: Blackwell.

Diamond, Cora (1991). *The Realistic Spirit: Wittgenstein, Philosophy, and the Mind*. Cambridge, Mass.: MIT Press.

Dilman, Ilham (1973). *Induction and Deduction: A Study in Wittgenstein*. Oxford: Blackwell.

——(1998). *Language and Reality: Modern Perspectives on Wittgenstein*. Brussels: Peeters.

Dummett, Michael (1978). *Truth and Other Enigmas*. London: Duckworth.

——(1991). *The Logical Basis of Metaphysics*. London: Duckworth.

Fish, Stanley (1989). *Doing What Comes Naturally: Change, Rhetoric, and the Practice of Theory in Literary and Legal Studies*. Oxford: Oxford University Press.

Frege, Gottlob (1952). 'On sense and reference', in P. Geach and M. Black (eds), *Selections from the Philosophical Writings of Gottlob Frege*. Oxford: Blackwell. pp. 56–78.

Gefwert, Christoffer (1998). *Wittgenstein on Mathematics, Minds and Mental Machines*. Aldershot: Ashgate.

Gödel, Kurt (1962). *On Formally Undecidable Propositions of Principia Mathematica and Related Systems*, trans. B. Meltzer. New York: Basic Books.

Goodman, Nelson (1955). *Fact, Fiction and Forecast*. Cambridge, Mass.: Harvard University Press.

Griffin, James (1964). *Wittgenstein's Logical Atomism*. Oxford: Clarendon Press.

Hacker, P.M.S. (1996a). *Wittgenstein: Mind and Will*. Oxford: Blackwell.

——(1996b). *Wittgenstein's Place in Twentieth-Century Analytic Philosophy*. Oxford: Blackwell.

Hart, W.D. (ed.) (1996). *The Philosophy of Mathematics*. Oxford: Oxford University Press.

Hume, David (1978). *A Treatise of Human Nature*. Oxford: Clarendon Press.

Janik, Allan and Stephen Toulmin (1973). *Wittgenstein's Vienna*. New York: Simon & Schuster.

Johnston, Paul (1993). *Wittgenstein: Rethinking the Inner*. London: Routledge.

Katz, Jerrold J. (1998). *Realistic Rationalism*. Cambridge, Mass.: MIT Press.

Kitcher, Philip (1983). *The Nature of Mathematical Knowledge*. Oxford: Oxford University Press.

Klenk, V.H. (1976). *Wittgenstein's Philosophy of Mathematics*. The Hague: Nijhoff.

Kripke, Saul (1982). *Wittgenstein on Rules and Private Language: An Elementary Exposition*. Oxford: Blackwell.

Lewis, David (1973). *Counterfactuals*. Oxford: Blackwell.

Lewis, David (1986). *On the Plurality of Worlds*. Oxford: Blackwell.

McDowell, John (1994). *Mind and World*. Cambridge, Mass.: Harvard University Press.

Malcolm, Norman (1975). *Knowledge and Certainty: Essays and Lectures*. Ithaca, N.Y.: Cornell University Press.

——(1977). *Thought and Knowledge*: *Essays*. Ithaca, N.Y.: Cornell University Press.

Marsonet, Michele (ed.) (2002). *The Problem of Realism*. Aldershot: Ashgate.

McGuiness, Brian F. (1988). *Wittgenstein: A Life*, Vol. 1, *Young Ludwig, 1889–1921*. London: Duckworth.

Miller, Alexander and Crispin Wright (eds) (2002). *Rule-Following and Meaning*. Chesham: Acumen.

Monk, Ray (1990). *Ludwig Wittgenstein: The Duty of Genius*. London: Jonathan Cape.

——(1996). *Bertrand Russell: The Spirit of Solitude*. London: Jonathan Cape.

——(2000). *Bertrand Russell: The Ghost of Madness*. London: Jonathan Cape.

Munz, Peter (1985). *Our Knowledge of the Growth of Knowledge: Popper or Wittgenstein?* London: Routledge & Kegan Paul.

Nagel, Thomas (1997). *The Last Word*. Oxford: Oxford University Press.

Norris, Christopher (1997). *Against Relativism: Philosophy of Science, Deconstruction and Critical Theory*. Oxford: Blackwell.

Norris, Christopher (2000). *Minding the Gap: Epistemology and Philosophy of Science in the Two Traditions*. Amherst, Mass.: University of Massachusetts Press.

Norris, Christopher (2002). *Truth Matters: Realism, Anti-realism and Response-dependence*. Edinburgh: Edinburgh University Press.

Penrose, Roger (1996). *Shadows of the Mind: A Search for the Missing Science of Consciousness*. London: Vintage Books.

Putnam, Hilary (1983). *Mathematics, Matter and Method*. Cambridge: Cambridge University Press.

Reck, Erich H. (ed.) (2002). *From Frege to Wittgenstein: Perspectives on Early Analytic Philosophy*. Oxford: Oxford University Press.

Russell, Bertrand (1905). 'On denoting', *Mind* **14**: 479–93.

——(1959). *My Philosophical Development*. London: Allen & Unwin.

——(1986). *The Philosophy of Logical Atomism* (ed.) J.G. Slater. London: Allen & Unwin.

——(1993). *Our Knowledge of the External World as a Field for Scientific Method in Philosophy*. New York & London: Routledge.

——(1994). *Foundations of Logic: 1903–05* (ed.) A. Urquhart. New York & London: Routledge.

Shanker, Stuart G. (ed.) (1996). *Philosophy of Science, Logic and Mathematics in the Twentieth Century*. New York: Routledge.

Shapiro, Stewart (2000). *Thinking About Mathematics: The Philosophy of Mathematics*. Oxford: Oxford University Press.

Sluga, Hans and David G. Stern (eds) (1996). *The Cambridge Companion to Wittgenstein*. Cambridge: Cambridge University Press.

Soames, Scott (1999). *Understanding Truth*. Oxford: Oxford University Press.

Stern, G. (1995). *Wittgenstein on Mind and Language*. New York: Oxford University Press.

Stich, Steven (1990). *The Fragmentation of Reason*. Cambridge, Mass.: MIT Press.

Stroud, Barry (2000). *Meaning, Understanding, and Practice: Philosophical Essays*. Oxford: Oxford University Press.

Tait, William W. (ed.) (1997). *Early Analytic Philosophy: Frege, Russell, Wittgenstein*. Chicago, Ill.: Open Court.

Vincenti, Walter G. (1990). *What Engineers Know and How They Know It: Analytical Studies from Aeronautical History*. Baltimore: Johns Hopkins University Press.

Waismann, Friedrich (1979). *Wittgenstein and the Vienna Circle* (ed.) B.F. McGuiness, trans. McGuiness and J. Schulte. Oxford: Blackwell.

Williams, Meredith (1999). *Wittgenstein, Mind and Meaning: Toward a Social Conception of Mind*. London: Routledge.

Williams, Michael (1996). *Unnatural Doubts: Epistemological Realism and the Basis of Scepticism*. Princeton, N.J.: Princeton University Press.

Winch, Peter (1958). *The Idea of a Social Science and its Relation to Philosophy*. London: Routledge & Kegan Paul.

——(1987). *Trying to Make Sense*. Oxford: Blackwell.

Wittgenstein, Ludwig (1953). *Philosophical Investigations*, trans. G.E.M. Anscombe. Oxford: Basil Blackwell.

——(1956). *Remarks on the Foundations of Mathematics*, trans. G.E.M. Anscombe. Oxford: Blackwell.

——(1961). *Tractatus Logico-Philosophicus*, trans. D.F. Pears and B.F. McGuiness. London: Routledge & Kegan Paul.

——(1969). *On Certainty* (ed.) G.E.M. Anscombe and G.H. von Wright. Oxford: Blackwell.

——(1973). *Letters to C.K. Ogden: with Comments on the English Translation of the Tractatus Logico-philosophicus* (ed.) G.H. von Wright. London: Routledge & Kegan Paul.

——(1974). *Philosophical Grammar* (ed.) Rush Rhees, trans. A. Kenny. Oxford: Blackwell.

——(1976). *Wittgenstein's Lectures on the Foundations of Mathematics* (ed.) Cora Diamond. Sussex: Harvester Press.

——(2000). *Wittgenstein's Nachlass: Text and Facsimile Version: The Completed Edition on CD-ROM*. Oxford: Oxford University Press.

Wright, Crispin (1980). *Wittgenstein on the Foundations of Mathematics*. London: Duckworth.

——(1992). *Truth and Objectivity*. Cambridge, Mass.: Harvard University Press.

3
Modularity, Nativism, and Reference-Fixing: On Chomsky's Internalist Assumptions

I

Noam Chomsky's objections to the Kripke/Putnam externalist or causal theory of reference have been developed in various books and articles over the past two decades (see for instance Chomsky 1986, 1988, 1992, 1993, 2000; also Kripke 1980; Putnam 1975a,b,c; Schwartz [ed.] 1977). They involve – as might be expected – a vigorous re-statement of his own internalist view that linguistic competence can be explained only on the basis of innate mental structures which are 'stimulus-free', that is, unconstrained by any causal relation to those various proximal objects or events which at most play a prompting or 'triggering' role in the process of language-acquisition. This goes along with his well-known case – deployed over the years against behaviourists of various stripe, from Skinner to Quine – that externalist approaches simply cannot work since they ignore the extent to which our shared (genetically programmed) capacity in this regard outstrips any possible explanation in terms of a naively empiricist psychology or a straightforward stimulus–response model (see Chomsky 1959, 1968; Quine 1961, 1969; Skinner 1957).

Chomsky has five main reasons for rejecting the Kripke/Putnam theory of naming, necessity, and natural kinds. First, it ignores this 'poverty of the stimulus' argument, namely, that infants are able to acquire language – and mature speakers to exhibit a command of complex linguistic forms – far beyond anything to which they have been exposed by training, observation, environmental input, and so forth. Second, it fails to distinguish our everyday linguistic competence – those innate (hard-wired or modular) capacities that define what it is to know or possess a language – from the kinds of specialised, for example, scientific knowledge which cannot be thought of as in any sense innate but on the contrary require a considerable labour of conceptual refinement and redefinition. Such would in particular be the knowledge required to grasp statements of the sort that figure as prototype examples for the Kripke/Putnam theory of reference. Thus 'water = H_2O' and 'gold = the metallic element with atomic number 79' are statements whose import depends on their belonging to a relatively expert discourse with its own, highly specific terms of reference (Kripke 1980; Putnam 1975a,b). Third, following from this, is the commitment of semantic externalism to a causal theory of reference-fixing which sharply diminishes the scope for creativity – for 'stimulus-free' expression – that forms such a striking feature of ordinary language use (Chomsky 1982). Whence (fourth) his reiterated point: that issues of reference had better be treated as belonging to the pragmatic dimension of language, that is, to the contextual (non-cognitive or extra-theoretical) domain, while issues of meaning had better be brought within the compass of a theory of syntax that does full justice to our modularised capacity for complex linguistic processing (Chomsky 2000; also McGilvray 1999). Lastly (fifth) there is the powerful consideration – as Chomsky sees it – that certain lexical items as well as logico-syntactic forms can be shown to involve a degree of pre-existent (innately specified) conceptual grasp that cannot be accounted for on any version of the externalist case. Thus he comes out flatly opposed to Putnam's claim that 'meanings just ain't "in the head"', and argues – on the contrary – that they *are and must be* 'in the head' if we are to make any sense of certain basic facts about human cognitive-linguistic competence (Chomsky 1975, 1993, 1995; cf. Putnam 1967, 1975a,d).

Chomsky also maintains – as against any form of modal-realist argument – that it is illicit to draw metaphysical conclusions (e.g., about the necessary, essential, or individuating properties of objects, kinds, or persons) from the sorts of merely intuitive self-evidence that Kripke and Putnam typically deploy in their reasoning on such matters (see also Hintikka 1999). Thus he accepts that Richard M. Nixon would still have been Richard M. Nixon – the self-same, biologically identical and genetically specified individual – had he not been elected US President in 1968, whereas he would have been a different individual entirely (and a different kind of individual) should it turn out that in fact the bearer of that name was a silicon-based replica. Yet, according to Chomsky, '[this] follows from the fact that Nixon is a personal name, offering a way of referring to Nixon as a person; it has no metaphysical significance' (Chomsky 2000: 41–42). And again: '[i]f we abstract away from the perspective of natural language, which has no pure names in the logician's sense [. . .], then intuitions collapse: Nixon would be a different entity, I suppose, if his hair were combed differently' (ibid.: 42). This follows from Chomsky's staunch internalist conviction that what counts in such matters is the role of lexico-syntactic processes or structures of representation that serve to individuate the various items of our everyday-common sense experience, rather than the reference-fixing role of external (mind and language-independent) objects, persons, or natural kinds. He is keen to emphasise the point since it strikes him as bearing crucially on two main issues, that is, the 'creativity' requirement (that a theory of language make full allowance for the scope of human expressive freedom within certain specifiable rule-governed constraints) and the inevitable failure to meet this requirement on the part of any theory that adopts an externalist approach.

This in turn links up with Chomsky's well-known position on issues of freedom and justice in the moral-political sphere, that is to say, his claim that respect for such values is best promoted by a rationalist philosophy of mind that stresses the innateness of certain distinctively human traits and attributes, rather than – as the behaviourist would have it – their 'plastic' or malleable nature (Chomsky 1966, 1971, 1972). Where the former conception acknowledges our capacity for autonomous moral and political judgement the latter lends itself all too readily to the kinds of mass-indoctrination and 'manufactured consensus' that Chomsky has sought to expose in his writings on US foreign and domestic policy. (See especially Chomsky 1967, 1973, 1989, 1991, 1994, 1996; also Chomsky and Herman 1979, 1988.) Thus, despite his unwillingness to extrapolate directly from the specialised domain of linguistic science to issues in the 'everyday' socio-political realm, there is still a clear sense in which those two endeavours are linked through Chomsky's insistence on the absolute superiority of an internalist (and rationalist) philosophy of mind over any externalist (or causal) account. What 'E-language' approaches fail to grasp is the plain impossibility of their ever doing justice to the open-ended nature – the potential for producing an infinite range of new sentences from a finite stock of lexico-syntactic elements – which constitutes the single most remarkable feature of human linguistic competence. From an 'I'-perspective, conversely, one can capture just those aspects of language (its internal, individual, and intensional aspects) which explain not only that salient property but also the fact that a modular approach – despite its determinist overtones – can sit perfectly well with the emphasis on human creativity and freedom as regards other, less specialised (or encapsulated) mental functions (Chomsky 2000).

Hence Chomsky's unorthodox assignment of reference to the pragmatic domain where it depends on a host of speaker-related and context-specific variables rather than serving – as it does for Putnam – to fix the conditions for truth-apt statements. Hence also his equally unorthodox proposal that semantics be absorbed into the theory of syntax where it is best able to satisfy the constraints on a formal (scientifically adequate) account of linguistic structure. Where both arguments depart from the received philosophical account – whether Frege's descriptivist principle that 'sense determines reference' or Kripke's causal-realist inversion of that principle – is in rejecting the idea that reference must occupy an ultimately privileged role (Frege 1952; Kripke 1980). For Chomsky, on the contrary, these two seemingly opposed conceptions are in fact merely flipside versions of the same basic error, that is to say, the belief that meanings have to do with anything external to the processes or structures that constitute I-language. Thus Frege's insistence that senses are objective – that they should not be confused with ideas 'in the mind' of this or that individual speaker – is evidence enough of his having mislocated the source of our linguistic competence, that is, his having placed it outside (rather than within) those same processes and structures. And this error is compounded by the Kripke/Putnam theory of reference which pushes yet further in an externalist direction and denies that the meaning of our various expressions – whether lexical items or syntactic forms – can possibly be thought of as somehow existing 'in the head'. What then drops out of sight – on Chomsky's account – is everything that makes the crucial difference between E-language as a mere assemblage of behavioural traits or dispositions and I-language as the object of a genuine attempt to specify those various distinctive features that constitute the domain of linguistic enquiry, properly (scientifically) construed.

II

So there would seem, on the face of it, no way to reconcile Chomsky's programme in theoretical linguistics and cognitive psychology with the externalist account of reference-fixing proposed by Kripke and Putnam. On the Chomskian view it has to be something quite mysterious – 'a bit of a miracle', as Chomsky disarmingly admits – that our innate stock of meanings and concepts should somehow (at least for all practical and a good many scientific purposes) turn out to yield reliable knowledge of the world (cited from an unpublished manuscript source by McGilvray 1999: 93). All the same he is more than willing to grasp this particular nettle if it permits the construc-tion of a rationalist, nativist, and internalist theory that accords full weight to the arguments for linguistic creativity (within certain clearly specified constraints) and for the existence of hard-wired conceptual structures whose range and complexity far exceeds anything allowed by the externalist approach. As McGilvray puts it: '[w]hile the meaning of a lexical item might be related by a speaker to something in the world – by, for example, using a sentence with its meaning to speak about that thing – the fact that it is so related on an occasion of use is irrelevant to its meaning' (McGilvray 1999: 162).

This is why, on Chomsky's internalist account, issues of reference are best shunted off into the rich but inherently unformalisable (hence unscientific) domain of pragmatics whereas issues of meaning are much better treated through a theory of syntax with additional resources for dealing with various lexically manifest concepts and categories. The latter may exhibit a remarkable, indeed a well-nigh 'miraculous' degree of success in enabling our everyday commerce with the world and – beyond that – our construction of scientific theories which, in some cases at least, go a long way toward explaining the reasons for it. After all, they are 'mental entities that people employ in their cognitive dealings with the world, . . . mental items that we use to (it is dif-ficult to come up with another word) conceptualise experience and things'

(McGilvray 1999: 169). Nevertheless – crucially for Chomsky's programme – '[t]hat they are used by people to deal with the world does not entail that they be defined in terms of the things of the world, derived from them, or captured in terms of how they relate to them' (ibid.: 169). For if this were so – if the externalist argument were allowed to get so much as a toehold on the theory of meaning – then it would (so he thinks) undermine the three main pillars of that programme, that is, the nativist, rationalist, and internalist theses, along with the associated 'creativity' and 'poverty of the stimulus' arguments.

Now there is much that is persuasive – indeed compelling – about Chomsky's case when applied to hard-line Skinner-type behaviourism or Quinean radical empiricism (Chomsky 1959, 1968). However one may doubt that it applies with equal force to the Kripke/Putnam externalist theory of reference. For one thing, this pushes him into adopting a radically opposed (internalist and nativist) stance which has problems of its own when it seeks to explain how we could ever acquire knowledge of a mind-independent, objectively existent world. Thus Chomsky is obliged to postulate a vast range of innate ideas which include not only those abstract concepts and structures that play a role in our powers of syntactic and logico-semantic parsing but also numerous lexical items such as – among his favourite instances – 'house' = 'building made by humans, fit for human habitation, etc.' (Chomsky 1966). As it happens, he takes this particular example from the Cambridge platonist Ralph Cudworth who – along with Descartes, the Port-Royal grammarians, and Herbert of Cherbury – occupies a privileged place in the roll-call of Chomsky's rationalist precursors (Cudworth 1976[1731]). Cudworth especially he sees as a prophetic figure who laid out all the most powerful arguments against any version of empiricist psychology or philosophy of mind, that is to say, any notion of the mind as a passive 'receptacle' that acquires all its concepts from sensory or perceptual inputs. In answer to the question how innate ideas – like that of 'house' – could be thought to hook up with things in the world, Cudworth proposed a 'proleptic' theory of judgement according to which the mind *anticipates* all those various humanly intelligible objects, kinds, and forms that might come to play a role in our experience. For him, 'the inner engine that produces these concepts seems to be able to anticipate *anything*. . . . He spoke of the "potential omniformity" of intellect, which provides sufficient concepts of sufficient complexity and richness to be able to anticipate anything that the human might encounter – anything where "Occasion serves and Outward Objects invite"' (Cudworth 1976[1731]: 135; McGilvray 1999: 171).

Not that Chomsky is altogether willing to endorse so strongly teleological a view of the preordained harmony between mind and world, or so markedly platonist a conception of the way that Cudworthian 'ideas of intellect' transcend yet somehow represent or capture the objects of our everyday perceptual acquaintance. After all, he has some scathing comments elsewhere about the folly of adopting a full-fledged platonist approach – with regard to meanings, concepts, or other such abstract entities – when all one needs (from a naturalised rationalist viewpoint) is the straightforward acceptance that meanings, and so forth, *just are* whatever can be represented by an adequate account of those processes and structures innate to our shared competence as language users (Chomsky 1995, 2000). Indeed he takes the view that platonism of that sort, though historically important as a source of powerful arguments against empiricism, has now been overtaken – rendered otiose – by the advent of modern developments in neurophysiology and cognitive science. Yet Chomsky still accepts at least two major claims put forward by Cudworth and the Cambridge neo-platonists, namely their doctrine of the mind's 'anticipatory' power to produce all the concepts and categories required for our cognitive dealing with the world and their notion of those concepts as somehow pre-existing any causal or experiential input from it. Moreover, he sets a great store by the famous set-piece example from Plato's *Meno* where Socrates claims to demonstrate the existence of *a priori* knowledge – or truths self-evident to reason – by coaxing a math-ematically uneducated slave-boy to evince his understanding of Pythagoras' theorem along with the inter-related definitions of 'line', 'angle', 'hypotenuse', and so forth (Chomsky 1966). Chomsky's point in this is to reinforce his claim – very much like Socrates' 'midwife' analogy – that such knowledge requires only minimal prompting (or 'triggering') from the environment, rather than the kind of strong causal input that behaviourists, physicalists, or externalists would take as a decisive factor. Still his use of the *Meno* episode – along with his (albeit qualified) appeal to Cudworth on the 'potential omniformity' of intellect – suggest that Chomsky's philosophy of mind is more deeply indebted to the platonist tradition than can easily be squared with his naturalised approach to epistemological and language-related issues.

It seems to me that one main reason for this is Chomsky's resolute refusal to accept that an externalist theory of reference might provide a means to conjure away the 'miracle' involved – on his own admission – in explaining how innate concepts and categories apply to the objects of everyday perceptual experience. Here one could invoke a whole range of arguments from realist philosophy of science, among them (most aptly) the 'no miracles' argument which holds that we are rationally justified in supposing that 'terms in a mature scientific theory typically refer' and that 'laws of a mature scientific theory are typically approximately true' (Putnam 1975d: 290). For otherwise it would be nothing less than a miracle that those theories had managed to produce such a mass of well-confirmed empirical results, accurate predictions, high-yield explanatory laws, successful applications in technology, and so forth. Or again, there is the convergent-realist case which readily admits the partial character of scientific knowledge as we have it, but which takes this situation – now as in the past – to support its claim that science makes progress toward truth by offering ever more detailed descriptive, theoretical, and depth-explanatory hypotheses (see Aronson 1989; Boyd 1984; Psillos 1999; also – for a strongly dissenting view – Laudan 1981). If Chomsky is routinely unimpressed by such arguments – tending as they do (or as he thinks they do) to controvert his rationalist-nativist-internalist case – then one way out of this philosophic stand-off might be to look more closely at his claim that these options come as a package, or that you cannot have rationalism and nativism without adhering to the strict internalist line. For of course it is the latter commitment – the idea that meanings must be 'in the head' rather than explained by adverting to mind-external objects or referents – which motivates Chomsky's unyielding resistance to the Kripke–Putnam position. That is, there is no obvious reason to suppose that one cannot be a rationalist in philosophy of mind and a nativist in cognitive psychology while also accepting the externalist thesis that reference is fixed – at least for a certain range of scientifically or otherwise specified terms – by some causal interaction between knower and known. To regard this as an either/or choice or a straightforward instance of *tertium non datur* is to fall right back into the kind of dilemma that has plagued epistemology at least since Kant and whose upshot is all too visible in the various inconclusive debates between realists and anti-realists that have so often surfaced during the past few decades (Norris 2002a,b; also Farrell 1994; Williams 1996).

Thus Chomsky might do well to adopt a more ecumenical approach that would find adequate room for the main features of his own rationalist project while conceding the relevance – even the necessary role within that project – of certain externalist or causal-realist considerations. On this view there would be no problem in acknowledging that the Kripke/Putnam theory of naming, necessity, and natural kinds is one that does indeed explain a great deal about fixity of reference across theory-change and how we can get a conceptual grip on comparative or truth-evaluative claims in the history and philosophy of science (Putnam 1988). Beyond that, it would cover a range of non-natural or artefactual terms – such as 'house' – whose objects are picked out *both* through their possessing certain humanly cognisable features – 'building', 'place of domicile', 'fit for habitation', and so forth – and *also* in virtue of their being objects of just that physical or functional sort (see especially Burge 1979, 1986). Allowing that their reference is fixed in this way need not by any means entail the conclusion – as Chomsky takes it – that such fixing affords no possible role for the 'stimulus-free' (or creative) character of human linguistic and cognitive activity. On the contrary: in the case of natural kinds it would offer full scope for the exercise of our rational powers in finding out just those salient properties of the physical world – subatomic configurations, molecular structures, genetic-chromosomal attributes, and so forth – that must none the less be taken to exist independently of human knowledge. Indeed one advantage of the Kripke/Putnam approach *via* modal logic is that it does very clearly distinguish between the order of necessity pertaining to such *a posteriori* discoverable truths and those other kinds of (e.g.) mathematical or logical truth whose status – whether *a priori* or purely analytic – places them in a wholly different realm. From the Chomskian perspective, conversely, we are required to think that our grasp of natural-kind terms like *gold* and *water* or even of artefactual terms such as *house* must somehow be a product of *a priori* structures (or Cudworthian 'intellectual ideas') that refer to those items only by grace of preordained correspondence or innate foreknowledge. What drives him to this conclusion, I suggest, is the refusal to accept that an externalist approach might help to explain certain otherwise inscrutable facts about truth, reference, and the mind–world relationship.

Nor can such an explanation be had by adopting Chomsky's proposal and shifting the whole issue about reference from the domain of linguistic theory (or cognitive psychology) to that of pragmatics, very broadly, that is, 'unscientifically' conceived. For this is tantamount to saying that his programme is unequipped to cope with a dimension of language-use – whether in the everyday or other, more specialised contexts – which cannot be ruled beyond the pale of 'scientific' enquiry without hugely restricting the programme's scope and explanatory power. As McGilvray puts it: 'reference, thought of as essentially involving speakers as agents and mind-independent entities, can and should be absorbed into pragmatics, where it can be dealt with on its own terms, even if these terms do not suit the aims of serious theory' (McGilvray 1999: 102). This is a faithful gloss on Chomsky's proposal and is offered – like much of McGilvray's commentary – in a strongly approving (even fideist) mode of exposition. However it does raise some significant problems, among them the issue as to whether reference can be thought of as 'essentially' involving 'mind-independent entities' yet at the same time as 'essentially' involving the pragmatic appeal to speakers, agents, and their various context-specific aims and interests. Or again, in what precise sense can Chomsky claim to be dealing with reference 'on its own terms' – as distinct from the terms laid down in advance by his internalist programme – if he excludes any alternative theory of reference (such as the Kripke/ Putnam account) that would seek to explain how language refers to 'mind-independent entities' in some way other than a sheerly providential or downright 'miraculous' way? No doubt, as McGilvray says, '[h]is basic view on this matter seems to be that one cannot speak of word–world relationships without speaking of people as agents who use words and sentences to deal with the world, or for other purposes' (McGilvray 1999: 102). Such arguments are indeed familiar enough from the philosophical literature, including Strawson's well-known rejoinder to Russell on the topic of referring expressions (Russell 1905; Strawson 1950). However, in the present context, this notion of reference as wholly a matter of pragmatic, circumstantial, or speaker-relative meaning is one that undercuts any adequate (scientifically plausible) account of the language–world relationship. That is to say, it offers no means of explaining how language hooks up with reality save the rationalist (actually platonist) resort to a doctrine whereby the mind comes comprehensively stocked with 'intellectual ideas' which cannot but match – since they effectively create – the structure of perceived appearances.

This is why Chomsky comes out in broad agreement with a radical nominalist like Nelson Goodman for whom there exist as many world-versions – or as many different 'ways of worldmaking' – as there exist different kinds of projective schema or modes of symbolic representation (Chomsky 1995; Goodman 1978; McCormick [ed.] 1996). To be sure, he thinks Goodman's project is hobbled by its lack of any adequate scientific basis in cognitive psychology and computational linguistics. Had he (Goodman) only embraced the rationalist rather than the radical-empiricist option then he would surely have avoided this unfortunate upshot. Thus: '[w]e can think of naming as a kind of "worldmaking", in something like Nelson Goodman's sense, but the worlds we make are intricate and substantially shared thanks to a complex shared nature' (cited by McGilvray [1999: 169] from unpublished manuscript source). Yet in the end it is hard to see how Chomsky can square his commitment to a strong cognitivist theory of mental representations with anything like the Goodmanian ultra-nominalist idea that 'reality' *just is* whatever counts as such according to some favoured conceptual-interpretative scheme. For there could then be no distinguishing accurate (veridical) representations from those that serve well enough as a matter of common sense – or folk-psychological – wisdom but which possess no claim to validity or truth when assessed by other, more rigorous criteria of scientific warrant.

Of course it is a main plank in Chomsky's argument that different standards apply when one switches from the realm of everyday, competent language-use to the sphere of theoretical linguistics or cognitive psychology where any proper (scientifically adequate) account involves a high degree of conceptual abstraction from whatever goes on – pragmatically speaking – in this or that context of linguistic exchange. McGilvray links this to Strawson's distinction between 'what can be said about words and what can be said about the uses of words', a distinction that finds its equivalent in Chomsky's claim that 'in order to make sense of how words are used (in reference and reasoning), one must speak of persons as users of words' (McGilvray 1999; Strawson 1950). From which he concludes – very much in keeping with Chomsky's proposal – that reference must indeed be treated as dependent on pragmatic or contextual factors rather than as falling within the purview of a strictly scientific approach. Thus 'another motivation behind Chomsky's distinction is not found in Strawson', namely that 'it helps bound a domain where science can get a grip – the domain of words or language (or what they become in formal linguistic theory) – by distinguishing it from the domain of human action, where people use words and language' (McGilvray 1999: 39–40). However this requires us to think that what becomes of language in 'formal linguistic theory' is a construct that achieves theoretical (scientific) precision just in so far as it renounces the claim that reference could ever – in principle – be more than a matter of ad hoc adjustment to various localised contexts of utterance. In which case there might seem little to choose, practically speaking, between Chomsky's ultra-rationalist approach and the Quinean radical-empiricist approach according to which reference is 'fixed' only relative to some given ontological scheme or some favoured method for picking out objects from the otherwise undifferentiated flux of incoming sensory-perceptual data (Quine 1961).

To be sure, these positions are worlds apart as regards their express philosophical commitments. On the one hand there is Chomsky's strict internalist precept that meaning has to do with structures and representations in the mind of this or that individual speaker, while on the other there is Quine's programmatic claim that such mentalist talk should forthwith be abandoned in favour of a thoroughly naturalised approach which treats epistemology as a sub-branch of physical science (Quine 1969). It is just this distinction that Chomsky is so keen to uphold through his argument for the 'poverty' of environmental inputs and – in consequence – the inherently creative (i.e., the unbounded or 'stimulus-free') character of human thought and language. Thus 'the only grip science is likely to get [on this single most striking aspect of linguistic competence] concerns its relations to "other systems" in the head, not reference to things outside the head' (McGilvray 1999: 152). That is to say, it involves a modular conception of the mind and its various capacities wherein some (like the language-module) must be thought of as relatively 'encapsulated' or 'cognitively impermeable' since this alone explains our commonplace ability to talk straight ahead and make reasonable sense – to ourselves and others – on the basis of a shared (innate) linguistic competence (see also Fodor 1983, 1990, 1994). At the same time there must be certain channels of exchange with other, less specialised modules – perceptual, experiential, memory-based, and so forth – which explain how language effectively hooks up with our everyday practices and modes of being in the world. Chomsky no doubt wants to limit the extent of this permeability since he thinks that any excessive allowance for the role of causal or experiential inputs must compromise the claim for human linguistic, rational, and (not least) moral-political autonomy. Otherwise – so it seems – we should have to go along with some version of the Quinean empiricist (or behaviourist) approach that leaves no room for the exercise of any such distinctively human capacities. Hence his strong aversion to externalist accounts of reference-fixing – like those put forward by Kripke and Putnam – which deny that meanings are 'in the head' and locate them rather in our various modes of interaction with real-world (mind-independent) objects and properties.

However it is far from evident that the choice falls out between 'E-language' and 'I-language' approaches in the way that Chomsky presents it. That is, there is no reason why semantic externalism of the Kripke/Putnam type should place limits on the extent of our linguistic-cognitive potential, the scope of human intellectual achievement, or our self-image as rational agents with the freedom (both the right and the responsibility) to think for ourselves in matters of moral-political choice. Such an argument is perfectly justified when raised with respect to claims such as those of Skinnerian behaviourism or the Quinean project of naturalised epistemology. Here indeed there is a failure to allow for those normative values – of truth, rationality, informed criticism, active participant debate – which Chomsky identifies with the rationalist tradition in philosophy of mind and language (see especially Kim 1993; also Norris 2000). Thus on Quine's account epistemology does best when it emulates the methods of the physical sciences, excludes all reference to dubious 'internal' goings-on such as thoughts, concepts, meanings, intentions, and so forth, and adopts a strictly behaviourist approach to the various assenting or dissenting dispositions of subjects exposed to a certain range of observable sensory stimuli. At this point 'epistemology, or something like it, simply falls into place as a chapter of psychology and hence of physical science' (Quine 1969: 82). Or again: '[t]he relation between the meagre input and the torrential output is a relation that we are prompted to study for somewhat the same reasons that always prompted epistemology; namely, in order to see how evidence relates to theory, and in what ways one's theory of nature transcends any available evidence' (ibid.: 93). When expressed in these terms the programme very plainly lies open to Chomsky's standard objection, that is, that it fails to provide anything like an adequate answer to the rationalist's threefold argument from 'poverty of the stimulus', conceptual-linguistic creativity, and the 'unboundedness' of human cognitive powers in comparison to what Quine himself describes as the 'meagre' supply of sensory promptings. All that he can offer by way of response is the vague idea of pragmatic 'adjustment' between beliefs affected – confirmed or infirmed – by the range of incoming stimuli and the overall 'fabric' of beliefs-held-true at that particular time (Quine 1961). In which case any such belief might conceivably have to be revised, from empirical observation-statements (since these are always subject to the limits and vagaries of human perceptual grasp) to the ground-rules of classical logic (as for instance – Quine's example – if they turn out to conflict with certain well-attested quantum phenomena).

What drops out completely on this account is the conception of scientific knowledge as typically advancing through stages of increased theoretical scope and explanatory power joined with increased observational precision or capacity for accurate measurement. There is simply no room for such objective standards of epistemic warrant in the Quinean view of science as always involving some negotiated trade-off between logic, theory, empirical observation, and the overall requirement that beliefs hang together in a broadly coherent fashion. So one can see well enough why Chomsky and others have objected to the lack of rational or normative criteria for choice among competing theories entailed by this particular version of the argument for a naturalised (that is to say, full-fledged physicalist or behaviourist) epistemology. What is not so clear is why Chomsky should think that the same objection applies to the Kripke/Putnam argument for modal realism – that is, the existence of *a posteriori* necessary truths – as a means of overcoming various problems with descriptivist theories of sense and reference. After all, that argument is aimed precisely *against* the Quinean veto on modal talk or on any conception of logical form beyond that provided by the standard apparatus of the first-order quantified predicate calculus (for further discussion, see Hintikka 1969; Linsky [ed.] 1971; Marcus 1993). Yet there is an obvious sense – as modal logicians are fond of pointing out – in which modal concepts must be taken as prior to those of classical deductive logic since the latter depends on a notion of necessity (of what necessarily follows from what as a matter of strict entailment) which cannot be justified unless in modal-logical terms. For Quine, such arguments are wholly misconceived since modal logic can be shown to produce various problems about quantifying into opaque contexts or to generate all sorts of philosophic mischief with statements like 'the number of planets is necessarily greater than seven' (Linsky [ed.] 1971). For Kripke and Putnam, conversely, it is a means of accounting for the way that scientific knowledge accrues with respect to a real-world domain of objects, kinds, and properties whose existence is by no means *dependent upon* but progressively *revealed and clarified through* our various investigative methods.

Besides, a chief purpose of this approach is to explain why the argument for fixity of reference across episodes of theory-change need not entail – as Chomsky thinks – any conflict with the claim that such episodes involve far more in the way of rational (and creative) thought than could possibly figure in a Skinner-type behaviourist or Quinean radical-empiricist account. Thus the point about *a posteriori* necessary truths – like 'water = H_2O' or 'gold is the metallic element with atomic number 79' – is that they pick out salient (microstructural) properties of just those natural kinds in any world physically compatible with ours. Moreover the kinds existed – together with their properties – long before we attained knowledge of them even though their discovery required a good deal of highly resourceful and intelligent scientific investigation (Kripke 1980; Putnam 1975a,b; also Abbott 1997). In other words the case for fixity of reference is one that has to do with *metaphysical* issues – of identity across a certain range of possible worlds resembling our own in certain specified respects – and which entails no *epistemological* limits on the extent to which rational thought-procedures can transcend the raw data of sensory stimuli. To suppose that it does – that semantic externalism fixes not only the reference of terms but also the scope of human linguistic-cognitive or creative-exploratory thought – is to conflate two very different (indeed sharply opposed) philosophies of mind and language. That is to say, it assumes that any claim for the existence of real-world (reference-fixing) properties or attributes must amount to a claim that the process of human knowledge-acquisition is likewise subject to an order of implacably determinist causal explanation. Chomsky has always rejected such ideas with the utmost vehemence, whether in the context of linguistic theory (as against hard-line behaviourists like Skinner) or in his political writings, where it forms a main part of his passionate crusade against various techniques of mass-indoctrination or 'manufactured consent' (Chomsky 1989; Chomsky and Herman 1988; also Barsky 1996; Edgley 2000). However – as I have said – there is no good reason for supposing the causal theory of reference to entail any such untoward consequences either in the realm of linguistics and cognitive science or in the wider socio-political sphere. Rather it might more usefully be seen as providing just what is needed to resolve some otherwise intractable problems with the Chomskian approach, among them – not least – its internalist/nativist commitment to a vast range of *a priori* concepts and the issue as to how these could possibly hook up with real-world objects and properties. At any rate there is nothing in the nature of semantic externalism that places such a prospect of reconciliation beyond hope of achievement (Silverberg 1998).

III

Here again it is Chomsky's unswerving allegiance to rationalism in its strongest, most avowedly 'mentalist' form that leaves him without any credible means of bridging the divide between subject and object, word and world, or representations and whatever they (more or less accurately) represent. McGilvray bites the bullet on this and takes Cudworth to have shown – beyond reasonable doubt – that objects and properties *must* be viewed as products of our innate *a priori* powers of mind, rather than existing 'out there' in the world and awaiting human discovery. Thus: '[t]hese ideas... *cannot* arise from things "outside"; there is nothing in the physical world that could have the ideas (properties) that we assign to them in the form in which we conceive them' (McGilvray 1999: 170). And again: '[h]ouses as understood by the intellect have the function of being fit for human habitation, because that "feature" is contained in – or is at least definitely relevant to – the concept *house*. But, he argues, there is nothing in the physical world outside the head with the feature *fit for human habitation*; there are only atoms (Atomical Particles)' (ibid.: 171). And from here it is no great distance to Chomsky's rationalist-internalist claim that issues of reference must be taken as falling outside the domain of linguistic theory, properly conceived, since the former have to do with pragmatic considerations (who refers to what, in which particular context of utterance) while the latter is concerned with syntactic and logico-semantic structures whose description requires a rigorous bracketing of all such extraneous factors. In short: 'once you deal with language in a way that goes outside the head, you are in the domain of language use – in the domain of representing the world, the community's role, correctness, and appropriateness of use. You are not dealing with anything that can be identified (for theory) as a language at all' (ibid.: 108). However this statement begs some large philosophical questions, among them – most pressingly – the question as to whether 'language' is here defined in such a specialised (theoretical) way that it fails to find room for so basic a function as that of linguistic reference.

Of course it is one of Chomsky's central claims that any science, beyond a certain stage of development, will need to devise certain terms and concepts that have no place in ordinary language, and whose usage cannot be governed – or explained – by appealing to the kinds of innate conceptual structure that characterise everyday linguistic competence. Thus where people may talk common sensically enough about 'the meaning of a word' as if that meaning were somehow contained within it this idea makes no sense from a scientific standpoint, or only on condition that ' "word", "meaning", and "of" are read technically, in the way they are in Chomsky's theory' (ibid.: 163). Otherwise the science of theoretical linguistics could never have acquired conceptual resources beyond those available to any competent speaker working on a basis of straightforward, unaided intuition. Yet there is something odd about a theory which credits natural-language speakers with an *a priori* grasp of the various distinctive features of the concept *house* – such that, for instance, if one says 'Ralph is painting the house' one means that he is painting it outside rather than inside – while treating their intuitive ideas about language as at best unscientific and at worst grossly misleading. After all, on the innateness-hypothesis combined with Chomsky's rationalist approach to issues of mind and knowledge they should possess at least a fair measure of native expertise in this regard.

What is additionally odd about the *house* example is the fact that conceptual attributes like 'fit for habitation' are self-evidently features which have to do with human purposes and interests, that is, with *house* as a certain sort of custom-built artefact rather than a natural kind (such as *water* or *gold*) which may be thought to possess its constituent (molecular or subatomic) features as a matter of physical necessity. By choosing this example – and others like it – Chomsky makes it easier to argue the case for an internalist approach that sharply downplays (even excludes) the role of the 'outside world' in deciding theoretically relevant issues with regard to language and mind. Yet it also tends to undercut that case by suggesting that the argument only works when applied to artefacts, like houses, which lend themselves readily to just such treatment in virtue of their answering certain specifiable human needs. Moreover, there is the obvious objection – from a realist or externalist standpoint – that Chomsky has still not convincingly explained how the stock of presumed innate or *a priori* concepts can be thought to make contact with anything beyond the self-insulated realm of mental representations. For it does seem pre-requisite to any adequate philosophy of mind and language that it acknowledge at least one basic tenet of realism, that is, that the world contains certain objects (and properties thereof) which must exert some referential constraint on our everyday linguistic competence. And this applies just as much to those other, more specialised languages of science – including theoretical linguistics – whose aim is to specify their object of study with a greater degree of descriptive exactitude and conceptual precision. According to Chomsky such benefits are to be had only by abstracting from the everyday contexts of language-use – along with naïve (realist) ideas about meaning and reference – and constructing a model that meets the requirements for a strictly internalist ('I-language') approach. Thus on his account linguistic theory can only go wrong if it seeks to address 'scientifically' irrelevant concerns such as that of how language hooks up with the world or how various (putative) referring expressions either succeed or fail in picking out some item of extra-linguistic reality. This is why Chomsky subscribes to Goodman's strong-constructivist idea that there exist as many 'ways of worldmaking' – or diverse projective schemes – as there exist human purposes, communicative contexts, relevance-conditions, and so forth (Goodman 1978). Where he differs sharply with Goodman is in his claim that this argument can be saved from outright relativism (i.e., from renouncing any basis for comparison or evaluative judgement between different world-versions) through the appeal to innate conceptual structures which offer enough in the way of shared cognitive-linguistic grasp.

However it is not at all clear why Chomsky should go part-way toward endorsing Goodman's extreme (ultra-nominalist) version of the Quinean empiricist doctrine when he comes out implacably opposed to that doctrine in its original form. That is to say, Goodman is doing no more than pushing right through with Quine's argument that all we have to go on – epistemo-logically speaking – are the raw data of sensory stimuli plus a variety of frameworks, paradigms, or conceptual schemes whereby to achieve maximum coherence in the range of beliefs held true at any given time. In which case one would expect Chomsky to treat Goodman's argument with as great a degree of philosophical disdain – not to mention moral opprobrium – as he brings to the critique of other empiricist or behaviourist approaches. What swings him in Goodman's favour, I think, is the latter's more explicit emphasis on the mind's freedom to create – or project – all manner of alternative 'world-versions' subject only to certain conventional constraints. This squares well enough with Chomsky's case for the inherent creativity of human intelligence and its demonstrable power (as per the 'poverty of stimulus' argument) to come up with forms of linguistic expression and other cognitive achievements far beyond anything explainable in behaviourist terms. All the same there is a problem – as Goodman's critics have been quick to point out – with the idea that such creative freedom can be bought only at the cost of accepting an open multiplicity of projective schemas, none of which can lay any privileged claim to truth or veridical warrant (McCormick [ed.] 1996). For this amounts to just a further variation on

Quine's radical-empiricist theme, that is, the notion that 'truth' in any given context of enquiry is simply a matter of pragmatic adjustment between the range of incoming sensory stimuli and whatever conceptual framework we can adopt with least disturbance to existing habits of belief.

Thus Chomsky is ill-advised – or so one might think – to go along even partly with the kind of projectivist or strong-constructivist approach that would claim to secure a working space for the exercise of human rational and creative powers by placing them beyond reach of whatever goes on at the stage of our causal interactions with the world. That is to say, he inherits the problem – familiar enough from the long and troubled history of post-Kantian epistemological debate – as to how one can possibly overcome the vexing dualisms of subject and object, mind and world, or the concepts and categories of *a priori* knowledge and the deliverance of sensuous (phenomenal) intuitions (Kant 1964). This was the main dividing-point among philosophers like Fichte and Schelling who claimed to pursue Kant's arguments to their logical conclusion. Such thinking took the form either of an all-out Fichtean subjective idealism that counted objective (mind-independent) reality a notion well lost in comparison to the ego's world-constitutive powers, or a Schellingian objective idealism that pinned its faith to nature's all-encompassing (mind-inclusive) reality. (For a detailed and highly informative account, see Beiser 1987.) Since then the debate has been played out in various ways, among them Strawson's 'descriptivist' attempt to talk Kant down from the giddy heights of metaphysical abstraction and – most recently – John McDowell's more elaborate and (often) tortuous efforts in a similar vein (McDowell 1994; Strawson 1966; also Norris 2000: 172–96 and 197–230).

Meanwhile other thinkers, such as Richard Rorty, have accepted the dualism at full stretch and recommended that we give up even trying to explain how the 'brute causal impact' of incoming sensory data can somehow be taken as providing justificatory grounds for this or that particular (scientifically warranted) interpretation of the evidence. Thus, according to Rorty, we can be as 'realist' as we like about the impact of photons on Galileo's eyeball without supposing that any such raw (uninterpreted) physical event could possibly settle the issue between detractors and upholders of the new cosmology. After all, '[t]he astronomers of Padua took it as merely one more anomaly which had somehow to be worked into a more or less Aristotelian cosmology, while Galileo's admirers took it as shattering the crystalline spheres once and for all' (Rorty 1991: 81). To think otherwise – to believe that such evidence can count decisively in favour of one or the other hypothesis – is merely to reveal one's attachment to an outworn metaphysics of mind and nature. Or again, '[t]o say that we must have respect for unmediated causal forces is pointless. It is like saying that the blank must have respect for the impressed die. The blank has no choice, neither do we' (ibid.: 81).

My point is that Rorty arrives at this position simply by accepting what he takes to be the negative upshot – the inevitable failure – of all attempts (like those of McDowell and numerous thinkers after Kant) to resolve the mind/ world dualism, or the problem of explaining how 'raw' physical stimuli could ever give reason for endorsing or rejecting any interpretation of them. It is, to be sure, a position utterly remote from Chomsky's insistence on the capacity of human minds to exercise their powers of rational-creative intelligence and thereby accomplish a range of otherwise impossible feats, from everyday native competence in language-use to the most advanced forms of scientific, mathematical, and psychological enquiry. Thus Chomsky would have no time for the Rortian strong-descriptivist idea that these research-programmes amount to no more than a range of optional 'discourses' or 'language-games' whereby to signal one's membership in this or that 'interpretive community' (Rorty 1989, 1991). Nevertheless, his arguments lie open to construal on just those terms in so far as they equate the creative ('stimulus-free') dimension of human cognitive activity with a strictly internalist theory of mind which requires that it operate in total isolation from real-world sensory or causal inputs, and hence that issues of reference be shunted into the non-scientific (pragmatic) domain. For this leaves him awkwardly placed when it comes to explaining how we could ever gain knowledge of the world – or indeed knowledge of our own cognitive processes – without some means of establishing the link between mental concepts or representations and that which they (more or less adequately) represent. Thus Chomskian rationalism is always at risk of providing unintended support for a full-scale Goodmanian constructivist (or Rortian descriptivist) approach according to which there is simply no point in worrying about such matters since truth *just is* what we take it to be under some particular projective scheme or culture-relative description.

Of course Chomsky thinks that this objection is adequately met by building in the rationalist innateness-hypothesis as a means of accounting for the trans-cultural uniformity of certain distinctive (uniquely human) mental capacities. And to critics – like Quine – who argue against that hypothesis in the name of a naturalised epistemology with no need for such delusive transcendental guarantees, Chomsky has two well-practised lines of response. The first, as we have seen, is that their kind of reductive physicalist naturalism cannot offer a remotely adequate account of human creativity (or rational 'unboundedness') with respect to language and related aspects of higher-order cognitive processing. The second – taking the argument onto their own chosen ground – is that his kind of rationalism (unlike other, more traditional varieties) comes equipped with a biological component which draws upon the resources of neurophysiology in fruitful conjunction with those of cognitive science and computational linguistics (Chomsky 1995, 2000). Thus Chomsky can assert, *contra* the old-style behaviourists and empiricists, that any viable 'naturalised' epistemology will need to incorporate certain crucial insights from the rationalist tradition in philosophy of mind while any viable rationalist account will need to take stock of certain relevant findings in that branch of natural science devoted to the brain and its neuro-chemical workings. In other words there is a way to address such issues – that of 'biological rationalism' – which at last promises to break the hold of those various tenacious dualisms that have plagued the discourse of philosophy for the past three centuries and more.

However this solution does not offer much help with the other main problem of Chomskian linguistics and cognitive science, namely its failure to explain how concepts or structures of representation might actually provide us with more or less reliable knowledge of the world. Indeed there is a growing body of work in various fields – among them evolutionary episte-mology – that adopts a naturalistic approach to this question in terms of our capacity to pick out just those objects (and properties thereof) that best enable our survival and flourishing as creatures in a certain physical environment (Kornblith [ed.] 1985; Kornblith 1993). Such an argument would clearly go along well enough with Chomsky's biological rationalism, since the latter finds room – indeed accords a large explanatory role – for evolu-tionary factors and considerations. Yet it just as clearly comes into conflict with his internalist principle that any adequate (scientific) account of language and mind must treat issues of reference as belonging to the realm of pragmatics, broadly conceived, and hence as lying beyond the purview of linguistics and cognitive psychology. It seems to me that Chomsky has boxed himself into a corner here and that this results mainly from his fixed idea that any referential constraints upon thought and language from the 'outside' world would constitute a threat to the autonomy and creativity of human intelligence. However, to repeat, this threat exists only if the kinds of constraint involved are such as would result from adopting a behaviourist stimulus–response psychology of the type that Chomsky has convincingly shown to fail the most basic tests of empirical (as well as theoretical) adequacy.

Thus there is no justification in principle for extending his usual counter-arguments, like those from linguistic creativity and poverty of the stimulus, to externalist theories of reference – such as the Kripke/Putnam account – which can perfectly well be construed on terms compatible with Chomsky's rationalist programme. Of course it may be said that they are equally open to a reading that lays maximum stress on the reference-fixing role of physical stimuli, causal inputs, or other such external (mind-independent) factors, and which hence amounts to just a back-door variant of old-style behav-iourist doctrine. Either that, so the charge might run, or they leave the way clear for someone like Rorty to accept the whole story about 'causal impacts on our retinas' (etc.) while claiming that this applies only at the level of raw sensory data and exerts no constraint on what we make of those data through various perceptual, cognitive, theoretical, or explanatory schemes.

('Causation is not under a description', as Donald Davidson puts it in an aphorism much quoted by Rorty, 'but explanation is' [e.g., Rorty 1991: 81].) From which Rorty concludes that language (or interpretation) goes all the way down for all practical purposes since however 'hard' the sensory data – or unmediated causal inputs – they count for nothing when it comes to the business of assessing rival hypotheses, theories, or truth-claims. In short, one can be as 'realist' as one likes about the physical world and our placement in it as creatures hard-wired (at that basic level) to react in certain ways to certain physical stimuli. But this carries absolutely no implications for epistemology or issues of knowledge and truth. Indeed, Rorty thinks, such issues are no longer of genuine interest from a philosophic standpoint – after so much fruitless wrangling – and are hence best treated (in pragmatist fashion) as so many optional language-games or styles of talk whose worth is to be judged solely in terms of their relevance to the ongoing 'cultural conversation' (Rorty 1989).

As I have said, this outlook could scarcely be further from Chomsky's rationalist belief in the power of human intelligence to arrive at truths – about its own nature and also (implicitly) about its cognitive functions with regard to the non-mental or extra-linguistic domain – which are not just projections of some currently favoured conceptual scheme. After all, if there is one central claim that links his writings on linguistics, cognitive science, and issues of ethics and politics it is the case for a rationalist philosophy of mind that explains how individuals can think their way beyond habitual modes of response or ideologically inculcated values and beliefs. Yet Chomsky comes close to undermining this claim when he endorses Goodman's strong-constructivist claim that the world and all its furniture – its constituent objects and properties – must be treated as products of mental representation rather than conceived as existing quite apart from whatever we think or believe concerning them. For there could then be no substance to his epistemological *or* his ethico-political arguments, that is to say, no objective truth of the matter with regard to statements concerning the nature of human cognitive-linguistic faculties or the extent (say) of covert US involvement in sponsoring the overthrow of various democratically elected regimes and the installation of various brutal right-wing military dictatorships (Chomsky 1973, 1989, 1991, 1994). That is to say, without some realist (externalist) account of what makes such statements objectively (mind-independently) true or false it is hard to see how Chomsky can sustain his case for the freedom and autonomy of moral conscience as a means of mounting critical resistance to state propaganda and media disinformation.

No doubt he is right to stress the connection between certain kinds of 'manufactured consensus' – those that involve the massaging of public opinion through compliance on the part of mainstream intellectuals, journalists, or media pundits – and a certain kind of causal-determinist thinking which lends itself readily to recruitment in just that cause (Chomsky and Herman

1988). This was of course Chomsky's main charge against the types of crudely reductive behaviourist psychology that prevailed across large sectors of the human and social sciences at an earlier period of intensive effort to indoctrinate people in a mindset conducive to the maintenance of Cold War strategic and political aims. More recently he has taken a similar line against proponents of various likewise reductionist but philosophically more sophisticated doctrines – such as eliminative materialism – which claim to provide a fully adequate account of human cognitive functioning without any need to invoke redundant ('folk-psychological') concepts such as thought, belief, meaning, intention, propositional attitudes, or the like. Here again Chomsky mounts a two-pronged attack which involves both their failure to account for the facts of human cognitive-linguistic competence and their promoting a drastically deflationist view of our rational and moral capacities most aptly epitomised in the title of Paul Churchland's book *Scientific Realism and the Plasticity of Mind* (Churchland 1979; also 1984). However – to repeat – these objections apply only to the kind of hard-line reductionist approach that holds out the prospect of completely eliminating 'mentalist' (intentional) talk through the advent of a neurophysiological discourse with no room for such antiquated concepts. Where they *do not* apply – except by a confusion of two quite distinct lines of argument – is in the realm of philosophical semantics (more precisely: the theory of reference) which has to do with the truth-conditions that obtain for various orders of statement. Here it is a matter of reference-fixing *not* through some combination of brute causal impacts and hard-wired (passively receptive) responses but rather – as Chomsky should surely be willing to accept – through the active processing of informational data that may or may not (depending on our powers of rational grasp) provide us with an accurate representation of objects and events 'outside the head'. For otherwise it is strictly impossible to explain how the exercise of human reason could be brought to bear on issues ranging from theoretical linguistics and cognitive psychology to history, politics, and ethics.

To be sure, this externalist claim will seem stronger when applied to issues in the physical rather than the social and human sciences. Yet it can scarcely be denied – above all by a theorist with Chomsky's strongly naturalistic bent – that even in the case of disciplines such as linguistics and cognitive psychology there must be some determinate object-domain or focus of descriptive-explanatory treatment that is not just a product of internal representation. After all, if this were the case – if eidetic self-evidence or *a priori* warrant were the sole source of knowledge with respect to our cognitive-linguistic powers – then, quite simply, those disciplines could never have achieved the status of genuine sciences. And of course it is a chief tenet of Chomsky's updated (naturalistic) version of the rationalist argument that they *can* yield a knowledge of the mind and its workings which involves no such desperate resort to dualist ideas of immaterial essence or the 'ghost in the machine'.

However this claim comes distinctly into conflict with his demand that linguistics and cognitive psychology must eschew any recourse to externalist theories of reference lest they end up by endorsing some form of revived behaviourist doctrine. I would suggest, on the contrary, that his project is much better served by an approach that goes further in renouncing its ties with that old Cartesian tradition, and which sees no need for a straightforward choice between 'I-language' and 'E-language' perspectives. For this places Chomsky in the awkward predicament – epistemologically and ethico-politically speaking – of one who argues with passionate conviction for the mind's capacity to discriminate in matters of objective truth and falsehood while grounding that capacity in nothing more than its internal powers of thought and representation.

IV

McGilvray takes a very different view since he agrees with Chomsky on the main point at issue, that is, that any adequate rationalist approach must also adopt an internalist perspective which treats mental processes as wholly independent of causal inputs or 'outside' information-sources. Thus he lays great stress on the 'creativity' and 'poverty of the stimulus' arguments, taking them to show beyond doubt that linguists, psychologists, and cognitive scientists are on a false trail if they allow any more than a strictly pragmatic (scientifically extraneous) role to external modes of reference-fixing. This goes along with a firm commitment to Chomsky's rationalist position on issues of moral and political conscience, that is to say, his belief – as against the purveyors of mass-induced consensus ideology – that the human mind is innately capable of exerting resistance to various forms of manipulative thought-control.

McGilvray provides plentiful evidence of Chomsky's superb investigative work on the complicity of numerous US administrations – together with well-placed media hacks and academic camp followers – in a whole range of frauds, cover-ups, illicit arms deals, political assassinations, terrorist attacks, military coups, and assorted large-scale brutalities conducted in furtherance of their economic and geo-strategic aims (see for instance Chomsky 1967, 1989, 1991, 1994). One can fully accept his eloquent case for Chomsky's role as the greatest living voice of US intellectual and moral dissent, along with his argument – despite the latter's express reservations – that there exists a close link between his technical work in cognitive-linguistic theory and his socio-political writings. Among the main reasons for Chomsky's reticence in this regard is his belief that such technical work – like all scientific disciplines – involves a high degree of theoretical abstraction from its first-order (natural linguistic) subject-domain. Thus it is carried on at a large remove not only from the realm of innate human competence in language and cognitive processing but also from the sphere of shared interests, values, and concerns that Chomsky seeks to address in his other, politically engaged books and articles. Besides, he is wary – justifiably so, given the kinds of attack often launched by some of his right-wing critics – about laying himself open to the charge that his technical work has been influenced (even primarily motivated) by his ideological views (Sampson 1979, 1989). So one can count McGilvray right in his claim that the two projects have a great deal in common – crucially their joint dependence on a critical-rationalist philosophy of mind – while accepting that Chomsky has good reason for denying that they stand or fall on the same theoretical grounds.

Nevertheless, there is something askew about Chomsky's need to assert this dual perspective as a matter of philosophic principle as well as a means of heading off irrelevant (ideologically motivated) objections. For on the rationalist account – whether in linguistics and cognitive science or in the ethico-political sphere – there should always be some means of linking up the judgement of competent ('native') subjects to the kinds of more specialised argument that occupy linguists, psychologists, and ethical philosophers. Of course Chomsky accepts this constraint in so far as linguists have to check their hypotheses against the evidence provided by native speakers, or in so far as moral and political theorists had better keep their judgements reliably in touch with what counts – among non-experts – as the right or wrong course of action in any case. Indeed this is just his point in distinguishing the specialist sphere of the sciences, physical and human, from the sphere of those innately given and humanly shared cognitive capacities which may become the objects of scientific study but whose practical exercise entails no such specialist knowledge. Thus people can talk straight ahead and get the grammar right without any grasp of theoretical linguistics, just as they can reason to good effect about issues of justice and moral conscience without having read Kant, Rawls, or whomever. So far as language is concerned this results from the fact that it belongs to a modular faculty of mind whose operations are amenable to scientific treatment precisely on account of its 'encapsulated' nature, or its not depending on inputs from a range of other such modules or widely distributed mental functions. In the case of moral judgement, conversely, it has to do with the global (i.e., non-modular) character of practical reason and the fact that getting things right in such matters comes about through a capacity for achieving wide reflective equilibrium over complex issues which could never be reduced to any abstract system of formal representations.

Thus 'competence' in language and 'competence' in issues of practical reason must both be counted as native endowments whose exercise need not involve any specialised knowledge on the speaker's or reasoner's part. Where they differ – crucially so – is in virtue of the fact that linguistic competence is modular and therefore subject to scientific methods of computational analysis whereas judgement draws upon a range of skills, capacities, and aptitudes that inherently elude any such formal specification. Moreover (as Jerry Fodor has argued) this applies equally to higher-level cognitive processes like abduction – or inference to the best explanation – which cannot be construed in modular terms, since they clearly involve a much greater degree of complex interactive exchange between different aspects or functions of human intelligence. In Fodor's words:

> there are lots of syntactical facts about each representation other than the ones that comprise its constituent structure; in particular, there are lots of facts about its syntactical relations to other representations. And, on the one hand, these facts are not ipso facto accessible to computations for which the representation provides a domain; and, on the other, globality considerations suggest that they may well be essential to determining how the representation behaves in cognitive processes. (Fodor 2000: 30)

So there is a problem about any argument for 'massive modularity' that ignores this crucial point and attempts to extend the computational approach into areas of cognitive psychology where global considerations must play a role (see also Fodor 1983, 1990). That is, it conspicuously fails to explain how thought can go beyond the limits of formal (logico-syntactic) representation and draw upon other, more complex or widely integrated modes of cognitive processing. This is the main reason for drawing a line between matters of innate (hard-wired or modular) competence and matters that involve the exercise of mental powers beyond whatever can be captured in purely formal or computational terms.

However this distinction is somewhat blurred – or rendered more problematic – by Chomsky's way of raising these issues in a markedly epistemological register, that is, as having to do with questions of *knowledge*, whether tacit and preconscious (as in the case of native linguistic competence) or subject to rational evaluation in a wider cognitive context. Thus (Fodor again):

> Chomsky's nativism is primarily a thesis about knowledge and belief; it aligns problems in the theory of language with those in the theory of knowledge .... the grammar of a language specifies what its speakers/ hearers have to *know* qua speakers and hearers; and the goal of the child's language acquisition process is to construct a *theory* of the language that correctly expresses this grammatical knowledge. Likewise, the central problem of language acquisition arises from the poverty of the 'primary linguistic *data*' from which the child effects this construction; and the proposed solution of the problem is that much of the knowledge that linguistic competence depends on is available to the child *a priori* (i.e., prior to learning). (Fodor 2000: 11)

This creates problems when it comes to explaining just how and where the line can be drawn between modular and non-modular processes, or those that can be represented in formal-computational terms and those that must involve wider (global) aspects of human cognition. For if both have to do with 'knowledge' in some sense of the term then both entail a certain *normative* conception of what should count as a competent exercise of the function, capacity, or rational procedure concerned. In the case of language, according to Chomsky, this normativity constraint is provided by reference to native speakers' intuitions with respect to grammatical well-formedness or preservation of sense across various (e.g., active/passive) transformations. In the case of non-modular processes it derives from the shared human capacity for reasoning on the evidence, arriving at justified (rationally warranted) conclusions, or exercising moral and political judgement in accordance with standards of social justice and humanitarian concern. Clearly such standards cannot be accounted for on anything like the modular conception of a hard-wired faculty for preconscious data-processing whose operations are autonomous (or fully 'encapsulated') and which therefore exhibits no dependence on inputs from other information-sources. Yet it is then hard to see how the argument for linguistic 'creativity' – or for the 'unboundedness' of human cognitive-linguistic powers *vis-à-vis* the poverty of ambient stimuli – could possibly lend philosophical support (as Chomsky claims) to the rationalist argument for human autonomy in issues of moral and socio-political judgement.

What seems to be involved is a dual application of these terms – 'knowledge', 'creativity', 'autonomy' – whereby they assume radically different senses in different contexts of enquiry. Thus in the one context they are taken to denote mental powers that involve only tacit or preconscious 'knowledge', that exhibit 'creativity' only in the sense of producing a potentially infinite range of well-formed grammatical sentences from a finite stock of syntactic resources, and which exhibit 'autonomy' just in so far as they are assumed to operate according to modular (domain-specific) rules. In the other context – as applied to more global capacities of mind – they denote the kinds of rational, problem-solving, intellectually inventive, and morally responsive thinking which require that those terms be construed in line with a normative conception of human nature that is subject to no such specialised constraints. However, to repeat, this places sharp limits on the relevance of Chomsky's technical work in theoretical linguistics and cognitive psychology to his wider concerns with moral and political issues. Thus it raises the awkward question as to why any argument from the demonstrable facts of linguistic knowledge, creativity, and autonomy should be thought to carry substantive implications for our view of how those 'same' powers might be exercised to best advantage in matters that involve our capacity for rational, reflective, or deliberative thought. More than that: if we suppose some connection to exist – as Chomsky often (albeit cautiously) suggests – then this creates further problems with his case for the freedom of individual conscience as brought to bear in those matters. On the one hand it runs the risk of implying a wider extension of the modularity thesis (or a claim for its pertinence in other domains) that would drastically diminish the scope for such freedom. On the other it risks lending support to a weakened construal of that thesis which takes it that syntactic forms, semantic representations, propositional contents, and so forth, are more context-sensitive – or less constrained by the requirements of modular autonomy – than could ever be allowed for on Chomsky's version of the argument. That is to say, Fodor has a strong point when he remarks on the tendency of Chomskian epistemological nativism to resuscitate certain long-standing philosophic problems, among them – not least – the freewill/determinism issue.

It seems to me that this results from his strict internalist approach in philosophy of mind and his outright rejection of any alternative account – such as that provided by the Kripke/Putnam causal theory of reference – which strikes him as posing a threat to that approach. However, there is no reason to take such a view if one accepts that claims for the fixity of reference with regard to matters of *a posteriori* necessary truth can go along perfectly well with claims for the exercise of rational intelligence and creative problem-solving activity in science as in other disciplines. What this involves is nothing more mind-constrictive or inimical to Chomsky's rationalist programme than a straightforward subscription to the basic premises of scientific realism. These are (1) that there exist certain objective (belief-independent) truths about physics, mathematics, history, psychology, cognitive-linguistic structures, and so forth, (2) that they fix the truth-conditions for any well-formed statement we make concerning them irrespective of whether we are adequately placed to know or determine its truth-value, and (3) that we gain knowledge of the world – and also of our own place in it as physically embodied, sentient, and mindful beings – through various modes of truth-seeking enquiry whose success (or otherwise) ultimately depends on the way things stand with regard to their particular object-domain. (See for instance – from a range of philosophical perspectives – Alston 1996; Devitt 1986; Norris 2002b; Soames 1999.) To which may be added (4) the equally basic realist premise that minds – like physical objects and properties – exert certain causal powers and dispositions which (again) might always turn out to exceed our utmost capacities of descriptive-explanatory grasp yet whose existence and workings it is the business of science to find out so far as possible (Harré and Madden 1975). Thus, in Kripkean modal parlance, any well-formed statement with respect to such objects, properties, or powers must contain certain terms which – if the statement is true – will have their reference fixed (necessarily so) by the existence or reality of just those same objects, properties, or powers (Kripke 1980; also Schwartz [ed.] 1977; Wiggins 1980).

What is distinctive about modal realism is the fact that it makes explicit allowance for different orders of truth-claim, among them the self-evident (*a priori*) truths of mathematics and logic which hold good across all possible worlds and the *a posteriori* necessary truths of the physical sciences which can be known to hold good only with reference to worlds that duplicate our own in the relevant (e.g., subatomic, molecular, genetic, or neurophysiological) respects. It seems to me that this approach should recommend itself to a thinker like Chomsky in so far as it helps to avoid the sorts of problem that typically arise when a rationalist commitment to the values of freewill, autonomy, and creativity comes up against the strongly determinist pull of a naturalistic or biologically based account. Chomsky attempts to get around these problems – as we have seen – by pinning the blame on causal (or externalist) conceptions of reference and then shunting reference off into a branchline where it can best be dealt with by relevance-theorists, students of speech-act implicature, and other pragmatically minded types (Grice 1989; Sperber and Wilson 1986). For the field is then free for linguistics and cognitive psychology to get on with their task of specifying just those respects in which language and mind must be taken to exhibit powers of rational grasp beyond anything remotely explicable in stimulus–response terms.

However this argument has problems of its own, chief among them that of explaining how to square the nativist hypothesis (the idea of mind as programmed in advance to acquire and manifest certain forms of cognitive-linguistic competence) and the claim for intellectual creativity as the single most distinctive feature of human intelligence. Moreover, the problem is compounded by two further aspects of Chomsky's approach, namely his stress on computational models of mental processing and his baseline appeal to biology (brain science) as our best present and future source of advances in cognitive psychology. This is not the place for a review of the debate among philosophers, psychologists, and others as to whether any such advance toward a better, more detailed understanding of neurophysiology could possibly explain 'what it is like' to experience certain sensations, moods, perceptual states, subjective qualia, and so forth. (See for instance Chalmers 1996; Flanagan 1992; Kirk 1994; McGinn 1999; Papineau 2002; Shear [ed.] 1997.) Likewise philosophers frequently deny that we could ever – in principle – explain the workings of human moral and social conscience with reference to various processes or events in the central nervous system. At any rate Chomsky's biologism and nativism – along with his modular-computational approach – are apt to strike anyone versed in that debate as posing the freewill/determinism problem with no less force than those behaviourist doctrines that he finds so utterly repugnant.

My point is that Chomsky invites this kind of *tu quoque* response by adopting an extreme version of the internalist thesis which leaves no room for the kinds of complex interaction between mind and world that typify the process of knowledge-acquisition, whether in the natural or the human sciences. Had he not taken so strong a line against Kripke-type externalist (as distinct from Skinner-type behaviourist) theories of reference then he could readily have made such allowance and avoided the sorts of dilemma that I have outlined above. Thus the trouble with Chomsky's I-language approach is that it swings so far in an internalist direction as to exclude those normative values of truth, objectivity, and causal-explanatory grasp which apply in the physical sciences and also – one would think – to any science of language that purports to do more than construct purely abstract hypotheses whose theoretical power is inversely related to their purchase on the everyday-communicative aspects of linguistic grasp. In his view this is just the price one has to pay for producing an adequate scientific theory, that is, an account of speaker-competence that satisfies the nativist, rationalist, and internalist constraints and which does not get side-tracked into strictly extraneous (pragmatic or context-specific) fields of research. However, as I have said, it is far from clear that this programme can be carried through without giving up any claim to capture certain crucial dimensions of our cognitive-linguistic dealing with the world. Amongst these latter must be counted our capacity to represent that world in ways that provide some mutually intelligible means of assessment in point of their objective truth or falsehood. For we should otherwise be quite at a loss to explain how language has evolved – as Chomsky could scarcely deny – in close conjunction with our cognitive powers of attaining and communicating knowledge of a world that exerts certain definite constraints on the range of admissible (truth-conducive) theories and hypotheses. In which case there is simply no need for Chomsky's rigorous distinction between internalist ('I-language') and externalist ('E-language') methodologies. Rather we can take it that his strongly argued claims for linguistic creativity and rational autonomy would in no way be compromised by conceding the existence of such real-world objective and referential constraints. On the contrary: it is just this salient feature of our cognitive-linguistic dealings with the world that explains how a naturalised theory of language and representation can avoid coming into conflict with a rationalist account that prizes the values of truth and intellectual creativity (Papineau 1993).

V

This might also help to resolve some other problems with Chomsky's approach, among them his insistence on the sharp methodological divide between everyday-common sense modes of understanding (like our native competence as language-users) and the sorts of scientific theory-construction – such as Chomskian linguistics and cognitive psychology – that should be thought of as belonging to a realm quite apart from their first-order 'natural' object-domain. For there is (to repeat) something odd about a theory that relies so heavily on speaker-intuition – on native judgements with regard to grammatical well-formedness – while none the less imposing such a sharp distinction between linguistic science and everyday linguistic performance.

Of course it may be argued that this is the case for any specialised field of enquiry where the kind of theoretical knowledge that experts seek has little in common with the kinds of practical-experiential grasp that characterise our normal, preconscious, or intuitive modes of being in the world. Thus one does not need an ability to solve complex equations in dynamics in order to ride a bike or catch a ball, or require even the most rudimentary grasp of genetics and molecular biology in order to propagate one's kind with a fair measure of success. Moreover this applies to the human sciences – including linguistics and cognitive psychology – in so far as they involve a degree of theoretical abstraction from the first-order business of thinking straight or of talking ahead and getting the grammar right. Such performances could only be impeded – or rendered downright impossible – if success depended on our consciously grasping the structures and generative mechanisms that the theorist takes to subtend and explain our native competence. Yet in these cases, unlike the situation in physics or molecular biology, there is still a clear need for what the theorist advances by way of scientific explanation to represent at least a plausible account of what goes on – no doubt at some preconscious level – in the minds of normally equipped reasoners and speakers. That is to say, if the science becomes too remote from the first-order (natural) practice or object-domain then it will tend to generate just the sorts of problem – about linguistic creativity or rational autonomy *versus* the implicitly determinist claims of scientific method – that I have outlined above. For this makes it all the harder to envisage a naturalistic and computational approach to cognitive psychology that would not end up by placing sharp limits on the capacity of human subjects to exhibit the required degree of freedom in just that regard.

The same goes for Chomsky's nativist hypothesis when applied to issues of moral and political judgement. Here, as I have said, he adopts a two-pronged line of approach, on the one hand assembling a vast range of detailed and meticulously documented facts concerning the extent of US global involvement in various war-crimes, atrocities, and covert military operations while on the other arguing with passionate conviction for the capacity of moral agents – except when subject to forms of mass-indoctrination – to comprehend and resist what has been done in their name by successive administrations. And whence could such resistance arise, he asks, if not from their innate disposition to distinguish those facts from the various falsehoods put about through techniques of 'manufactured consent', and furthermore to apply their best efforts of morally discriminative judgement to the issues concerned. Thus '[t]he acquisition of a specific moral and ethical system, wide ranging and often precise in its consequences, cannot simply be the result of "shaping" and "control" by the social environment' (Chomsky 1988: 152–53). And again:

[t]he environment is too impoverished and indeterminate to provide this system to the child, in its full richness and applicability... [In which

case] it certainly seems reasonable to speculate that the moral and ethical system acquired by the child owes much to some innate human faculty. The environment is relevant, as in the case of language, vision, and so on; thus we can find individual and cultural divergence. But there is surely a common basis, rooted in our nature. (ibid.: 153)

Now I think that this is true – vitally so for Chomsky's ethical case – and that some such appeal to innate (or natural) facts about human intellectual, cognitive, and moral dispositions is indispensable to any argument that would locate the values of trust and reciprocity in the sphere of shared human concerns. More specifically, it offers a strong basis for the kind of consequentialist (but none the less principled) approach which avoids the twin poles of an abstract moral discourse on rights, obligations, civic responsibilities, and so forth, and a communitarian outlook that rejects such notions but also – along with them – the idea of morality as sometimes requiring an exercise of individual conscience that goes clean against the consensual values of a given society or culture. The terms of this somewhat typecast 'liberal *versus* communitarian' debate are familiar enough from the recent literature and need not be rehearsed in any detail here (see for instance Paul, Miller and Paul [eds] 1996; Rasmussen [ed.] 1990; also Edgley 2000). What is crucial for Chomsky – as a dissident political thinker – is that liberalism should find adequate room for the appeal to universal yet not merely formal or abstract principles of justice, while the claims of community or shared ethico-political allegiance should not override those of freely exercised moral choice. For of course it is a leading point of his work on the theme of 'manufactured consensus' that there *can and must* be an appeal open from the realm of received (e.g., media-dominated) opinion to the sphere of informed participant debate wherein the voice of individual conscience should always have a fair hearing.

All the same – to repeat – it is a necessary presupposition of any such argument that moral conscience must have something to work with – that is, some access to relevant truths that are not just projections of its own innate capacity for judging moral issues in the abstract – if this case is to carry the kind of weight that Chomsky requires of it. And it is hard to conceive how that capacity could be exercised to any practical effect in the absence of real-world (mind-external) constraints that make all the difference – epistemologically and morally speaking – between striving to ascertain the truth in such matters and passively endorsing a prevalent consensus of ideological beliefs. To be sure, if one takes it (as Chomsky does) that the choice falls out between nativist rationalism and a crude stimulus–response psychology, then '[t]he environment is too impoverished and indeterminate to provide this [moral] system . . . . in its full richness and applicability' (Chomsky 1988: 153). On this view there is room only for the minor concession that such inputs may have a certain pragmatic or context-specific role to play, but not – emphatically – one that would grant them a place in any self-respecting rationalist philosophy of mind. No doubt '[t]he environment is relevant, as in the case of language, vision, and so on; thus we can find individual and cultural divergence' (ibid.: 153). But these factors are strictly beside the point if one is concerned with the innate capacity of human thought to derive certain truths about our rational nature and its attendant ethical and socio-political obligations that cannot be explained – much less morally justified – through any appeal to the causal interaction between world and mind. Rather, as Chomsky puts it, there is 'a common basis, rooted in our nature' which can be captured only by an internalist conception, one that in principle eschews any recourse to causal theories of reference or external sources of knowledge and belief. For this Kripke/Putnam alternative – he thinks – is a form of updated behaviourist doctrine that draws on more highly developed theories of the relation between environmental input and linguistic output, yet which still conspicuously fails to make room for the exercise of human rational and moral-evaluative powers.

It seems to me that Chomsky is wrong about this and that he needs something like that alternative account – some non-behaviourist version of the argument for external reference-fixing – in order to save his theory from the kinds of problem described above. That is to say, it is otherwise open to a range of closely related objections, among them (1) that its biologism might well lead to a form of determinist doctrine with drastic claims on the scope and limits of our freedom, (2) that its nativism goes so far as to exclude (or put down to mere 'cultural divergence') those significant conflicts of view that may arise with respect to real-world matters of fact, and (3) that its adopting so strict an internalist line on issues of mental content or representation is such as to create an insuperable gulf between mind and world, or our faculties of cognitive-linguistic processing and that which they (more or less adequately) serve to describe, explain, and communicate. What is lacking in Chomsky's approach – I would suggest – is a theory of reference that allows for the existence of objective (mind-independent) truths while neither placing such truths beyond our utmost epistemic reach nor restricting the scope of human knowledge to a passive registration of incoming sensory data (Norris 2002a,b). That he rejects the best current candidate for just that role (i.e., the Kripke/Putnam theory) is perhaps understandable given its stress on the causal nature of reference-fixing and Chomsky's resistance to any claim that meanings or mental contents are determined by environmental factors beyond the domain of autonomous rational thought. Yet it is clear enough from Putnam's more extensive and detailed development of the theory that it need not involve any such affront to Chomsky's leading principles. Thus the causal tie between name and referent – fixed through an act of inaugural 'baptism' – and the existence of *a posteriori* necessary truths concerning the essential (kind-constitutive) properties of various items should be treated as strictly *metaphysical* claims that entail no restriction on our capacity to find such properties out through rational conjecture and inventive hypothesis-testing (Kripke 1980;

Putnam 1975a,b). Still less can they be seen as inimical to Chomsky's programme if taken in conjunction with Putnam's idea of the 'linguistic division of labour', that is, his allowance that speakers can successfully refer to all kinds of things without possessing an expert (scientific) knowledge of just what makes them things of that kind (Putnam 1988; also Burge 1989). So laypersons can talk reliably enough about everyday referents like 'gold', 'water', and 'tigers' or even about recondite items such as 'atoms', 'molecules', and 'chromosomes' just so long as they know that there are experts around – physicists, chemists, and molecular biologists – who could supply the relevant specification if required.

VI

What this helps to make clear in the context of Chomsky's quarrel with the causal theory of reference is the fact that such a theory allows wide scope (as much as the rationalist could possibly require) for speakers to exercise their native reasoning capacities in ways untrammelled by a hard-line determinist conception of reference-fixing. Thus it makes full provision for the extent to which knowledge may often be advanced through a complex interaction of special expertise and the kinds of everyday-practical grasp – whether in language or the process of scientific theory formation – that constitute the basis or enabling condition of all such advances. On this account there is no sharp distinction (such as Chomsky requires) between the modes of cognitive-linguistic competence exhibited by native reasoners or speakers and the specialised treatment to which their performances are subject once brought within the sphere of cognitive psychology or theoretical linguistics. Rather it will seem more plausible to argue – by analogy with Putnam's 'linguistic division of labour' – that these are two expressions of a common human capacity whose first-order manifestation in the form of preconsciously structured grammatical utterance is just what provides the linguist not only with her object of analysis but also with the means (the theoretical resources) whereby to elucidate its deeper regularities.

Of course this goes without saying in so far as the linguist must always check her theoretical claims against the evidence of native intuitions with regard to what counts as a well-formed sentence or a case of genuinely sense-preserving active/passive transformation. Chomsky is the first to acknowledge this constraint and indeed makes it a chief plank in his argument for the innate (i.e., the universal or trans-culturally valid) character of human linguistic competence. Yet his argument pulls in an opposite direction when he stresses the difference between talking straight ahead and getting the grammar right – a matter of native human endowment – and the specialised business of producing scientific theories which purport to explain that phenomenon. It seems to me that Chomsky is forced into this position through his endorsement of the strong internalist case against referential 'inputs' of whatever kind and his consequent idea that any adequate theory of language must firmly reject the kinds of explanation that would take some account of our everyday cognitive-exploratory dealings with the world. That is, if he relaxed this stringent demand – if he allowed that such dealings legitimately fall within the remit of linguistic science rather than the merely pragmatic domain – then he would have no problem in likewise allowing for the continuity between native competence and those other, more specialised kinds of knowledge that characterise his own theoretical project.

Also he would have less need to insist – often, one suspects, very much against the rationalist grain – on the error of imputing too close a connection between that project and his work as a political dissident or left-wing 'public' intellectual. As I have said, it is perhaps understandable that Chomsky should adopt this cautious position, given the way that his opponents on the right have attempted to discredit his work in linguistics and cognitive psychology through a kind of guilt-by-association technique. Nevertheless the connection does run deep – as Chomsky sometimes makes clear – and indeed plays a central role in his case for the native capacity of thinking individuals to exercise their powers of rational, moral, and political judgement when placed in possession of the relevant facts, as opposed to the barrage of state-sponsored media disinformation. However, that case could only be weakened if one took Chomsky too much at his word either with regard to the strict separation between specialist and non-specialist domains, or with regard to the rigorous requirement that specialised work in linguistics and cognitive psychology should adopt a strictly internalist approach which leaves aside issues of reference and factual truth.

To be sure, this would spike the guns of his detractors on the right who could then scarcely claim that Chomsky's entire theoretical apparatus was merely a projection of his own political views, or a show of special expertise put up to conceal his primary (ideological) intent. Yet it would also undermine the very point of his argument that reflection on the kinds of intelligence manifest in our ordinary (native) powers of linguistic and cognitive grasp has large – indeed decisive – implications for our view of ourselves as rational agents equipped to take a properly informed and principled stand on issues of political conscience. For if this argument is to carry much philosophic weight then there has to be a close relationship – much closer than he is fully willing to proclaim – between the sorts of criteria that Chomsky applies in his specialist (theoretical or scientific) work and the sorts of criteria that he takes to apply in matters of real-world moral and political debate. Moreover, it has to involve some adequate dealing with just that recalcitrant aspect of language – that is, its referential dimension – which, according to Chomsky's internalist approach, had better be consigned to the non-scientific (i.e., the pragmatic or extra-theoretical) domain. For there is a straightforward sense – maintained by philosophical realists from Aristotle down – in which truth must be conceived as that which might always turn out to transcend our present-best state of belief, or again (more prosaically) as that which we might always bump up against despite our firmly held preconceptions to the contrary (Devitt 1986; Leplin [ed.] 1984).

This conviction is present throughout Chomsky's writings on the 'political economy' of truth and the extent to which people can be persuaded to adopt false beliefs through techniques of mass-media manipulation and subtle (though none the less coercive) ideological conditioning (Chomsky and Herman 1979, 1988). Yet it would lack any force – whether as a philosophic thesis or as a matter of ethico-political faith – were it not for his espousing the realist view that there exist certain truths (e.g., about US involvement in various covert campaigns to destabilise democratically elected governments around the world) whose objective warrant is entirely independent of whatever we may happen to think or believe concerning them. On the other hand – as anti-realists are quick to point out – this argument must collapse into manifest incoherence if we take it that such truths are *by very definition* beyond our utmost powers of ascertainment or epistemic grasp (see especially Dummett 1978; Luntley 1988; Tennant 1987; also Norris 2002b; Wright 1987). What is needed in order to avoid this sceptical upshot is a theory that makes due allowance for the inherent fallibility of human cognitive powers yet which also grants due weight to those various knowledge-conducive methods and procedures that possess a fair claim to put us right about matters of objective truth and falsehood. Such is the thought of causal realists like Kripke and the early Putnam when they argue that our usage of certain (prototypically natural-kind) terms is 'truth-tracking' or 'sensitive to future discovery' (Kripke 1980; Putnam 1975; also McCulloch 1995). That is to say, the reference of 'water', 'gold', 'atom', 'electron', or 'gene' was fixed from the outset – when relatively little was known about their kind-constitutive natures or proper-ties – and has since held firm throughout various advances in our state of knowledge concerning them. In which case we can also suppose that these terms will continue to pick out identical referents despite and across any future (perhaps revolutionary) changes in the fields of physics, chemistry, or molecular biology. For the claim that reference is fixed in this way – as a means of maintaining trans-paradigm comparability between different stages in the progress of scientific knowledge – has no bearing whatsoever on the issue about human rationality or the scope and limits of creatively applied intelligence. Indeed, as I have said, it is just the sort of claim that best goes along with Chomsky's rationalist case for the capacity of mind to arrive at truths about itself and the world that cannot be sustained except on the basic realist premise that such truths are objective and would none the less obtain quite apart from our current best state of knowledge or belief.

This applies just as much to his specialised work in theoretical linguistics and cognitive psychology as to his other, more exoteric writings on politics, society, and the mass media. Thus he is clearly committed to a realist position as regards the existence of mental contents, propositional forms, linguistic universals, structures of logico-semantic representation, and – not least – those various mathematical entities (numbers, sets, classes, etc.) which provide so much of the requisite framework for Chomsky's computational approach. At any rate, despite his odd attraction to Goodman's ultra-nominalist stance, it appears that Chomsky *must* be so committed if he is to justify his case for treating those various abstract entities as something more than products of theoretical convenience (see also Hale 1987; Katz 1998; Norris 2002b; Soames 1999). Nor need his platonism in this regard, that is, his endorsing an object-ivist philosophy of mathematics and the formal sciences, be taken as in any way dependent upon – or inextricable from – the kinds of neo-platonist doctrine that he finds so appealing in Cudworth and other representatives of the seventeenth-century rationalist tradition. As we have seen, this appeal has to do mainly with their taking a strong stand on the innate or *a priori* capacity of thought to transcend any possible account of its own cogitative powers in terms of environmental inputs, sensory stimuli, causal interactions, or other such 'impoverished' means of explanation. Yet there is a problem here – and one that Chomsky is strangely unwilling to confront – in so far as the history of the formal sciences at least since Kant has thrown up a series of increasingly powerful challenges to the claim that *a priori* modes of reasoning might be a reliable source of guidance with respect to truths about math-ematics, logic, or (least of all) the necessary presuppositions of our knowledge concerning physical reality (Coffa 1991). Thus philosophers – the later Putnam among them – are still much exercised by the issue as to whether there can possibly exist any such self-evident (rationally grounded) truths in the wake of non-Euclidean geometry, relativity-theory, quantum mechanics, and other such affronts to our *a priori* knowledge of the world (Putnam 1983). That Kant's entire argument in the First *Critique* relied so heavily on this idea – that the truths of Euclidean geometry and Newtonian space-time physics were secure beyond intelligible doubt – is perhaps one reason why Chomsky so seldom refers to Kant and looks farther back (to the seventeenth-century rationalists) in his quest for elective precursors (Chomsky 1966). However this can only raise the same problem in a yet more acute form since, as Kant argued, their conception of *a priori* knowledge was based on a failure (or dogmatic refusal) to recognise the limits of pure reason as a source of reliable – cognitively grounded – understanding of the physical world.

Thus Chomsky's rationalist approach to issues in linguistics and cognitive psychology may not, after all, be best served by his commitment to the full-strength nativist-internalist hypothesis. Indeed these two commitments can be seen as coming into conflict if one considers how far modern (post-Kantian) developments in mathematics, logic, and physical theory have narrowed the range of defensible *a priori* truth-claims to the point where – as Putnam somewhat pyrrhically suggests – perhaps the sole surviving contender for such status is a statement that runs: 'not every statement is both true and false' (Putnam 1983a). Yet this need not entail any serious challenge to the rationalist component of Chomsky's programme just so long as that component is decoupled from the claim that any truths thus discovered must be thought of as sheerly self-evident since deriving from a stock of innate ideas that require no input from external (mind-independent) sources. For there are strong arguments from philosophy of mathematics, logic, and the formal sciences which hold that one can perfectly well maintain a realist conception of abstract entities without inviting the standard charge – much exploited by anti-realists – of supposing us to have epistemic access to them through some kind of quasi-perceptual epistemic contact (Katz 1998; Penrose 1995; Soames 1999). Such, most famously, was Gödel's platonist claim that we can acquire knowledge of certain mathematical truths that exceed the limits of formal computation and are clearly subject to no kind of empirical discovery-procedure yet which still possess a force of rational self-evidence to anyone who grasps the relevant proof, even (or especially) an incompleteness-proof that places certain ultimate limits on the scope of formal provability (Gödel 1962, 1983). Other thinkers – including some with strong ties to the Chomskian project – have developed this case for an outlook of 'realistic rationalism' which maintains the existence of abstract entities that confer an objective truth-value on our various statements concerning them whatever the kinds of epistemic restriction imposed by our finite computational resources (Katz 1998).

So there is a range of well-developed alternative arguments which preserve the main features of Chomsky's rationalist approach while avoiding its problematical commitment to the twin doctrines of full-strength nativism and strict internalism. On the one hand they come from philosophy of the formal sciences where realism with respect to abstract entities is still very much a live option in current debate. Most importantly, it offers a way beyond the sceptical dilemma – as proposed by Paul Benacerraf in a well-known essay – that we can *either* have (the notion of) objective mathematical truth *or* mathematical knowledge within the bounds of human ascertainment but most assuredly not both, unless at the cost of endorsing some version of the epistemic contact thesis (Benacerraf 1983; also Hart [ed.] 1996). On the other hand such arguments come from the quarter of Kripke–Putnam type modal realism where they provide just the kinds of philosophical resource that Chomsky needs in order to explain how reference can be fixed to the extent that his wider commitments require without any compromise to his rationalist principles. Thus he can perfectly well maintain the case for human autonomy and intellectual freedom *versus* any form of causal determinism along with the case for semantic realism and hence – in the socio-political sphere – for our capacity to sift and evaluate statements with respect to their objective truth-value, as distinct from their ideological currency or their function in promoting various forms of placid consensus belief.

Nobody who has read very far into Chomsky's massive volume of work on the conduct of US foreign and domestic policy could be in any doubt that he subscribes to each of the above principles. So the problems, as I have presented them here, are chiefly philosophical in character and have more to do with issues raised in his generalised reflections on mind and language than with the force and moral impact of his political writings or the value of his technical work in linguistics and cognitive psychology. All the same such reflections have always been central to Chomsky's project, from his earliest endeavours to link that project with the heritage of seventeenth-century rationalist thought to his current engagement with issues concerning the modularity of mind. Thus it is not just philosophical nit-picking if one points out the various tensions that exist within Chomsky's project and which might be resolved if he abandoned the strict nativist hypothesis and adopted a more accommodating line on the issue of semantic externalism. However there is no question that he has done more than any contemporary thinker to raise these topics to a new level of theoretically informed as well as morally and politically responsible debate.

References

Abbott, Barbara (1997). 'A note on the nature of "Water"', *Mind* **106**: 311–19.

Alston, William P. (1996). *A Realist Theory of Truth*. Ithaca, NY: Cornell University Press.

Aronson, H. (1989). 'Testing for convergent realism', *British Journal for the Philosophy of Science* **40**: 255–60.

Barsky, Robert F. (1996). *Noam Chomsky: A Life of Dissent*. Cambridge, MA: MIT Press.

Beiser, Frederick C. (1987). *The Fate of Reason: German Philosophy from Kant to Fichte*. Cambridge, MA: Harvard University Press.

Benacerraf, Paul (1983). 'What numbers could not be', in Benacerraf and Putnam (eds). pp. 272–94.

Benacerraf, Paul and Hilary Putnam (eds) (1983). *The Philosophy of Mathematics: Selected Essays*, 2nd edn. Cambridge: Cambridge University Press.

Boyd, Richard (1984). 'The current status of scientific realism', in Leplin (ed.). pp. 41–82.

Burge, Tyler (1979). 'Individualism and the mental', *Midwest Studies in Philosophy* **4**: 73–121.

——(1986). 'Individualism and psychology', *Philosophical Review* **95**: 3–45.

——(1989). 'Wherein is language social?', in George (ed.). pp. 175–91.

Chalmers, David J. (1996). *The Conscious Mind: In Search of a Fundamental Theory*. Oxford: Oxford University Press.

Chomsky, Noam (1959). 'A review of B.F. Skinner's *Verbal Behavior*'. *Language* **35**: 126–58.

——(1966). *Cartesian Linguistics*. New York: Harper & Row.

——(1967). *American Power and the New Mandarins*. New York: Pantheon.

——(1968). 'Quine's empirical assumptions', *Synthèse* **19**: 53–68.

——(1971). *Problems of Knowledge and Freedom*. New York: Pantheon.

——(1972). *Language and Mind*. New York: Harcourt, Brace, Jovanovich.

——(1973). *Towards a New Cold War*. New York: Pantheon.

——(1975). *Reflections on Language*. New York: Pantheon.

——(1982). 'A note on the creative aspect of language use', *Philosophical Review* **91**: 423–34.

——(1986). *Knowledge of Language: Its Nature, Origin, and Use*. New York: Praeger.

——(1988). *Language and Problems of Knowledge: The Managua Lectures*. Cambridge, MA: MIT Press.

——(1989). *Necessary Illusions*. Toronto: Anansi.

——(1991). *Deterring Democracy*. London: Verso.

——(1992). 'Discusion of Putnam's comments' in B. Beakley and P. Ludlow (eds), *The Philosophy of Mind: Clasical Problems/Contemporary Issues*. Cambridge, MA: MIT Press. pp. 411–22.

——(1993). *Language and Thought*. London: Moyer Bell.

——(1994). *World Orders Old and New*. New York: Columbia University Press.

——(1995). 'Language and nature', *Mind* **104**: 1–61.

——(1996). *Powers and Prospects*. Boston: South End Press.

——(2000). *New Horizons in the Study of Language and Mind*. Cambridge: Cambridge University Press.

Chomsky, Noam with Edward Herman (1979). *The Political Economy of Human Rights*. Montreal: Black Rose.

——(1988). *Manufacturing Consent*. New York: Pantheon.

Churchland, Paul M. (1979). *Scientific Realism and the Plasticity of Mind*. Cambridge: Cambridge University Press.

——(1984). *Matter and Consciousness*. Cambridge, MA: MIT Press.

Coffa, J. Alberto (1991). *The Semantic Tradition from Kant to Carnap: To the Vienna Station*. Cambridge: Cambridge University Press.

Cudworth, Ralph (1976 [1731]). *A Treatise Concerning Eternal and Immutable Morality*. New York: Garland.

Devitt, Michael (1986). *Realism and Truth*, 2nd edn. Oxford: Blackwell.

Dummett, Michael (1978). *Truth and Other Enigmas*. London: Duckworth.

Edgley, Alison (2000). *The Social and Political Thought of Noam Chomsky*. London: Routledge.

Farrell, Frank B. (1994). *Subjectivity, Realism, and Postmodernism: The Recovery of the World in Recent Philosophy*. Cambridge: Cambridge University Press.

Flanagan, Owen J. (1992). *Consciousness Reconsidered*. Cambridge, MA: MIT Press.

Fodor, Jerry (1983). *The Modularity of Mind*. Cambridge, MA: MIT Press.

——(1990). *A Theory of Content and Other Essays*. Cambridge, MA: MIT Press.

——(1994). *The Elm and the Expert*. Cambridge, MA: MIT Press.

——(2000). *The Mind Doesn't Work That Way: The Scope and Limits of Computational Psychology*. Cambridge, MA: MIT Press.

Frege, Gottlob (1952). 'On sense and reference', in P. Geach and M. Black (eds), *Selections from the Philosophical Writings of Gottlob Frege*. Oxford: Blackwell. pp. 56–78.

George, Alexander (ed.) (1989). *Reflections on Chomsky*. Oxford: Blackwell.

Gödel, Kurt (1962). *On Formally Undecidable Propositions of* Principia Mathematica *and Related Systems*, trans. B. Meltzer. New York: Basic Books.

——(1983). 'What is Cantor's continuum hypothesis?', in Benacerraf and Putnam (eds). pp. 470–85. New York: Basic Books.

Goodman, Nelson (1978). *Ways of Worldmaking*. Indianapolis: Bobbs-Merrill.

Grice, H.P. (1989). *Studies in the Ways of Words*. Cambridge, MA: Harvard University Press.

Hale, Bob (1987). *Abstract Objects*. Oxford: Blackwell.

Harré, Rom and E.H. Madden (1975). *Causal Powers*. Oxford: Blackwell.

Hart, W.D. (ed.) (1996). *The Philosophy of Mathematics*. Oxford: Oxford University Press.

Hintikka, J. (1969). *Models for Modalities*. Dordrecht: D. Reidel.

——(1989). 'Logical form and linguistic theory', in George (ed.). pp. 41–57.

——(1999). 'The emperor's new intuitions', *Journal of Philosophy* **96**: 127–47.

Kant, Immanuel (1964). *Critique of Pure Reason*, trans. Norman Kemp Smith. London: Macmillan.

Katz, Jerrold J. (1998). *Realistic Rationalism*. Cambridge, MA: MIT Press.

Kim, Jaegwon (1993). *Supervenience and Mind*. Cambridge: Cambridge University Press.

Kirk, Robert (1994). *Raw Feeling: A Philosophical Account of the Essence of Consciousness*. Oxford: Clarendon Press.

Kornblith, Hilary (1993). *Inductive Inference and its Natural Ground: An Essay in Naturalistic Epistemology*. Cambridge, MA: MIT Press.

——(ed.) (1995). *Naturalizing Epistemology*. Cambridge, MA: MIT Press.

Kripke, Saul (1980). *Naming and Necessity*. Oxford: Blackwell.

Laudan, Larry (1981). 'A confutation of convergent realism', *Philosophy of Science* **58**: 19–49.

Leplin, Jarrett (ed.) (1984). *Scientific Realism*. Berkeley & Los Angeles: University of California Press.

Linsky, Leonard (ed.) (1971). *Reference and Modality*. Oxford: Oxford University Press.

Luntley, Michael (1988). *Language, Logic and Experience: The Case for Anti-realism*. London: Duckworth.

Marcus, Ruth Barcan (1993). *Modalities: Philosophical Essays*. New York: Oxford University Press.

McCormick, Peter J. (ed.) (1996). *Starmaking: Realism, Anti-realism, and Irrealism*. Cambridge, MA: MIT Press.

McCulloch, Gregory (1995). *The Mind and its World*. London: Routledge.

McDowell, John (1994). *Mind and World*. Cambridge, MA: Harvard University Press.

McGilvray, James (1999). *Chomsky: Language, Mind, and Politics*. Cambridge: Polity Press.

McGinn, Colin (1999). *The Mysterious Flame: Conscious Minds in a Material World*. New York: Basic Books.

Norris, Christopher (2000). *Minding the Gap: Epistemology and Philosophy of Science in the Two Traditions*. Amherst, MA: University of Massachusetts Press.

——(2002a). *Hilary Putnam: Realism, Reason, and the Uses of Uncertainty*. Manchester: Manchester University Press.

——(2002b). *Truth Matters: Realism, Anti-realism and Response-Dependence*. Edinburgh: Edinburgh University Press.

Papineau, David (1993). *Philosophical Naturalism*. Oxford: Blackwell.

——(2002). *Thinking About Consciousness*. Oxford: Clarendon Press.

Paul, Ellen F., Fred D. Miller and Jeffrey Paul (eds) (1996). *The Communitarian Challenge to Liberalism*. Cambridge: Cambridge University Press.

Penrose, Roger (1995). *Shadows of the Mind: A Search for the Missing Science of Consciousness*. London: Vintage.

Psillos, Stathis (1999). *Scientific Realism: How Science Tracks Truth*. London: Routledge.

Putnam, Hilary (1967). 'The Innateness Hypothesis', *Synthèse* **17**: 12–22.

——(1975). *Mind, Language and Reality*. Cambridge: Cambridge University Press.

——(1975a). 'Is semantics possible?', in Putnam (1975). pp. 139–52.

——(1975b). 'Explanation and reference', in Putnam (1975). pp. 196–214.

——(1975c). 'The meaning of meaning', in Putnam (1975). pp. 215–72.

——(1975d). 'Language and reality', in Putnam (1975). pp. 272–90.

——(1983). *Realism and Reason*. Cambridge: Cambridge University Press.

——(1983a). 'There is at least one *a priori* truth', in Putnam (1983). pp. 98–114.

——(1988). *Representation and Reality*. Cambridge, MA: MIT Press.

Quine, W.V. (1961). 'Two dogmas of empiricism', in *From a Logical Point of View*, 2nd edn. Cambridge, MA: Harvard University Press. pp. 20–46.

——(1969). *Ontological Relativity and Other Essays*. New York: Columbia University Press.

Rasmussen, David (ed.) (1990). *Universalism versus Communitarianism: Contemporary Debates in Ethics*. Cambridge, MA: MIT Press.

Rorty, Richard (1989). *Contingency, Irony, and Solidarity*. Cambridge: Cambridge University Press.

——(1991). *Objectivity, Relativism, and Truth*. Cambridge: Cambridge University Press.

Russell, Bertrand (1905). 'On denoting', *Mind* **14**: 479–93.

Sampson, Geoffrey (1979). *Liberty and Language*. Oxford: Oxford University Press.

——(1989). 'Language acquisition: growth or learning?'. *Philosophical Papers* **18**(3): 203–40.

Schwartz, Stephen P. (ed.) (1977). *Naming, Necessity, and Natural Kinds*. Ithaca, N.Y.: Cornell University Press.

Shear, Jonathan (ed.) (1997). *Explaining Consciousness: The 'Hard Problem'*. Cambridge, MA: MIT Press.

Silverberg, Arnold (1998). 'Semantic externalism: a response to Chomsky', *Protosociology* **11**: 216–44.

Skinner, B.F. (1957). *Verbal Behavior*. Englewood Cliffs, N.J.: Prentice-Hall.

Soames, Scott (1999). *Understanding Truth*. Oxford: Oxford University Press.

Sperber, Dan and Deidre Wilson (1986). *Relevance: Communication and Cognition*. Oxford: Blackwell.

Strawson, P.F. (1950). 'On referring', *Mind* **59**: 320–44.

——(1966). *The Bounds of Sense: An Essay on Kant's Critique of Pure Reason*. London: Methuen.

Tennant, N. (1987). *Anti-realism and Logic*. Oxford: Clarendon Press.

Wiggins, David (1980). *Sameness and Substance*. Oxford: Blackwell.

Williams, Michael (1996). *Unnatural Doubts: Epistemological Realism and the Basis of Scepticism*. Princeton, N.J.: Princeton University Press.

Wright, Crispin (1987). *Realism, Meaning and Truth*. Oxford: Blackwell.

4
The Perceiver's Share (1): Realism, Scepticism, and Response-Dependence

I

There is a large recent literature on the topic of response-dependence, ranging over issues in ontology, epistemology, philosophy of mind, political theory, ethics, aesthetics, and various other branches of the social and human sciences. (See for instance Edwards 1992; Holton 1992; Johnston 1992, 1993; Pettit 1991, 1992, 1998a,b; Powell 1998; Wedgwood 1998; Wright 1988a, 1998.) Much of this literature is highly technical or concerned with intra-theoretical debates which can be of interest only on the shared premise that a response-dependent (or response-dispositional: henceforth interchangeably 'RD') approach is capable of yielding valid answers to a range of well-defined philosophic problems. My intention here is not so much to engage with these often quite arcane disputes but rather to ask, in a general way, whether that approach can indeed live up to the kinds of expectation placed upon it by some contributors to the current discussion. My answer will be a qualified 'no', but one that credits the theorists concerned with having raised a number of pertinent questions and having usefully clarified the terms of debate.

In brief, their claim is that it holds out the prospect of resolving the issue between realists and anti-realists, or those who maintain an objectivist (recognition-transcendent) concept of truth for any given area of discourse and, on the other hand, those who argue that truth cannot possibly transcend our best methods of proof or verification. Thus realists uphold an alethic conception wherein truth-values are fixed by the way things stand in reality, quite apart from our state of knowledge concerning them or even, at the limit, our utmost capacities of cognitive or rational grasp (Alston 1996; Katz 1998; Soames 1999). Anti-realists uphold an epistemic conception according to which truth-values – or values of 'warranted assertibility' – are assignable just to the extent that we possess some means of reliably finding them out (Dummett 1978, 1991a; Luntley 1988; Wright 1993). For the realist our statements are potential truth-bearers which either correspond or fail to correspond with objective truth-makers such as empirical facts, valid theorems, logical laws, mathematical verities, or real-world (past or present; maybe future) states of affairs. These latter hold good irrespective of whatever we happen to think or believe, and despite our no doubt limited range of perceptual, cognitive, or epistemic powers. For the anti-realist, this claim is strictly unintelligible since we cannot conceive of truth except on the basis of those various criteria – standards of proof or verification – through which we are enabled to acquire and to recognise the conditions of assertoric warrant. Thus where the realist considers it absurd (a flagrant instance of the epistemic fallacy) that truth should be thought of as in any way subject to the scope and limits of human knowledge, the anti-realist considers it equally absurd – a self-refuting argument if ever there was one – that we should claim to have cognisance of that which exceeds our capacities of epistemic grasp. To which the realist predictably responds that this is to mistake the whole issue since her case is *not* that we can somehow (impossibly) assign determinate truth-values to statements that cannot be verified or falsified but rather that such statements, so long as they are well formed, are necessarily *either* true *or* false depending on whether or not they correspond to states of affairs which happen to elude our best evidence or means of probative warrant. However this is just what anti-realists like Michael Dummett deny since on their account statements of the 'disputed class' (i.e., those lacking such warrant) must be treated as neither true nor false *so far as we can possibly know*, and hence as falling outside the domain of classical (bivalent) logic (Dummett 1978).

It is on these grounds that Dummett asserts – again quite absurdly, to the realist's way of thinking – that any 'gaps in our knowledge' concerning some particular area of discourse must also be construed as 'gaps in reality', or as marking the existence of an indeterminate realm that cannot decide the truth-value of our speculative statements or hypotheses. For the realist that realm is best conceived as a kind of *terra incognita*, a region of hitherto unexplored country which possesses the full range of objectively existent geographical features, but whose contours and landmarks do not yet feature on any reliable map. For the anti-realist – to pursue the metaphor – it is more like an imaginary country or a virtual-reality game which we are all too apt (in realist fashion) to endow with quasi-objective attributes that are merely the result of our projecting truth-values where no such values properly apply. Thus the anti-realist is happy enough to accept the exploration-metaphor just so long as its implications are held within bounds, that is, taken as a handy way of thinking about the various procedures by which we explore (say) the evidential sources for past events, or the significance for particle physics of observing tracks in a Wilson cloud-chamber, or the consequence of certain mathematical or logical theorems when drawn out through formalised methods of elaboration and proof. Where it becomes actively misleading – he will urge – is at the point where those procedures are construed as 'exploring' a domain of objective (recognition-transcendent) features which exist quite apart from our acquired knowledge of the landscape, that is say, our capacity for finding our way around and applying such know-how to the business of mapping any unfamiliar regions. For it then gives rise to the illusory idea that we can somehow advance intelligible truth-claims concerning matters that inherently transcend our recognitional capacities or acquired powers of perceptual-conceptual grasp.

Dummett is much drawn to an alternative metaphor, that of the artist's creative or imaginative way of exploring new worlds of possibility which cannot be thought of as existing 'out there' until someone happens to discover them, but which none the less exert certain limits and constraints on the process of artistic creation (Dummett 1978: xxv). This seems to fit best with Dummett's intuitionist approach to the philosophy of mathematics, that is, his idea that mathematical truths are not 'objective' in the sense of pre-existing and transcending our various methods or proof-procedures, but are rather discovered *in and through* the very act of creative-exploratory thought (Dummett 1977). On the face of it he is proposing nothing more than a generalised principle of tolerance that makes full allowance for the differing criteria that apply from one investigative context to another. To the extent that anti-realism has any 'programme', Dummett suggests, it should adopt a duly tentative approach and test its claim across a range of subject-areas (mathematics, the physical sciences, history, ethics, aesthetics, and so forth) in order to decide just where and how far that claim matches our best intuitions. If this were indeed how the programme worked out then the realist might willingly endorse it as a means of sharpening our sense of the distinction between areas of discourse where objective truth-values properly obtain and areas which seem better suited to appraisal in terms of epistemic warrant, rational consensus, or communal agreement according to the norms of this or that culture. However this is *not* how it works out in practice, as can readily be seen from Dummett's espousal of a strong intuitionist (or constructivist) approach to the philosophy of mathematics, and likewise from his various anti-realist pronouncements with regard to 'gaps' in historical reality or the error of supposing that bivalence holds for *any* statement of the 'disputed class'. What these passages bring out is the sheer impossibility – on Dummett's account – that we could ever be logically or metaphysically justified in taking truth to transcend the capacities of human knowledge or reason.

II

Response-dependence (RD) theory looks a lot better suited to respect this diversity of subject-areas and the corresponding range of appropriate criteria or truth-evaluative standards. Its two chief sources in the classical literature are Plato on the objectivity (or otherwise) of moral judgements and Locke on the epistemological status of 'secondary qualities' such as colour, taste, texture, or smell. In this section I shall be concerned mainly with the debate around Plato's *Euthyphro*, and in Section III with some issues that arise from the RD theorists' reading of Locke. However, as will soon become apparent, one problem with this whole line of approach is that while claiming to respect the different standards that apply to different areas of discourse – on a scale running from objective to subjective (radically response-dependent) criteria – it none the less exhibits a strong tendency to focus on just those instances that best support the RD position. That is to say, there is an inbuilt bias toward the epistemic (as opposed to the alethic or objectivist) conception of truth according to which truth-values cannot possibly transcend the limits of attainable 'best judgement' or optimised human response.

In the *Euthyphro* Plato raises the question: do the gods approve pious acts on account of their godlike (omniscient) capacity to track or detect moral virtue? Or is it not rather the case that the gods' approval is itself what constitutes the virtuous character of just those acts? (Plato 1977; also Allen 1970). On the first view – that of Socrates – moral judgements are accountable to standards of truth or falsehood that transcend our limited (human, all-too-human) capacities and which moreover determine the truth-conditions even for the kinds of verdict delivered by possessors of the highest moral authority. Thus the gods may always be right in such matters but only because they are sure to be right in so far as their divine intelligence precludes the possibility of error. On the second view (that of Euthyphro) the gods cannot possibly be wrong because they decide – by absolute fiat – what shall count as an instance of moral goodness or badness. From which it follows, transposing this argument into secular terms, that the ultimate authority in moral issues is best opinion (or optimised judgement) as represented by some given juridical body or accepted constitutional power.

No doubt there is a sense in which this whole debate might seem like a case of philosophical hair-splitting since the same acts will turn out pious (or impious) whether they possess that character intrinsically or in consequence of its being conferred through divine or idealised human approbation. However it becomes a genuine, non-trivial issue when raised in the context of current disputes between ethical realists and anti-realists, or those who maintain that moral values might always transcend the deliverance of best opinion by some such body as the US Supreme Court and those who hold, on the contrary, that best opinion necessarily – by very definition – constitutes the highest, the sole legitimate, or ultimate ground of appeal. Where the RD theorists claim to break new ground is by showing that this is a false dilemma and that one can have all the objectivity one needs through appealing to a suitably specified construal of what constitutes 'best opinion' in any given case. That is to say, if best opinion (or optimal response) is defined with sufficient care and with due regard to the various factors that make up an ethically valid judgement then there is simply no need for realists to worry about the notional gap between moral truth and truth according to the standards or criteria of those best qualified to judge. What is required in order to resolve this dilemma is a quantified biconditional of the form (1): 'any action x is pious, good, worthy of moral approbation (etc.) if and only if that action is such as to elicit an approving response on the part of moral agents fully apprised of the relevant facts and circumstances and possessing an adequate discriminative power to arrive at the right (ethically justified) verdict'. Or again (2): 'any social or political system can lay valid claim to justice if and only if its virtues are such as to elicit the approval of those whose authority derives from their being best placed to adjudicate that claim from a standpoint informed by all the relevant moral, social, and political considerations'.

Of course it might be said that this amounts to no more than a circular argument which identifies truth, goodness, or justice with what counts as such by very definition and therefore cannot fail to satisfy the relevant criteria. Hence the concern of some RD theorists – Crispin Wright among them – to head off such criticism by requiring that those criteria be specified in substantive, that is, non-circular terms and not as just a matter of 'whatever it takes' (or 'fill in as appropriate') for the judgement to be deemed valid (Wright 1988b; also Johnston 1989). However it is far from clear that this non-triviality condition can be met without going so far in a realist direction as to render the RD case pretty much redundant. That is to say, if the criteria are adequately specified so as to avoid the circularity charge then they would have to include a whole range of factors such as those instanced in (1) and (2) above, factors that are taken as defining what shall count as an apt, fitting, morally judicious, or duly authorised response but which have to be based on a realist assessment of some given ethical predicament or socio-political situation. So, for instance, we might claim that the statement 'Slavery is wrong', uttered by an abolitionist in antebellum America, was a justified (morally authoritative) statement in so far as it took account of certain salient truths concerning the extent of human suffering, racial persecution, blighted lives, oppressive legal practices, selective definition of 'human rights', and so forth, which afforded the utterer adequate factual and moral-evaluative grounds for reaching that particular verdict. Or again, in the case of pre-1990 South Africa, anyone who offered the judgement '*Apartheid* is wrong' would implicitly be putting that claim forward for assessment in the context of known or documented facts with regard to that system and its social, political, and human consequences. Thus the RD thesis – as expressed in the standard quantified-biconditional form – can be saved from manifest triviality or circular argument only in so far as the 'substantive' conditions invoked by Wright and others are specified in terms that amount to an endorsement of the realist case and which thereby deprive the thesis itself of any genuine (substantive) content.

The alternative is to take a stronger, less concessionary RD line and maintain – with Euthyphro – that optimal response or best opinion constitute the ultimate ground of appeal and must hence be thought to determine – rather than to 'track' or 'detect' – the class of pious acts, virtuous dispositions, or just and equitable socio-political arrangements. However, this alternative runs straight into the opposite problem, namely that it cannot take adequate account of those real-world constraints upon moral judgement which enable us to say, without undue arrogance, that 'best opinion' may sometimes be wrong, as for instance when the practice of slavery was widely thought to involve no conflict with principles laid down in the Bill of Rights, or when *Apartheid* was enshrined in numerous provisions of South African law (see Dyzenhaus 1991, 1998). The main trouble with this line of thought is that it tends very often to equivocate on two senses of the phrase 'best opinion', switching between them as happens to suit the immediate context of argument. Thus one works out as an implicit endorsement of whatever the best, that is, the most highly placed or widely respected judges may happen to deem right, just, or constitutional, while the other defers to what *would* ideally or counterfactually be the case if all the evidence were in and if they exercised a sovereign (morally infallible) power of discriminating right from wrong. Both conceptions are Euthyphronic – though in differing degrees – since both involve the normative appeal to human judgement (or response) as the final arbiter in all such matters. That is to say, even the second conception stops short of taking the ethical-realist view that what constitutes the judges' infallible knack of always coming up with the right verdict is their capacity to 'track' or 'detect' moral virtue whenever they encounter an instance of it. Where they differ is on the issue as to whether best opinion should be taken as vested in some currently accredited body – such as the US Supreme Court – with the presumed constitutional authority to make just decisions or whether there is always an appeal open to some higher standard of natural justice which might – perhaps in the wisdom of enlightened retrospect – be thought to render those decisions unjust or invalid (Beard 1962; Kurland [ed.] 1965; Pacelle 2001).

What distinguishes these two positions is the meaning they assign to the term 'constitutional' and its various cognates. Thus 'best opinion' may be taken to *constitute* moral or juridical authority in the strong-RD sense that it determines what shall count as a valid judgement and hence precludes any possible (legitimate) appeal to standards, values, or principles that transcend such *de facto* 'constitutional' warrant. Or again, 'best opinion' may taken as referring to the kinds of judgement or moral reasoning that *would* counterfactually prevail among respondents (e.g., Supreme Court judges) possessed of all the relevant evidence and capable of reaching an enlightened verdict on matters of shared, community-wide ethical and socio-political concern. Clearly there is a genuine distinction here, one that in effect marks the difference between a pragmatist conception of truth, justice and right as values that consensually count as such according to some given set of beliefs and an optimised conception which in principle allows for those beliefs to be challenged or struck down in response to some future-possible advance in our powers of discriminative judgement. However – to repeat – both arguments stop short of granting the ethical-realist case that the truth-value of *any* such judgement may transcend not only our present-best responses (or those vested in some highest constitutional authority) but also – conceivably – the kinds of response that would issue from human valuers optimally placed to survey, comprehend, and adjudicate the full range of evidence. Unless, that is, 'best opinion' is so defined as to make it a sheerly tautological truth that their deliverances *must* coincide with whatever would pass the optimality-test. Such would indeed be the case with Plato's omniscient or godlike intelligences, those concerning whom it makes no difference whether their judgements are infallibly spot-on in virtue of their superhuman tracking ability or whether it is their own divine edict that determines (or constitutes) values of right and wrong.

However this Euthyphronist way of framing the issue is one that should afford little comfort to the RD theorist who is concerned, after all, with the scope and capacities of *human* evaluative response and whose case can scarcely be strengthened by an argument based on circular reasoning or the appeal to some ultimate (purely notional) source of authority. In Plato the question is squarely posed as a matter of realist *versus* anti-realist conceptions of moral good, with the gods brought in as a convenient (quasi-allegorical) means of making the point. Thus it is clear enough that when Socrates defends a realist conception of ethical values, as against Euthyphro's RD account, he does so without any ultimate appeal to divine sanction or warrant, and more with a view to defending their objective (rather than judgement-relative) status. However this point tends to get lost in recent discussions of the issue where the choice falls out between two possible construals of the RD thesis, on the one hand a version that equates best opinion with whatever consensually counts as such, and on the other a version which avoids that outcome by deferring to whatever it would notionally take for human judgements to meet the required standard. That is to say, this approach manifests an inbuilt bias against the ethical-realist case that truth in such matters has to do with the way things actually stand with respect to the measure of weal or woe – whether human, non-human animal, or environmental – that results from our acting on this or that set of moral-evaluative precepts. As Peter Railton puts it: '[w]hat matters [in the moral case] is not who is making the judgement, but *of whom* the judgement is being made, which can be constant across differences in observers' (Railton 1998: 77). And again, 'our vocabulary of intrinsic value is primarily geared to the task of asking what to seek and what to avoid, depending on whether it would be (in some sense) a positive or negative thing intrinsically to lead a given life' (Railton 1998: 77). Thus the problem with response-dispositional accounts – at any rate from a realist viewpoint – is their failure to acknowledge the standing possibility of widespread error in judgement, whether as concerns some *de facto* consensus of 'best opinion' or even (at the limit) some optimised state of human moral insight and wisdom.

This problem is posed most sharply in the case of our judgements with regard to issues of non-human animal welfare and matters of environmental concern where any appeal to *human* 'best opinion' will be apt to strike the realist as anthropocentric and hence as missing the ethical point in certain crucial respects. After all, as Railton remarks, '[h]uman approbation of its torment would not in the least improve the experience of a dog being kicked or a horse being whipped. . . . Rather, it is the intrinsically unliked character of the torment such conduct would cause its recipients – a torment which is unaffected by our attitude – that makes the behaviour wrong' (Railton 1998: 82). No doubt there is an ambiguity here as to just what is meant by the 'intrinsically unliked' character of cruelty to animals, that is to say, whether the property is 'intrinsic' to the kinds of conduct concerned (those that involve the wanton infliction of suffering on sentient creatures) or whether it is 'intrinsic' to the kinds of response (disapproval, revulsion, moral condemnation) that do or should accompany our witnessing such behaviour. That Railton is here writing specifically in the context of RD debate – albeit from a largely dissenting (ethical-realist) standpoint – is perhaps one reason why his phraseology lets in this apparent passing concession to a response-dispositional approach. However it is clear from his whole line of argument that he regards that approach as unduly anthropocentric and as failing to acknowledge the prior claim of facts about (e.g.) animal suffering or environmental degradation that might quite conceivably elude the best opinion of well-placed (even maximally sensitive) human respondents. In other words there is no version of the RD case, however tuned up to compliance with standards of idealised ethical warrant, that can adequately answer the realist charge of its inability to cope with cases like this.

Moreover the argument transposes directly into an ethico-political context, as can be seen from debates about the moral authority of certain (especially US) constitutional powers, or the issue as to whether such powers may be subject to abrogation if they contravene other, more basic principles of right or natural justice. This question tends to be aired most often at times of political crisis, moral uncertainty, or widespread disagreement over issues – such as abortion or capital punishment – when Supreme Court edicts can effectively determine what shall count (constitutionally speaking) as an ultimate, consensually binding expression of authorised best judgement. Those citizens who dissent from the prevailing view must find themselves questioning not only the particular verdict arrived at through the process of judicial review – say the moral justifiability of capital punishment or more stringent anti-abortion laws – but also the Court's constitutional authority to speak the last word in such matters. Here again, as in the case of cruelty to animals, argument will turn on the intrinsic character of certain practices or provisions, among them the barbarous practice (as some would have it) of inflicting cruel and inhumane treatment on death-row prisoners, or the infringement of a woman's natural right to exercise choice in a matter of uniquely intimate bodily and psychological concern. Of course there are contrary arguments in each case which might also claim – in a more liberal climate where Supreme Court judgements were going the opposite way – that mere 'best opinion' was no adequate guide to morals and that natural justice offered good grounds for rejecting the abolitionist stance on capital punishment or the pro-choice stance on abortion. However this would still involve a realist appeal to certain putative truths about, for instance, the deterrent effects of capital punishment, the intrinsic justice of taking a life for a life, or the status of the human embryo at this or that stage in its development. That is to say, it would share at least this much common ground with the opposing liberal viewpoint, namely the belief that 'best opinion' even when backed by the highest constitutional authority may sometimes be morally in the wrong and hence such as to justify rejection on grounds of ethical or socio-political conscience.

I should add that this is *not* to derive any version of the ethical-relativist view according to which such issues are either too 'deep' (i.e., too metaphysically loaded) to permit of rational adjudication, or so much a matter of shifting, culturally determined beliefs and values that they cannot be subject to any kind of comparative (let alone decisive) moral assessment. It seems to me, on the contrary, that a realist approach to the issue concerning capital punishment is one that will lead any morally responsive and right-thinking assessor to the conclusion that this practice is indeed cruel and inhumane. In which case any constitutional body – like the US Supreme Court in recent years – that sanctions and promotes that practice is thereby contravening certain basic principles of natural justice and hence undermining its own claim to moral and juridical authority. No doubt there are phrases in this previous sentence ('it seems to me', 'morally responsive', 'right-thinking') which might well seem to let go the case for ethical realism and allow for a construal along Euthyphronist or best-opinion lines. Thus it is always open to the RD theorist or the committed constitutionalist to claim that no matter how fallible the record up to now still there is a further appeal to be made, that is, an appeal to those opinions or judgements that *would* (counterfactually) prevail just so long as all respondents – Supreme Court justices or concerned citizens – were optimally placed to survey and evaluate the full range of evidence. But again, this strategy avoids endorsing a *de facto* consensualist theory of moral truth only through the somewhat desperate recourse to an open-ended, that is, 'whatever-it-takes' conditional clause, or a circular (trivial) equation between 'truth' and what must (by very definition) count as such among those best qualified to judge. So the realist point is that this kind of reasoning gets the matter back-to-front and that only by accepting the existence of objective (non-judgement-relative) truths can ethical discourse respect the claims of natural justice or a due regard for interests and priorities that might lie beyond our powers of evaluative grasp.

This issue is posed with particular force if one considers the case of a Supreme Court ruling – like that handed down in the 2001 US election – which declares in favour of a manifestly flawed vote-counting method whose result is to disenfranchise portions of the electorate in a key marginal state, and thus to ensure the return to office of an unrepresentative government. On the 'strong' constitutionalist view – implicitly subscribed to by many RD theorists – there is no appeal beyond the deliverance of 'best opinion' enshrined in that Supreme Court verdict, issuing as it does from the highest juridical authority and possessing as it does the presumed mandate of due electoral process. However, the ethical realist will argue, this mandate and that authority can be lost if the Court is so packed with partisan judges as to lay itself open to the charge of complicity with vested interests of precisely the kind that worked to secure the 'election' of President George W. Bush. What sustains such a charge is again the appeal to certain standards of natural justice, in this case standards having to do with the self-avowed values of a democratic system supposedly exempt from such distorting pressures and influences. The same argument applies, as I have said, to earlier cases where judicial 'best opinion' may be thought to have gone lamentably wrong, as for instance at the time when slavery was thought to entail no infringement of basic (constitutionally enshrined) human rights, or when it seemed self-evident to reason that women should not be entitled to vote. Here again it is hard to see how a RD approach – one that takes best opinion to constitute the highest court of appeal – can yield any adequate philosophical account of why those attitudes should strike us now as involving a failure to respect certain elementary precepts of natural justice.

No doubt it may be said, in defence of that approach, that the standards we apply in reaching such a verdict are themselves unavoidably response-dependent, or the result of our having since then acquired a different (presumptively more liberal, inclusive, or humanitarian) capacity of moral judgement. Nor should this argument be lightly dismissed, given the kinds of objection most often brought against it, whether from a cultural-relativist standpoint that rejects the very notion of moral progress as strictly incoherent, or on the typically postmodernist sceptical grounds that history has delivered a standing rebuke to 'enlightenment' notions of reason, truth, and justice (Lyotard 1984; also Norris 1993). After all, there is a manifest *non sequitur* involved in the notion that wars, sectarian strife, political oppression and other such continuing large-scale evidence of man's inhumanity to man should somehow be thought to invalidate our judgement that in certain areas – like those mentioned above – some cultures have managed to achieve some degree of moral and socio-political progress. Thomas Spragens puts the opposite case in his book *The Irony of Liberal Reason* where he acknowledges the prejudicial blind spots that have marked every stage of liberal thinking to date, but also makes the point that this tradition incorporates a way of reflecting critically on its own less-than-perfect record which cannot be found in other, more conservative or complacent habits of thought (Spragens 1981). Thus liberalism at least has the virtue of not claiming the last word in matters of moral conscience, and of holding open the constant possibility of progress beyond whatever counts as the present-best state of informed or enlightened opinion. In this respect the 'irony' of liberal reason – as Spragens construes it – is not to be confused with the outlook of 'liberal ironism' recommended by Richard Rorty, one that subscribes to the values of 'North Atlantic bourgeois postmodern liberal pragmatist' culture, and which rejects any notion of holding them answerable to standards that might not be acknowledged by members of that same community (Rorty 1989). Where the irony comes in, on Rorty's account, is through the modest proposal that creative individuals (philosophers hopefully among them) do best – or at any rate do least harm – when they cultivate the private 'self-fashioning' virtues and resist the temptation to lay down precepts for the wider (let alone universal) human good. Nothing could be further from the liberal tradition of thinkers – from Mill to Habermas and Rawls – who, whatever their differences of ethico-political standpoint, have taken it as self-evident that any progress achieved in our moral sentiments must go along with a corresponding progress in the public sphere of participant debate on matters of shared concern. (See for instance Calder, Garrett and Shannon [eds] 2000; Evans [ed.] 2001.) So there is a case to be made that 'best opinion' can transcend any merely *de facto* consensus of belief and, moreover, that a suitably specified (optimised) response-dispositional account can allow for advances in moral understanding which find no place in the consensualist approach adopted by thinkers like Rorty.

All the same, as I have argued, this RD account falls short in one crucial respect, namely its refusal – at the limit – to acknowledge the existence of moral truths that transcend not only the judgemental capacities of those presumed to know best but also the deliverance of verdicts indexed to an optimal conception of human judgement at the end of moral enquiry. For if it is not to invite the triviality charge – 'best opinion' = 'whatever it takes for judgements to come out morally right' – then this approach falls prey to the equally damaging criticism that it makes no allowance for the inherent fallibility of even the best, that is, the most sensitive and highly developed powers of human response. Hence – to repeat – the moral realist's case that what makes our judgements right or wrong is in no way a matter of their happening to meet the standards, however specified, of those presumptively best fitted (or constitutionally authorised) to judge. Rather it is a question of whether we are responsive to just those morally salient aspects of real-world flourishing or suffering which constitute the intrinsic goodness or badness of some given situation. Thus the wrong that is done through our wantonly inflicting pain on animals would still be a wrong even if – through some large-scale mutation in our moral sensibilities – it should come to be thought of as perfectly acceptable (indeed meritorious) by every human being on the planet (Railton 1998). Or again, the advance from widespread endorsement to near-universal disapprobation of slavery would still have marked a genuine advance even if – through some similar moral catastrophe – everyone were suddenly to take the view that abolition had itself been a retrograde step and that natural justice allowed (even required) the revival of that excellent practice. Such thought-experiments may seem bizarre but they serve to bring out what is crucially lacking in the appeal to best opinion – or optimal response – as a baseline criterion of rightness in moral judgement.

III

It is the same problem that typically emerges when RD theorists engage with epistemological issues of truth, knowledge, and evidence. Most often they adopt this approach in the hope of steering an alternative path between, on the one hand, an outlook of alethic realism committed to the existence of objective or verification-transcendent truths and, on the other, a range of subjectivist, projectivist, or anti-realist positions which are firmly committed to denying that claim. In this context debate has very often focused on Locke's conception of 'secondary qualities' such as colour, taste, texture, or odour. These latter are taken as paradigm cases for a response-dispositional approach since they cannot be thought of as existing 'out there' among the features of an objective, mind-independent reality but rather involve an intrinsic refer-ence to the way that we normally or typically perceive them under certain specifiable ambient conditions. Thus, for Locke, they contrast with 'primary qualities' such as shape or extension which depend not at all on our innate range of perceptual powers or capacities, and must therefore be conceived as objectively existent so far as we can possibly know. As he puts it in a much-cited passage:

[t]he ideas of primary qualities of bodies are resemblances of them, and their patterns do really exist in the bodies themselves, but the ideas pro-duced in us by these secondary qualities have no resemblance of them at all. There is nothing like our ideas existing in the bodies themselves. They are, in the bodies we denominate from them, only a power to produce those sensations in us; and what is sweet, blue, or warm in idea is but the certain bulk, figure, and motion of the insensible parts, in the bodies themselves, which we call so. (Locke 1969, Book II, Ch. 8, Sect. 15: 69)

Where the RD approach seeks to improve upon Locke's somewhat vague formulation is by providing a more detailed, carefully specified account of the various conditions that have to be met for a perceptual response to count as normal, that is, for judgements such as 'that looks red', 'this tastes sweet', 'that is an acrid smell', and so forth, to fall within the range of duly authorised (non-deviant) assertions. This can be done most effectively – so the argument goes – by constructing a quantified biconditional of the type first proposed by Mark Johnston, namely: '[i]f the concept associated with the predicate "is C" is a concept interdependent with or dependent upon concepts of certain subjects' responses under certain conditions, then something of the following form will hold *a priori*: x is C iff in conditions K, Ss are disposed to produce x-directed response R (or: x is such as to produce R in Ss under conditions K)' (Johnston 1989: 141). Thus the claim is that an RD account can point a way beyond the quarrel between realists and anti-realists by laying down the terms on which human perceptual responses can be factored into the equation without giving up the normative appeal to standards of correctness or failing to allow for the possibility of error.

Where it needs filling out most crucially – the theorists agree – is with respect to those ambient conditions K which ensure that subjects are optimally placed to deliver the right sorts of judgement and also with respect to those subjects' capacities of perceptual-cognitive processing. That is to say, this requires (1) that the conditions be specified so as to exclude distorting factors, masking effects, illusory appearances, and so forth, and (2) that the subjects are themselves not prone to perceptual aberrations such as colour-blindness or impaired (non-standard or deviant) sensory response. These requirements can be met, so it is claimed, by building in a range of normative criteria on the right-hand side of the quantified biconditional which specify just those physical conditions under which suitably equipped subjects can reliably, predictably, or safely be supposed to produce accurate responses. Thus, in the case of colour-perception, the relevant clause might run: 'when viewed by normal observers in normal lighting conditions', or again, more specifically: 'when viewed by such observers at midday in moderately cloudy (non-dazzling) conditions and with no proximal light-source which might create visually distorting interference-effects'. The RD literature contains quite a number of ingenious counter-examples, most of them involving variations on the latter theme which purport to show how subjects confronted with some elaborate *trompe l'oeil* set-up can indeed be expected to misidentify colours *even though* their perceptual responses are perfectly in order and the set-up (apparently) not such as to fall outside the specified range of normative criteria. To which, predictably, the RD theorists reply by extending or refining those criteria so as to exclude such counter-examples from the relevant comparison-class, or to count them among the kinds of case ruled out on a more adequate specification (Johnston 1992, 1993).

I shall not here go into the details of this often intriguing but highly specialised debate. Sufficient to say that the RD approach takes the instance of colour – or other such Lockean 'secondary qualities' – as a basis for arguing that realists get it wrong (and box themselves into a sceptical corner) when they maintain an objectivist or alethic conception of truth that places it, in principle, beyond our utmost epistemic reach. Rather they should adopt a more flexible, pluralist conception that acknowledges the variety of truth-conditions (or conditions of warranted assertibility) which properly apply to different areas of discourse, from mathematics, physics and the natural sciences to ethics, politics, social theory, and aesthetics (see especially Wright 1999). However, this pluralism often tends to reveal a marked anti-realist bias which results from its predisposition toward an RD account and from the inbuilt tendency of any such account to privilege those areas that best lend themselves to treatment in just such terms. Thus Wright puts forward a number of criteria – among them 'superassertibility' and 'cognitive command' – that would (supposedly) accommodate the realist case with regard to certain such areas while avoiding what he takes to be the problems with any outright commitment to 'metaphysical' (i.e., alethic or objectivist) realism. A statement may be counted as superassertible 'if and only if it is, or can be, warranted and some warrant for it would survive arbitrarily close scrutiny of its pedigree and arbitrarily extensive increments to or other forms of improvement of our information' (Wright 1992: 48). That is to say, its truth (or assertoric warrant) may go beyond anything knowable on the basis of our existing proof procedures, evidential sources, or current-best means of ascertainment. All the same – as emerges very clearly from Wright's phrasing – this is still an epistemic, rather than an alethic conception of truth-values, one that makes truth dependent *at the limit* on our capacity to gain knowledge of it, even if through 'arbitrarily extensive' advances in the range of investigative methods or techniques through which such know-ledge might ultimately be acquired. In other words it is a conception of idealised epistemic warrant which stops just short (though by a crucial distance) of conceding any version of the realist case for the existence of objective, recognition-transcendent truths. This point comes out with particular (though perhaps unintended) force when Wright specifies that '[s]uper assertibility . . . is, in a natural sense, an *internal* property of the statements of a discourse – a projection, merely, of the standards, whatever they are, which actually inform assertions within the discourse' (Wright 1992: 61). And again, more explicitly: '[i]t supplies no external norm – in a way that truth is classically supposed to do – against which the internal standards might *sub specie Dei* themselves be measured, and might rate as adequate or inadequate' (p. 61).

This may remind us of the current RD debate about Plato's *Euthyphro*, involving as it does the idea of a choice between realism conceived as a godlike claim to omniscience in matters of moral understanding and response-dependence as a sensible accommodation to the scope and limits of human ethical judgement. What is ruled out by this pre-emptive *tertium non datur* is the realist argument that ethical values are *neither* 'recognition-transcendent' in the sense of surpassing any mundane reference to human needs, interests, or priorities, nor reducible to the deliverance of 'best opinion' among those presumptively best qualified to judge. Rather they are a matter of the weal or woe enjoyed or suffered by those – so to speak – on the receiving end of the actions, policies, or decision-procedures adopted by agents with the power to determine the outcome in any given case. Thus, as Railton puts it, '[w]hat matters is not who is making the judgement, but *of whom* the judgement is being made, which can be constant across differences in observers' (Railton 1998: 77; see also Brink 1989; Haldane and Wright [eds] 1993; Sayre-McCord [ed.] 1988). That is to say, what counts in any adequate moral reckoning is *not* the fact that it squares with best opinion – however defined – but the extent to which it captures certain salient truths about the welfare or otherwise of sentient creatures with a presumed capacity for experiencing pleasure or pain, fulfilment or non-fulfilment of their instincts, desires, life-opportunities, natural (unthwarted) social inclinations, and so forth. No doubt it can be said that this is still a 'RD' approach in so far as it accords priority to certain normative conditions, that is, those that are taken to characterise the typical response of humans (or non-human animals) when placed in some given situation or exposed to some given range of beneficial or maleficent factors that impinge on their own life-experience. However it differs crucially from the standard RD account in adopting what I have called the 'receiving-end' view, or in attaching primary significance to *their* responses rather than to *our* (no matter how optimised) powers of responsive or moral-evaluative judgement. In this respect Jeremy Bentham got the emphasis right when he declared, concerning animals, that we should ask not so much 'Can they speak?' or 'Can they reason?', but rather 'Can they suffer?' (Bentham 1823: 283).

Thus the trouble with an RD approach to ethical issues is that it tends always to shift the emphasis from considerations of right and wrong construed in such realist terms to considerations of what best fits with our own repertoire of consensual, normalised, or idealised moral responses. To this extent it manifests the same bias that typifies RD discussions of epistemology and the role of 'best opinion' as a mediating term between outright 'metaphysical' (alethic or objectivist) realism and various kinds of internalist, projectivist, or discourse-relativist argument. Such – to repeat – is Wright's idea of 'superassertibility', proposed as a means of avoiding any recourse to merely *de facto* or consensual standards of evidential warrant, but also quite explicitly rejecting the idea of certain truths as perhaps – for all that we can know – transcending the limits of human cognitive grasp. After all, as Wright says, this is 'an *internal* property of the statements of a discourse – a projection, merely, of the standards, whatever they are, which actually inform assertions within the discourse' (Wright 1992: 61). In which case, surely, he might as well concede that what makes a statement 'superassertible' is nothing more than what makes it assertible according to the best opinion of those who are willing to 'project' in well-established ways from the standards of evidence currently prevailing within this or that discourse. Thus it goes no way toward meeting the realist objection that the truth-value of certain statements (like 'Goldbach's Conjecture is true' or 'There exists a duplicate solar system in some radio-telescopically inaccessible region of the expanding universe') must be taken as fixed quite independently of us and our limited epistemic resources.[1]

So likewise with Wright's somewhat stronger notion of 'Cognitive Command', intended to head off realist objections – especially with regard to areas of discourse where they possess the strongest intuitive appeal – but in the end turning out to support what amounts to an idealised epistemic construal. 'When a discourse exhibits Cognitive Command', Wright suggests, 'any difference of opinion will be such that there are considerations quite independent of the conflict which, if known about, would mandate withdrawal of one (or both) of the contending views' (Wright 1992: 103). One could spend a lot of time analysing the way that this sentence swings back and forth between a quasi-objectivist appeal to 'considerations' that would (counter-factually) decide the issue if all the evidence were in, and an optimised RD approach according to which such truths would *even at the limit* depend on their somehow being 'known about' or entering our range of relevant, humanly recognisable 'considerations'. What is clear at any rate is the impossibility of keeping both options in play, that is to say, of maintaining the qualified RD thesis that truth-values are *ultimately* dependent on our best knowledge, optimal judgement, most advanced proof-procedures, most refined investigative techniques, and so forth, while none the less maintaining that truth might conceivably transcend those same epistemic standards. Wright puts the case that we can perfectly well avoid this pseudo-dilemma if we just accept that different 'areas of discourse' require different standards or criteria of truth. Thus some such areas – like mathematics or the physical sciences – will seem best suited to a realist (all-but-objectivist) conception where truth-values are minimally constrained by standards of epistemic or assertoric warrant. Elsewhere, as for instance with our savouring of jokes or comic situations, objectivism seems simply out of the question since responses vary so widely across cultures, generations, classes, genders, or individual temperaments. Thus the best we can have is a loose appeal to localised and period-specific communal norms which specify what counts as a fairly typical response among fairly representative sample groups. However in that case the RD quantified biconditional can amount to no more than a trivial statement to the effect that 'joke x or situation y is funny, comical, mildly amusing (or whatever) just on condition that it is apt to evoke such responses among those whose comic sensibility approximates to the relevant group norm'.

Thus the problem here is just the opposite of that which RD theorists confront in the case of statements like those about the truth of Goldbach's Conjecture or the duplicate (epistemically inaccessible) solar system. Where comedy is response-dependent to a degree which empties the biconditional of any substantive (i.e., non-trivial) content, well-formed mathematical and astronomical statements have a truth-value that is entirely independent of our knowledge or beliefs concerning them, and which thus leaves the biconditional devoid of conceptual or explanatory purchase. It seems to me that these discussions have been regularly sidetracked by the prominence accorded to Lockean 'secondary qualities' as a paradigm instance for the kind of approach that would seek to resolve or overcome the dispute between realists and anti-realists. This is not to deny that some protagonists, Wright among them, have entered certain explicit reservations with regard to any overly direct analogy between the case of colour-perception and the cases of moral, mathematical, and other kinds of judgement (Wright 1988). All the same there is a constant bias toward the idea that secondary qualities provide at very least a useful and constructive *via media*, that is, an approach that holds out the prospect of talking the objectivist down from the heights of 'metaphysical' delusion while talking the relativist or subjectivist around from their likewise untenable position. Moreover (as we shall see in Section IV) this approach very often works out in practice as a tendency to treat certain areas of discourse – such as mathematics – which the realist would regard as prime candidates for ascription of objective truth-values in terms that render them more amenable to a qualified RD construal.

Elsewhere it appears to have a contrary intent, that is, to oppose various kinds of projectivist or anti-realist thinking with regard to areas that might seem *prima facie* well suited to just such treatment. Thus '[a]t first approximation', according to Wright, 'comic discourse is disciplined by the objective of irreproachability in the light of a community of comic sensibility' (Wright 1992: 106). However this apparent reversal of emphasis – the claim to establish relatively strong normative criteria for modes of response that might otherwise be thought irreducibly culture-specific or idiosyncratic – is undercut by Wright's rather shifty choices of phrasing. After all, this claim holds only 'at first approximation', and the appeal to communal warrant goes against any notion that comic responses might indeed be 'disciplined' by standards beyond or above those of localised agreement in judgement. Moreover, the idea that 'irreproachability' is the 'objective' of comic discourse in no way sanctions any realist claim – implausible enough in this context – that the standards concerned might be 'objective' in a stronger sense, for all that Wright's language tends to convey some such misleading impression. So this approach in the end does little to shake our standing intuition that what different people (or small-scale communities) happen to find amusing is response-dependent to such a degree that it gives no hold for a substantively specified RD biconditional, that is to say, for a filling-out of the normative criteria that would count some responses apt or fitting and others deviant in this or that respect. Also – as I have argued at length elsewhere – the ambiguity in Wright's treatment of comic discourse can likewise be seen to affect his thinking when it comes to matters of moral-evaluative judgement

(Norris 2002). For there is an easy slide from the 'strong' RD approach which defends a relatively sturdy (short of objectivist) conception of moral values to the 'weak' version that treats such values as bearing comparison with other, more culturally variable standards of good taste or refined sensibility in matters of social etiquette.

Nor is this surprising, given that – for instance – our judgements as to what counts as a fit subject for jokes will sometimes be affected by our moral judgement that certain topics are definitely off-bounds, while others tread a fine line in this respect and may be acceptable when told by certain people in certain kinds of company. Thus it is a matter of fairly common experience – not only among readers of Henry James – that the distinction between moral and 'good-taste' criteria is often very hard to draw and, in certain contexts, ethically beside the point. Such is famously the case with Jewish jokes as told by Jewish or non-Jewish jokesters, or with the current generation of tough-minded 'topical' comedians who constantly risk causing offence if they overstep the mark of acceptability with regard to the kinds of topic they exploit, their own (e.g.) ethnic or gender status, and the per-ceived make-up of their audience on some particular occasion of delivery. To this extent there will often be situations where it is neither desirable nor (ultimately) possible to draw any clear line between issues of moral or political conscience and issues of good taste. However it does become a problem if we take it that *all* such values are in some degree response-dependent, so that any distinction must have to do with the scope they offer for appeals to 'best opinion', the latter presumed to carry more authority or pertinence in moral issues than in matters of social tact. For if the relevant criteria are specified in RD rather than 'receiving-end' terms, then the kinds of response which lay claim to approval will always have reference to what counts *for us* – or some optimally specified version of ourselves – as good or acceptable behaviour. And in so far as this approach tends to play down the element of objectivity in moral judgement, that is to say, its responsibility to interests and values not (or not necessarily) our own, it will also tend to blur the distinction between moral judgements and judgements on grounds of tact, good taste, or social etiquette. What is missing is precisely the additional constraint that comes of our acknowledging the limits of 'best opinion' and the existence of a moral value-sphere which includes – among other things – the absolute wrongness of certain kinds of behaviour even if such behav-iour should suddenly gain universal human recognition as perfectly right and proper.

It seems to me that this problem with the RD approach to moral issues results very often from the privilege it grants to the instance of Lockean 'secondary qualities' as a touchstone for discussion in other fields. According to Wright, 'when the element of subjectivity is properly located, it poses no threat to the objectivity of secondary quality ascription, or to the idea that an object's secondary qualities constitute material for cognition, in a proper sense of that term' (Wright 1988b: 2). So by transposing Locke's proto-RD account of qualities like colour to the case of moral values we can find a way beyond the sterile debate between ethical realists on the one hand and projectivists, subjectivists, and anti-realists on the other. Wright has certain worries about this line of argument, among them the likely objection that it leaves insufficient room for the exercise of *responsible* moral judgement by underrating the distinctive kind of objectivity involved in ethical choice, and by fixing its sights too rigidly on the model of colour-perception and other such perceptual-epistemic modes of response. All the same – despite these misgivings – he thinks it a useful analogy and one that promises to break the hold of that vexing pseudo-dilemma. Yet Wright's sanguine conclusion in this regard is not such as would carry conviction with the ethical realist who requires something more than a compromise solution along vaguely analogical lines. Here again Railton pinpoints the problem when he remarks that, 'in thinking about value, it is altogether too easy to project, conflating the familiar and conventional with the natural and inevitable' (Railton 1998: 84). And again: '[o]ne could write a pocket history of progress in moral sensibility in terms of the successive unmasking of such conflations – with respect to slavery, inherited rule, the status of women, and the borders of tribe, "people", or nation' (Railton 1998: 84). That is to say, such 'unmaskings' can be understood only on condition that judgement is answerable to standards that require the transcendence of any rigidly projected moral response. Only thus can one make sense of the claim that advances in moral sensibility occur through a willingness to think and reason beyond the deliverance of accredited best opinion. Otherwise – if moral judgements were 'fixed' (like responses to Lockean secondary qualities) by the way that we normally tend to respond when exposed to this or that stimulus – then there could be no accounting for moral progress except on a Rortian strong-descriptivist account which views them as mere periodic shifts in our choice of preferential vocabulary (Rorty 1989, 1991).

This is why the RD approach swings across so readily from a quasi-realist theory of moral response that treats it by analogy with normalised colour-perceptions to a theory which allows such leeway for variant responses that moral judgement shades off imperceptibly into nuances of good taste. It is the same drastic dichotomy that Rorty falls into when he talks, on the one hand, in a realist mode about 'hard' causal impacts or sensory stimuli that are fully 'objective' since under no description, while on the other insisting that they place no constraint upon the range of theories or interpretations which different observers may arrive at. Thus 'the pragmatist agrees that there is such a thing as brute physical resistance – the pressure of light waves on Galileo's eyeball, or of the stone on Dr. Johnson's boot. But he sees no way of transferring this nonlinguistic brutality to *facts*, to the truth of sentences' (Rorty 1991: 81). That is to say, Galileo and the orthodox astronomers of Padua can safely be assumed – in some rock-bottom sense – to have 'seen the same thing' when they peered through his telescope at the moons of Jupiter. But in the sense that matters – at the point where their theories diverged – this claim no longer holds good since plainly they did not 'see the same thing' once those incoming stimuli were brought under two, radically conflicting descriptions. Any notion that Galileo got it right because his was the theory that best, most accurately matched or corresponded with the causal impacts is just the kind of quaintly moralistic idea that realists endorse when they think of us as having a *duty* to ensure that our sentences or descriptions achieve the desired match. In short, it is much like the primitive belief that 'the gods can be placated by chanting the right words' (Rorty 1991: 80). Or it is as if one should hold that epistemic virtue consists in an attitude of proper deference to those powers (physical or divine) which hold us more or less willingly in thrall. Thus, as Rorty puts it: '[t]o say that we must have respect for unmediated causal forces is pointless. It is like saying that the blank must have respect for the impressed die. The blank has no choice, neither do we' (Rorty 1991: 81). Yet we do have a choice – limited only by the range of vocabularies on offer – when it comes to working our perceptions up into the form of observation-sentences, theories, or astronomical worldviews. For as Donald Davidson puts it, in a passage much cited by Rorty, even if 'causes are not under a description', nevertheless 'explanations are' (see for instance Rorty 1991: 81). In which case one can perfectly well be a 'realist' about the impact of photons on Galileo's eyeball or of the stone on Dr Johnson's boot while denying that such baseline realism has any implication for the kinds of issue typically debated by philosophers and historians of science.

This is not to say that Rorty's argument would cut much ice with Wright or other thinkers of a broadly RD persuasion. Indeed, their main purpose in adverting to Locke on the topic of secondary qualities is to offer what they see as a promising alternative way between the twin poles of hard-line, objectivist realism and its Rortian 'strong'-descriptivist counterpart. However, as I have said, this project misses its mark in so far as it tends to assimilate moral discourse to the kinds of epistemic response (like correctly perceiving an object to be red under normal lighting conditions) which, if the analogy holds, can offer no scope for the exercise of distinctively moral capacities or powers of judgement. Either that, or it displays the opposite (reactive) tendency to exaggerate the scope for variable standards of taste, sensibility, civilised conduct, and so forth, by taking insufficient account of those real-world (morally salient) facts about creaturely flourishing or suffering which depend not at all on their happening to strike a responsive chord with us or with some notional optimised community of subjects-presumed-to-know. This is why, as Railton puts it, '[o]bjectivity about intrinsic and moral good alike calls for us to gain critical perspective on our own actual responses, not to project their objects rigidly' (Railton 1998: 84). For the 'rigidified' conception of response-dependence is one that, like Rorty's rock-bottom appeal to 'unmediated causal forces', gets us nowhere in explaining the normative dimension of enquiry, whether as concerns the quest for scientific truth or the attempt to achieve a more just, humane, or equitable moral and socio-political order.

This is of course no problem for Rorty since he thinks it the merest of delusions – though one to which philosophers are chronically prone – that we could ever get from 'realism' in the baseline (causal-impact) sense to 'realism' in a sense that could possibly bear such a weight of epistemic or moral-evaluative baggage. Thus he is happy enough that our scientific theories and descriptions should float entirely free of their notional 'real-world' moorings, just as he is happy that our various private-individual projects of creative 'self-fashioning' should float entirely free of the public domain wherein ethical and socio-political thinkers elaborate their theories for the common good. Indeed, we had much better keep these realms firmly apart since otherwise there is always the risk that strong self-fashioners such as Nietzsche or Foucault will manage to impose their values on the wider community, most likely with untoward (morally and politically disastrous) results (Rorty 1989; also Norris 2000). And if the earnest social improvers are allowed to encroach on the private-individual domain – if we start taking lessons in self-description from theorists like Habermas, Nozick, or Rawls – then this will close off the very possibility of making our lives more creative, adventurous, inspiring, or aesthetically fulfilled. Whence, as I have said, Rorty's idea of the 'liberal ironist' who is enough of a liberal to share the social hopes of progressive thinkers but also (importantly) enough of an ironist not to treat their – or his own – values as somehow enjoined upon all right-thinking persons.

Of the various, widely canvassed objections to Rorty's way of treating these issues one in particular has pointed relevance in the context of RD debate (see Brandom [ed.] 2000; Festenstein and Thompson [eds] 2001; Geras 1995; Malachowski [ed.] 1990). This is the fact that he fails to make allowance for the existence of truth-values – whether scientific, historical, moral, or socio-political – that might always conceivably transcend the deliverance of accredited 'best opinion'. Moreover, Rorty counts it a chief virtue of the 'liberal-ironist' outlook that it dissuades us from vainly thinking to achieve such a God's-eye view from outside and above the consensual mores of our own time and place. That this results – to say the least – in a degree of complacency with regard to the merits of present-day US (or 'North Atlantic bourgeois postmodern liberal pragmatist') culture is a case that has been pressed repeatedly by various critics and to which Rorty has most often responded with a polite though dismissive liberal-ironist shrug (Festenstein and Thompson [eds] 2001; also Rorty 1999). Complacent acquiescence in the norms and values of a given (as it happens globally dominant) culture is not a charge that could fairly or plausibly be levelled at Wright and other RD theorists. However there is a sense in which this approach *cannot but* endorse a consensualist appeal to best opinion, one that no doubt works well enough when applied to instances like colour-perception – where it reliably falls square with normalised modes of response – but which creates large problems when applied to other areas of discourse such as mathematics, scientific enquiry, or moral judgement. For in these cases it is always possible that 'best opinion' might just be wrong, whether for lack of empirical evidence, restrictions on our scope of epistemic access, the finite capacity of human reason, or again, through the limits of moral intelligence among this or that (no matter how socially well-placed) group of respondents. Of course – to repeat – this objection can be got around by simply redefining 'best opinion' as that upon which they are destined to converge at the ideal limit of enquiry when all the evidence is in and assuming them to exercise optimal powers of conceptual-evaluative judgement. But then the argument becomes merely trivial since any such deliverance is, *per definiens*, true, valid, or morally justified and human responses no longer play any but a nominal or place-holder role.

IV

Such is most strikingly the case when thinkers of a qualified RD persuasion apply themselves to subject-areas, like that of mathematics, where realists and anti-realists divide along sharp and (as it might seem) strictly non-negotiable lines. Here again the idea is to make such disputes appear misconceived by staking out a middle-ground position – 'humanised platonism', as Alex Miller describes it – whereby we can have as much objectivity as the realist can sensibly require while not pushing that demand so far that mathematical truth recedes into a realm of inherently unknowable abstract platonic entities. Miller has a colourful passage where he calls this the 'sublimated' realist conception by analogy with Freud's diagnosis of the male pathological fixation on images of woman as idealised sexless angel or vilified whore (Miller 1998: 178; also Divers and Miller 1999). In the same way, hardcore mathematical platonists cling to a notion of objective (recognition-transcendent) truth which places it beyond epistemic reach and which thus gives rise to various kinds of reactive (e.g., anti-realist or fictionalist) doctrine. (For further discussion, see Benacerraf and Putnam [eds] 1983; also Field 1980.) Much better give up that unworkable notion – the belief (say) in numbers, sets, or classes as belonging to a realm of absolute ideal objectivity – and settle for a humanised platonist approach that brings mathematical truth back within the compass of attainable knowledge.

However the attempt to construe mathematics on this qualified RD account is one that must inevitably fail to explain why such truths might always transcend or surpass our best methods of proof or ascertainment. That is to say, it cannot avoid a whole range of simply untenable conclusions, such as that Fermat's Last Theorem was neither true nor false until Andrew

Wiles came up with his recent celebrated proof, or that Goldbach's Conjecture ('every even number is the sum of two primes') is likewise devoid of an objective truth-value since unprovable by any currently existing formalised procedure, or that it somehow became true that 311 successive iterations of the digit '1' is a prime number just at the moment when this truth was established through application of enhanced computational resources. Miller wants to coax the platonist down from the delusive metaphysical heights by arguing the merits of a 'humanised' conception on which truth can be thought of – reassuringly enough – as answering to standards that are not just those of currently accepted best belief but which do not (like the 'sublimated' realist conception) have the untoward consequence of placing truth beyond our utmost epistemic reach. On this alternative view, he writes, 'we deliberately separate the idea that best opinions play an extension-determining role from the idea that they constrain rather than track the facts about the extension of the relevant predicate; in humanised platonism we view best beliefs as playing a constraining role with respect to the applicability of a predicate *only in virtue of the fact that they infallibly track its extension*' (Miller 1998: 193; author's italics). However this sounds very much like a case of having one's philosophic cake and eating it, or making 'best belief' do double service as a source of *epistemic* (RD-compatible) 'constraints' on our processes of knowledge-acquisition and also as that which 'infallibly' puts us in touch with mathematical truths. On the former construal it clearly falls short of meeting the realist's requirement, while on the latter it does so only by dint of an optimising clause which simply equates 'best opinion' with 'truth', and which thus (in effect) cuts out the appeal to response-dependence in whatever qualified or minimalist form. At any rate it is hard to conceive what other interpretation could be placed on Miller's infallibility-clause.

One idea that has motivated much of this debate is the claim that an approach along these lines might provide an answer to Saul Kripke's Wittgensteinian rule-following paradox (Wittgenstein 1953: Part 1, Sects 201–92 *passim*; also Boghossian 1989; Hale 1997; Kripke 1982; McDowell 1984; Miller and Wright [eds] 2002). That paradox is held to arise when one asks for any reason – any 'deep further fact' about meanings, intentions, or rule-governed ways of proceeding – that would define what it is to get things right according to the rule in question. So it might just be, on this 'Kripkensteinian' view, that somebody was following a nonstandard or (to us) plain crazy 'rule' which they could none the less spell out, on demand, in (to them) perfectly correct and consistent terms. For instance, when posed an arithmetical question like 'What is the sum of $68+57$?' they might answer '5' and go on to justify that response, if challenged, by adducing the rule: 'add up in the manner standardly prescribed *unless* the sum is greater than 68, in which case the correct answer must always be 5'. Kripke's point is that there is nothing – communal agreement apart – that can settle the issue between 'us' right-thinking types trained up on principles such as recursivity throughout the entire sequence of natural numbers and those other, presumptively deviant types who just do not get it according to our own agreed-upon methods or criteria. More generally: there is no fact of the matter (no eidetic or introspectible truth) concerning what speakers or reasoners mean – what they manifestly have in mind – when applying some rule or carrying out some recursively specified task. Rather it must always be open to doubt whether they have applied the correct (by our own lights) rule or whether they are following some alternative procedure which just happens *not yet* to have produced answers that come out wrong by accepted communal standards. For there is nothing to prevent the deviant reasoner from producing a rule that perfectly explains and justifies his 'incorrect' response and which thus (by his own lights) shows *us* to have followed a wrong or inappropriate rule. To conclude otherwise – to think that he must have some problem in seeing how the 'same' rule (that of elementary addition) applies both to smaller and larger numbers – is to beg the whole question as to what constitutes a rule and how (by what objective or practice-transcendent criterion) we are entitled to impute this presumptive failure of grasp.

Kripke makes the case in more general terms by supposing that the out-of-step respondent is working on a rule (that of *quaddition*) which has so far produced results in accord with the standard procedure for addition but which might turn out – at some arbitrary point on the numerical scale – to require a non-standard or non-communally warranted response. That is to say, all that we (or they) have to go on in a case of this sort is the evidence of their answers up to that point, answers that fail to provide any guidance when it comes to deciding just which rule (addition or quaddition) they have been working on all along. Thus they might have meant *quus* rather than 'plus' and yet have given answers that apparently showed them to have grasped the correct rule of addition just so long as the sum was less than 68. In which case we should surely be inclined to say that they were suffering some curious limitation on their powers of rational-recursive thought which enabled them to add correctly up to that point but which then – unaccountably – induced them to go off the rails (i.e., answer '5' rather than '125') when required to calculate the sum of $68 + 57$. However, once again, this takes it for granted that we *know* what rule they must have been following in order to produce the right answers within that numerically restricted range and hence to *know* that they must have gone wrong (failed to apply the rule consistently) as soon as their responses started to diverge from our own. Yet we are simply not placed to make that assumption if, as Kripke argues, there is something inscrutable about all rule-following behaviour, that is say, something that inherently eludes any normative account requiring our shared access to whatever it is that constitutes the rule in question. For given this practice-based conception of arithmetic knowledge – one that rejects the platonist conceit of our somehow having epistemic access to a realm of objectively existent arithmetical truths – there is no holding deviant reasoners accountable to standards which do (or which should) govern their performance quite apart from what properly counts *for them* as 'following a rule'. And moreover, just as we lack any sure criterion for judging them objectively right or wrong in that regard, so likewise they – the 'deviant' reasoners – lack any sure criterion for knowing whether or not they have applied the 'same' rule when essaying some problem in arithmetic that involves numbers greater than anything they have dealt with up to now.

In short, the Kripkensteinian argument entails that they (and we) can have no privileged access to a realm of thoughts, meanings, intentions, or ideal objectivities of the platonist sort by which to ascertain that any new result either counts or demonstrably fails to count as an instance of correctly carrying on in accordance with this or that rule. For there is nothing – no evidence from some finite range of previous responses – that could prove them (or us) to have been working on the standard addition-rule that requires uniform recursive application, rather than the alternative 'quaddition'-rule whereby that principle ceases to apply for any sum beyond a certain arbitrary order of magnitude. Thus our own ideas about what constitutes an instance of properly rule-governed behaviour – such as adding 68 and 57, and coming up with the answer 125 – cannot be accorded normative force without inviting the Kripkean charge that they involve a version of the old, discredited Cartesian appeal to indubitable grounds of self-validating knowledge or truth. Such is the consequence – as Kripke sees it – of Wittgenstein's argument against the possibility of a 'private language', an argument epitomised in his famous example of the man who buys two copies of the daily newspaper so that he can use the second to check that everything the first copy says is true (Wittgenstein 1953: Part 1, Sect. 265). It is just as absurd, Kripke's Wittgenstein maintains, to think that we could somehow monitor the correctness of our own rule-following activities by checking them against (what else?) the standards of correctness that are presupposed by our own rule-following behaviour. Any reasoning of this sort is either viciously circular or subject to an equally vicious regress which involves rules for the application of rules for the application of rules (and so forth *ad infinitum*).

Hence the radically sceptical upshot of Kripke's (on the face of it) modest suggestion that we should interpret Wittgenstein's private-language argument in conjunction with his thoughts about 'following a rule'. For the result – if Kripke's argument goes through – is to engender doubts that could we could ever be warranted in holding ourselves or others accountable to standards of consistency, correctness, or truth that allowed for the possibility of error or the failure to apply such standards from one deliberation to the next. The only solution, in his view, is a Kripkensteinian 'sceptical solution' which appeals to the idea of communal warrant as the furthest we can get toward deciding what should count as a correct response to some problem in logic, arithmetic, evidential reasoning, or making sense of our own (or other people's) meanings and intentions. In which case there is nothing – apart from such communal warrant – that could justify our deeming certain practices right (like that which interprets the rule of addition as a strictly recursive rule applying right up through the sequence of natural numbers) and other practices wrong (like that which routinely delivers the answer '5' beyond some arbitrary cut-off point). Thus, according to Kripke, the notion that there should or must be some such standard is one that merely betrays our hankering for objective (practice-transcendent) criteria of truth and falsehood apart from the deliverance of fallible human judgement. Such is the realist (or platonist) conception according to which there exist certain abstract entities – numbers, sets, classes, or functions – that decide the truth-value of our well-formed statements concerning them irrespective of whether we happen to possess an adequate proof-procedure. For an anti-realist such as Michael Dummett that claim cannot be upheld since the meaning of a statement is given by its conditions of warranted assertibility and those conditions, in turn, by its belonging to the class of effectively decidable statements (Dummett 1978, 1991a). Otherwise – failing this – it must fall within Dummett's 'disputed class', that is, the class of nonbivalent (neither-true-nor-false) statements for which we lack any method of proof or verification. Thus the only candidates for ascription of objective truth-values are those ascertainable by methods that lie within our scope of perceptual, epistemic, or logico-mathematical grasp. From which it follows that a whole vast range of (on the face of it) perfectly well-formed and truth-apt though unverifiable statements must be taken to lack such a truth-value in so far as they cannot be confirmed or disconfirmed by any means at our disposal.

Dummett stops short of Kripke's sceptical conclusion in so far as he acknowledges that at least certain statements (those that are capable of formal proof or empirical verification) should be taken as falling outside the 'disputed class', and hence as properly up for assessment in terms of 'warranted assertibility'. That is to say, he rejects – or at any rate nowhere endorses – the idea that correctness in rule-following can amount to no more than the habit of conformity with this or that set of agreed-upon standards among this or that community of like-minded reasoners. This line can be held (so Dummett believes) by insisting on Frege's more moderate version of the context-principle – that terms acquire sense *and* reference through their truth-functional role in various propositions – while eschewing any wholesale contextualist appeal to the role they play in some particular language-game, discourse, or cultural life-form (Dummett 1981). Yet it is just this latter Wittgensteinian conception that Dummett draws upon in arguing his case for the impossibility of assigning truth-values except in so far as those values can be specified according to accepted (communally ratified) standards of proof or verifiability. Thus there is, to say the least, an unresolved tension between Dummett's rejection of the full-fledged holistic approach (since it fails to explain how we could ever acquire or recognise the truth-conditions for any given truth-evaluable statement) and his anti-realist commitment to the thesis that truth cannot possibly transcend or surpass the criteria of assertoric warrant among those best qualified to judge. For there is no stopping short of the radically holistic or full-scale contextualist doctrine once it is granted (with Frege) that 'sense determines reference' and moreover – according to Wittgenstein – that any truth-talk is internal to this or that language-game or communal 'form of life'.

Dummett strenuously resists this conclusion, along with its allied and (in his view) disastrous entailment of the theory-laden character of observation-statements and the underdetermination of theory by evidence (Dummett 1991b; Fodor and LePore 1991; also Kuhn 1970; Quine 1961). For if the meaning of a sentence is given by its truth-conditions and if these are relativised to the entirety of beliefs-held-true among some extant community of enquirers then it becomes impossible to explain – along Dummettian lines – how we could ever grasp the meaning of any particular such sentence (see especially Dummett 1991b: 237–48).[2] This is why, in his view, one has to adopt a compositional approach whereby meaning is treated as a function of the sentence's component parts and the speaker's competence defined in turn as comprising her ability to acquire and to recognise the criteria for its truth (or assertoric warrant). Otherwise – quite simply – we could not make a start in learning or manifesting such competence since, as Quine argues, there is a limitless range of conceivably variant contextual factors that might always be adduced in support of one or another interpretation. Dummett is likewise opposed – and for similar reasons – to the Kripkean take on Wittgenstein's rule-following paradox, one that entails the impossibility of knowing for sure what constitutes a standard of correctness in such matters since (1) there is no appeal to some ultimate (objective) criterion of truth or falsehood, and (2) there is no 'fact' about utterer's meaning or intent that could serve as a fixed point of reference enabling us to judge whether or not they are applying the rule consistently with their own past practice. For Dummett such scepticism is misconceived in so far as it ignores the epistemic and logical constraints on our various well-established procedures of evidential reasoning, arithmetic calculation, and meaning-attribution on the basis of acquired and manifestable linguistic grasp. In which case Kripke is completely off beam in proposing his 'sceptical solution' to Wittgenstein's rule-following paradox, that is to say, his idea that communal warrant (or correctness by the lights of some shared practice, language-game, cultural life-form, or whatever) is the furthest we can get toward providing a justificatory account.

However it is not at all clear how Dummett can succeed in answering the Kripkean challenge, given both his anti-realist conviction that it makes no sense to conceive the existence of objective (recognition-transcendent) truths, and his jointly Fregean and Wittgenstein-derived insistence that truth-values can only be assigned through a grasp of the criteria that standardly apply within this or that context of usage. For it is then open for the sceptic to claim – with warrant from Quine – that any move toward a moderate context-principle such as Frege's (one that makes the meaning of a sentence functionally dependent on its component parts which in turn acquire a truth-value from their function within the sentence as a whole) *cannot but* give way to a full-fledged version of the argument whereby this compositionality-requirement has to be abandoned in favour of contextualism *sans frontières* (Frege 1952; Quine 1961). From here it is a short and, as Kripke would maintain, a logically inevitable step to the 'sceptical solution' which frankly acknowledges communal agreement as our last, best hope for avoiding the kinds of problem – that is, those of infinite regress or vicious circularity – that supposedly ensue from the rule-following dilemma.

Thus, whatever Dummett's statements to contrary effect, there is clearly a sense in which his arguments conduce to a sceptical-communitarian outlook which finds no place for criteria of warranted assertibility except in so far as they accord with some prevailing (whether relatively specialised or community-wide) currency of belief. In which case Kripkensteinian scepticism is the end of the road that Dummett is travelling, despite his logico-semantic approach *via* Frege and his refusal to countenance any extension of the context-principle beyond what is required for explicating sentences in terms of their compositional structure as given by a truth-functional analysis. All of which helps to explain why Dummettian anti-realism has so often been taken – *malgré lui* – as a far-gone instance of meaning-scepticism with large (and highly counter-intuitive) epistemological consequences (Devitt 1986; Grayling 1982). Nor are such readings altogether wide of the mark if one considers the above-cited examples of how Dummett's arguments work out when applied, say, to Goldbach's Conjecture, to Fermat's Last Theorem (until just recently), or to the case of the remote duplicate solar system. For in each instance the upshot of a Dummettian anti-realist approach is to place those statements firmly within the 'disputed class', and hence to deny the realist's claim that they do – indeed must – possess an objective truth-value quite apart from our lack of any proof-procedure or means of verification.

V

And so back to the main topic of this chapter: whether or not there is any help to be had from an RD approach that would purport to offer a workable *via media* between the twin extremes of objectivist realism and Kripke's sceptical-communitarian 'solution'. For of course – as recent commentators have emphasised – this is just the kind of chronic dilemma that has so often surfaced in epistemological debate, with the realist asserting the existence of objective (recognition-transcendent) truths, and the sceptic routinely responding that such truths, if they exist, are *ex hypothesi* beyond our utmost powers of epistemic grasp, and hence of no avail to the hard-pressed realist (Williams 1996). Such arguments very often focus on the case of mathematics since here the issue is posed with particular force. Thus mathematical anti-realists deride the idea – the typecast 'platonist' idea – that we could somehow have epistemic access to abstract objects (numbers, sets, classes, etc.) that 'exist' in a realm which by very definition eludes our utmost perceptual or cognitive capacities. To which, predictably, realists respond by denying that their argument involves any such self-contradictory claim – any notion of our having quasi-perceptual 'contact' with such abstract entities – and asserting the *sui generis* status of objective mathematical truths (for further discussion, see Alston 1996; Hale 1987; Katz 1998; Soames 1999). Where the confusion comes in, they argue, is through the idea that *any* realist approach to mathematics must fall into the original platonist trap of positing a supra-sensory domain of 'forms', 'essences', 'ideas', or suchlike, and then – absurdly – staking its claim on the notion of 'privileged epistemic access.

This skewing of the issue has been pointed out by various defenders of a realist approach, among them most notably Kurt Gödel, whose incompleteness-theorem – so far from supporting the anti-realist case – requires that mathematical truth *can and must* transcend the deliverance of any formalised proof-procedure (Gödel 1962; also Nagel and Newman 1971; Shanker [ed.] 1987). However there is still a widespread presumption – clearly visible in Dummett's writings – that mathematical realism self-destructs on the platonist idea of epistemic access to non-epistemic (objective or verification-transcendent) truths. So it is that Dummett proceeds to argue for a verificationist approach to other statements in the 'disputed class', that is to say, for denying the existence of objective truth-values as applied to a range of well-formed claims or hypotheses (scientific, historical, and so forth) for which we lack any means of definitive proof or decisive empirical warrant. Thus a great deal depends on whether an RD approach can successfully meet the anti-realist challenge and come up with some argument – other than Kripke's communitarian pseudo-solution – for rejecting an outlook of wholesale scepticism with regard to our accustomed notions of following a rule or reasoning consistently on the evidence. That is to say, such an outlook – if taken at its word – threatens to undermine not only the axiomatic foundations of arithmetic but also the entirety of our scientific knowledge and (beyond that) any claim we might have to conduct our social, political, and moral lives in accordance with standards that are *not* merely those of short-term evidential warrant or compliance with the currency of localised best belief. So the issue concerning arithmetical truth – whether or not an RD account can head off this Kripkean sceptical line of attack – is one with much wider ramifications quite apart from its obvious central importance in philosophy of mathematics.

If there is one common source to which this whole debate points back it is the late-Wittgensteinian idea of communal 'agreement in judgement' as the furthest that enquiry can possibly get in its otherwise deluded quest for ultimate 'foundations' that would serve to guarantee the objectivity or truth of our various utterances (Wittgenstein 1953, 1969, 1976). That idea has spawned a great range of responses, from Kripke's extreme sceptical ruminations on the rule-following paradox to the claim of those moderate Wittgensteinians who adduce his quietist counsel – that 'philosophy leaves everything as it is' – in order to maintain that one can still be a realist with respect to any area of discourse just so long as such realism finds criterial warrant in the language-game, practice, or communal life-form concerned (see for instance Crary and Read [eds] 2000; Diamond 1991; Wright 1992). Then there are Wittgensteinian social scientists, anthropologists, ethnographers, political theorists, and moral philosophers who mostly (if in varying degrees) subscribe to Peter Winch's cultural-relativist thesis that we cannot comprehend – let alone criticise – beliefs or value-systems other than our own since understanding requires that we share the criteria by which they make sense to members of the relevant community (Winch 1958). And of course there is the Wittgenstein-derived approach to philosophy of mathematics which holds that our reasonings cannot possess better (more adequate or certain) warrant than the fact of their belonging to a communal practice which alone decides what shall count as a well-formed theorem, a correct arithmetical result, or a valid proof-procedure (Wright 1980).

No doubt, as Wittgenstein remarks in *On Certainty*, there are some such community-wide agreements – like acceptance of the axioms of elementary arithmetic – which go so deep that they strike us as simply undeniable or as *a priori* truths that constitute the very grounds and conditions of rational intelligibility. In his famous metaphor they are like the bed of a river which pursues its (seemingly) inexorable course undisturbed by the surface swirls and eddies that represent our changeable beliefs about matters of empirical or *a posteriori* warrant (Wittgenstein 1969: Sects 95–9; also 319–21). Yet if one takes this metaphor at face value then it still leaves room for the standing possibility that a river may eventually change its course and hence that our notions of *a priori* truth might undergo some gradual change brought about by the long-term erosive effect of those same surface conditions. Thus Wittgenstein is perfectly prepared to accept that the logical 'laws of thought' – even that of non-contradiction – might come down to agreements in judgement that exercise a well-nigh unbreakable hold on our normative practices of reasoning but whose authority cannot be other (or higher) than the warrant of communal practice. So there is nothing in Kripke's sceptical 'solution' to Wittgensteinian's sceptical paradox that goes much beyond what Wittgenstein himself has to say on the matter, apart from his (Kripke's) sharpening the issue to a point where it threatens even the stability of a communal or consensus-based theory of assertoric warrant.

It is here – in responding to just this ultra-sceptical challenge – that the RD theorists would claim to have shifted the grounds of debate and come up with an *a priori* yet suitably provisoed account of what truth amounts to in terms that respect the operative scope and limits of human knowledge. However, that account breaks down through its failure to acknowledge the various ways in which truth might always transcend or elude the capacities of best judgement. In the physical sciences this claim has to do with the range of as-yet undiscovered (perhaps by-us undiscoverable) objects, properties, attributes, microstructural features, causal dispositions, and so forth, which fix the truth-value of any statement or conjecture we might make concerning them. Such statements are 'truth-tracking' or 'sensitive to future discovery' – as Hilary Putnam phrases it – quite apart from the verification-conditions or the standards of warranted assertibility that characterise our present state of knowledge (Putnam 1975; also McCulloch 1995). In certain cases, like that of the conjectured duplicate solar system in some epistemically inaccessible region of the expanding universe, they must be thought to possess an objective truth-value even though we could never be in a position to verify or falsify the claim. Moreover this realist argument extends to theorems in mathematics – such as Goldbach's Conjecture – that are capable of well-formed (truth-apt) expression but whose truth-value lies beyond the reach of our current-best or even (perhaps) our best-attainable proof-procedures.

Of course there is no question of Putnam's causal-realist theory with respect to natural kinds and their properties transposing directly to the abstract domain of numbers, sets, or suchlike mathematical entities. Indeed – as we have seen – it is a standard argument adduced in support of mathematical anti-realism that the realist approach entails the impossible idea of our somehow having epistemic contact with 'objects' that inherently elude any such mode of quasi-perceptual cognitive grasp. All the same there is a sense in which those abstract entities can properly be thought of – on a realist construal – as likewise determining the truth-conditions of our various statements concerning them, or again (where we possess no adequate method of proof) as existing, like the duplicate solar system, in a realm that is none the less real for lying beyond our epistemic ken (Katz 1998; also Hale 1987, 1994; Wright 1983). The anti-realist can make no sense of this claim and is thereby driven to espouse the idea that numbers, sets, classes, and so forth, must be treated either as constructions out of some accepted proof-procedure or else as notional (fictive) entities whose role is to facilitate the business of devising empirically adequate physical theories (Field 1980).

It is chiefly in order to avoid this sceptical upshot – along with the Kripkean *reductio* – that an RD account suggests we should abandon any full-fledged objectivist approach and instead make room for a suitably provisoed appeal to best judgement or optimal response. However, as I have said, that account lies open to the stock Kripkean rejoinder: namely, that there is nothing in the nature of such a response – no determinable 'fact' as to just what competent reasoners must have in mind – which could meet this challenge on terms that the sceptic has so shrewdly set in advance. For it either comes down to the trivial (tautologous) claim that best opinion *necessarily* equates with truth at the idealised end of enquiry or else advances a 'stronger', more substantively RD-specified version of the case which then affords the sceptic full scope for exploiting the 'no private language' or vicious-regress strategies of argument. So despite the high hopes entertained by some of its advocates there seems little prospect that an RD approach will provide the resources for an adequate rejoinder to current forms of anti-realist or sceptical thinking. What emerges most plainly is the fact that no such third-way alternative can avoid the choice between a realist conception of alethic (recognition-transcendent) truth and an epistemic theory that makes truth dependent on the scope and limits of human cognitive powers. This clarification of the issue may yet prove the most important, albeit negative outcome of RD debate in those various fields – among them ethics and philosophy of mathematics – where anti-realism has been felt to pose an especially keen challenge.

Notes

1. I take this example from Soames (1999).
2. Thus, according to Dummett, in some instances 'Wittgenstein built upon doctrines of Frege in order to produce what is not only a legitimate, but the only true, development of them', while in other respects '[h]e fought against the power of Frege's thought; and in such cases, I believe, he was almost always at his worst' (1991b: 239). What Dummett most forcefully rejects – for reasons discussed above – is Wittgenstein's wholesale contextualist doctrine of meaning-as-use, as opposed to Frege's compositional and truth-functional account of sentence meaning.

References

Allen, Reginald E. (1970). *Plato's Euthyphro and the Earlier Theory of Forms*. London: Routledge & Kegan Paul.
Alston, William P. (1996). *A Realist Theory of Truth*. Ithaca, N.Y.: Cornell University Press.
Beard, Charles A. (1962). *The Supreme Court and the Constitution*. Englewood Cliffs, N.J.: Prentice-Hall.
Benacerraf, Paul and Hilary Putnam (eds) (1983). *Philosophy of Mathematics: Selected Readings*, 2nd edn. Cambridge: Cambridge University Press.
Bentham, Jeremy (1823). *An Introduction to the Principles of Morals and Legislation*. Oxford: Clarendon Press.
Blackburn, Simon and Keith Simmons (eds) (1999). *Truth*. Oxford: Oxford University Press.
Boghossian, Paul (1989). 'The rule-following considerations', *Mind* **98**: 507–49.
Brandom, Robert B. (ed.) (2000). *Rorty and his Critics*. Oxford: Blackwell.
Brink, David O. (1989). *Moral Realism and the Foundations of Ethics*. Cambridge: Cambridge University Press.
Calder, G., Garrett, E. and Shannon, J. (eds) (2000). *Liberalism and Social Justice: International Perspectives*. Aldershot: Ashgate.
Crary, Alice and Rupert Read (eds) (2000). *The New Wittgenstein*. London: Routledge.
Devitt, Michael (1986). *Realism and Truth*. Oxford: Blackwell.

Diamond, Cora (1991). *The Realistic Spirit: Wittgenstein, Philosophy, and the Mind.* Cambridge, MA: MIT Press.

Divers, John and Alex Miller (1999). 'Arithmetical Platonism: reliability and judgement-dependence', *Philosophical Studies* 95: 277–310.

Dummett, Michael (1977). *Elements of Intuitionism.* Oxford: Oxford University Press.

—— (1978). *Truth and Other Enigmas.* London: Duckworth.

—— (1981). *Frege: Philosophy of Language*, 2nd edn. London: Duckworth.

—— (1991a). *The Logical Basis of Metaphysics.* London: Duckworth.

—— (1991b). *Frege and Other Philosophers.* Oxford: Clarendon Press.

Dyzenhaus, David (1991). *Hard Cases in Wicked Legal Systems: South African Law in the Perspective of Legal Philosophy.* Oxford: Clarendon Press.

—— (1998). *Judging the Judges, Judging Ourselves: Truth, Reconciliation and the Apartheid Order.* Oxford: Hart Publishing.

Edwards, Jim (1992). 'Best opinion and intentional states', *Philosophical Quarterly* 42: 21–42.

Evans, Mark (ed.) (2001). *The Edinburgh Companion to Contemporary Liberalism.* Edinburgh: Edinburgh University Press.

Festenstein, Matthew and Simon Thompson (eds) (2001). *Richard Rorty: Critical Dialogues.* Cambridge: Polity Press.

Field, Hartry (1980). *Science Without Numbers: A Defence of Nominalism.* Oxford: Blackwell.

Fodor, Jerry and Ernest LePore (1991). *Holism: A Shopper's Guide.* Oxford: Blackwell.

Frege, Gottlob (1952). 'On sense and reference', in *Selections from The Philosophical Writings of Gottlob Frege* (eds) P.T. Geach and M. Black. Oxford: Blackwell. pp. 56–78.

Geras, Norman (1995). *Solidarity in the Conversation of Mankind: The Ungroundable Liberalism of Richard Rorty.* London: Verso.

Gödel, Kurt (1962). *On Formally Undecidable Propositions of* Principia Mathematica *and Related Systems*, trans. B. Meltzer. New York: Basic Books.

Grayling, A.C. (1982). *An Introduction to Philosophical Logic.* Brighton: Harvester.

Haldane, John and Crispin Wright (eds) (1993). *Realism, Representation, and Projection.* Oxford: Oxford University Press.

Hale, Bob (1987). *Abstract Objects.* Oxford: Blackwell.

—— (1994). 'Is Platonism epistemologically bankrupt?', *Philosophical Review* 103: 299–325.

—— (1997). 'Rule-following, objectivity, and meaning', in Hale and Wright (eds). pp. 369–96.

Hale, Bob and Crispin Wright (eds) (1997). *A Companion to the Philosophy of Language.* Oxford: Blackwell.

Holton, Richard (1992). 'Response-dependence and infallibility', *Analysis* 52: 180–84.

Johnston, Mark (1992). 'How to speak of the colours', *Philosophical Studies* 68: 221–63.

—— (1989). 'Dispositional theories of value', *Proceedings of the Aristotelian Society* 63: 139–74.

—— (1993). 'Objectivity refigured', in Haldane and Wright (eds). pp. 85–130.

Katz, Jerrold J. (1998). *Realistic Rationalism.* Cambridge, MA: MIT Press.

Kripke, Saul (1982). *Wittgenstein on Rules and Private Language.* Oxford: Blackwell.

Kuhn, Thomas S. (1970). *The Structure of Scientific Revolutions*, 2nd edn. Chicago: University of Chicago Press.

Kurland, Philip B. (ed.) (1965). *The Supreme Court and the Constitution: Essays in Constitutional Law from* The Supreme Court Review. Chicago: Phoenix Books.

Locke, John (1969). *An Essay Concerning Human Understanding* (ed.) A.S. Pringle-Pattison. Oxford: Oxford University Press.

Luntley, Michael (1988). *Language, Logic and Experience: The Case for Anti-realism*. London: Duckworth.

Lyotard, Jean-François (1984). *The Postmodern Condition: A Report on Knowledge*, trans. G. Bennington and B. Massumi. Manchester: Manchester University Press.

McCulloch, Gregory (1995). *The Mind and its World*. London: Routledge.

McDowell, John (1984). 'Wittgenstein on following a rule', *Synthèse* **58**: 325–63.

Malachowski, Alan R. (ed.) (1990). *Reading Rorty: Critical Responses to* Philosophy and the Mirror of Nature. Oxford: Blackwell.

Miller, Alexander (1998). 'Rule-following, response-dependence, and McDowell's debate with anti-realism', *European Review of Philosophy* **3**: 175–97.

Miller, Alexander and Crispin Wright (eds) (2002). *Rule-Following and Meaning*. Chesham: Acumen.

Nagel, Ernest and James Newman (1971). *Gödel's Theorem*. London: Routledge & Kegan Paul.

Norris, Christopher (1993). *The Truth About Postmodernism*. Oxford: Blackwell.

——(2000). 'Ethics, autonomy and self-invention: debating Foucault', in *Deconstruction and the 'Unfinished Project of Modernity'*. London: Athlone Press. pp. 119–35.

——(2002). *Truth Matters: Realism, Anti-realism, and Response-Dependence*. Edinburgh: Edinburgh University Press.

Pacelle, Richard (2001). *The Supreme Court in American Politics*. Boulder, Col.: Westview Press.

Pettit, Philip (1991). 'Realism and response dependence', *Mind* **100**: 597–626.

——(1992). *The Common Mind: An Essay on Psychology, Society, and Politics*. Oxford: Oxford University Press.

——(1998a). 'Are manifest qualities response-dependent?', *The Monist* **81**: 3–43.

——(1998b). 'Noumenalism and response-dependence', *The Monist* **81**: 112–32.

Plato (1977). *Plato's Euthyphro, Apology of Socrates, and Crito* (ed.) John Burnet. Oxford: Clarendon Press.

Powell, Mark (1998). 'Realism or response-dependence?', *European Review of Philosophy* **3**: 1–13.

Putnam, Hilary (1975). *Mind, Language and Reality*. Cambridge: Cambridge University Press.

Quine, W.V. (1961). 'Two dogmas of empiricism', in *From a Logical Point of View*, 2nd edn. Cambridge, MA: Harvard University Press. pp. 20–46.

Railton, Peter (1998). 'Red, bitter, good', *European Review of Philosophy* **3**: 67–84.

Rorty, Richard (1989). *Contingency, Irony, and Solidarity*. Cambridge: Cambridge University Press.

——(1991). *Objectivity, Relativism, and Truth*. Cambridge: Cambridge University Press.

——(1999). *Philosophy and Social Hope*. Harmondsworth: Penguin.

Sayre-McCord, Geoffrey (ed.) (1988). *Essays on Moral Realism*. Ithaca, N.Y.: Cornell University Press.

Shanker, S.G. (ed.) (1987). *Gödel's Theorem in Focus*. London: Routledge.

Soames, Scott (1999). *Understanding Truth*. Oxford: Oxford University Press.

Spragens, Thomas A. (1981). *The Irony of Liberal Reason*. Chicago: University of Chicago Press.

Wedgwood, Ralph (1998). 'The essence of response-dependence', *European Review of Philosophy* **3**: 31–54.

Williams, Michael J. (1996). *Unnatural Doubts: Epistemological Realism and the Basis of Scepticism*. Princeton, N.J.: Princeton University Press.

Winch, Peter (1958). *The Idea of a Social Science and its Relation to Philosophy*. London: Routledge & Kegan Paul.

Wittgenstein, Ludwig (1953). *Philosophical Investigations*, trans. G.E.M. Anscombe. Oxford: Blackwell.

——(1969). *On Certainty* (trans. and ed.) G.E.M. Anscombe and G.H. von Wright. Oxford: Blackwell.

——(1976). *Lectures on the Philosophy of Mathematics* (ed.) Cora Diamond. Chicago: University of Chicago Press.

Wright, Crispin (1980). *Wittgenstein on the Foundations of Mathematics*. Cambridge, MA: Harvard University Press.

——(1983). *Frege's Conception of Numbers as Objects*. Aberdeen: Aberdeen University Press.

——(1988a). 'Realism, antirealism, irrealism, quasi-realism', *Midwest Studies in Philosophy* **12**: 25–49.

——(1988b). 'Moral values, projection, and secondary qualities', *Proceedings of the Aristotelian Society* **62**: 1–26.

——(1992). Truth and objectivity. Cambridge, Mass.: Harvard University Press.

——(1993). *Realism, Meaning and Truth*, 2nd edn. Oxford: Blackwell.

——(1998). 'Euthyphronism and the physicality of colour', *European Review of Philosophy* **3**: 15–30.

——(1999). 'Truth: a traditional debate reviewed', in Blackburn and Simmons (eds) pp. 203–38.

5
The Perceiver's Share (2): Deconstructive Musicology and Cognitive Science

It is now more than twenty years since Joseph Kerman published his much-cited essay 'How we got into analysis, and how to get out' (Kerman 1980). Significantly enough, it appeared in the US journal *Critical Inquiry*, which adopted as one of its principal aims the encouragement of inter-disciplinary exchange across the more usual, professionally defined boundaries of academic discourse. The emphasis was on textual-hermeneutic approaches that derived chiefly from post-1970 literary theory, but whose influence was then being felt in other fields, among them art-criticism, cultural history, and the social sciences. Kerman took up this challenge on behalf of the musicological profession, and in the process declared himself squarely at odds with most of its predominant values, priorities, and working methods.

Thus he called for a radical re-thinking of the role of music 'theory' *vis-à-vis* music 'criticism'; for the opening up of criticism to a range of theoretical ideas far beyond its current, conservative remit; and – above all – for a critical questioning of 'analysis', one that would challenge its hegemonic status among theorists trained on a naive ('positivist') conception of musical structure and form. That conception – he argued – goes hand in hand with a narrow and ideologically determined view of the musical 'canon', a view that inevitably works to promote just the kinds of music that are best suited to analysis in terms of thematic development, motivic integration, and complex tonal structure (Kerman 1983). In particular it takes for granted the idea of 'organic form' as an absolute aesthetic value, that is to say, the premise that all great works – those that truly merit the analyst's attention – should manifest a deep-laid unity of style and idea, whatever their apparent (surface) lack of any such unifying features. The result, according to Kerman, is a kind of vicious circle whereby analysts prove their worth through seeking out ever more recondite or depth-structural traits of organic form while the music in question retains (or acquires) classic status precisely in so far as it rewards their efforts. Yet why should we accept this organicist doctrine, grounded as it is in nothing more than a professional need – or an ideological imperative – to justify the analyst's vocation by singling out those particular works that constitute the musical canon? All the more so since it has often led – notoriously in Schenker's case – to a likewise 'organicist' conception of musical history which amounts to the same doctrine writ large, that is, construed in terms of cultural as well as of formal (motivic-thematic) development. For there is a close connection between, on the one hand, Schenker's attachment to 'absolute' musical-aesthetic values like that of organic form and, on the other, his contemptuous dismissal of any music – like Debussy's – which failed to meet the required standard. (See Schenker 1973, 1979; also Beach [ed.] 1983; Blasius 1996; Forte and Gilbert 1982; Narmour 1977; Siegel [ed.] 1990; Yeston [ed.] 1977.)

Thus the vicious circularity of analysis takes on a yet more sinister aspect when it serves as an evaluative touchstone, a means of distinguishing the central from the marginal (or the authentic from the inauthentic) with respect to entire musical cultures. For it is a short step from this version of aesthetic ideology – the formalist imperative to seek out 'evidence' of large-scale thematic integration – to the belief that some (and not other) such cultures have a special claim to pre-eminent status in just that regard. Hence the privilege granted to a certain, presumptively classical line of descent whose great central figures were Haydn, Mozart, and Beethoven. Then there were the various elective precursors going back through Bach to the Renaissance polyphonists and, arguably, certain more 'developed', that is, forward-looking since tonally suggestive forms of liturgical plainchant. Thereafter the line was continued – with various 'organic' developments along the way – by composers such as Schubert, Schumann, (maybe) Mendelssohn, Brahms *or* Wagner (according to taste), Bruckner, Mahler, and of course Schoenberg and the Second Viennese School. After all, Schoenberg claimed to stand squarely within that tradition and indeed to have secured the cultural dominance of Austro-German music through his invention of the twelve-tone method as a means of imposing unity on the otherwise disintegrating language of tonal music in the post-Romantic era (Schoenberg 1984, 1995).

So Kerman's argument is presented not merely as a corrective to the kinds of partial or distorting view that often result when analysts remain naively in the grip of their own favoured metaphors. Rather, there is a strong implication that the *very practice* of analysis – in so far as it draws upon Schenker's organicist model – is to that extent bound up with some deeply prejudicial and politically suspect values. During the past two decades his challenge to mainstream musicology has been erected into a full-scale deconstructive programme by younger critics who routinely denounce the guilty liaison (as they see it) between 'analysis' in whatever guise and concepts of musical unity, development, or organic form. (See for instance Bergeron and Bohlman

[eds] 1992; Korsyn 1993; Solie [ed.] 1993; Street 1989; Subotnik 1996.) What I propose to do here is examine these arguments, along with their various source-texts, and enter some strong reservations with regard to the widespread turn against analysis in recent music theory. I shall argue – in short – that analytically informed (or 'structural') listening is the only kind of musical experience that can put up resistance to 'aesthetic ideology', or enable us better to perceive and understand those recalcitrant musical structures that do not fit in with preconceived, habitual modes of listener response. Moreover I shall make the case that much of what passes – among music theorists – as a discourse radically opposed to 'aesthetic ideology' is one that operates at so great a distance from our cognitive involvement with music that it becomes, in effect, a discourse not so much about music as about certain abstract theoretical issues that often have little or no bearing on our perception of musical works.

II

Of course these terms – 'perception', 'cognition', 'experience', the musical 'work' as a putative 'object' of analysis – have all been exposed to intense deconstructive scrutiny and treated as likewise complicit with a form of naive aestheticist thinking (see especially Goehr 1992). However, I suggest, this drastic devaluation of the work-concept, along with the role of analysis in sharpening or heightening our powers of musical perception, is often carried so far that – 'in theory' at least – it leaves no room for any active, critically informed engagement with music. One is put in mind of Hermann Hesse's prescient novel *The Glass-Bead Game* where an elite community of intellectuals devote their time to devising new mathematico-combinatorial possibilities on the basis of existing scores rather than do anything so vulgar as create, perform, or enjoy music like those outside their well-guarded retreat (Hesse 1990). Most probably this tale was intended as a satire on serialism and high modernist musical culture, as well as the sorts of purebred analytical approach that fostered such (as he saw them) untoward developments. However it can also be interpreted – in the present context – as a satire on those kinds of theoretical discourse that reject 'analysis' as the tool of an aesthetic ideology deeply in hock to organicist concepts and values. Indeed, this reading gains an added force in so far as analysis – perceptive and intelligent analysis – has the virtue of staying reliably in touch with the listener's musical experience, whereas the discourse that purports to deconstruct such claims does so, very often, from the vantage point of a theory that seems quite devoid of substantive perceptual or experiential content. So my argument will utilise certain ideas from recent cognitive psychology in the hope of providing a viable alternative to Kerman's drastically revisionist proposal that music critics should get into theory as a means to get out of analysis. For there is no reason – academic prejudice aside – why analysis should not be thought of as always open to refinement through modes of theoretical critique, just as musical perceptions are open to refinement through modes of analytic commentary.

The main source here has been Paul de Man's writings on 'aesthetic ideology', that is to say, his claim that such thinking results from a deep misconception concerning the relationship between subject and object, mind and nature, or language and phenomenal experience. (See especially de Man 1984, 1986, 1996; also Norris 1988 and 1989.) For de Man that relationship is most aptly figured by prosaic tropes like metonymy and allegory as opposed to quintessentially poetic tropes like metaphor and symbol. Where the latter suggest a power of language to transcend those vexing antinomies – to reconcile mind and nature through an act of creative imagination – the former manifest a stubborn resistance to such forms of delusory 'totalising' thought (de Man 1983a, 1979). Their virtue is to keep us constantly aware of the impossibility that language might attain a condition of transcendent communion with nature, the 'one life within us and abroad' that exerted such a powerful hold on the thinking of Goethe, Schiller, Wordsworth, Coleridge and other romantic poet-critics. Metonymy 'undoes' the claims of metaphor since it operates through chains of contiguous detail – or the associative linkage between them – and thereby draws the attention of a vigilant reader to metaphor's ultimate reliance on just such prosaic devices. Allegory likewise 'undoes' the kinds of imaginative truth-claim vested in symbolic language since it involves a codified system of interpretation which openly acknowledges its own artificial or conventional character, and thus works to deconstruct the idea of a consummate, quasi-mystical union between mind and nature (de Man 1983a).

Moreover, the process of allegorical reading is one that unfolds through a temporal sequence of narrative events and which permits no escape into some realm of transcendent communion exempt from the inherently limiting conditions of our time-bound perceptual and cognitive experience. Thus it acts as a check upon the symbolist idea that poetry – or language at its moments of greatest expressive power – can somehow break free of those irksome constraints and hence achieve access to an order of timeless or eternal truths. Just as metaphor turns out – on closer inspection – to self-deconstruct into chains of metonymic displacement, so the language of symbolism likewise reveals its dependence on a temporal dimension (that of allegory) which shows such language to be still caught up in a linear, consecutive mode of reading that constantly belies its own more elevated claims. According to de Man, this is no mere exercise in textual gamesmanship but a powerful means of rhetorical demystification which makes all the difference between reading texts in a naive, uncritical, or ideologically complicitous way and reading those same texts with an eye to their resistant or disruptive potential. As he puts it (no doubt with provocative intent): '[t]hose who reproach literary theory for being oblivious to social and historical (that is to say ideological)

reality are merely stating their fear at having their own ideological mystifi-
cations exposed by the tool they are trying to discredit. They are, in short,
very poor readers of Marx's *German Ideology*' (de Man 1986: 11).

Thus de Man's chief purpose in his later work is to foreground the moments
of textual complication when these high claims for metaphor and symbol
can be shown to involve a duplicitous recourse to the tropes of metonymy and
allegory. By so doing we can best resist the appeal of an aesthetic ideology
whose effect is not only to confuse our thinking about matters of literary
theory but also to promote an organicist conception of language and art
which – as de Man darkly warns – may come to exert a far-reaching and malign
political influence. That is to say, such thinking all too readily consorts with
the Heideggerian claim that certain languages have privileged access to a truth
that other languages cannot express or even obliquely summon to remem-
brance (Heidegger 1962). In part this has to do with de Man's turning-away
from a Heidegger-influenced 'jargon of authenticity' – to adopt Adorno's telling
phrase – which accords special status to just those languages (classical Greek
and modern German) that can still, albeit at a distant remove, evoke some
sense of a primordial mode of Being 'covered over' by the subsequent accre-
tions of Western metaphysics (Adorno 1973b; de Man 1983b). But it also
results from de Man's conviction that aesthetic ideology – this potent mixture
of mythical, linguistic, cultural, and quasi-historical themes – has in turn
given rise to an 'aestheticisation of politics' whose upshot can be seen in the
fascist idea of the nation-state as a kind of surrogate artwork expressing the
will of a visionary populist leader, one with the charisma to mobilise mass
support for that same idea (de Man 1984 and 1996; also Lacoue-Labarthe
and Nancy 1988). And of course, in Heidegger's case, this argument gains
credence from the fact of his notoriously having declared himself a staunch
supporter of the Nazi cause and having placed his philosophical project at
the service of Nationalist Socialist aims and ideals (Wolin 1990). Thus it is
not, after all, such a wild or exorbitant claim that certain elements in the
discourse of post-romantic aesthetics – in particular the stress on metaphor
and symbol as figures transcending the prosaic conditions of everyday perceptual experience – have helped to engender an organicist conception of
national culture that opened the way to a fascist politics of the spectacle. Nor
is de Man exploiting this connection for merely dramatic or rhetorical effect
when he writes that the 'totalising' power of such figures – their capacity to
conjure delusions of aesthetic transcendence – is deeply complicit with their
'totalitarian' character, that is to say, their potential deployment as a means
of suasive mass-propaganda.

This is not the place for a detailed rendition of Heidegger's readings of
philosophers from Plato and Aristotle to Descartes, Kant, and Husserl
(Heidegger 1962). Nor have I room for an adequate rehearsal of de Man's
deconstructive strategies, aimed as they are toward challenging the kinds of
ideological 'blindness' that go along with this depth-hermeneutic drive, this

quest for a primordial ground of Being and truth that supposedly precedes the modern (European) division of languages and cultures, but which none the less grants authoritative status to a certain – that is, Graeco-German – line of cultural-linguistic descent (de Man 1983). Sufficient to say that de Man pursues his critique of aesthetic ideology through a deconstructive reading of various texts – philosophical, poetic, fictive, and literary-critical texts – all of which display a marked tension between, on the one hand, a seductive rhetoric of transcendence characterised by the predominance of metaphor and symbol, and, on the other, a counter-rhetoric whose effect is to undo such delusory claims by revealing their constitutive dependence on tropes such as metonymy and allegory. Thus 'Nietzsche's final insight', according to de Man, 'may well concern rhetoric itself, the discovery that what is called "rhetoric" is precisely the gap that becomes apparent in the pedagogical and philosophical history of the term. Considered as persuasion, rhetoric is performative but when considered as a system of tropes, it deconstructs its own performance' (de Man 1979: 131). That is to say, a rhetorically aware (critical or deconstructive) reading of texts is the only kind of reading that can muster resistance to the power of rhetoric in its other, more persuasive or ideologically beguiling forms. Elsewhere de Man makes a kindred distinction between rhetoric conceived 'pragmatically', that is, as a matter of bringing about certain desired effects in the reader or listener, and rhetoric conceived as an 'epistemology of tropes', or a means of exposing the various mechanisms by which such effects are typically achieved (de Man 1986: 18–19). In other words the term harbours within itself a crucial ambiguity – or semantic tension – which he sees as having marked the entire history, from Aristotle down, of attempts to teach 'rhetoric' as an art of persuasion while also paradoxically promoting resistance to it by laying bare its manipulative techniques.

Hence his otherwise extravagant claims for the virtue of deconstruction as a mode of 'rhetorical' analysis that is uniquely effective in countering the kinds of naive or complicitous reading that would simply go along with a text's 'rhetorical' design on the unsuspecting recipient. 'To empty rhetoric of its epistemological impact', he writes, 'is possible only because its tropological, figural dimensions are being bypassed' (de Man 1986: 18–19). The political connection is most explicit in an article on Heinrich Kleist's strange essay 'Ueber das Marionettentheater' ('Concerning the Puppet-Theatre'), which de Man reads in conjunction with Friedrich Schiller's *Letters on Aesthetic Education* (de Man 1984a; Kleist 1947; Schiller 1967). What these texts have in common is a certain idea of the aesthetic as involving a degree of formal perfection most aptly figured in the metaphor of the dance as a pattern of co-ordinated movements and gestures. Thus – in Schiller's words – 'everything fits so skilfully, and yet so spontaneously, that everyone seems to be following his own lead, without ever getting in anyone's way' (Schiller 1967: 300). However Kleist's essay brings out a more disturbing, even sinister aspect to this analogy, namely its suggestion that the 'state' here envisaged – the state of perfect harmonised accord between dancers moving in precise obedience to a sequence of minutely choreographed steps – is one that finds its highest embodiment in a purely mechanical contrivance such as the puppet-theatre. 'The point', de Man writes, 'is not that the dance fails and that Schiller's idyllic description of a graceful but confined freedom is aberrant. Aesthetic education by no means fails; it succeeds all too well, to the point of hiding the violence that makes it possible' (de Man 1984a: 289).

More than that: Schiller's ideal of 'aesthetic education' is likewise premised on a notion of art as enabling the various human faculties – knowledge, reason, and imagination – to transcend their everyday dissociated state and achieve a kind of harmonious balance (or 'freeplay') wherein such conflicts of interest or priority no longer exist. This is the condition of aesthetic grace, as de Man ironically describes it: 'a wisdom that lies somehow beyond cognition and self-knowledge, yet can only be reached by ways of the process it is said to overcome' (de Man 1984a: 265). That is to say, if we read Schiller's choreographic metaphor as it asks to be read, then we shall think of the dance as indeed presenting an image of formal perfection, but one that points beyond any sheerly mechanistic construal to a realm of aesthetic transcendence where the antinomy between freewill and determinism no longer has any hold. De Man is quite aware that such ideas have exerted, and continue to exert, a powerfully seductive (or 'eudaimonic') appeal since they play upon the natural desire to believe that the experience of dance, literature, or music might indeed grant access to this wished-for state of achieved reconciliation. However, he cautions, we can and should resist the desire to go along with Schiller's ideal of aesthetic education in so far as it involves a 'totalising' rhetoric that hides or dissimulates the 'violent' operations that make such a rhetoric possible. On the one hand these are the prosaic operations of a language whose basis in metonymy – in the image of the dance as a sequence of rigorously programmed moves from one position to the next – is sufficient to 'violently' undo or subvert the truth-claims vested in a language of metaphor and symbol. On the other it is the 'violence' of a metaphoric vision which strives to efface all the signs of that other violence in pursuit of an ideal that requires nothing less than total, uncritical compliance on the reader's part.

Thus '[t]he "state" that is here being advocated is not just a state of mind or of soul, but a principle of political value and authority that has its own claims on the shape and the limits of our freedom' (de Man 1984a: 264). And again: what the Kleist essay brings out when read in conjunction with Schiller's (on the face of it) more sublime or elevated thoughts is 'the trap of an aesthetic education which inevitably confuses dismemberment of language by the power of the letter with the gracefulness of a dance' (ibid.: 290). This sentence would bear a great deal of conceptual unpacking but I shall mention only those aspects of it which bear on our immediate concern with de Man's conception of aesthetic ideology. When he refers to the 'dismemberment of language by the power of the letter' what he chiefly has in mind – so I take it – is a deconstructive reading that focuses intently on the letter of the text and is thereby enabled all the better to resist the blandishments of metaphor or symbol. At the same time de Man is ironically aware that this way of reading is itself 'violent' in so far as it conceives the text as obtruding a stubborn materiality – like the mechanised movements of Kleist's puppet theatre – that blocks any recourse to consoling ideas of aesthetic transcendence. For it is precisely his point that such readings are sure to encounter resistance or provoke strong reactions since they go clean against the conventional wisdom about literature and literary criticism. That is, they counsel an attitude of extreme scepticism with respect to just those kinds of appreciative reader-response – like the pleasure taken in a telling metaphor or a powerfully suggestive symbol – which critics up to now have mostly accepted pretty much at face value. For de Man, on the contrary, such pleasures are by no means innocent and require the most strenuous efforts of critical vigilance if we are not to be seduced by an aesthetic ideology with its own design on 'the shape and limits of our freedom'. Yet this self-denying ordinance carries certain costs, among them – not least – the violence involved in a deconstructive practice of textual 'dismemberment' which reduces metaphor to chains of metonymy, and symbol to an allegory of its own perpetual undoing through the temporal condition of all language and experience.

In short, deconstruction 'upsets rooted ideologies by revealing the mechanics of their workings; it goes against a powerful philosophical tradition of which aesthetics is a prominent part; it upsets the established canon of literary works and blurs the borderline between literary and non-literary discourse' (de Man 1986: 11). This is why, as de Man mock-ruefully reflects, the resistance to deconstruction has run so high not only among more conservative scholars and critics but also among literary theorists of various other (e.g., formalist, structuralist, Marxist, or 'New Historicist') persuasions. For they also have a strong investment – so he claims – in a certain conception of literary language that cuts across these methodological divides and which entails the reduction of rhetoric either to a systematic taxonomy of tropes or to a function that places texts in the service of a naive 'phenomenalist' (quasi-natural) relation between language and reality. Thus '[t]he resistance to theory...is a resistance to language itself or to the possibility that language contains factors or functions that cannot be reduced to intuition' (de Man 1986: 12–13). So it is not just a matter of widespread institutional resistance – as with the 'theory wars' that have raged in many university departments of literature – but also (more crucially) a kind of internal, self-generated resistance that is sure to emerge once theory encounters the conflict between its systematic claims and the mechanisms of figural language as revealed by a deconstructive reading. This is the point, de Man asserts, 'at which literariness, the use of language that foregrounds the rhetorical over the grammatical and logical functions, intervenes as a decisive but unsettling element which, in a variety of modes and aspects, disrupts the inner balance of the model and, consequently, its extension to the nonverbal world as well' (de Man 1986: 14). To ignore that disruptive element is to run the risk of endorsing an aesthetic ideology whose pleasurable yield must be offset against its tendency to 'aestheticise politics' by extending an organicist conception of art to an organicist conception of culture, language, history, the nation-state, and the individual's strictly subservient role *vis-à-vis* those transcendent values. Deconstruction thus serves – like Kleist's parable as de Man reads it – to caution us against such delusory ideas of a higher freedom that consists in perfect submission to interests of state or the laws of historical development. Yet in order to perform this necessary task it is obliged 'violently' to dismember those texts and those habituated modes of reader-response that would otherwise appear to offer consolation – or the promise of aesthetic transcendence – in the face of such threats to our autonomy and freedom.

The most extraordinary statement of de Man's ambivalence in this regard comes toward the end of his essay 'The Resistance to Theory' and takes the form of a series of wiredrawn paradoxical statements. Thus:

> technically correct rhetorical readings may be boring, monotonous, predictable and unpleasant, but they are irrefutable. They are also totalizing (and potentially totalitarian) for since the structures and functions they expose do not lead to the knowledge of an entity (such as language) but are an unreliable process of knowledge production that prevents all entities, including linguistic entities, from coming into discourse as such, they are indeed universals, consistently defective models of language's impossibility to be a model language. They are, always in theory, the most elastic theoretical and dialectical model to end all models and they can rightly claim to contain within their own defective selves all the other defective models of reading-avoidance, referential, semiological, grammatical, performative, logical, or whatever.... Nothing can overcome the resistance to theory since theory *is* itself this resistance. The loftier the aims and the better the methods of literary theory, the less possible it becomes. Yet literary theory is not in danger of going under; it cannot help but flourish, and the more it is resisted, the more it flourishes. (de Man 1986: 19)

The reader might bear this passage in mind when I now go on to discuss in more detail the way that deconstruction has been applied to issues in music theory, especially the issue concerning 'analysis' and its supposed complicity with a suspect (ideologically contaminated) notion of 'organic form'. For it seems to me that this way of thinking – already evident in Kerman's 1981 essay – holds dangers of its own once erected into a wholesale anti-aestheticist creed with orthodox sanctions attached. That is to say, it calls for just the kind of critical 'resistance' that de Man constantly invokes, but which his followers often fail to apply when it comes to the more programmatic claims of deconstructive musicology.

III

Thus, to start with the most obvious question: is there *really* such a close and disreputable link between 'analysis' as practised by music theorists from Schenker down and an ideology of organic form with such large (presumptively malign) implications for our thinking about history and politics? In fact there are three distinct questions here which have not been sufficiently disentangled by adherents to this line of argument. One has to do with the basic issue as to whether organicist conceptions in aesthetics, criticism, and music-historical discourse can indeed have such a crucial bearing – as de Man claims – on 'the shape and limits of our freedom'. For it might well be argued that this claim derives from a literalisation or over-extension of the metaphor which piles an absurd weight of significance onto what is, in its proper domain, a useful and critically productive way of thinking about music. (For a range of views, see Bent and Drabkin 1987; Cook 1989; Dahlhaus 1981 and 1983; Dunsby and Whittall 1988.)

Of course this rejoinder would not impress de Man who makes a virtue of respecting the stubborn 'literality' of texts and who regards any saving appeal to metaphor as itself complicit with aesthetic ideology in one or another guise. Still there is room to doubt whether *every* such use of the organicist metaphor must be thought of as somehow mortgaged in advance to a deeply conservative (indeed proto-fascist) mystique of linguistic, cultural, and national identity (de Man 1996; also Lacoue-Labarthe and Nancy 1988). I shall have more to say about this later on but would here just remark – with a glance toward Adorno – that the idea of musical works as exhibiting certain formal traits which make for a sense of long-range thematic or tonal integration is perfectly capable of going along with a keen awareness of those other, more recalcitrant features whose effect is to disrupt or to complicate our usual expectations (see especially Adorno 1973a, 1997). Indeed it is widely accepted among music theorists – even those with a strong analytic or formalist leaning – that without this resistance to simplified (stereotypical) ideas of 'unity' and 'form' no work could rise above the routine conventions of its time and achieve the kind of distinctive character that repays detailed analysis. At any rate there is something crudely reductive – almost, one might say, 'totalitarian' – about a theory that equates the very notion of formal coherence with an *echt*-Schenkerian drive to promote certain deeply suspect musical values and, along with them, a certain hegemonic conception of musico-historical development.

Whence the second question, one that has again received nothing like its due share of attention from the New Musicologists. This has to do with the relationship between 'theory' and 'analysis', a relationship nowadays conceived by many as involving a sharp conflict of interests, or a state of downright mutual antagonism. Kerman sounded the first note of this emergent hostility when he called for musicologists to embrace theoretical ideas from other disciplines – chiefly literary criticism – and thereby break the hold of those taken-for-granted values and priorities that formed the agenda of old-style analysis. Thus, Kerman advised, the best way forward for music criticism was to loosen its unfortunate ties with the workaday business of musical journalism and become theoretically informed to a point where it could undertake the task of deconstructing those hegemonic values that were broadly shared by analysts and music historians (Kerman 1985). Chief among them – predictably enough – was the priority attached to notions of organic form, offering as they did a means to assimilate work-based judgements of aesthetic value to larger claims for the pre-eminent standing of a certain, narrowly exclusive musical tradition.

What seemed, at the time, a radical statement is now more likely to be viewed as a feather in the wind, or a moderate rendition of various ideas that were later to acquire orthodox status among the New Musicologists. Thus Kerman enlists the resources of 'theory' in order to expose what analysts are loath to admit, that is, the fact that their supposedly objective methods are in truth deeply wedded to a set of ideological values and imperatives. No doubt this case finds plentiful support when applied to Schenker and other analysts in the same line of descent whose particular understanding of 'organic form' goes along with a highly prescriptive (and restrictive) idea of what counts as 'great' music. Here again, de Man gives a diagnostic lead when he shows – in his early book *Blindness and Insight* – how literary critics tend to project their favoured notions of form, unity, structural coherence, and so forth, onto texts which very often turn out (on a closer reading) to resist any such blandly homogenising treatment (de Man 1983). But there is still a fairly obvious sense in which de Man, like the New Musicologists, relies on 'analysis' to make his point and to challenge those prevalent ideological conceptions.

In his case the kind of analysis involved is a deconstructive reading of various literary or philosophical texts which foregrounds their rhetorical elements – what he calls the 'epistemology of tropes' – and which thereby seeks to subvert or undermine their other, more 'totalising' claims (de Man 1979, 1986). Among the New Musicologists it takes the form of a resolute scepticism directed toward any work-based conception of unity, development, or thematic coherence that gives a hold for 'analysis' on the terms laid down by a prevalent musicological tradition. Yet here also there is simply no alternative but to put forward a *different kind* of analysis that singles out features of the work in hand – hitherto unnoticed or 'marginal' features – whose effect (once recognised) is to complicate our sense of what constitutes a structural or noteworthy element. Such approaches may indeed be more 'theoretically' informed in so far as they evince a greater awareness of the presuppositions and the value-laden character of musical perceptions or judgements. However they will surely count for nothing unless their claims are convincingly borne out through a cogent and detailed analytical account of why certain works elude or resist the best efforts of mainstream analysis (Dempster and Brown 1990; Dunsby and Whittall 1988; Pople [ed.] 1994). In other words – as de Man often implies but is mostly (not always) too tactful to say – it is no use claiming to 'deconstruct' the canonical reading of this or that text unless one can demonstrate a keener grasp of precisely those recalcitrant details that have hitherto escaped critical notice. Thus if 'nothing can overcome the resistance to theory since theory *is* itself this resistance', then likewise there is no question of theory overcoming or discrediting the claims of analysis since analysis provides an indispensable means of showing how prevalent analytical paradigms fail to make good their own more ambitious or 'totalising' claims (de Man 1986: 19).

So, to repeat, the second main question with regard to this dispute between 'theory' and 'analysis' is the question whether theory can ever dispense with the kinds of analytical approach – the detailed attention to the 'words on the page' or the 'notes in the score' – that alone give an adequate handle for comparison between different, organicist and deconstructive modes of critical engagement. And this connects in turn with the third question, namely the issue as to just what role theoretical ideas can be thought to play in our actual *experience* of literature or music, that is to say, our responses as readers or listeners when not primarily concerned with matters of high-level theoretical debate. For de Man, as we have seen, such intuitive responses are always suspect since they typically involve some seductive or 'eudaemonic' appeal to notions – such as that of aesthetic transcendence through the unifying power of metaphor or symbol – which should not be allowed to pass unchallenged since they render us susceptible to various forms of ideological blindness. According to the New Musicologists, likewise, we can only be deluded – in the grip of a naive organicist metaphor with suspect historico-political implications – if we listen to music in the way prescribed by advocates of mainstream analysis. For that whole approach is premised on the idea of certain works as intrinsically capable of yielding the intuitive pleasure that results from a heightened perception of those various developmental structures – motivic, thematic, tonal, and so forth – which thereby serve as a sure criterion of authentic musical worth. And from here, so the New Musicologists contend, it is no great distance – or no great stretch of that same organicist metaphor – to the Schenkerian idea of musical history as unfolding through a preordained process of development and growth wherein certain select national or cultural traditions are conceived as exerting a privileged claim to the analyst's attention.

However, once again, this creates a large problem for the New Musicologists since they are placed in the awkward (contradictory) position of maintaining on the one hand that we need theory as a guard against the kinds of ideological delusion that result from naively intuitive modes of response, while on the other hand suggesting that *theory itself* – at least in its hitherto prevalent forms – has itself been the primary means of enforcing a dominant ideological consensus. Of course it is 'analysis', rather than 'theory', that is mostly singled out as the discourse responsible for producing this drastically narrowed focus on just the sorts of work that provide fit material for just that sort of approach. Hence the fallacy, as de Man describes it, which leads critics to project their favoured values – unity, coherence, and organic form – onto texts which supposedly embody or exemplify such values, but which always turn out, on a closer (deconstructive) analysis, to resist or obstruct such delusory projections (de Man 1983). However this applies just as much to 'theory' as to 'analysis' since, as I have argued, the distinction between them is one that breaks down as soon as one asks how theory could find any valid application apart from the detailed analysis of works, or again, how analysis could ever proceed except on the basis of certain theoretical presuppositions. In which case the question surely arises: what can be the source of that 'resistance to theory' (or resistance to analysis) that is supposed to play so crucial a role in unmasking the effects of aesthetic ideology?

For de Man such resistance can only be located in the stubborn 'literality' of texts, that is to say, in the sheerly 'material' resistance that reading encounters when it strives for a sense of aesthetic transcendence through figures like metaphor or symbol, but finds that desire constantly blocked or thwarted by prosaic tropes such as metonymy or allegory. Yet it is hard to see what de Man can mean by this appeal to linguistic 'materiality', given his claim that such rhetorical readings achieve their most decisive effect by offering strictly 'irrefutable' evidence that 'language contains factors or functions that cannot be reduced to intuition' (de Man 1986: 10–11). And it is yet harder to conceive what music theorists might have in mind when they endorse de Man's outright rejection of the claim that there exists some relationship between perceptual (or phenomenal) experience and whatever gives meaning or value to such experience (Street 1989). For there is a certain plausibility to de Man's argument that literary critics who make that claim are in the grip of a 'Cratylist' delusion, that is to say, the idea – put forward by Cratylus in Plato's eponymous dialogue – that this relationship is one of natural affinity and not just a matter of the purely conventional ('arbitrary') link between signifier and signified (Plato 1997). Thus: '[t]o the extent that Cratylism assumes a convergence of the phenomenal aspects of language, as sound, with its signifying function as referent, it is an aesthetically oriented conception' (de Man 1986: 9). But in the case of music this argument is much less plausible since here we have to do with a mode of perceptual experience which is also – inseparably – one that evokes whatever meaning or significance the music is taken to possess. In other words there is simply no room for a deconstructive 'reading' of music that would seek to expose the workings of aesthetic ideology by drawing attention to the non-coincidence between its 'phenomenal aspects (as sound)' and 'its signifying function as referent'. Indeed this whole way of stating the issue must seem oddly off-the-point given that music has no 'referent', unless one subscribes to a naively mimetic or programmatic conception of musical 'meaning' that few if any music critics would nowadays endorse.

Indeed there is an earlier essay by de Man – on Rousseau and, more specifically, on Jacques Derrida's deconstructive reading of Rousseau – where he makes this point with maximum emphasis (de Man 1983c; Derrida 1976; also Norris 1987, 1992, 2000, 2002). What emerges from Rousseau's writings on music despite and against their manifest intent is the 'empty' character of the musical sign, that is, the fact that no mimetic or representationalist philosophy of music can possibly account for its capacity to 'mean' something more than could ever be put into words or spelled out in the form of a programme (see also Barry 1987; Norris 1989). Thus music provides something like a deconstructive object-lesson for literary critics who are tempted to short-circuit the difficult business of formal analysis and press straight through to some 'thematic' interpretation that purports to explain what the text is all about. However, there is an obvious problem with any claim that deconstruction presents a powerful challenge not only to certain prevalent ideas of musical form which figure in the discourse of mainstream musicology but also to the kinds of phenomenal (i.e., perceptual or cognitive) response that constitute our experience of music. For what could be the force of such a challenge – or whence its justification – if that experience is thought of as merely the product of those same illusory ideas? Or again: if we take it on de Man's terms that aesthetic ideology results from a downright category-mistake – a 'phenomenalist' confusion between language and sensory perception – then it is hard to see how this argument could apply to music (or musicological discourse) in the same way that perhaps it applies to literary, philosophic, or other kinds of written text. For there is just no sense in which the experience of music – its phenomenal aspect – can be shown up, like the Cratylist error, as involving a naive metaphorical transference from the realm of natural processes and events to that of linguistic representations.

Of course this case looks a lot more plausible when directed against those ways of *writing about* music, or those approaches to musical analysis, which invoke notions of 'organic form', 'germinal' motifs, thematic 'growth', stylistic 'evolution', and so forth. At least it finds a measure of support, as I have said, in the various critiques that have lately been directed toward Schenkerian analysis and its clear affinity with certain forms of 'national-aestheticist' thinking. But de Man's argument goes farther than that, as can be seen when he nominates *music* (along with these ways of conceptualising music) as no less subject to a deconstructive reading that would question its phenomenal attributes or properties. Thus, if 'literature involves the voiding, rather than the affirmation, of aesthetic categories', then 'one of the consequences of this is that, whereas we have traditionally been accustomed to reading literature by analogy with the plastic arts and with music, we now have to recognise the necessity of a non-perceptual, linguistic moment in painting and music' (de Man 1986: 10). That is to say, the critique of aesthetic ideology requires that we remain on guard not only against those organicist metaphors which have captured the prevailing discourse of musical criticism but also against those perceptual modalities that we take – naively – to constitute the very nature of musical experience. For this idea is on a par (so de Man implies) with the Cratylist delusion which supposes all language to manifest a 'natural' link between signifier and signified, or a kind of generalised onomatopoeia whereby certain words are 'naturally' suited to evoke the experience of certain real-world objects, processes, and events.

Such is the fallacy of imitative form which few linguists or literary theorists would explicitly endorse but to which they are none the less committed – he thinks – through the aestheticist appeal to modes of heightened sensory perception that supposedly result from the power of poetry or music to renovate our otherwise jaded habits of perceptual response. Yet this is itself the merest of critical clichés, a metaphor that draws its suasive force from the standard (aesthetically grounded) conflation of linguistic and phenomenal realms. For '[i]f literariness is not an aesthetic quality, it is not primarily mimetic, [since] mimesis becomes one trope among others, language choosing to imitate a non-verbal entity just as paranomasia "imitates" a sound without any claim to identity (or reflection on difference) between the verbal and non-verbal elements' (de Man 1986: 10). And with respect to music we are likewise mistaken – in the grip of a naive mimeticist doctrine – if we suppose that its 'phenomenal' or sensory-cognitive aspect could bear any other than an arbitrary relation to those meanings or significant structures that analysis seeks to reveal. No doubt there are works – or passages of works – that exhibit certain obvious mimetic effects, such as Haydn's famous evocation of chaos in the opening bars of *The Creation*, or Beethoven's episodes of scene-painting at various points in the *Pastoral Symphony*. However – so de Man's analogy suggests – these should be treated as the equivalent of onomatopoeia in verbal language, that is to say, as strictly fortuitous or random effects which can have no place in any adequate conception of musical language. To suppose otherwise – to accord them a more significant status – would be just another version of the old Cratylist delusion, or (in this case) the crude mimeticist idea that music has its origin and achieves its highest goal in the faithful 'imitation' of nature (Neubauer 1986).

IV

However there are problems with de Man's argument that have not been sufficiently addressed by those – whether literary theorists or New Musicologists – who follow his lead in these matters. Most striking is the problem as to how language or music can be thought of as offering 'resistance' to aesthetic ideology if there is nothing in the nature of language or music – or in the nature of our responses to them – that could constitute the source of such resistance. To be sure, de Man makes a cardinal distinction between 'materiality' and 'phenomenality', where the former evokes the letter of the text – prior to any imposition of semantic values – while the latter has to do with those 'aestheticised' (hence delusory) modes of pseudo-cognition that conceive language by analogy with perceptual experience, itself conceived on the model of organic (natural) processes and events. Thus a 'non-phenomenal linguistics' would be one that redirected our attention to the 'material' aspect of language, that is, to those functions that cannot be subsumed under any such erroneous model. Moreover, de Man claims, it would 'free the discourse on literature from naive oppositions between fiction and reality, which are themselves the off-spring of an uncritically mimetic conception of art' (de Man 1986: 10–11). For what is brought into question through a deconstructive reading is not 'the referential function of language' but rather 'its authority as a model for natural or phenomenal cognition' (ibid.). And again, lest this point fail to register with critics who mistake deconstruction for some kind of wholesale anti-realist doctrine: '[l]iterature is fiction not because it somehow refuses to acknowledge "reality", but because it is not *a priori* certain that language functions according to principles which are those, or which are *like* those, of the phenomenal world' (ibid.).

All the same one may reasonably doubt whether it makes sense to postulate a 'material' substrate of language that somehow exists – and puts up resistance to 'naive' or 'aberrant' readings – quite apart from, or prior to, any ascription of semantic values. This claim is crucially important to de Man since it underwrites his notion of deconstructive reading as a practice that involves sedulous attention not only to the 'words on the page' but also to the very *letter* of the text as that which exerts a dislocating force on received (ideological) habits of thought. Hence – to repeat – his talk of the 'violence' or 'dismem-berment' of language that often results from such a reading but whose salutary effect is to heighten our awareness of other, more coercive or insidious kinds of violence, such as that which masks behind idealist notions of aesthetic transcendence. However it is hard to comprehend how language construed in this 'material' way could possibly perform the kind of work that de Man requires of it, that is, the work of resisting or subverting such forms of aesthetic ideology. For 'language' so conceived is *not yet* language in any meaningful sense of the term, namely, any sense that would involve something more than the mute, asemic, non-signifying 'matter' of vocal sounds or written marks. Yet how could such sheerly material sounds or marks exert the least resistance to modes of reading which, no matter how 'naive' on de Man's account, take for granted the existence of meanings or semantic values which transcend this primitive (strictly pre-linguistic) level of materiality? Indeed the only way to interpret his claim is to take it as referring to just those kinds of merely accidental property – such as onomatopoeia – whose appeal to a mimetic (sensory-perceptual) mode of response is such as to exclude them from con-sideration as elements of 'language', properly so called. But in that case what becomes of de Man's vaunted distinction between 'phenomenality' and 'materiality' as radically opposed ways of reading, the one falling in with aesthetic ideology in its various seductive forms, while the other resists such delusory ideas through its scrupulous attention to the letter of the text? For if a 'material' reading of this kind is one that steadfastly abjures any recourse to prior notions of semantic value then its resistance to those values can only come from our *sensing* or *perceiving* the existence of certain marks on the page, marks which can only register as such – only exert this supposed power to dislocate naturalised modes of response – in so far as they enter our field of phenomenal cognition. Yet of course it is precisely this 'phenomenalist' conception of language that de Man is out to deconstruct since he considers it the chief and continuing source of that potent strain of 'aesthetic ideology' which may otherwise exert its malign pressure on 'the shape and limits of our freedom'. (For further discussion, see especially Gasché 1998.)

This problem with de Man's line of argument is still more acute when his terms are transposed to the discourse of musical criticism and theory. For here, as I have suggested, there is something highly implausible – even absurd – about the notion that we might break free from 'phenomenalist' conceptions of musical experience and hence utterly transform not only the ways in which we write or talk about music but also our very modes of perceptual-cognitive response. Of course this is *not* to maintain – just as absurdly – that our musical responses are 'natural' in the sense of involving some deep-laid, permanent repertoire of innate predispositions that lead us to assign certain meanings, emotions, or values to certain kinds of melodic feature or harmonic progression. Such a charge demonstrably misses its mark even when brought against a work like Deryck Cooke's *The Language of Music*, which in fact – on closer reading – turns out to qualify this claim by making some allowance for the extent to which musical responses are informed by shifting cultural and theoretical expectations (Cooke 1962; also Pople [ed.] 1994). So there is a sense – albeit a limited sense – in which de Man is clearly right to reject any approach that would naturalise those responses to the point of denying their historically changeable character. However he goes way too far in the opposite direction when he claims that music, like literature, requires of us a resolutely deconstructive 'reading' whose effect is to break *altogether* with phenomenalist (or 'aesthetically oriented') modes of cognition. For here again the question arises as to how music could ever resist our more routine perceptual dispositions if not in virtue of its actually possessing certain salient features – melodic, harmonic, thematic, or structural features – which the acute listener is able to grasp *against and despite* her acquired knowledge of the background conventions that make up a musical genre or period style (Meyer 1967).

No doubt it may be said – on de Man's behalf – that it is precisely those 'material' (i.e., non-phenomenal) elements that resist the imposition of preconceived meanings or patterns of significance and thereby enable listeners to withstand the seductions of aesthetic ideology. But this argument is no less problematical here – and indeed, one might think, even more so – than when applied to literary language. For with music there is just no escaping the fact that any details, structures, or formal attributes which can plausibly be thought of as mounting such resistance must surely be heard (or perceived) to do so, rather than playing some notional role in a deconstructive *theory* of music that on principle eschews all recourse to 'naive' phenomenalist categories. Perhaps it is the case, as de Man says, that in literary criticism the 'resistance to theory' is 'a resistance to language itself', or 'to the possibility that language contains factors or functions that cannot be reduced to intuition' (de Man 1986: 10–11). But this is not to say – far from it – that the sole alternative to naive intuitionist, phenomenalist, or 'aesthetic' conceptions of literary language is a 'materialist' conception that voids such language of semantic or signifying content. On the contrary, this leaves us at a loss to explain how it could ever pose any credible challenge to received notions of literary meaning and form. And with music, likewise, it is a curious approach that stakes its claim to transform or radicalise our perceptions on a wholesale critique of aesthetic ideology which devalues the role of perceptual response to the point of theoretical negation.

What I think is going on in these passages of de Man is a justified reaction against certain, no doubt naive mimeticist assumptions, but one which, in the process, swings right across to the opposite extreme of a 'linguisticist' approach that rejects any appeal to perceptual experience as merely a product of ideological delusion. Thus the 'linguistics of literariness' becomes, for de Man, a veritable touchstone of authentic critical insight, as opposed to the kinds of blindness that result from critics' attachment to phenomenalist metaphors or analogies. However there is good reason to doubt that this programme can be carried through without giving rise to problems more acute than de Man or his followers seem willing to acknowledge. Those problems are particularly striking when the New Musicologists adopt de Man's critical apparatus and set it to work against established paradigms of music analysis or received ideas of the musical canon which they take to involve an illicit conflation of aesthetic and historical categories (Solie [ed.] 1993). What often emerges is a strongly marked linguistic-constructivist bias, that is to say, a tendency to suppose – very much in line with de Man's thinking – that any such appeal to modes of perceptual or cognitive experience can only be a product of the various ways in which that experience is described, analysed, or narrated.

Of course this bias is not so apparent in the field of literary theory since here – more than anywhere – we have to do with a metalinguistic discourse whose object-domain is likewise linguistic and which thus lends credence to the argument that language (in some sense) goes all the way down, to the extent of 'voiding' those aesthetic values that de Man takes as his chief target. All the same, even here, it fails to explain how literary texts could muster the kind of 'material' resistance to aesthetic ideology which that argument crucially requires. And in the case of music it is yet more difficult to conceive how a sheerly materialist conception – one that somehow operates prior to all ascriptions of meaning or value – could provide the basis of an ideological critique that claims to deconstruct certain prevalent meanings and values. For the consequence of de Man's anti-phenomenalist stance is to push criticism so far in the opposite direction – that is, toward a linguistically oriented approach – that his disciples in the musicological camp end up by talking not so much about *music* as about the kinds of language (or critical discourse) that supposedly constitute 'music' in so far as we can talk about it at all. Thus 'organic form' is no longer conceived – perish the thought! – as referring to features of the musical work that the critic might hope to reveal through perceptive, intelligent, and historically informed analysis. Rather it is the product of a hegemonic discourse which foists that conception onto various canonical works and which of course finds its own methods and values perfectly mirrored thereby. In other words, as de Man argues, organic form is not so much a feature of the poem or the musical work as a result of the predisposed 'intent at totality' which typifies various (hitherto dominant) modes of critical discourse (de Man 1983). But again this prompts the obvious question – 'obvious' from any but a linguistic-constructivist viewpoint – as to how music could muster resistance to the currency of ideological values at any given time. For if criticism is always, inevitably trapped in this hermeneutic circle – if there is nothing 'in' the work that might check or oppose our preconceived (ideologically motivated) habits of response – then such resistance can only be thought of as resulting from the kinds of linguistic or rhetorical aporia that figure so largely in the discourse of present-day musical theory. In which case the critique of aesthetic ideology is one that operates at a level so remote from the music itself (or from anything that analysis might hope to uncover) that it becomes entirely detached from its object and enters a realm of speculative theory devoid of any genuine critical purchase.

The trouble is that these commentators are often not clear as to just what target they have in view or just how far their more programmatic claims are supposed to extend. Thus when New Musicologists routinely denounce the notion of 'organic form' it is sometimes (one gathers) a certain type of *discourse* on music that they have in mind, but sometimes – more ambitiously – the very idea that music might manifest structural features that are aptly described in such terms. So likewise with various recent assaults on the notion of the musical canon, taken up by cultural-materialist critics who seek to deconstruct received ideas of (say) the 'English Musical Renaissance', or by feminist scholars who argue that the normative values of mainstream musicology are shot through with patriarchal or sexist attitudes (Burnham 1996; McClary 1991; Solie [ed.] 1993; Stradling and Hughes 1993). Some of these approaches seem chiefly out to challenge a certain prevalent discourse of canonical values, along with its favoured analytic techniques, while others seem bent upon rejecting any notion that music might possess the kind of intrinsic value that would justify our making comparative judgements with respect to its structural interest, thematic inventiveness, capacity to transform or renew our musical perceptions, and so forth.

Most often – as with Kerman – the argument proceeds without coming down firmly on either side and is thus able to retain some residual or qualified commitment to the merits of musical analysis while also professing a sympathy with critics who would call that whole enterprise into question. Elsewhere – especially among recent theorists – there is a constant oscillation between claims to deconstruct the discourse of mainstream musicology and claims (such as those of feminists like Susan McClary) to reveal how music enacts within itself the workings of an oppressive social or patriarchal order (McClary 1991). Or again, some theorists greatly influenced by de Man – including Alan Street in a well-known essay – make a case for 'reading' music allegorically as a perpetual reflection on the self-undoing of organicist models and metaphors through the covert operation of rhetorical figures that inherently resist such 'totalising' treatment (Street 1989). However there is still some doubt as to whether this argument goes all the way with de Man's iconoclastic talk of 'dismemberment', 'disarticulation', radical 'materiality', and so forth, and hence with the claim that musical works – as distinct from the discourse about them – can be shown to deconstruct under pressure of their own internal complications. For it is hard to see how this could be the case if we are to take Street at his de Manian word and accept that such 'allegorical' reading is sufficient to undo not only the notion of organic form but also the naive phenomenalist idea that particular features of the musical work can call forth particular kinds of intuitive (or sensory-cognitive) response.

Here again, this confusion results from the way in which a linguistically oriented criticism starts out by shifting the focus of attention from music to musicological discourse, and then proceeds to treat musical works as *nothing more* than so many constructs or products of our various ways of talking about them. One version of the argument is that which holds that concepts such as 'sonata form' – and other such staples of mainstream analysis – can be shown to have entered the lexicon of music criticism only a century-or-so *after* composers were (supposedly) producing works that embodied those same principles. So is it not a blatant anachronism and another plain instance of 'aesthetic ideology' when critics apply such concepts to the first movement of a Haydn string quartet, or a Mozart symphony, or a Beethoven piano sonata? Or again, are not analysts indulging a kind of retroactive teleological illusion when they claim to discover signs of an emergent 'progressive tonality' in works by composers (such as Beethoven or Bruckner) who would not have described their music in just that way? And of course the same argument is regularly applied to notions of 'organic form', extended as they are – very often – to periods, genres, or musical styles whose practitioners would scarcely have understood the term (see Burnham 1996; Cook and

Everist [eds] 1999; Treitler 1989; also – for a useful source-text – Damschroder 1990). However this thesis is no more convincing than the claim by some literary theorists that 'literature' has existed only since the time – somewhere around the late eighteenth century – when the term underwent a semantic shift from 'printed material of whatever sort' (or, at an earlier period, 'the discourse of the cultivated, literate classes') to its present, more specific asso-ciation with works of a creative or imaginative kind (Williams 1976 and 1977). In both cases the argument rests on a linguistic-constructivist fallacy, namely the idea that it is senseless to talk of generic attributes that could have played no role in the language – or even the conscious awareness – of composers or writers whose works are now said to exhibit them. After all, the joke about Molière's M. Jourdain is that he *had* been talking prose all that time without knowing it, rather than talking something else which he later (happily) mistook for 'prose' when the term entered his vocabulary.

Thus cultural theorists miss the point when they argue from the changed semantic currency of 'literature' to the notion that 'literary' attributes or values are really nothing more than the product of a certain, currently prevailing but historically short-term ideological discourse. And music theorists commit the same fallacy when they generalise from the claim that sonata-form cannot have existed before analysts came along and 'invented' the idea, to the claim that such notions are *always* just a figment of so-called 'aesthetic ideology'. No doubt this is a crude version of the case when compared with de Man's far subtler deconstructive variations on the theme or with some (not all) of the arguments put forward by New Musicologists. But it does share the basic presupposition that musical experience is always linguistically mediated, or that perceptual modalities – such as our capacity to register thematic, harmonic, or tonal structures – can only have to do with the language (or 'discourse') through which such perceptions achieve articulate form.

Now indeed there is an element of truth in this since our responses to music undoubtedly involve a great range of social experience, cultural knowledge, generic expectations, and so forth, in the absence of which we should simply not be *hearing* it as music (Pople [ed.] 1994; Swain 1994). So de Man is quite right – and the New Musicologists also – in arguing that critics are apt to be misled by that particular strain of organicist thought which purports to derive principles of meaning or value from the perceptual experience of music without making due allowance for these various, broadly 'linguistic' factors. As he puts it, in the context of literary theory, '[t]he phenomenality of the signifier, as sound, is unquestionably involved in the correspondence between the name and the thing named, but the link, the relationship between word and thing, is not phenomenal, but conventional' (de Man 1986: 10). That is to say – transposed to the musical context – it may well be allowed that our perceptual responses are responses to something in the nature of music (its tonal, harmonic, or structural properties) which constitute the basis of musical experience and which are, to that extent, phenomenally 'given' as a matter of sensory-cognitive grasp. Where 'ideology' comes in is with the further (illicit) move that metaphorically extends this natural condition of musical experience to a set of far-reaching evaluative claims for the intrinsic superiority of certain works – and certain musical traditions – as displaying quasi-natural forms of development, growth, or stylistic evolution.

This idea most often goes along – as in Schenker's case – with the privilege attached to the Western tonal system as itself a kind of natural resource with its own developmental laws (Schenker 1977; also Yeston [ed.] 1997). Thus the history of music can be written as a progressive exploration of tonal possibilities which remain firmly within that system while moving into ever more adventurous regions of harmonic discovery. Even Schoenberg – as I have said – felt compelled to justify his break with established conventions by asserting that so-called 'atonal' music involved nothing more radical than an abandonment of clearly marked key centres and a willingness to exploit tonal relationships which ventured farther out along the circle of fifths, that is, the harmonic overtone-series that still provided a 'natural' grounding for his experiments in twelve-tone compositional technique (Schoenberg 1984). What is more, he conjoined this legitimising ploy with the claim – ironically enough, given his personal predicament as an exile from Nazi persecution – to have thereby secured the continuing dominance of Austro-German musical tradition beyond the post-romantic 'crisis' engendered by the exhaustion of hitherto-existing tonal resources. So the New Musicologists do have a point when they argue for the link between 'aesthetic ideology' and a phenom-enalist conception of music which exploits the vaguely analogical appeal to certain intrinsic 'laws' of musico-historical development grounded in the very nature of the overtone-series. And this in turn goes along with a marked disposition, on the part of some analysts, to devalue or to marginalise any music which does not fit in with an organicist conception of what constitutes musical greatness.

However the 'linguisticist' orientation of much New Musicological writing is itself a very definite *parti pris* and one with its own, highly selective way of addressing these issues. Thus what de Man (1986) calls 'the voiding of aesthetic categories' brought about by a 'linguistics of literariness' is here erected into a full-scale doctrine that privileges theory – in its deconstructive mode – above any mode of analysis premised on 'naive' (undeconstructed) values such as those of formal integrity, thematic development, harmonic complexity, long-range tonal progression, and so forth. More than that, it takes the Schenkerian approach as a cautionary instance of what is bound to happen when analysis becomes mixed up with certain kinds of aesthetically deter-mined evaluative judgement and these, in turn, with a cultural politics whose end-point is 'national aestheticism' in its full-blown totalitarian form (Lacoue-Labarthe and Nancy 1988). Yet there is something drastically reduc-tive about this whole line of argument, suggesting as it does that *all* analysis must be headed in the same direction, or that *any* talk of 'organic form' is complicit with fascist ideology, or again – with the customary nod to de Man – that those among the old-style analysts or musicologists who reject that diagnosis are thereby manifesting a 'resistance to theory' with its own dark design upon the 'shape and limits of our freedom'. What this amounts to is a highly prescriptive – even, one might say, coercive or 'totalitarian' – assertion of theory's claim to legislate in all matters concerning the relationship between theory, analysis, and musical perception. And of course, given its strongly marked anti-phenomenalist bias, this priority of theory can only entail a devaluation of perceptual response in favour of a deconstructive (linguistically oriented) approach that also finds little use for analysis in so far as the latter is presumed to involve a naive supposition that musical structures are *there* to be perceived and analysed. Thus 'theory' comes out in sharp hostility to the kinds of justificatory argument often advanced on behalf of analysis: that it serves to heighten our conscious perception of details and structural relationships which we might hitherto not have noticed or perhaps been aware of only at a preconscious or intuitive level (Cook 1994 and 1996; Dunsby and Whittall 1988). For if the theorists are right then this supposed 'justification' is in truth nothing more than a telling exposure of the way that analysis readily falls in with an ideologically loaded concept of 'intuitive' perceptions and responses.

There is an odd (paradoxical) sense in which this whole line of approach both *overvalues* the role of theory in offering resistance to established procedures of musical analysis and *undervalues* the extent to which theory can inform our intelligent (analytically educated) modes of musical response. (For further discussion from a range of viewpoints, see Baker *et al.* 1997.) The overvaluation involves the idea that theory does best – promotes such resistance most effectively – when it deconstructs the premises of mainstream analysis from a meta-linguistic standpoint which rejects any notion of analysis as answering to genuine musical perceptions that are *not* just products of 'aesthetic ideology'. Hence the regular shift – as I have argued – from the idea of theory as a discourse in the service of sharpened musical perception to the idea of theory as a discourse that aims to discredit such delusory ways of thinking. Where the undervaluation appears is in the strange refusal to credit theory with any capacity to *inform and enhance* our musical responses as distinct from providing some alternative currency of musicological debate. However there is no good reason to think that these options exhaust the field, or that critics are faced with the stark choice between subscribing *either* to a naive 'phemonenalist' account of aesthetic experience *or* to a full-scale linguistic-constructivist approach that completely rejects such perceptual categories. For if this were indeed the case – *pace* Kerman and other promoters of the current theoretical line – then music criticism could hardly exist as such. That is to say, it would be 'critical' only to the extent that it deconstructed any grounds for claiming that the discourse on music had something to do with our intuitive modes of response. And, conversely, it would be 'musical' only in so far as it managed completely to ignore this critical challenge and thereby protect its belief that perceptive and intelligent analysis *can* have something of value to contribute to our better understanding of music. Neither option seems very attractive, on the face of it, so there might be some merit in considering alternative proposals.

V

One such alternative is that put forward by music theorists with an interest in certain areas of cognitive psychology. What has chiefly sparked this interest is the question as to whether – or just how far – our 'intuitive' responses are theoretically informed by various cultural inputs, such as our reading of musical analyses or our knowledge of music history. Mark DeBellis has taken a lead from the philosopher Jerry Fodor in suggesting this line of approach so I shall summarise the relevant arguments here and hope that readers will go on to consult the original sources (DeBellis 1995; Fodor 1976, 1983, 1990). Fodor's central claim has to do with what he calls the 'modularity of mind', that is to say, his thesis that certain fairly basic cognitive functions are such as to require a rapid response under given ambient conditions (like that of avoiding some immediate physical threat) and have hence evolved in a way that entails no complex processing of data from a range of informational sources. These functions are relatively 'encapsulated' or 'cognitively impervious' (Fodor's terms) since they work best – or most effectively ensure our survival – by avoiding such lengthy and complicated detours through neural networks that are specialised for other, more advanced or sophisticated purposes.

Thus, for instance, one would not expect a high level of complex intermodular exchange for perceptions of rapidly moving objects in our proximate visual field, or for tactile sensations of heat, since here what is required is a more or less reflex response that enables us to take evasive action or save ourselves from getting burnt. Also there are modules – like that concerned with language in its grammatical aspect – which likewise function to a large extent in isolation from other inputs since their main job is to facilitate communication (e.g., by allowing us to talk straight ahead and get the grammar right) and not involve too much interpretative processing along the way. However the case is very different with language in its other (semantic or pragmatic) aspects since here there is a need to draw upon whole large areas of background information, cultural knowledge, interpersonal skills, contextual adjustments, and so forth, in order to make ourselves understood or to understand what others are saying. So the main challenge for cognitive psychology in this modularised form is (1) to describe the kinds and degrees of relative 'encapsulation', and (2) to explain how the theory works out when applied to more complex, that is, cognitively 'permeable' modes of mental processing.

According to DeBellis, music provides an interesting test-case for the Fodor approach since musical perceptions – unlike more straightforward or reflex kinds of auditory response – do seem to change quite markedly in consequence of our learning to read a score, or to recognise complex patterns of thematic development, or to hear such patterns as a striking departure from established generic or stylistic norms (DeBellis 1995). So if indeed there is a 'module' specialised for musical perception then it must be one that exhibits only a limited degree of encapsulation, or that leaves enough room for inputs from various sources such as the listener's progressive exposure to more refined forms of musical analysis or more extensive acquaintance with other works in the pertinent reference-class. Perhaps there are certain very basic perceptual capacities – like hearing a temporal (melodic) succession of notes or perceiving a vertical (harmonic) relationship between different notes in a chord – that equate, roughly speaking, with grammar in verbal language, or with the kinds of 'hard-wired' syntactic regularity that transformational grammarians take to underlie the surface features of different languages (Chomsky 1957). To this extent musical perceptions may be said to manifest a high degree of cognitive impermeability, or to operate in virtual isolation from that whole range of other, theoretically informed or culturally acquired modes of response.

However, DeBellis argues, we shall not get far toward understanding the experience of music if we over-emphasise this 'dedicated' modular component and hence ignore the surely self-evident fact that our perceptions *can* be affected – sometimes in decisive ways – through the general process of music education, a process that includes (not least) our reading of analytic commentaries or works of musical theory. For there would otherwise seem little profit to be had from such reading except as a kind of mandarin distraction from the business of actually listening to music and allowing it to make its perceptual impact through the module specialised for just that purpose. In other words – though DeBellis does not draw this lesson – we should end up in the position of those deconstructive theorists who raise the critique of 'phenomenalism' to a high point of abstract doctrine and who can thus conceive of no middle ground between naive, theoretically untutored habits of response and a discourse (their own) that lacks any genuine purchase on our modes of musical experience.

What this amounts to, in short, is a strong case for the inter-involvement of perceptual responses with conceptual categories, or of musical 'intuition' with all those sources of sharpened critical awareness which most listeners presumably seek from analysts, theorists, and musicologists. It is therefore a conception far removed from that relentless deconstructive hermeneutics of suspicion that entirely discounts the appeal to phenomenal (or quasi-phenomenal) modes of perception and which thus drives a wedge between listener-response and the kinds of counter-intuitive claim that characterise the discourse of present-day 'advanced' musical theory. As we have seen, this hostility also extends to the practice of musical analysis, at least in so far as that practice assumes (1) that certain works possess certain salient (perceptible) structural features, and (2) that analysis is best deployed in describing those features and making them more consciously available through the process of enhanced (analytically informed) listening. But there is something very odd – not to say perverse – about a theory that is committed to the outright denial of both these claims in the interest of promoting a resistance to forms of aesthetic ideology which could only be resisted – in so far as one accepts this general diagnosis – through a better, more acute, more *musically* perceptive understanding of the music itself. For it is hard to conceive how such resistance could arise from a discourse that stakes its radical credentials on a 'voiding' of all aesthetic categories along with all notions of musical structure that might offer any hold for detailed critical analysis.

This issue is posed with particular force in a well-known exchange between Alan Street and Jonathan Dunsby on Brahms's sequence of piano *Fantasies,* Op. 116 (Dunsby 1981, 1983; Street 1989; also Korsyn 1993). Street takes the line – very much in keeping with his de Man-inspired deconstructive approach – that these pieces cannot (or should not) be heard as manifesting a degree of thematic coherence or interlinked 'organic' development that belies and transcends their seemingly small-scale, episodic character. So when other analysts – Dunsby among them – profess to detect such signs of coherence they must be in the grip of an aesthetic ideology that promotes a purely circular form of reasoning, that is, from the 'self-evident' premise that organic unity is a prime aesthetic value to the equally 'self-evident' conclusion that Brahm's music must exhibit that feature in the highest possible degree since plainly it is music of great aesthetic value. In which case – according to Street – it is the proper business of deconstruction to reveal this inherent circularity at work and thereby demonstrate how far the values of mainstream musical analysis are complicit with those of an organicist doctrine that does not so much *discover* as *project* those favoured musical attributes.

De Man makes the point in a passage that is worth citing at length since it seems to have provided Street and others with the chief inspiration for such claims. 'Literary "form"', he writes,

is the result of the dialectic interplay between the prefigurative structure of foreknowledge and the intent at totality of the interpretative process. This dialectic is difficult to grasp. The idea of totality suggests closed forms that strive for ordered and consistent systems and have an almost irresistible tendency to transform themselves into objective structures. Yet, the temporal factor, so persistently forgotten, should remind us that the form is never anything but a process on the way to its completion. The completed form never exists as a concrete aspect of the work that could coincide with a sensorial or semantic dimension of the language. It is constituted in the mind of the interpreter as the work discloses itself in response to his questioning. But this dialogue between work and interpreter is endless. (de Man 1983: 31–32)

For Street, this indicates the fallacy involved in any sort of musical analysis which purports to identify perceptually salient features of the work 'itself', and which then proceeds to assimilate those features to a concept of organic form premised on just such naive objectivist assumptions. What is needed, rather, is an 'allegorical' reading in the de Manian mode whereby the analysis can be shown to self-deconstruct through its recourse to various 'totalising' metaphors that always break down, on closer inspection, into chains of merely contiguous metonymic detail or the temporal flux of discrete events. For Dunsby, on the other hand, such arguments are misconceived since they fail to acknowledge what should be audible to anyone with sufficiently acute musical perception and with the capacity for long-range structural grasp that comes of knowing the pieces well and listening for just such kinds of thematic inter-relationship. From this point of view Street has gone wrong by allowing his (potential) musical perceptions to be skewed or overridden by a theory – a de Manian 'allegory of reading' – whose effect is to devalue our perceptual experience of music to the point where it becomes just a product of deep-laid ideological prejudice. As Street sees it such responses are predictably blind to their own motivating interests, that is, their investment in a mode of analysis that all too readily complies with the dictates of aesthetic ideology. Thus any such appeal to 'experience' or 'perception' must be thought to involve a naive metaphorical projection from the realm of natural processes and events onto the discourse of musical meaning or form. In which case the only proper antidote is a deconstructive reading of those texts – Dunsby's among them – which espouse that delusive organicist idea, rather than a detailed counter-analysis that would pick out other (recalcitrant) features of the musical work but thereby confirm the self-same kinds of aesthetic value.

DeBellis's approach *via* Fodor and debates within cognitive psychology seems to me to provide one useful alternative to this way of thinking. That is to say, it lends strong support to the case for treating our musical perceptions as 'cognitively permeable', and therefore as subject to progressive refinement – to 'aesthetic education' in a sense very different from de Man's usage of the phrase – through our reading of intelligent analytic commentaries or critically informed scholarship. Moreover, it offers grounds for rejecting both the false idea that equates 'phenomenalism' with aesthetic ideology, and the equally false conception of analysis as always and everywhere complicit with a deep-laid conservative mystique of organic form. For this conception is based on a narrow understanding, one that takes Schenker's very overt ideological bias as somehow built into the very practice of analysis. Yet it has surely been the experience of many listeners – myself included – that analysis can and often does provide an insight into processes of tonal development, thematic transformation, subtle cross-reference between movements, and so forth, which had perhaps registered already in some subliminal way but which achieve far greater impact and expressive power once raised to the level of conscious awareness. Nor are such analyses always premised on a notion of organic unity whose effect – as the deconstructionists argue – is to repress or to marginalise any recalcitrant detail that does not fit in with their preconceived 'totalising' schema. Here again, this charge has a certain plausibility when brought against Schenker or analysts in the *echt*-Schenkerian line of descent, but amounts to no more than a wilful caricature if applied to 'analysis' in general. Thus, for instance, it is way off beam with respect to Donald Tovey's highly perceptive, intelligent, broadly formalistic but also (at times) decidedly anti-organicist essays in musical analysis (Tovey 1949). Nor can the general charge be sustained if one thinks of Hans Keller's more acerbic and shrewdly paradoxical reflections on music's resistance to certain kinds of orthodox analytic approach (Keller 1986, 1987, 1994). Indeed, one feature of any analysis worth reading – as likewise of any work that truly merits such treatment – is its capacity to foreground just those details or formal structures that *do not* fall in with routine (naturalised) habits of listener-response.

Of course it may be said – and has been said by theorists from Kerman down – that this is just the point of readings which challenge the very practice of analysis in so far as it (supposedly) lends support to such naive 'phenomenalist' assumptions. But then one has to ask what could possibly count as 'resistance' to aesthetic ideology if not our critically informed *perception* of salient formal or structural elements which are there *in the work* – and available to analysis – rather than figuring merely as constructs of a certain theoretical discourse on music. For this latter approach marks a crucial shift from the kind of criticism that makes some claim to actually engage with our musical experience to the kind of linguistic (or metalinguistic) theory that treats such claims as nothing more than a figment of naive organicist thinking. It is a shift clearly visible if one compares Adorno's writings on music with the sorts of writing that have lately captured the high ground of music-theoretical thought. (See especially Adorno 1991a,b, 1998a,b; also Paddison 1993.) To be sure, he sharply rejects any straightforward appeal to 'perception' or 'experience' that would treat such notions as somehow providing a solid basis for judgement as opposed to the giddy gyrations of abstract theory (Adorno 1982b). Thus if one thing typifies Adorno's thinking about music, literature, and philosophy alike it is his relentless critique of the positivist idea that we could ever have 'immediate' perceptual acquaintance with those sense-data that supposedly constitute the very foundation of knowledge (Adorno *et al.* 1976). Hence his 'negative-dialectical' approach, derived from Hegel in so far as it insists on the culturally or socially mediated character of perception, but rejecting Hegel's premature appeal to a knowledge (that of 'Absolute Reason') that would finally transcend all such limiting perspectives (Adorno 1974, 1997).

So to this extent Adorno is in agreement with the deconstructionists, that is to say, in his resolute refusal to countenance any notion of musical meaning or form that derives from the illicit (metaphorical) projection of naive phenomenalist categories. However he goes nothing like so far toward a purely linguistic or rhetorical approach that would treat all talk of musical 'perception' or 'experience' as resulting from a straightforward failure to acknowledge the discursively constructed character of music and – moreover – the role of 'analysis' as a discourse that functions entirely in the service of aesthetic ideology. For it is Adorno's leading contention that music (like language) possesses a certain stubborn 'particularity' which cannot be subsumed under models or metaphors – such as that of 'organic form' – that derive from some preconceived interpretative schema. Of course de Man makes a similar claim for the 'materiality' of language in so far as this is conceived as a kind of non-signifying substance or substrate that precedes and (somehow) effectively resists the imposition of ideological meanings and values (de Man 1986, 1996). However there is no making sense of such a claim if, as I have argued, it blocks the appeal to those language-constitutive (i.e., semantic) attributes that define *what counts* as an item of meaningful utterance, rather than a sequence of pre-articulate noises or senseless (purely 'material') textual inscriptions.

At any rate it is clear that Adorno has nothing like this in mind when he stakes his case for the capacity of music or literature to resist our ideological preconceptions on their harbouring of certain recalcitrant features that cannot convincingly be brought under some generalised conceptual scheme. Indeed this constantly reiterated stress on the tension between 'particular' and 'universal' is the driving force of Adorno's negative dialectic and the chief justification of his claim for the emancipatory power of certain musical and literary works (Adorno 1973a, 1974, 1997). Thus, despite his staunch Hegelian insistence that 'immediacy' is the merest of phenomenalist illusions, Adorno still holds out for the idea that our critically informed experience of music must be responsive to something *there* in the work, even though – as he is equally at pains to remind us – such experience is always subject to complex forms of social and cultural mediation. For it would otherwise be sheerly nonsensical to argue that music has this capacity to challenge our acculturated habits of response and hence to resist various kinds of deeply entrenched aesthetic ideology.

This is also why Adorno – unlike the New Musicologists – comes out strongly in defence of 'analysis' as a means of sharpening our musical perceptions, whether as listeners or performers. Indeed in one of his last published essays – transcribed from a radio talk – Adorno makes this point *via* a consideration of the way that 'structural listening' has become ever more crucial to the experience of music as composers have themselves been driven to explore ever more complex and demanding forms of musical expression (Adorno 1982a). That is to say, any adequate (perceptive and intelligent) rendition of a Schoenberg quartet, or a work that resists our more accustomed intuitive modes of response, will necessarily involve a great deal of analysis, some of it no doubt at a preconscious level, which makes all the difference between just playing the notes and playing them with a grasp of this deeper structural logic. Analysis begins precisely at the point where conventional commentary ends, that is, with the critically informed perception of just those salient 'particularities' of detail and structure that are strictly immanent to the work in hand and cannot be subsumed under broad generic concepts or notions of typical 'period' style. Above all it is Adorno's contention that performers and listeners who manifest a grasp of such details are thereby exercising the kind of musical intelligence that the composer must already have exercised in relation to his or her inherited range of tonal, thematic, or developmental resources. In other words, 'structural listening' of this kind is *not* just one way of listening among others – perhaps (as some New Musicologists would claim) an elitist or culturally mandarin practice – but the means of coming as close as possible to a true understanding of the work. Nor does it betoken a falling-in with established, academically canonised conceptions of form, meaning, and value which reveal nothing more than the analyst's professional self-interest or ideological complicity. Rather it provides the only hope of resisting those pressures of cultural commodification and regressive, fetishised musical perception which – according to Adorno – have well-nigh extinguished the capacity of listeners to engage with music at a level beyond the most banal and cliché-ridden habits of response (Adorno 1991c).

VI

One characteristic of the New Musicology is its extreme ambivalence toward Adorno. This comes out most strikingly if one compares two books by Rose Rosengard Subotnik, the earlier of which (*Developing Variations*, 1991) bears clear marks of his influence, while the second (*Deconstructive Variations*, 1996) adopts a far more sceptical view, especially with regard to the idea of 'structural listening'. Thus she now considers this to be merely an expression of Adorno's narrowly formalist aesthetic values, his snobbish attachment to 'high' musical culture, and – worst of all – his downright contempt for any kind of music (or musical experience) that involves straightforward enjoyment, rather than a strenuous self-denying ordinance and effort of analysis on the listener's part. For why should we suppose that the latter is any more valuable or that we ought to give up such simple satisfactions for the sake of some highly abstract idea of music's critical-emancipatory power? Or again, what is the virtue of any approach – like Adorno's – that would have us sternly reject those pleasures for the sake of a heightened analytical awareness that (supposedly) empowers us to resist the commodification of musical experience and the blandishments of the culture industry? In short, the idea of 'structural listening' is one that imposes its own criteria for what counts as genuine musical experience, namely the kind of culturally and socio-economically privileged experience that comes of a commitment to canonical values as enshrined in the 'great tradition' of Western art-music and the modes of analysis that have grown up around it. Much better – Subotnik now thinks – that we should jettison this whole elitist conception and accept the sheer variety of musical pleasures, including those that Adorno would doubtless regard as exposing its adherents to the worst, most degrading and manipulative forms of mass-cultural production (Adorno 1991c).

If one wishes to explain this turn against Adorno in Subotnik's later writing then it has to do mainly with two lines of argument that play a relatively low-key role in her earlier book but which emerge at full blast in *Deconstructive Variations*. One is the cultural-relativist idea that issues of musical form, structure, meaning, or value can be addressed only from some given social perspective or from within some particular 'discourse' which will always interpret those issues in keeping with its own ideological agenda. Thus Adorno's commitment to analysis and structural listening is enough to mark him out as an upholder of cultural values that can have not the least purchase on other, less 'complex' but just as valuable modes of musical experience. Along with this goes Subotnik's increasing scepticism with regard to the Adornian claim that certain works – and certain analytically describable features of them – might put up a resistance to dominant forms of 'regressive' listening or cultural commodification. In short, she has moved a long way toward endorsing the two chief tenets of deconstruction, at least as the New Musicologists conceive it: the discursively constructed character of musical values and – closely allied to that – the fallacy of thinking that value-judgements could ever be grounded in veridical perceptions of musical structure or form. So – my examples, not hers – should any listener prefer (say) Michael Nyman to Beethoven, or Philip Glass to J.S. Bach, or Arvo Pärt to William Byrd, then we had better just say that these judgements are culture-relative (or listener-dependent) and in no way capable of ranking on a scale of perceptual acuity or structural grasp. For this would be to fall straight back into the trap of an aesthetic ideology that failed to acknowledge its own deep investment in prevailing ideas of what properly counts as a perceptive or musically informed response to works whose self-evident canonical status requires nothing less.

At this point the reader may protest that I am talking not so much about *deconstruction* in a musicological context as about the much wider cultural phenomenon of *postmodernism* in so far as it has influenced recent debates on and around music. (See Jameson 1991; Kramer 1995; Lochhead and Auner [eds] 2002; McClary 2000; Norris 1990, 1993.) After all, in so far as the term 'postmodernism' has any specific application here, then it signifies something very like the kinds of argument that I have summarised in the above few paragraphs. Thus to call oneself a musical postmodernist is presumably to endorse most of the claims put forward in Subotnik's *Deconstructive*

Variations. These are, in brief: (1) the obsolescence of 'high' modernist values such as those embodied in the music of Schoenberg and his disciples, along with the canonical tradition of great works to which Schoenberg claimed to stand as revolutionary heir and successor; (2) the irrelevance (or at any rate the strictly limited scope) of music analysis or 'structural listening' as criteria of aesthetic worth; and (3), following directly from this, the open multiplicity of styles, genres, listening practices, pleasures, socio-cultural contexts, and so forth, that cannot be brought under any such reductive or monolithic standard of value. To which might be added (4) the linguistic or narrative 'turn' in much postmodern theorising which rejects any single, privileged discourse or master-narrative – like that of mainstream musicology – and replaces it with the notion of multiple 'first-order natural pragmatic' narratives, each of them valid on its own terms, but none of them possessing any claim to ultimate authority (Lyotard 1984).

So when Subotnik (1996) intersperses her more 'theoretical' discussions with sundry illustrative anecdotes from her musical, professional, and personal experience this is very much a part of her wider attack on the governing norms of 'serious' academic discourse (see also DeNora 2000). What she is out to deconstruct is precisely the idea – raised to a high point of doctrine by formalists or analysts – that such discourse has no place for such merely 'extraneous' narratives since its sole legitimate concern is with 'the work', or with structural features of the work that best ensure respect for its properly autonomous status. And the same applies to that organicist metaphor of musical 'growth' and 'development' which has lent credence to a certain prevalent musicological narrative, one that elevates just those works – and just those aesthetic values – that keep the analysts in business. So a further strategy for opening up the canon is by telling alternative stories (such as that of Subotnik's repeated put-downs by the musicological establishment) that highlight her sense of increasing disenchantment with the kinds of academic discourse to which she had once (with whatever reservations) implicitly subscribed. Whence the postmodern-cultural-relativist claim that in the end there is nothing more to musical value or judgement than those various stories – or narrative constructions – that constitute the musical experience of various listeners (Solie [ed.] 1993). No doubt the analysts have their own favoured narrative, albeit one that admits of some disagreement as to just which composers, works, or structural aspects should count as most 'intrinsically' valuable. But theirs is a story that likewise involves certain culture-specific criteria, among them – not least – the very idea of 'intrinsic' musical value and, along with it, the closely associated notions of formal complexity, organic unity, and 'developing variation'. That this was Subotnik's choice of title for her earlier (1991) book is a measure of the distance that she has travelled from a qualified commitment to critical theory in the Adornian mode to a full-fledged postmodernist approach that finds no room for such 'elitist' conceptions of musical form and value.

So there is, to be sure, a sense in which my reader is right to protest that what I have been describing in parts of this chapter – especially the last few pages – has more to do with musical postmodernism than with deconstructive musicology. And I would grant that the work of de Man-inspired exegetes like Street has little in common (superficially at least) with the kinds of post-modernist writing that summarily reject any claim for analysis as conducive to modes of 'structural listening' that can actually enhance our appreciation of music. Still the main tendency of deconstruction when carried across from the reading of verbal to non-verbal (e.g., musical) 'texts' is to lay great stress on the discursively constructed character of all perceptions and hence to minimise the role of music *itself* in contesting or subverting received analytical procedures. Here again Adorno provides the most instructive counter-example, insisting as he does on the 'language-character' of music, that is, its ineluctable mediation by various discourses of meaning, value, and cultural significance, but also on its power to challenge ideological preconceptions through its stubborn particularity of detail and structure. This is also where Adorno can be seen to come out in strong opposition to the kinds of modish value-relativism that leave no room for comparative judgement on grounds of thematic integration, harmonic resourcefulness, formal complexity, or long-range structural development. Indeed one can readily imagine Adorno's response had he lived on to witness the current minimalist vogue or the respectful treatment mostly accorded – even by 'serious' critics and reviewers – to the music of Philip Glass or Michael Nyman. For he would surely have viewed such developments as further confirmation of his gloomy prognosis with regard to the 'regressive' or 'fetishised' character of musical perception in an age given over to the commercial dictates of mass-cultural consumption (Adorno 1991c).

It is worth recalling Kerman's original plea – in that 1980 essay – for a music criticism that would have the courage to expand its intellectual horizons, chiefly by meeting the challenge of ideas from other 'theoretical' quarters, but also – concomitant with that – by loosening the hold of a concept of 'analysis' deeply bound up with suspect ideological values. That both wishes have since come true (perhaps beyond Kerman's wildest hopes) is a fact that cannot fail to strike anyone who has followed debates in the more 'advanced' journals of music theory over the past two decades. Still one may doubt that the resultant benefits have been altogether what Kerman envisaged when he launched his reformist crusade. For there has now grown up a kind of counter-orthodoxy, one that routinely presses so far in its critique of analysis and its 'deconstruction' of musical perceptions and judgements as to risk altogether losing touch with the music which provides its (increasingly notional) object-domain. Of course it is the case – one borne out by any valid or convincing piece of analysis – that our perceptions can be changed quite decisively through the reading of texts that adopt a 'theoretical' line on some issue regarding the detailed structure of specific musical works. This applies just as much to deconstructive analyses – like Street's – as to those, like Dunsby's, which espouse a more 'conservative' idea of organic form. However there is a problem about any theory which purports to deconstruct the very idea that analysis can indeed sharpen our musical perceptions rather than promote an aesthetic ideology whose source is precisely that 'phenomenalist' appeal to modes of perceptual (no matter how refined or theoretically informed) experience.

I have suggested that certain recent developments in cognitive psychology might offer the best way out of this curious dilemma. Fodor himself suggests as much when he begins an essay with the engagingly upfront statement: 'The thing is, I hate cultural relativism' (Fodor 1990: 23). What he chiefly has in mind is the kind of relativist thinking that has resulted from certain ideas in post-empiricist philosophy of science, among them Thomas Kuhn's influential claim that scientific theories are always 'underdetermined' by the best available evidence, and that evidence is always 'theory-laden' to the extent of precluding any decision between rival hypotheses on the basis of straightforward empirical warrant (Kuhn 1970). Fodor's idea – as developed in *The Modularity of Mind* – is that this kind of far-gone epistemic relativism can best be countered by drawing a distinction between, on the one hand, those faculties that are relatively 'encapsulated' or 'cognitively impervious' and, on the other, those that are open to a wider range of perceptual or cognitive inputs (Fodor 1983). So there is simply no need to take the Kuhnian paradigm-relativist path and conclude that every major episode of scientific theory-change involves such a drastic shift in the currency of knowledge that it must affect not only what counts as an observational datum but also what counts as a 'basic' theoretical truth or even – at the limit – a hitherto unquestioned axiom of logic (see also Quine 1961). Fodor finds this a wholly unacceptable conclusion since it fails to explain how we could ever have knowledge of the growth of scientific knowledge. Thus he puts forward the modularity thesis as a means of distinguishing between those truths that are 'hard-wired' or integral to the nature of rational thought and those empirical findings that might just be subject to revision or modification under pressure of recalcitrant evidence. That is to say, it is the degree of cognitive 'permeability' that enables us to make such distinctions and thereby effectively hold the line against Kuhnian, Quinean, and other versions of the wholesale paradigm-relativist approach.

This is not the place for a detailed discussion of Fodor's arguments in epistemology and philosophy of science. However they do have a useful bearing on the issue as to whether our musical perceptions are theoretically informed or – as the cultural relativists would have it – 'constructed' through and through by various modes of discursive or narrative representation. On Fodor's account (suitably modified) one can make a strong case for the veridical character of certain musical perceptions even though they are always, in some degree, informed by a knowledge acquired from various extra-perceptual sources, among them – not least – our reading of analytic commentaries or musico-historical studies. On the deconstructivist account, conversely, any such appeal to 'perception' must be thought to betray a lingering attachment to the values enshrined in aesthetic ideology and a refusal to acknowledge that language (or discourse) goes 'all the way down'. This is the musicological equivalent of what Fodor has in mind when he excoriates cultural relativists for blithely endorsing a doctrine that would collapse every last distinction between truth and falsehood, knowledge and belief, or science and pseudo-science. Thus in both cases there is a failure to conceive that certain cognitive processes exhibit a high degree of 'encapsulation', that is, of uniform functional role despite and across otherwise large differences of cultural, socio-historical, or idiosyncratic response. Such would be, for instance, the processes involved in relatively abstract mental operations like logical reasoning, mathematical thought, or the ability to use and to comprehend language in its syntactic as distinct from its semantic or pragmatic aspects. With regard to the latter – as Fodor remarks – there is always a need for regular inputs from a wide range of informational sources that are processed by other, more 'cognitively pervious' or context-sensitive modules, and which therefore require a more holistic approach. Where the relativists go wrong is in thinking that holism applies right across the board, that is, not only to matters of culturally informed interpretation but also to functions – like logical reasoning or grammatical competence – whose distinctive nature is precisely their need to maintain this degree of insulation from other experiential inputs in order to do their specialised job (see also Fodor and LePore 1991).

So when relativists standardly invoke Kuhn on the 'underdetermination' of theory by evidence and the 'theory-laden' character of observation-statements, the best counter-argument (Fodor thinks) is one that deploys the modularity-thesis in order to explain why certain forms of conceptual reasoning and certain modes of perceptual response are exempt from such holistic treatment. And when music theorists likewise suggest that our perceptions are 'constructed' by various ideologically prevalent discourses then perhaps the best argument is one that stresses the relative 'encapsulation' of perceptual experience and the trans-cultural validity of certain analytic concepts and categories. On the other hand – as signalled by those words 'perhaps' and 'relative' – there are problems with any too-direct application of Fodor's approach in cognitive psychology to the sorts of issue that typically arise with respect to musical experience and judgement. For here, as I have said, there is a strong case for holding that perceptual responses are always informed – albeit not wholly determined – by certain acquired theoretical concepts as well as by a range of cultural and socio-historical values. So it looks as if the modularity-thesis will need at least some modification or local tweaking if it is to offer much help with the issues presently at hand.

This problem will naturally seem least pressing if one accepts a theory – like that advanced by Lerdahl and Jackendoff (1983) – which explicates the structure of tonal music through a transformational-generative model derived from Chomskian linguistics, one with its source in just the kind of modular cognitive-psychological approach that Fodor also champions. For it is then not difficult to make the case for musical 'competence' – like our competence in verbal language – as primarily a matter of certain *syntactic* regularities which display the required degree of encapsulation, that is, the functional capacity to operate at a 'deep' level sufficiently removed from surface variations of meaning and style. However, as is well known, this early-Chomskian approach soon ran into problems when it sought to account for those other (semantic and pragmatic) dimensions of linguistic competence which clearly played a more than 'surface' role in enabling speakers to distinguish grammatically well-formed from grammatically ill-formed sentences (cf. Chomsky 1957 and 1966). Thus a good deal of Chomsky's later work – and that of his like-minded colleagues in cognitive psychology – has been devoted to revising the unidirectional ('syntax-first') model and developing a theory of 'generative semantics' with the scope to accommodate just such cases. However this also has certain implications for the 'strong' modularity-thesis, that is to say, for the functionalist idea of language – at any rate the syntactic component of language – as 'encapsulated' or 'cognitively impermeable'. For that claim must be subject to more or less extensive revision depending on the degree to which speakers' intuitions with regard to grammatical correctness are affected by the kinds of semantic or pragmatic knowledge that cannot be treated in any such 'hard-wired' modular terms. And this applies even more in the case of music since here, as I have said, there is something highly implausible about the notion of a grammar (or syntax) of musical response that functions independently of inputs from our wider, theoretically informed or musically literate experience.

VII

All of which bring us back to Kerman and his shrewdly provocative phrasing of the question 'how we got into analysis, and how to get out'. One is tempted – in view of developments since 1981 – to suggest that the question now be re-phrased as 'how we got into theory, and how to get out'. Nevertheless this temptation ought to be resisted given the extent to which 'theory', in one form or another, enters into all our musical experience and affects the very character of that experience, whether consciously or not. (See especially DeBellis 1995; also Cook 1993; Deutsch [ed.] 1999; Dowling and Harwood 1986; Francès 1988; Hargreaves 1986; Krumhansl 1990; Parncutt 1989; Sloboda 1985.) My own view – as should be clear by now – is that theory does best when it remains closely in touch with the findings of musical analysis, which in turn does best when it retains a respect (though not an uncritical reverence) for our intuitive musical perceptions. Any theory that rejects the claims of analysis – or 'structural listening' – as nothing more than a product of aesthetic ideology will be prone to over-estimate the role of theoretical discourse in promoting such resistance and, by the same token, to under-estimate music's intrinsic capacity to challenge or unsettle our habituated modes of response. Indeed, this whole debate has tended to unfold very much along the lines that Kerman laid down when he offered critics a straightforward *choice* between established and newly emergent paradigms, as if getting 'into' theory were somehow the precondition – as well as the reward – for getting themselves 'out' of analysis. But there is nothing to be gained and a great deal to be lost by promoting such a downright Manichean attitude. What is needed, rather, is a sensible acknowledgement that our understanding of music along with the kinds of ideological discourse that have grown up around it is best served through a joint application of theoretically informed analysis and analytically informed perception.

Here one might recall de Man's paradoxical statement, in his essay 'The Resistance to Theory', that 'technically correct' (i.e., deconstructive) readings are at once 'irrefutable' in so far as they result from a rhetorically alert construal but also 'potentially totalitarian' in so far as they close down other, perhaps more rewarding possibilities. Thus (to repeat): 'since the structures and functions they expose do not lead to the knowledge of an entity (such as language) but are an unreliable process of knowledge production that prevents all entities, including linguistic entities, from coming into discourse as such, they are indeed universals, consistently defective models of language's impossibility to be a model language' (de Man 1986: 19). One way of grasping what has happened as a consequence of the deconstructive 'turn' in recent music theory is to run the fairly simple thought-experiment of substituting 'music' for 'language' (and 'musical' for 'linguistic') in the above-quoted passage. For it then becomes clear that the upshot of such theorising is not only to resist a certain kind of ideologically motivated discourse *about* music – just the kind of discourse that de Man targets in his essays on literature and philosophy – but also to deprive *music itself* of any power to muster such resistance through its intrinsic structural features. After all, there is some plausibility to de Man's claim that 'phenomenalist' readings are aberrant when applied to linguistic texts since 'it is not *a priori* certain that language functions according to principles which are those, or which are *like* those, of the phenomenal world' (de Man 1986: 11). Indeed – or so he would have us believe – this idea is just a variant of the 'Cratylist' delusion which posits some quasi-natural kinship or affinity between signifier and signified, and which thus gives rise to all manner of naive 'organicist' metaphors and concepts. But when applied to music the argument simply does not work since here there is no escaping the fact that our musical experience *must* be perceptually grounded, even if – as also needs stressing – our perceptions can always be modified, refined, or subject to challenge through exposure to analysis and theory.

Thus the 'Cratylist' charge has far less force in a context – that of music criticism – where it pertains only to the crudest sort of mimeticist thinking and not to the perfectly valid conception of music as involving a constant interplay between perceptual and analytically informed modes of listener-response. For if pressed too hard then it is apt to leave the theorist with nothing very much to talk about, that is, with no theme upon which to practise her deconstructive variations apart from a well-nigh ubiquitous notion of 'aesthetic ideology' that offers a convenient pretext or foil for just this kind of metalinguistic or arcane theoretical discourse. No doubt it is an excellent thing to keep open the channels of communication between disciplines, among them the disciplines of music criticism and literary theory. However, as I have argued, there are problems with any approach which carries this project to the point of denying that 'analysis' has anything of interest to contribute save an object-lesson in naive 'phenomenalist' errors and a constant unwitting demonstration of its own ideological complicity.

References

Aiello, Rita and John Sloboda (eds) (1993). *Musical Perceptions*. New York: Oxford University Press.

Adorno, T.W. (1973a). *Philosophy of Modern Music*, trans. W. Blomster. London: Sheed & Ward.

——(1973b). *The Jargon of Authenticity*. London: Routledge & Kegan Paul.

——(1974). *Negative Dialectics*, trans. E.B. Ashton. London: Routledge & Kegan Paul.

——(1982a). 'On the problem of music analysis', trans. Max Paddison. *Music Analysis* 1(2): 170–87.

——(1982b). *Against Epistemology: A Metacritique*, trans. Willis Domingo. Oxford: Blackwell.

——(1991a). *Alban Berg: Master of the Smallest Link*, trans. Juliane Brand and Christopher Hailey. Cambridge: Cambridge University Press.

——(1991b). *In Search of Wagner*, trans. Rodney Livingstone. London: Verso.

——(1991c). *The Culture Industry: Selected Essays on Mass Culture* (ed.) J.M. Bernstein. London: Routledge.

——(1997). *Aesthetic Theory*, trans. Robert Hullot-Kentnor. London: Athlone.

——(1998a). *Beethoven: The Philosophy of Music*, trans. Edmund Jephcott. Oxford: Polity.

——(1998b). *Quasi Una Fantasia: Essays on Modern Music*, trans. Rodney Livingstone. London: Verso.

Adorno, T.W. *et al.* (1976). *The Positivist Dispute in German Sociology*, trans. Glyn Adey and David Frisby. London: Heinemann.

Baker, James M., David W. Beach and Jonathan W. Bernard (eds) (1997). *Music Theory in Concept and Practice*. Rochester, N.Y.: University of Rochester Press.

Barry, Kevin (1987). *Language, Music and the Sign*. Cambridge: Cambridge University Press.

Beach, David (ed.) (1983). *Aspects of Schenkerian Theory*. New Haven: Yale University Press.

Bent, Ian and William Drabkin (1987). *Analysis*. Basingstoke: Macmillan Press.

——(ed.) (1996). *Music Theory in the Age of Romanticism*. Cambridge: Cambridge University Press.

Bergeron, Katherine and Philip V. Bohlman (eds) (1992). *Disciplining Music: Musicology and its Canons*. Chicago: University of Chicago Press.

Blasius, Leslie D. (1996). *Schenker's Argument and the Claims of Music Theory*. Cambridge: Cambridge University Press.

Burnham, Scott (1996). 'A.B. Marx and the gendering of sonata form', in Bent (ed.) (1996). pp. 163–86.

Chomsky, Noam (1957). *Syntactic Structures*. The Hague: Mouton.

——(1966). *Topics in the Theory of Generative Grammar*. The Hague: Mouton.

Cook, Nicholas (1989). 'Music theory and "good comparison": a Viennese perspective', *Journal of Music Theory* 33: 117–42.

——(1993). 'Perception: a perspective from music theory', in Aiello and Sloboda (eds). pp. 64–94.

——(1994). *A Guide to Musical Analysis*. Oxford: Oxford University Press.

——(1996). *Analysis Through Composition*. Oxford: Oxford University Press.

Cook, Nicholas and Mark Everist (eds) (1999). *Re-Thinking Music*. Oxford: Oxford University Press.

Cooke, Deryck (1962). *The Language of Music*. Oxford: Oxford University Press.

Dahlhaus, Carl (1981). *Esthetics of Music*, trans. William Austin. Cambridge: Cambridge University Press.

——(1983). *Analysis and Value Judgement*, trans. Siegmund Levarie. New York: Pendragon Press.

Damschroder, David (1990). *Music Theory from Zarlino to Schenker: A Bibliography and Guide*. Stuyvesant, N.Y.: Pendragon Press.

DeBellis, Mark A. (1995). *Music and Conceptualization*. Cambridge: Cambridge University Press.

de Man, Paul (1979). *Allegories of Reading: Figural Language in Rousseau, Nietzsche, Rilke, and Proust*. New Haven: Yale University Press.

——(1983). *Blindness and Insight: Essays in the Rhetoric of Contemporary Criticism*. London: Methuen.

——(1983a). 'The rhetoric of temporality', in de Man (1983). pp. 187–208.

——(1983b). 'Heidegger's exegeses of Hölderlin', in de Man (1983). pp. 246–66.

——(1983c). 'The rhetoric of blindness: Jacques Derrida's reading of Rousseau', in de Man (1983). pp. 102–42.

——(1984). *The Rhetoric of Romanticism*. New York: Columbia University Press.

——(1984a). 'Aesthetic formalization in Kleist', in de Man (1984). pp. 263–90.

——(1986). 'The resistance to theory', in *The Resistance to Theory*. Manchester: Manchester University Press. pp. 5–20.

——(1996). *Aesthetic Ideology* (ed.) Andrzej Warminski. Minneapolis: University of Minnesota Press.

Dempster, Douglas and Matthew Brown (1990). 'Evaluating musical analyses and theories: five perspectives', *Journal of Music Theory* 34: 247–80.

DeNora, Tia (2000). *Music and the Everyday*. Cambridge: Cambridge University Press.

Derrida, Jacques (1976). *Of Grammatology*, trans. Gayatri Chakravorty Spivak. Baltimore: Johns Hopkins University Press.

Deutsch, Diana (ed.) (1999). *The Psychology of Music*. San Diego: Academic Press.

Dowling, W.J. and Dane L. Harwood (1986). *Music Cognition*. San Diego: Academic Press.

Dunsby, Jonathan (1981). *Structural Ambiguity in Brahms: Analytical Approaches to Four Works*. Ann Arbor: UMI Research Press.

——(1983). 'The Multi-piece in Brahms: *Fantasien*, Op. 116', in R. Pascall (ed.), *Brahms: Biographical, Documentary and Analytical Studies*. Cambridge: Cambridge University Press.

Dunsby, Jonathan and Arnold Whittall (1988). *Music Analysis in Theory and Practice.* New Haven: Yale University Press.

Fodor, Jerry A. (1976). *The Language of Thought.* Hassocks: Harvester Press.

——(1983). *The Modularity of Mind: An Essay on Faculty Psychology.* Cambridge, Mass.: MIT Press.

——(1990). *A Theory of Content and Other Essays.* Cambridge, Mass.: MIT Press.

Fodor, Jerry and Ernest LePore (1991). *Holism: A Shopper's Guide.* Oxford: Blackwell.

Forte, Allen and Steven E. Gilbert (1982). *Introduction to Schenkerian Analysis.* New York: Norton.

Francès, Robert (1988). *The Perception of Music,* trans. W.J. Dowling. Hillsdale, N.J.: Lawrence Erlbaum Associates.

Gasché, Rodolphe (1998). *The Wild Card of Reading: On Paul de Man.* Cambridge, Mass.: Harvard University Press.

Goehr, Lydia (1992). *The Imaginary Museum of Musical Works: An Essay in the Philosophy of Music.* Oxford: Clarendon Press.

Hargreaves, David J. (1986). *The Developmental Psychology of Music.* Cambridge: Cambridge University Press.

Heidegger, Martin (1962). *Being and Time,* trans. John Mcquarrie and Edward Robinson. Oxford: Blackwell.

Hesse, Hermann (1990). *The Glass Bead Game,* trans. Richard and Clara Winston. New York: Henry Holt.

Jameson, Fredric (1991). *Postmodernism, or, the Cultural Logic of Late Capitalism.* London: Verso.

Keller, Hans (1986). *The Great Haydn Quartets: Their Interpretation.* London: Dent.

——(1987). *Criticism.* London: Faber.

——(1994). *Essays on Music* (ed.) C. Wintle. Cambridge: Cambridge University Press.

Kerman, Joseph (1980). 'How we got into analysis, and how to get out', *Critical Inquiry* 7: 311–31.

——(1983). 'A few canonic variations', *Critical Inquiry* **10**: 107–25.

——(1985). *Musicology.* London: Fontana. (Published in the United States as *Contemplating Music,* Cambridge, Mass.: Harvard University Press.)

Kleist, Heinrich von (1947). 'Essay on the puppet theater', trans. Eugene Jolas, *Partisan Review* **14**: 57–62.

Korsyn, Kevin (1993). 'Brahms research and aesthetic ideology', *Music Analysis* **12**: 89–103.

Kramer, Lawrence (1995). *Classical Music and Postmodern Knowledge.* Berkeley: University of California Press.

Krumhansl, Carol (1990). *Cognitive Foundations of Musical Pitch.* Oxford: Oxford University Press.

Kuhn, Thomas S. (1970). *The Structure of Scientific Revolutions,* 2nd edn. Chicago: University of Chicago Press.

Lacoue-Labarthe, Philippe and Jean-Luc Nancy (1988). *The Literary Absolute: The Theory of Literature in German Romanticism,* trans. Philip Barnard and Cheryl Lester. Albany: State University of New York Press.

Lerdahl, Fred and Ray Jackendoff (1983). *A Generative Theory of Tonal Music.* Cambridge, Mass.: MIT Press.

Lochhead, Judy and Joseph Auner (eds) (2002). *Postmodern Music/Postmodern Thought.* New York & London: Garland.

Lyotard, Jean-François (1984). *The Postmodern Condition: A Report on Knowledge,* trans. Geoff Bennington and Brian Massumi. Manchester: Manchester University Press.

McClary, Susan (1991). *Feminine Endings: Music, Gender, and Sexuality*. Minneapolis: University of Minnesota Press.

——(2000). *Conventional Wisdom: The Content of Musical Form*. Berkeley: University of California Press.

Meyer, Leonard (1967). *Music, the Arts, and Ideas*. Chicago: University of Chicago Press.

Narmour, E. (1977). *Beyond Schenkerism: The Need for Alternatives in Music Analysis*. Chicago: University of Chicago Press.

Neubauer, John (1986). *The Emancipation of Music from Language: Departure from Mimesis in Eighteenth-century Aesthetics*. New Haven: Yale University Press.

Norris, Christopher (1987). *Jacques Derrida*. London: Fontana; Cambridge, Mass.: Harvard University Press.

——(1988). *Paul de Man: Deconstruction and the Critique of Aesthetic Ideology*. New York: Routledge.

——(1989). 'Utopian deconstruction: Ernst Bloch, Paul de Man and the politics of music', in Norris (ed.), *Music and the Politics of Culture*. London: Lawrence & Wishart. pp. 325–47

——(1990). *What's Wrong with Postmodernism: Critical Theory and the Ends of Philosophy*. Baltimore: Johns Hopkins University Press.

——(1992). *Deconstruction and the Interests of Theory*. Leicester: Leicester University Press.

——(1993). *The Truth About Postmodernism*. Oxford: Blackwell.

——(2000). *Deconstruction and the Unfinished Project of Modernity*. London: Continum; New York: Routledge.

——(2002). *Deconstruction: Theory and Practice*, 3rd edn. London: Routledge.

Paddison, Max (1993). *Adorno's Aesthetics of Music*. Cambridge: Cambridge University Press.

Parncutt, Richard (1989). *Harmony: A Psychoacoustical Approach*. Berlin: Springer-Verlag.

Plato (1997). *Cratylus*, in J.M. Cooper (ed.), *Plato: Complete Works*. Indianapolis, IN: Hackett.

Pople, Anthony (ed.) (1994). *Theory, Analysis, and Meaning in Music*. Cambridge: Cambridge University Press.

Quine, W.V. (1961). 'Two dogmas of empiricism', in *From a Logical Point of View*, 2nd edn. Cambridge, Mass.: Harvard University Press. pp. 10–46.

Schenker, Heinrich (1973). *Harmony* (ed.) Oswald Jonas, trans. Elisabeth Mann Borgese. Cambridge, Mass.: MIT Press.

——(1979). *Free Composition*, trans. and (ed.) Ernst Oster. New York: Longman.

Schiller, Friedrich (1967). *On the Aesthetic Education of Man, in a Series of Letters*, trans. E.M. Wilkinson and L.A. Willoughby. Oxford: Clarendon Press.

Schoenberg, Arnold (1984). *Style and Idea: Selected Writings of Arnold Schoenberg*, trans. Leo Black. London: Faber.

——(1995). *The Musical Idea and the Logic, Technique, and Art of its Presentation*, trans. Patricia Carpenter and Severine Neff. New York: Columbia University Press.

Siegel, Hedi (ed.) (1990). *Schenker Studies*. Cambridge: Cambridge University Press.

Sloboda, John (1985). *The Musical Mind: The Cognitive Psychology of Music*. Oxford: Oxford University Press.

Solie, Ruth A. (1980). 'The living work: organicism and musical analysis', *Nineteenth-Century Musicology* 4: 147–56.

——(ed.) (1993). *Musicology and Difference*. Berkeley: University of California Press.

Stradling, Robert A. and Meirion Hughes (1993). *The English Musical Renaissance, 1860–1940: Construction and Deconstruction*. London: Routledge.

Street, Alan (1989). 'Superior myths, dogmatic allegories: the resistance to musical unity', *Music Analysis*, **8**: 77–123.

Subotnik, Rose Rosengard (1991). *Developing Variations: Style and Ideology in Western Music*. Minneapolis: University of Minnesota Press.

——(1996). *Deconstructive Variations: Music and Reason in Western Society*. Minneapolis: University of Minnesota Press.

Swain, Joseph (1994). 'Musical perception and musical communities', *Music Perception* **11**: 307–20.

Tovey, Donald Francis (1949). *Essays and Lectures on Music* (ed.) Hubert Foss. Oxford: Oxford University Press.

Treitler, Leo (1989). 'Music analysis in a historical context', in Treitler, *Music and the Historical Imagination*. Cambridge, Mass.: Harvard University Press. pp. 67–78.

Williams, Raymond (1976). *Keywords: A Vocabulary of Culture and Society*. London: Fontana.

——(1977). *Marxism and Literature*. Oxford: Oxford University Press.

Wolin, Richard (1990). *The Politics of Being: The Political Thought of Martin Heidegger*. New York: Columbia University Press.

Yeston, Maury (ed.) (1977). *Readings in Schenker Analysis and other Approaches*. New Haven: Yale University Press.

6
Change, Conservation, and Crisis-Management in the Discourse of Analytic Philosophy

I

There has been much debate in recent years as to whether 'analytic philosophy' describes a distinctive tradition of thought or perhaps just a loosely related set of family-resemblance features. Here I put the case that it is characterised chiefly by a constant oscillation between, on the one hand, 'revolutionary' proposals of an often quite extreme or extravagant kind and, on the other, a normalising impulse to talk such proposals down to the point where they appear compatible with common sense ideas about truth, knowledge, and reality. Thus one way of writing the history of post-1930 'mainstream' analytic philosophy would be in terms of this alternating pattern between far-out sceptical or anti-realist doctrines and consequent attempts to find some middle-ground approach that would defeat scepticism by tailoring truth to the scope and limits of epistemic or assertoric warrant. However – I maintain – the latter tendency has often gone along with a willingness to lean so far in the sceptical direction that it ends up by offering only a nuanced or elaborately qualified version of the anti-realist case. My chapter pursues this theme through various strong-revisionist episodes such as Quine's attack on the two 'last dogmas' of Carnap-style logical empiricism, Rorty's postmodern-pragmatist idea that philosophers should 'change the conversation' and simply stop worrying about those old problems, and again – albeit from a very different quarter – Dummett's anti-realist line of argument as applied to sundry areas of discourse from mathematics to history and morals.

I also examine various attempts by Davidson, Putnam, Wright, and others to arrive at a workable compromise solution *via* some suitably adjusted or provisoed alternative to the claims of alethic (objectivist) realism. However these proposals all have the drawback that they yield crucial ground to the sceptic at just the point where scepticism gets a hold, that is, by asserting the impossibility that truth might transcend our utmost powers of recognition or verification. I conclude that this dilemma has marked the discourse of analytic philosophy from its origins in Russell-style logical atomism to its latest manifestations in the work of McDowell, Putnam, Wright, and others. What unites these thinkers – despite some otherwise large divergences of view – is the shared adherence to an epistemic paradigm which prevents them (often against their otherwise quite overt realist inclinations) from straightforwardly acknowledging the existence of objective, verification-transcendent truths. Yet the latter view has not only been defended to powerful effect by other thinkers within the analytic tradition but also has a strong claim to represent the default position for anyone concerned with explaining our knowledge of the growth of knowledge or – what amounts to the same thing – our grasp of how we (like previous enquirers) may in future turn out to have held false beliefs despite our firm assurance to the contrary. Hence, I suggest, the deceptive ease with which 'post-analytic' philosophers like Rorty can dismiss the whole enterprise as terminally hooked on problems of its own tedious and pointless devising.

II

'There is the bit where you say it', as J.L. Austin once remarked, 'and there is the bit where you take it back.' One thing that Austin famously said and then took back was the constative/performative distinction, proposed in the early chapters of *How to Do Things With Words* and then quickly dropped in favour of a three-term (locutionary-illocutionary-perlocutionary) approach when problems arose with assigning speech-acts exclusively to one or the other binary class (Austin 1963). That he could thus change tack without much sign of embarrassment is a clear mark of Austin's distance – or the distance of Oxford-style 'ordinary language' philosophy – from the mainstream analytic tradition descending from Frege and Russell.

To be sure, Austin's approach is 'analytic' in the broad-church, doctrinally neutral sense that it involves close attention to those features of everyday communicative discourse that are taken to reward such treatment by revealing hitherto unnoticed subtleties and nuances. More than that, he shares something of the mainstream belief – classically expressed in essays like Frege's 'On Sense and Reference' and Russell's 'On Denoting' – that we can best get straight about certain philosophical perplexities by examining the logical grammar of various otherwise misleading expressions (Frege 1952; Russell 1905). So if indeed, for Austin, 'ordinary language' is the definitive court of appeal, still it is the case that unpacking its complexities may well turn out to involve a good deal in the way of semantic, grammatical, and contextual analysis. Yet of course it is precisely Austin's point – as against the Frege–Russell tradition – that philosophy can leave confusion worse confounded if it thinks to correct or to regiment our commonplace modes of talk by applying other, supposedly more rigorous standards of logical accountability. Thus he never goes quite so far as Wittgenstein in the therapeutic aim of giving philosophy peace by coaxing it down to a sensible acceptance of the way things stand with our communal 'language-games' or acculturated 'forms of life' (Wittgenstein 1953). Analysis might properly attempt to straighten out those kinds of ambiguous or misleading expression that sometimes (exceptionally) get in the way of effective linguistic uptake. However this attempt should always go along with a due sense of the hubris entailed by any notion that ordinary language is chronically in need of such applied philosophical therapy.

Hence Austin's well-known remark in his essay 'A Plea for Excuses' that 'our common stock of words embodies connections and distinctions [that are] likely to be more numerous, more sound, since they have stood up to the long test of the survival of the fittest, and more subtle, at least in all ordinary and reasonably practical matters, than any that you and I are likely to think up in our armchairs of an afternoon – the most favoured alternative method' (Austin 1961: 182). So when the term 'analytic' is stretched so far as to encompass Austin's project then it begins to look more like a label of convenience – or a loose-knit 'family resemblance' concept – than one that marks a distinctive school of philosophical thought or (still less) a well-defined set of philosophical methods and techniques. If it is taken to denominate a range of approaches, from Frege and Russell at the one extreme to Austin at the other, then perhaps we could place Gilbert Ryle somewhere near the mid-point on this scale with his idea of 'systematically misleading expressions' (Ryle 1954). These involve the kinds of category-mistake – or illicit transfer of concepts and predicates from one to another domain – that often cause philosophical confusion yet can scarcely be expunged from our language since they have played so central and enduring a role in our 'common sense' modes of belief. Indeed Ryle's ambivalence on this point is a major problem when assessing his arguments in *The Concept of Mind* against any version of Cartesian dualism or the myth of the 'ghost in the machine' (Ryle 1963). So there is undoubtedly a tension, here as elsewhere, between the claim of analysis to straighten out our naive, unexamined, or pre-philosophical modes of talk and the Austinian claim that – in the last analysis – such talk embodies our best, most reliable and time-tested source of wisdom.

However my chief purpose here is not to provide a full-scale taxonomy of various, more or less 'analytical' approaches, nor yet to adjudicate the issue between them. Probably Richard Rorty was right, in the Introduction to his anthology *The Linguistic Turn*, when he concluded that this was a pointless exercise since nothing could serve as a common criterion by which to rank their achievements (Rorty [ed.] 1967). Rather I shall ask just what it is about philosophy in the mainstream analytic tradition that makes it a distinctive enterprise, that constitutes its main agenda, and – more controversially – that now appears to have brought it out somewhere near the end of its intellectual tether. By this I do not mean to assert that there is no valuable work being done by philosophers who seek to continue that tradition, who inherit its main terms for debate, and who typically publish in the more prestigious peer-reviewed analytic journals. Much of that work has all the virtues that are standardly claimed for it, among them those of conceptual clarity and argumentative rigour. Also, at best, its practitioners are willing to follow Austin's genial example and 'take it back' – change their mind in public – if problems crop up with some erstwhile firmly-held item of philosophic faith. Hilary Putnam is perhaps most notable in this regard, that is to say, as a thinker who has constantly seen fit to revise, modify, or abandon positions that he once defended with the greatest resourcefulness and verve. (See especially Putnam 1990, 1992; also Norris 2002a.) However one could list many other cases – from Russell to Quine and Davidson – of analytic philosophers who have significantly shifted ground in response to criticism or emergent difficulties in defending their previous views.

So it is not so much a question, as some might think, of an 'analytic' mind-cast that disposes thinkers to stick to their philosophic guns and either flatly ignore any challenge or meet it on their own preferential terms through a redefinition of the issues. Rather it is a question of just how much there can still be left to say after so many sayings and takings-back, or of whether analytic philosophy might not be subject to the intellectual equivalent of a law of diminishing returns. Nor – to repeat – is this merely the kind of complaint often voiced by cultural pundits who deplore what they see as the arid technicality, the jargon-filled language, and the narrowly professional concerns of present-day academic philosophy. Such complaints miss the point that work of this kind – say in logic or philosophical semantics – is 'technical' by its very nature and just as much in need of a specialised vocabulary as work in theoretical physics or molecular biology. My argument here has more to do with the development of analytic philosophy since its early days and the impression one has, when surveying current debates, that there is not much left of the animating impulse – the sense of new possibilities – that comes across vividly in classic texts from the half-century or so of what one is tempted to call its heroic period.

To list those texts would be something of a party-game exercise and would no doubt divide opinion very quickly according to different philosophical perspectives. Still one could make a reasonable case for all or most of the following: Russell's 'On Denoting', Carnap's *The Logical Structure of the World*, Tarski's 'The Concept of Truth in Formalised Languages', Quine's 'Two Dogmas of Empiricism', Putnam's 'The Meaning of Meaning', Kripke's *Naming and Necessity*, and Davidson's 'On the Very Idea of a Conceptual Scheme' (see References section for bibliographical details). These all have three things in common, apart from their (more or less agreed) canonical status. First, they each articulate a distinctive position which responds to some previously dominant or widely held view, and which subjects that view to the kind of critique – on conceptual or logical grounds – that constitutes the hallmark of much work in the analytic mode. Second, they form an intelligible sequence in and amongst themselves which could well provide the basis for a narrative account of the chief debates in analytic philosophy of language and logic during the major part of the twentieth century. Third, they are all couched in the basically constructive or problem-solving idiom which can likewise be seen as a defining feature of that same collective enterprise, one that its subsequent critics and debunkers – Richard Rorty among them – have singled out as a main focus of attack (Rorty 1980, 1982). That is to say, they take for granted the existence of certain well-defined philosophical issues – primarily issues of language, logic, and truth – and also the prospect of finding some ultimate solution that will not be just a matter (as Rorty would have it) of switching the range of conversational topics.

Thus Russell thinks to solve the problem of empty or non-referring expressions by supplying a depth-logical analysis that discounts their misleading surface form and explains how precisely they fail to satisfy the norms of veridical utterance. Carnap and Tarski build upon Russell's achievement (including his treatment of the set-theoretical paradoxes) and seek to lay the ground for a logical-empiricist approach that would incorporate the full range of empirically verifiable observation-sentences on the one hand and logically necessary truths of reason on the other. Quine's 'Two Dogmas' subjects such claims to a thoroughgoing sceptical critique which rejects that distinction and argues the case that theories are always 'underdetermined' by the best empirical evidence and that evidence is always 'theory-laden' to the point where no statement (even the axioms of classical logic or the most straightforward of observation-sentences) can be held unrevisable 'come what may'. At which point – to continue my thumbnail sketch – there enters the 'new theory of reference' advanced by Kripke and the early Putnam, one that interprets this sceptical upshot (along with claims about the impossibility of translation across different languages or scientific paradigms) as proof that the standard descriptivist account bequeathed by Frege and Russell just won't work. Thus, according to the new theory, reference must be fixed and held steady throughout such changes in the currency of various observational or theoretical terms. It is fixed by an inaugural act of naming ('this is water', 'this is an electron') and held steady by the way that such names continue to apply despite and across those periodic shifts in the range of predicates that are taken to pick out genuine samples of the kind (see also Schwartz [ed.] 1977).

Meanwhile, on a different logico-semantic tack, Davidson claimed to expose the third, residual dogma of empiricism in Quine's continued espousal of a scheme–content dualism that opened the way to full-fledged ontological relativism. What he proposed in its place was a truth-based theory of interlingual and inter-theoretical translation which stressed those logical, syntactic, and conceptual features that all languages *must* have in common if they are

to function as an adequate means of communicative grasp. Where philosophers had typically gone wrong was in being over-impressed by the evidence
of semantic variation between one language and another, and under-impressed
by the range of formal attributes – devices for conjunction, disjunction, negation, quantification, cross-reference, and so forth – in the absence of which
they would lack any grounds for making such comparisons. So if 'syntax is
more sociable than semantics' (in Davidson's laconic phrase) it is because
these logico-syntactic resources are just what enable translation to occur
across such otherwise unbridgeable differences of language and culture
(Davidson 1984).

No doubt many readers will want to question my choice of landmark
texts, as well as the idea that a half-century of diverse philosophical debate
can be summed up in so brief and procrustean a fashion. Still I hope that
they will acknowledge my general point, that is, that mainstream analytic
philosophy has defined itself very largely as just the kind of thinking that in
principle addresses a circumscribed range of distinctive, well-defined, and
(again in principle) philosophically resolvable problems. Here again it
stands in marked contrast to that other way of doing philosophy, prototypically Austin's way, which also has a claim to the title 'analytic' – for want
of any handy alternative – but which eschews the quest for system and
method (or the problem-solving paradigm) in favour of a more pragmatic
approach to nuances of verbal implication. Of course this dichotomy soon
breaks down if one examines Austin's work – or that of other 'ordinary language' philosophers – and notes the constant tension between an attitude
of open-minded alertness to the complexities of everyday usage and the
residual desire to encompass those complexities within some generalised
speech-act theory or classificatory system. All the same, as I have said, in
Austin's case the tension is most often resolved through his readiness to let
the theory go (or redefine its operative terms) and allow that 'our common
stock of words' expresses 'connections and distinctions...more numerous,
more sound,...and more subtle...than any that you and I are likely to
think up in our armchairs of an afternoon' (Austin 1961: 182). This is
enough to place a large distance between his approach and the kinds of systematic speech-act theorising pursued by philosophers like John Searle,
albeit with constant reference to Austin's texts (Searle 1969). What Searle
chiefly wants to do is tighten up the theory's conceptual structure and then
use it – very much in the mainstream analytic fashion – as a means of
resolving certain tenacious philosophical problems, among them issues of
intentionality, of sense and reference, and even (most controversially) the
fact/value dichotomy. However this leads him to interpret Austin in a
highly selective way and to ignore those passages in Austin's writing – the
moments of methodological doubt and the numerous complicating anecdotes
from talk – which raise large questions with regard to any such problem-
solving claim.

To this extent (whatever the fixed preconception of most analytic philosophers) Jacques Derrida's deconstructive reading of Austin is far more in tune with the latter's express inclination to 'play old Harry' with these and other 'fetishised' philosophic topoi, rather than sorting them out into a structure of clearly marked conceptual or logico-semantic distinctions (Derrida 1977a,b, 1989; also Searle 1977). In fact the issue is more complex than that since it is Searle who accuses Derrida of muddying the waters of speech-act theory by requiring an impossible degree of conceptual rigour in its operative terms while it is Derrida who charges Searle with resorting to a 'merely approximative' pseudo-logic, and hence failing to register those symptomatic moments in Austin's text where that theory is forced up against the limits of coherent conceptualisation (Derrida 1989; Norris 2000). I have already – in Chapter 1 – discussed these matters at considerable length so will offer no further exegesis of the Derrida/Searle debate. However, the difference between Austin's and Searle's approaches to speech-act theory, as indeed between those of Derrida and Searle, may help to clarify my general point about the way that analytic philosophy works, namely on the premise that genuine advances are only to be had through a specification of problem-areas which can then be treated – and the problems resolved – through use of the appropriate conceptual tools. And this leads back to my opening question as to whether analytic philosophy in *this* sense (that is, the proprietary sense adopted by most mainstream practitioners) might now be at the stage of having pretty much exhausted its central, typical, or even self-constitutive topics of debate. That is to say, philosophers who identify with this tradition are now confronted with a choice between *either* re-engaging long-familiar issues in a different technical idiom *or* adopting alternative positions whose claim to novelty rests, most often, on their highly paradoxical or counter-intuitive character.

III

Such was at any rate my purpose in offering the brief run-down of major episodes – from Russell to Putnam and Davidson – two paragraphs above. While scarcely exhaustive it did lay out the main topics and parameters of analytic thinking as these have developed in the central areas of epistemology, philosophy of logic, and philosophical semantics. In what follows I shall try to make good my thesis through a number of examples which emphasise the point about its tendency to pour new wine into old (albeit re-labelled) bottles, or again – at risk of somewhat straining the metaphor – to concoct new brews whose inebriating qualities tend to disguise their dubious vintage. Thus a good deal of recent (post-1980) analytic philosophy shows all the signs of what Lakatos described as a 'degenerating research-programme', that is, an enterprise marked on the one hand by increasingly elaborate or baroque attempts to shore up an old paradigm, and on the other by proposals which avoid that nemesis only through a readiness to take on board some quite exorbitant claims (Lakatos 1977; also Lakatos and Musgrave [eds.] 1970).

One way of putting this case is to say that all analytic philosophy aspires to one or other of two ideals: to a discourse composed entirely of logical truths self-evident to reason or to a discourse of valid (verifiable or falsifiable) observation-statements whose truth-conditions are solely a matter of good empirical warrant. Such was the starting-point of analytic philosophy in its turn against the 'metaphysical' extravagances of previous, for example Bradleian-idealist thought, and its fixed resolve – as famously announced by Russell and Moore – to rule such extravagances firmly beyond the pale (see especially Hylton 1990). If early Russell-style logical atomism comes up for discussion nowadays it is mostly treated as a dead-end movement and one whose interest – if any – is confined to the history of bygone ideas rather than touching on issues of live philosophical concern (Russell 1986, 1993). In so far as it exerted an influence on later movements such as logical positivism and logical empiricism that influence is viewed as having generated problems that ultimately led to their own demise, problems such as that with the self-refuting nature of the Verification Principle or the impossibility – as Quine maintained – of upholding the logical empiricist distinction between analytic 'truths of reason' and empirical 'matters of fact'. (For a range of views, see Ayer [ed.] 1959; Parkinson [ed.] 1976; also Quine 1961.) Nevertheless there is a sense in which logical atomism not only prefigured those later problems in their sharpest, most intransigent form but also set the pattern for various attempts to resolve them by adopting different technical registers. Thus Davidson was able to show that Quine's purported demolition job on the two 'last dogmas' of logical empiricism was itself in hock to a third such dogma, that of the scheme/content dualism. Yet Davidson himself has proved oddly unable to resolve the main issue with regard to his own position, that is, the question as to whether his truth-based, Tarski-derived theory of 'radical translation' is one with substantive philosophical content or merely – as interpreters like Rorty would have it – a pragmatist approach that dare not quite speak its name (Davidson 1990, 2001; also Norris 1988; Rorty 1991, 1998).

Since then there have been various proposals for resolving this issue, among them epistemic theories which adjust the criteria for truth to the scope and limits of human knowledge, most often conceived as a limit-point notion that equates with idealised rational acceptability under optimal conditions of perceptual or cognitive grasp (Putnam 1981; Wright 1992). Yet these proposals still fall short of the realist requirement that truth should in principle transcend such limits and always be a matter of what is objectively the case rather than of what happens to lie within the compass of our own or even some idealised consensus of best opinion (Alston 1996; Katz 1998; Soames 1999). To which anti-realists like Dummett routinely respond that if truth is indeed recognition-transcendent or epistemically unconstrained then by very definition it cannot be known and must hence be discounted as an empty claim or a figment of metaphysical illusion (Dummett 1978, 1991). Indeed one could write a large part of the history of recent epistemological debate in terms of this effort to head off the threat of full-fledged scepticism concerning the existence of an 'external world' by accommodating truth to the scaled-down requirements of warranted assertibility or 'truth' in so far as it proves ascertainable by our best methods of demonstrative proof or empirical verification.

Anti-realism nowadays tends to take the form of an epistemological thesis with distinct metaphysical underpinnings, that is to say, a Dummett-style argument to the effect that it cannot make sense to posit the existence of truths that somehow (impossibly) transcend the utmost limits of human knowledge (see also Luntley 1988; Tennant 1987). All the same this position amounts to no more than a sophisticated update on the 'old' verification-principle, one that (in Dummett's case) makes greater allowance for conceivable advances in our range of mathematical proof-procedures or means of empirical investigation, but which still declares firmly in favour of the view that truth-talk is otiose and much better couched in terms of warranted assertibility. And the same goes for other versions of the argument – like that advanced by Putnam in his later writings – which profess to circumvent the sceptical challenge by renouncing any form of objective ('metaphysical') realism and adopting a sensible middle-ground approach which takes due account of those same epistemic limits (Putnam 1990, 1995). Thus truth can be defined for all practical purposes as that upon which enquiry is destined to converge at the limit-point of human knowledge or as simply coextensive with the range of statements that would gain assent from rational enquirers in possession of all the humanly available evidence. Yet of course it is just this qualifying clause – 'humanly available' – that the realist will reject outright since she will regard it as the merest of face-saving ploys designed to preserve some semblance of objectivity while in fact making terms with anti-realism at just the point where its arguments can be forced home to maximum effect (Norris 2002b).

To recapitulate briefly: my claim is that these debates have been conducted in such a way as to leave room only for two sorts of argument. On the one hand are those that rehearse a range of familiar moves within a normal paradigm (that of post-1930 analytic philosophy) which has, to be sure, undergone some fairly striking changes of technical register but which continues to focus on problems bequeathed by Russell and its other early proponents. These problems were raised in a particularly acute form by the doctrine of logical positivism and were then taken up and (supposedly) resolved by various later movements of thought – from the logical empiricists down – which can now be seen to have raised them again with fairly minor refinements of detail. Thus one could write a well-documented narrative account of recent analytic philosophy which treats it as a constant attempt to negotiate the gap between knowledge conceived as a matter of adequate epistemic warrant and truth conceived in objectivist terms as that which might always potentially transcend any such fallible means of ascertainment (Norris 2002b). On the other hand are those that adopt a more extreme position – like Dummettian anti-realism – whose upshot is decidedly counter-intuitive yet which still works out as a further variation on the same set of problematic topoi. Such arguments reject any middle-ground stance and push right through to the 'logical' conclusion that since we cannot acquire or manifest a knowledge of that which transcends our utmost powers of perceptual, epistemic, or conceptual grasp, we can be in no position to assert the existence of objective (recognition-transcendent) truths (Dummett 1978). So in the case of formally unproven, perhaps unprovable mathematical theorems like Goldbach's Conjecture – that every even number is the sum of two primes – we must accept that there exists a 'truth-value-gap' such that any statement of the theorem is neither true nor false to the best of our knowledge and hence neither true nor false *sans phrase*. The same goes for well-formed, intelligible statements with respect to putative historical events for which we possess no means of evidential or documentary proof, and which therefore belong to Dummett's 'disputed class', that is, the class of statements lacking a determinate truth-value. Quite simply, any 'gaps in our knowledge' must be taken to entail corresponding 'gaps in reality', and to leave no room for the realist belief that the truth or falsehood of such statements is decided by the way things stood historically, quite apart from the scope and limits of our knowledge concerning them. To which the realist predictably responds that this is an argument so drastically at odds with our best conceptions of truth, objectivity, and knowledge that it must be the product of some strong metaphysical *parti pris* or some misapplication of logical reasoning which has somehow led Dummett to endorse such a downright counter-intuitive thesis.

What I am calling 'normal' analytic philosophy – with a nod toward Thomas Kuhn – is the kind that strives to avoid such doctrinal extremes while accepting that they pose a genuine challenge and thus constitute a valid agenda for debate. Typical here would be the effort of certain thinkers, among them Crispin Wright, to defuse the issue between realists and anti-realists by adopting a flexible approach that assigns different criteria to different areas of discourse, these latter ranging all the way from areas like mathematics and the formal sciences where something *very like* objectivity seems to be in question to areas (like colour-perception or morals) that require some duly weighted allowance for the role of normal or optimal human response (Wright 1992). Thus Wright suggests various intermediate categories – such as 'superassertibility' and 'cognitive command' – which tend toward the objective end of the scale but which still fight shy of the realist requirement that truth be conceived as always potentially beyond our furthest powers of perceptual, cognitive, or epistemic grasp. In so doing he accepts at least the basic point of Dummett's anti-realist challenge, that is, that if truth is indeed recognition-transcendent then by very definition it cannot be known and must hence give rise to epistemological scepticism (see also Williams 1996).

Wright's answer – in short – is to try out alternative approaches which each have a claim to capture our working intuitions with respect to some particular topic-domain. Such, he maintains, is the best way to capture our strongly held belief (*contra* the anti-realist) that certain kinds of statement must surely possess an objective truth-value quite apart from any present or future limits on our means of proof or verification. What he will not quite concede – again with an eye to the standard sceptical riposte – is the full-fledged objectivist case that we are right about this and that epistemic criteria are simply out of place in the instance of well-formed but unproven mathematical conjectures, or sufficiently precise historical statements for which nevertheless we lack any firm documentary evidence. Rather than yield unnecessary hostages to fortune Wright goes some highly elaborate ways around in order to keep truth within the bounds of optimised epistemic warrant, or to close the gap (so easily exploited by anti-realists like Dummett) between truth and knowledge. Still the upshot – as with many response-dispositional approaches – is to lean so far in the opposite direction that any talk of 'objectivity' becomes little more than a fig leaf or a notional limit-point conception devoid of substantive content. (I argue this case more fully in Norris 2002b.)

No doubt it will be said that Wright's misgivings in this regard are of a specialised philosophical character and are thus far from 'normal' in the sense that they might be expected to strike most reflective persons with a well-developed interest in mathematics or history but without any knowledge of recent philosophical debate. That is, they are distinctly *abnormal* when set against the prevalent belief that mathematical truths are there to be discovered and in no way dependent on our knowledge of them, or again, that the truth-value of disputed or unverified statements with respect to historical events is a matter of what actually occurred rather than a question of what (as it happens) we are able to adduce by way of reliable evidence. However such misgivings are *philosophically* 'normal' in so far as they issue from a long tradition of sceptical doubt going back at least to Hume, and also – more directly – in so far as they represent the latest (analytically acceptable) version of a way of discussing these issues that has been central to the mainstream of post-1930 philosophy of language and logic. For those working within that tradition it has always been a matter of choice between middle-ground positions of the kind that Wright espouses and other, more provocative theses – such as Quine's radical empiricism or Dummett's strong anti-realist stance – which push further out on the range of available options. Thus 'normality' here is an essentially contested concept but one which still places certain limits on the sorts of argument that standardly count as belonging to the discourse or the topic-domain of 'genuine' philosophical debate. Roughly speaking, those limits are drawn so as to include even such extravagant proposals as Quine's or Dummett's just so long as they engage familiar issues in a certain, recognisably analytic register. Hence – to repeat – the widespread agreement that when a 'maverick' thinker like Derrida raises questions of a comparable philosophic import (questions concerning truth, reference, meaning, intention, speech-act validity, etc.) he does so in a 'literary' mode of address or a self-consciously performative style which can lay no claim to serious attention among those with an adequate grasp of the issues (Derrida 1977a,b). And this despite the fact – as I have argued at length elsewhere – that Derrida's reading of Austin (to mention just one example) is none the less perceptive, logically rigorous, and indeed analytically acute for its drawing out problematic aspects of Austin's argument which find no place within the normal discourse of speech-act theorists such as Searle (Norris 2000).

More than that: there is something decidedly odd about a conception of relative normalcy in philosophic discourse that adopts so dismissive an attitude with regard to certain, locally abnormal ways of treating these issues while allowing its own agenda to be set very largely by debates like those summarised above. That is to say, Quinean radical empiricism and Dummettian anti-realism are doctrines that could figure as normal, agreed-upon topics for discussion only in so far as that discussion had itself taken a markedly abnormal turn. Nor is it the case – as frequently claimed – that analytic philosophy is distinguished from recent (e.g., Derridean) 'continental' developments by its respect for the protocols of valid argument and conceptual rigour, and its non-reliance on 'literary' style as a substitute for just those prime philosophical imperatives. For there is a strong case to be made that an essay like Quine's 'Two Dogmas of Empiricism' gets away with advancing some extreme, paradoxical, and intensely problematic assertions chiefly on account of its adopting a rhetoric of down-to-earth, 'common sense' pragmatism which allows those assertions to be passed off as nothing more than straightforward (metaphysically unencumbered) statements of the obvious (Quine 1961). Thus 'Two Dogmas' has continued to exert great influence despite its commitment to a range of proposals – such as the radical underdetermination of theory by evidence, the theory-laden character of all observation-statements, the doctrine of ontological relativity, and the indeterminacy of translation across languages or conceptual schemes – which many would consider problematic to the point of philosophical incoherence. The same may be said of Quine's wider project of 'naturalised epistemology', involving as it does a physicalist (science-led) conception of what philosophy ought to become while failing to provide any normative criteria by which that enterprise might be informed or guided (Quine 1969; also Kim 1993; Kirk 1986). These criticisms are familiar enough and I shall therefore not pursue them any further here. More relevant for present purposes is the fact that 'Two Dogmas' has retained its classic status very largely through its claim to have moved discussion forward by demolishing the entire conceptual structure of old-style Carnapian logical empiricism. That is to say it offers another, prototypical instance of the way that analytic philosophy thrives on a constant renegotiation of the limits between 'normal' and 'abnormal' discourse, or by managing at once to engage constructively with previous (canonical) topics of debate and to bring about some more or less decisive shift in the terms of that engagement.

IV

Of course there is a sense – a fairly obvious sense – in which this is just the way that all enquiry proceeds, whether in philosophy, the physical sciences, or the social and humanistic disciplines. Thus one does not have to be a full-fledged Kuhnian to think that these disciplines typically alternate between longish periods of normal, workaday, or problem-solving activity and occasional brief periods of 'revolutionary' ferment (Kuhn 1970). Still less need one subscribe to Rorty's ultra-Kuhnian view that they would do much better to sustain themselves in a state of perpetual revolution and thus keep the conversation from becoming just a routine exchange of platitudes. This notion goes along with Rorty's belief that analytic philosophy has had its day – entered a phase of well-nigh terminal exhaustion – precisely on account of its ruling idea that there exist certain well-defined philosophical problems and constructive, philosophically adequate solutions to them (Rorty 1982). If they could just throw off their lingering attachment to this outworn analytic paradigm then philosophers would see their way clear to joining the poets, novelists, and other creative types who are best at coming up with brilliant new metaphors or narratives rather than stale old concepts and arguments (Rorty 1989). I should perhaps make it clear that my purpose in this chapter is not to endorse anything like Rorty's diagnosis of what has gone wrong with analytic philosophy or his ideas as to where philosophers should now be heading in their effort to play a more useful role in the 'cultural conversation of mankind'. What I am suggesting, rather, is that *certain aspects* of the analytic enterprise have resulted in a tendency to swing back and forth between a narrowly defined set of core problems that are taken as defining the very terms for serious philosophical debate and a conception of progress with regard to those same issues which involves periodic claims to have transvalued the entire preceding discourse. Thus Quine's demolition of the two 'last dogmas' of Carnapian logical empiricism makes way for Davidson's critique of the third residual dogma in Quine, that is, his attachment to the dualism of scheme and content, and this in turn to Rorty's somewhat gentler chiding of Davidson for his not pressing right through with a full-fledged pragmatist conception of truth as what's currently and contingently 'good in the way of belief' (Rorty 1991, 1998). My point – once again – is that the standard for 'normality' in analytic discourse is one that leaves room for quite radical challenges to the currency of previous debate but only in so far as those challenges are mounted on terms laid down in advance by a prevalent consensus as to just what counts as an adequate, constructive, or professionally competent address to the problems concerned.

Where Rorty goes wrong, I think, is in mistaking this particular feature of mainstream analytic philosophy for a general malaise that infects the entire philosophical enterprise and which can only be cured through a wholesale change in its current self-image as an expert discipline devoted to solving (what else?) certain distinctively philosophic problems. One can see how Rorty arrived at this verdict from a growing sense of disenchantment with the kinds of overly technical and ultra-specialised debate that have typified a good deal of recent work in the mainstream analytic tradition. One can also see why he took to recommending that philosophers should turn their attention elsewhere – to the American pragmatists, 'continental' thinkers like Heidegger and Derrida, as well as the poets and novelists – if they hoped to strike a more responsive chord in readers outside their own, narrowly academic or professional community. All the same Rorty's conversion-experience has resulted not so much in an attitude of straightforward indifference to those tedious old topics as in a curious habit of rehearsing them over and again – often on fairly technical terms – just in order to show that they cannot be resolved and should therefore quite simply be let drop with a view to promoting some wider shift in the ongoing 'cultural conversation' (Rorty 1991, 1998). Indeed it could be said that Rorty's position is just another stage in the working-out of those inherited problems about truth and knowledge that were first posed by the logical positivists and empiricists, then finessed (or purportedly resolved) in various ways by Quine, Davidson, and other thinkers in the post-1950 period. What these arguments – Rorty's included – all have in common is the odd combination of a radical or strong-revisionist rhetoric, one that claims to have emerged on the far side of those same inherited problems, with a willingness to take them as setting the agenda for informed philosophical debate. Thus when Rorty puts his case for junking the concerns of mainstream analytic philosophy he does so through the same kind of rhetorical move that Quine deployed against the logical empiricists and which Davidson deployed against Quine (among others). That is to say, there is a standard analytic way of proceeding which consists in (1) taking up certain problems from previous thinkers, (2) declaring those problems to result from a failure to think things through consistently, and (3) concluding that they simply don't exist – or exist only as pseudo-problems – once viewed from a different (less 'metaphysically' or philosophically encumbered) standpoint.

Given time one could easily extend this story though the various efforts of McDowell, Wright and the theorists of response-dependence to come up with some alternative formulation of the 'problem of knowledge' that would resolve the issue on terms acceptable to all (or most) parties. (See McDowell 1994; Wright 1992;

also Norris 2002b, for a critical survey of the response-dependence (RD) literature.) However my point – more generally – is that what has come to count as a valid move within the mainstream of analytic thought is one that respects this dual imperative of venturing some 'new' proposal with regard to certain inherited problems while ensuring that the novelty of any such move is effectively restrained by a due regard for certain agreed-upon protocols or topics of debate. These are still very much the same topics that preoccupied philosophers in the heyday of 'old-style' logical empiricism, as can be seen if one considers the kinds of issue that typically arise with respect to the claims of RD theory. Thus debate turns mainly on the question as to whether – or just how far – the Lockean idea of secondary qualities (those that involve some intrinsic appeal to normal or optimal modes of human perceptual response) might apply to other areas of discourse from mathematics to morals and the social sciences. (See especially Locke 1969, Book II, Chapter 8, Sect. 15; also Haldane and Wright [eds] 1993; Johnston 1992, 1993; Pettit 1991, 1992; Powell 1998; Railton 1998; Wedgwood 1998; Wright 1988a, 1998b.) In so far as it does, the RD theorists maintain, it should always be possible to construct a formula – a quantified biconditional – of the same type that standardly holds for the paradigm (Lockean) instance of colour-perception. In this latter case the sentence might run: 'x is red if and only if perceived as such by normal (perceptually well-equipped) subjects under normal lighting conditions', these latter to be specified in some detail, for example, 'at noon on a moderately clouded day and in the absence of any proximal light-source that might create interference-effects or other forms of optical illusion'. If there exists such a formula which (1) captures our best working intuitions for the area of discourse concerned, and (2) allows for an adequate (substantive) spelling-out of the relevant criteria, then – so it is argued – we shall have good grounds for adopting a response-dispositional account which should perfectly satisfy the realist (since it gives her all she needs in the way of normative epistemic grounds) while yielding no unnecessary hostages to sceptical fortune. That is to say, it blocks the sceptic's usual line of anti-realist response: that if truth-values are indeed objective or 'recognition-transcendent' then *ex hypothesi* they cannot be known to us – even at the ideal limit of enquiry – and are hence non-existent or strictly irrelevant for all philosophic purposes.

What the RD theorist thus hopes to provide is a solution to this seeming dilemma which grants sufficient weight to the role of duly normalised or optimised human response (thus avoiding the sceptical nemesis) while it allows that responses may sometimes come apart from standards of veridical perception (thus meeting the realist's chief demand). And if it works in the case of colour-perception then surely there is reason to think that the approach might be extended to other topic-areas by adjusting the range of normative criteria which define what shall count as a correct, valid, or adequate response under suitably specified conditions. With respect to moral-evaluative issues the formula would run somewhat as follows: 'act or decision x is virtuous if and only if deemed so by persons of superior moral judgement who are apprised of all the relevant facts, circumstances, motivating interests, conflicts of principle, and so forth'. And with respect to mathematics, logic, or the formal sciences it could always be provisoed so as to accommodate the realist's strong intuition that here, if anywhere, one has to acknowledge the existence of objective truth-values that might always in principle transcend or surpass our current-best means of proof or ascertainment. Thus: 'statement x is true (or theorem y is valid) if and only if it would gain assent from mathematicians or logicians possessing the requisite means of proof or the conceptual resources to determine its truth'. Alex Miller calls this a philosophy of 'humanised platonism', as distinct from the kind of pure-bred platonism that conceives numbers, sets, or classes as somehow existing in a realm of absolute, ideal objectivity (Divers and Miller 1999; Miller 1998; also Norris 2002b: 130–64). On the latter view – so anti-realists maintain – it becomes a complete mystery how we could ever have knowledge of mathematical truths, if not through some quasi-perceptual mode of epistemic contact with items that by very definition cannot be known in such a way (Hart [ed.] 1996). Hence (as I have said) the sceptical argument that 'nothing works' in philosophy of mathematics since any viable conception of knowledge entails giving up the idea of objective (recognition-transcendent) truth while any theory that posits the existence of objective mathematical truths must place them forever beyond our epistemic reach (Benacerraf 1983). Hence also the appeal of a 'humanised platonist' outlook according to which this dilemma can always be resolved by acknowledging the truth-constitutive role of best judgement (or optimised human response) but also taking care to define what counts as best judgement in terms which cannot but ensure its conformity with truth classically conceived. The solution requires nothing more than a willingness to see that such truths may be 'conceptually structured', that is, subject to the scope and limits of human cognisance yet still – crucially – a matter of getting things right by standards that are not just those of some prevalent communal practice or rule-following convention.

So the realist has nothing to lose, Miller thinks, by adopting a suitably provisoed RD approach while the anti-realist or the hard-line sceptic has everything to gain by renouncing the surely absurd idea that 'nothing works' in the philosophy of mathematics when mathematics itself has enjoyed such spectacular success in various fields of scientific knowledge. All the same this line of argument will scarcely satisfy the objectivist about mathematical truth since it still involves the notion that standards of correctness must *at some point* be referred to the human capacity for grasping or applying those standards. Moreover she will maintain that the objection holds good even if the biconditional is phrased or provisoed in such a way as to locate that point at the epistemic limit where best judgement attains maximal convergence with truth classically conceived. For this still leaves room for the

Kripkean sceptic or the Dummettian anti-realist to come back with their standard rejoinder, namely, that we cannot make sense of the idea of recognition-transcendent truths, or of the claim that what renders our statements true or false is the way things stand in mathematical reality and not the way things stand with respect to our best methods of proof or verification. In short, the realist will be apt to view this approach as just another instance of the epistemic fallacy, that which confuses ontological issues concerning the existence of numbers, sets, functions, and the objective truth-value of state-ments about them with issues concerning the scope and limits of human knowledge, irrespective of whether the latter is defined in normalised, optimal, or ideal (limit-point) terms. At any rate this will be her likeliest objection in so far as the RD emphasis falls on those various provisos to the right-hand side of the quantified biconditional that specify what counts as a valid response among suitably qualified subjects whose suitability consists in their possessing the right kinds of knowledge or conceptual powers. When construed in this way the RD claim amounts to no more than a roundabout or elaborately nuanced concession that anti-realists are right – though prone to overstate their case – in arguing against the very possibility of objective (recognition-transcendent) truths.

Of course there is another construal of that claim which shifts the empha-sis away from those detailed provisos and which simply equates best judge-ment (or optimal response) with a fail-safe disposition to endorse all and only that range of statements whose truth is a matter of objective math-ematical fact. This seems to be implied by the RD requirement that, in any given case, the quantified biconditional should possess not only intuitive warrant but also a force of self-evident or *a priori* truth. That is to say, it must follow *by very definition* that the formula provides a necessary link between the truth-value of some candidate statement and the specified kinds of condition under which its utterance meets the requisite standards of epistemic, assertoric, or judgmental warrant. However there is a problem in squaring this demand with the claim – much canvassed by theorists like Wright – that the RD approach does not come down to just an empty tautology or a trivial (purely circular) form of identity-statement (Wright 1988a; also Johnston 1992). Such would be the case if the right-hand provisos were framed in so vague or indefinite a way as to equate best judgement with 'whatever it takes', or with a clause to the effect 'fill out as required' from one topic-area to the next. Rather the provisos have to be substantive and to specify just the kinds of criteria – or the kinds of validating warrant – that apply in each instance. Yet it is hard to see how this could ever be achieved if the resultant biconditional is also to satisfy the *a priori* requirement, that is, that it should represent a truth self-evident to reason in virtue of its logical structure and the meaning of its various component terms.

This is why, as I suggested earlier, one can view the whole debate about response-dependence as a re-run of certain unresolved issues that first arose in the wake of Russellian logical atomism, that were taken up by the logical positivists and empiricists, and which have since re-surfaced at regular intervals in various contexts of argument. Chief among them – as Quine famously remarked – was the problem of distinguishing empirical content from logical form, or explaining just how any such line could be drawn between observation-statements that might always be revised under pressure from recalcitrant evidence and analytic 'truths of reason' that were thought to hold firm come what may. No doubt there is still room for disagreement as to whether Quine's argument carried the day or whether he was justified in pushing so far toward a radically holistic approach (Fodor and LePore 1991; Harding [ed.] 1976; Norris 1997a,b). All the same his essay can now be seen to have marked not so much a turning point in the history of mainstream analytic thought as a strong-revisionist intervention which, if anything, left philosophers with yet more problems on their hands.

This is nowhere more apparent than in the difficulty faced by RD theorists when it comes to explaining how the quantified biconditional can be thought of *both* as a suitable candidate for *a priori* status *and* as making adequate room for the specification of substantive validity criteria. For these latter must inevitably have to do either with certain empirical conditions that determine what shall count (say) as an instance of veridical colour-perception or with certain kinds of conceptual, for example, logico-mathematical competence that determine what shall count as a valid statement in the formal sciences. Yet in neither case does it seem at all plausible to treat the resultant biconditional as possessing *a priori* warrant or as true just in virtue of its logical form and the meaning of its various constituent terms. Thus when applied to perceptual qualities its normative claims amount to no more than a generalisation from our working knowledge of various intersubjectively endorsed criteria which dispose us to utter and approve such judgements as 'this is red', 'that tastes sweet', 'there's a high-pitched whistling noise', or whatever. And when applied to mathematical statements – such as 'Fermat's Last Theorem is true', uttered at some time after Andrew Wiles produced his celebrated proof – then their status is wholly unaffected by the formal device of constructing an appropriate biconditional along standard RD lines. For in so far as the resulting formula satisfies the requirement of apriority (or analyticity) it will yield nothing specific in the way of truth-conditions for the statement concerned or validity-conditions for mathematical proofs of the type in question. Rather, what renders such statements true and such proofs valid – assuming this to be the case – is (1) their mathematical correctness as a matter of objective (recognition-transcendent) warrant, and (2) their having been arrived at through a process of adequate formal, that is, axiomatic-deductive reasoning.

No doubt one can set up the quantified biconditional so as to incorporate just these requirements and make it *a priori*, in the case of mathematics, that the class of true statements and adequate proofs is by very definition the class of those endorsed by mathematicians infallibly disposed to produce the right answers by the right kinds of reasoning procedure. This is what the RD theorists do – or what they must logically be doing – when they claim that the biconditional holds as a matter of analytic truth-by-definition or (as they are somewhat misleadingly wont to phrase it) on *a priori* grounds. In that case, however, one is entitled to ask what has become of their other chief precept, namely the requirement that any provisos on the right-hand side of the biconditional be *not* just a matter of 'whatever it takes' for best judgement to coincide with truth but a matter of substantive specification with respect to the standards that properly apply in this or that area of discourse. Of course there is a sense – a trivial sense – in which this problem can be solved at a stroke by simply defining it away. For if indeed it is the case that the biconditional holds beyond peradventure (i.e., through suitable adjustment of the optimising clause) then the class of true statements *cannot but* equate – extensionally speaking – with the class of statements that would gain assent from those respondents definitionally best placed to determine their truth-value. However, once again, this saving device ends up by rendering the formula trivial or sheerly redundant since it leaves the provisos with no substantive work to do.

Thus in Plato's *Euthyphro* (a text much cited in the RD literature) Socrates takes the objectivist view that pious acts are those that the gods approve because the gods are always right in such matters and hence infallibly equipped to distinguish pious from impious acts (Plato 1977; Wright 1992). That is to say, the gods' verdict is truth-tracking – or 'detectivist' – in so far as it is constrained by objective moral standards that exist quite apart from their considered judgement but which they always endorse in virtue of (what else?) their divine moral wisdom. According to Euthyphro, conversely, it is the gods who must have the last word – whose judgement must decide the issue – since there exists no higher tribunal before which their verdicts might be challenged or overturned. That is to say, pious or impious acts *just are* those which the gods approve or disapprove, and there is simply no question (as Socrates would have it) of their judgement being answerable to any such objective constraint. From a certain point of view this dispute must look trivial since, after all, it is the same class of acts that will count as pious or impious irrespective of whether one espouses the Socratic or Euthyphronist approach. As Wright puts it:

it is open to each of the antagonists in this debate to acknowledge that pious acts extensionally coincide with those which, at least potentially, are loved by the gods. Socrates is contending that the piety of an action is, as it were, constituted independently of the gods' estimate of it, and Euthyphro is denying this, but each can agree that the two characteristics invariably accompany one another. (Wright 1992: 80)

On the other hand it is crucial from an RD viewpoint that this distinction should be thought of as marking a genuine difference since, after all, the main argument for any such approach is that it makes room for the active role of knowledge and judgement in assessing or evaluating truth-claims (whether moral or mathematical) that would otherwise surpass the utmost powers of human cognitive grasp. That is, it promises – like Miller's idea of 'Humanised Platonism' – to achieve a workable *modus vivendi* between those in the hard-line realist camp who reject any notion of truth as epistemically constrained and those in the hard-line anti-realist camp who deny the very possibility of objective or recognition-transcendent truths. All that is needed is for both parties to agree (1) that the class of pious acts or mathematical truths must be coextensive whether one adopts a Socratic (realist) or Euthyphronist (best-judgement) approach, and (2) that by devising a suitably provisoed biconditional for each area of discourse one can satisfy both the realist's demand for something more than *de facto* communal assent and the anti-realist's requirement that truth be brought within the compass of humanly attainable knowledge. In which case such wranglings could henceforth cease and the rival parties learn to accept that their quarrel was merely the upshot of a failure to adopt this ecumenical view.

All the same one may suspect that the RD approach is not so much a genuine solution to the realism/anti-realism dispute as a means of shifting that dispute onto different ground through a reformulation of its basic terms which leaves all the same problems firmly in place. Thus there is still the big question – noted above – as to whether this approach can consistently claim to formulate certain necessary truths with regard to the constitutive role of best judgement in various fields of knowledge while also yielding a substantive (non-trivial) account of just what it takes for best judgement to play that truth-preservative role. That is to say, Wright's point about the extensional equivalence between the class of pious acts on either interpretation is one that could easily be turned back against this whole idea of response-dependence as means of escape from all our epistemic woes. For if the issue between Socrates and Euthyphro – or between realism and anti-realism – can always be finessed by taking this line then some disputants on both sides might well conclude that it is a non-issue, or one with no interest beyond the sphere of hypercultivated RD debate. At the same time those on either side who wished to maintain their doctrinal position could interpret Wright's equivalence-argument as having absolutely no impact on it, or indeed as providing welcome support when construed on their own favoured terms. Thus the realist might claim – plausibly enough – that in so far as 'best judgement' is *analytically* defined as that which by very definition equips its possessors to 'track' or to 'detect' the class of veridical statements, pious acts, or whatever, then why not cut out all this otiose talk and accept her argument for the objective, that is, recognition-transcendent character of truth? Yet the anti-realist would have just as good warrant – granted the extensional-equivalence thesis – for maintaining that any such objectivist position is a piece of sheer metaphysical extravagance which runs into all the well-known problems about reconciling truth with knowledge. In which case surely we might as well drop it in favour of the view that truth just is what corresponds to the deliverance of optimised response or best judgement, these latter (after all) being so defined – *via* the standard quantified biconditional – as to exclude *a priori* any possibility of error on the part of suitably equipped respondents.

Thus it looks very much as though the RD approach is one that can scarcely advance debate beyond the kinds of problem that have loomed periodically in the discourse of mainstream analytic philosophy since the heyday of logical empiricism. That is, this approach tends constantly to veer between the twin poles of its aim to produce some purely definitional (hence tautologous) account of the necessary link between truth and best judgement, and its need to avoid the charge of empty circularity by offering some adequate (substantive) account of what best judgement actually involves with respect to this or that specified topic-domain. Thus it replicates the difficulty faced by logical empiricists – as likewise by earlier logical positivists such as Schlick and Neurath – when they strove to explain how sense-data (phenomenalistically construed) might somehow be conjoined on the one hand with a credible realist epistemology and on the other with those logical 'laws of thought' which provided the necessary means for any valid reasoning on the evidence (Achinstein and Barker [eds] 1969; Hanfling [ed.] 1981). In the case of RD theory this problem is further compounded by the tendency to take a proto-type instance – the Lockean empiricist conception of 'secondary qualities' like colour or taste – and extend it to the treatment of other, often very different domains such as mathematics, logic, and the formal sciences. Or again, there is the RD approach to moral philosophy which likewise very often starts out from a set-piece topic of debate (i.e., the *Euthyphro* contrast) and constructs its agenda on just the terms – as I have argued, the restrictive and at times even trivialising terms – which are thus laid down in advance. What results is a kind of chronic oscillation between claims whose logical self-evidence or unrestricted range of application renders them empirically vacuous and claims that are tailored so specifically to this or that area of discourse (*via* the RD provisos) that they lack the required degree of *a priori* warrant.

V

This problem is among the most abiding features of analytic philosophy from Russell to the present day. It is one that cuts across the so-called 'linguistic turn' and which figures just as much in Tarski's treatment of the concept of truth in formalised languages as in the kinds of epistemo-metaphysical debate that characterised 'old-style' Russellian logical atomism (Russell 1986, 1993; Tarski 1956). Thus the chief difficulty with attempts, like Davidson's, to extract a substantive account of truth from Tarski's original theory is that it comes down on the one hand to a purely tautological definition (' "snow is white" is true if and only if snow is white') and on the other to a statement of the conditions for truth relative to some particular – albeit logically regimented – language (Davidson 1984, 1990, 2001). So this theory is subject to the twofold charge of reducing to sheer vacuity as a matter of formal truth-by-definition and of failing to provide any guidance as to how those formal conditions might apply across or between languages. More than that, it places large problems in the way of philosophers like Davidson who rest their case on its applicability to natural languages – or its promise of resolving issues such as Quinean 'radical translation' or Kuhnian 'incommensurability' across paradigms – but who then have to tactfully ignore Tarski's express reservations in that regard. It is not hard to see how these problems are carried over into the discourse of RD theory with its constant vacillation between claims of purely logical, analytic, or *a priori* warrant and its assertion that those claims are not *merely* tautological (or vacuous) since they are subject to qualification by way of the relevant provisos. What this purported solution fails to acknowledge is the fact that any gain in substantive (discourse-specific) content is bought at the cost of its declared aspiration to the status of *a priori* truth while any move to strengthen the latter claim goes along with a strictly unavoidable loss of relevance to this or that topic-domain.

I have taken RD theory as test-case for my wider thesis that analytic philosophy – or one major branch of it – can be seen as a series of repeated (unsuccessful) attempts to resolve those problems that first arose in the wake of logical atomism and which thereafter set the terms for any 'new' approach that purported to shift the debate onto different ground. Thus there is sense in which all such projects, from logical positivism down, have involved on the one hand a logicist commitment to the idea that every discourse should ultimately aspire to the status of the analytic proposition, and on the other – strictly incompatible with this – a desire to avoid any charge of merely tautological, vacuous, or circular argument by introducing various kinds of empirical constraint or domain-relative (topically specified) proviso. Nothing could more strikingly illustrate the point than McDowell's recent efforts to resolve this problem through a return to Kant or, more specifically, to certain passages in Kant's First *Critique* which lend themselves – so he thinks – to a 'detranscendentalised' reading that might yet succeed in bridging the gulf between sensuous intuitions and concepts of understanding (Kant 1964; McDowell 1994). Thus we are to think of Kantian 'spontaneity' and 'receptivity' as inter-involved or mutually reliant to the extent that such dichotomies simply fall away and there is no longer any 'problem of knowledge' of the kind that has created so much trouble for philosophers over the past century. 'If we restrict ourselves to the standpoint of experience itself', McDowell writes,

> what we find in Kant is precisely the picture I have been recommending: a picture in which reality is not located outside a boundary that encloses

the conceptual sphere...The fact that experience involves receptivity ensures the required constraint from outside thinking and judging. But since the deliverances of receptivity already draw on capacities that belong to spontaneity, we can coherently suppose that the constraint is rational; that is how the picture avoids the pitfall of the Given. (McDowell 1994: 41)

However – as I have argued at length elsewhere – this proposal only succeeds in resurrecting all the same vexatious dualisms (of mind/world, subject/object, empirical experience/conceptual scheme) that have marked the discourse of analytic philosophy from its earliest stage and whose ultimate source, ironically enough, is Kant's failed attempt to reconcile the claims of 'transcendental idealism' and 'empirical realism' (Norris 2000: 172–230). Moreover, these problems are often evident in the tortuous character of McDowell's arguments, such as the claim that 'reality is not located outside a boundary that encloses the conceptual sphere', where his purpose is presumably to show that we can have all the 'reality' we need even if that reality is in some sense conceptually structured, but where the claim is wide open – on closer inspection – to construal in transcendental-idealist terms. Here again, as with Miller's proposal for a 'humanised platonist' approach to the philosophy of mathematics, what we are offered is a form of quasi-realism which attempts to strike a working balance between objectivist and RD conceptions of truth but which ends up by swinging much further in the latter direction.

Of course McDowell is well aware of this and makes a point of disowning those other, problematical aspects of Kantian thought that have led to various more recent (e.g., logical empiricist) forms of the same impasse. Thus:

Kant also has a transcendental story, and in the transcendental perspective there does seem to be an isolable contribution from receptivity. In the transcendental perspective, receptivity figures as a susceptibility to the impact of a supersensible reality, a reality that is supposed to be independent of our conceptual activity in a stronger sense than any that fits the ordinary empirical world. (McDowell 1994: 41)

If we can just set aside these metaphysical excrescences then Kant can be taken as pointing the way toward a naturalised epistemology that has managed, at last, to dismount from the 'seesaw' – or to damp down the otherwise unstoppable oscillating movement – created by dualist conceptions of mind and world. Rather, according to McDowell, 'we should understand what Kant calls "intuition" – experiential intake – not as a bare getting of an extra-conceptual Given, but as a kind of occurrence or state that already has conceptual content' (ibid.: 9). Yet what can this mean if not that 'reality' (or reality so far as we can know it through various kinds of 'experiential uptake') is conceptually structured and hence – as in Kant – a product of the mind's *a priori* synthesising powers? No doubt there is great merit in McDowell's suggestion that we should try to overcome the dualist impasse and, so far as possible, loosen the hold of those other formulations in Kant's First *Critique* – like his talk of the mind's power, through the exercise of judgement, to bring phenomenal intuitions under adequate concepts – that have subsequently wrought such large-scale epistemological havoc. Thus '[t]he original Kantian thought was that empirical knowledge results from a co-operation between receptivity and spontaneity. (Here "spontaneity" can be simply a label for the involvement of conceptual capacities.) We can dismount from the seesaw if we can achieve a firm grip on this thought: receptivity does not make an even notionally separable contribution to the co-operation' (ibid.: 9). Yet once again there no escaping the clear implication that those 'conceptual capacities' are always already in play and hence that any notion of 'empirical knowledge' must always be subject to the transcen-dental-idealist proviso: 'knowledge within the scope and limits of human conceptualisation'.

Of course this would be nothing short of self-evident – the merest of epistemological truisms – if McDowell were only saying that we cannot know more than we are equipped to know through our various powers of perceptual, cognitive, or conceptual grasp. However his claims appear to go much farther than that, as can be seen from the above-cited passage where he speaks of 'reality' – not just our knowledge of reality – as somehow 'not located outside a boundary that encloses the conceptual sphere'. That is to say, McDowell's argument takes a markedly idealist (and anti-realist) turn at the point where its claims extend beyond the realm of epistemological debate and purport to have a bearing on ontological issues or questions of objective (verification-transcendent) truth. His 'solution', in brief, is to treat such questions as fundamentally misconceived since they entail the idea – the impossible idea – that reality could somehow fall outside the sphere of jointly operative 'spontaneity' and 'receptivity' which alone renders our experience meaningful or intelligible. That is, he concurs with the RD theorists thus far at least: that the realism issue is much better treated not on the drastically dichotomous terms of objectivist *versus* verificationist conceptions of truth but through a sensible allowance for the role of human judgement as a means of reconciling their otherwise endless and strictly unresolvable dispute. Yet here again his approach works out, like theirs, as one that maintains a semblance of even-handedness between the rival parties while in fact leaning very strongly in an anti-realist direction. For if indeed it is the case that 'reality' and truth cannot be thought of as somehow located 'outside a boundary that encloses the conceptual sphere' then plainly – to adapt early Wittgenstein – the limits of our world are the limits of whatever we can know or discover concerning it. Granted, there is a plausible reading of this claim that interprets 'our world' as the world of our perceptual experience, knowledge, or judgement and which thus brings it out in keeping with a common sense epistemological view. However in McDowell and the RD theorists that view very often gives way to the far from common sense idea that 'our world' thus construed is also – of necessity – the only kind of world that can reasonably figure in our thinking about issues of reality and truth. And from here it is no great distance to the Dummettian anti-realist or verificationist claim that the limits of our knowledge are indeed the limits of our world since truth *just is* whatever we are able to reliably assert, prove, or ascertain by the best formal or epistemic means at our command (Dummett 1978, 1991).

I think it fair to say that Dummett's position in this regard should count among the more extravagant varieties of recent philosophical doctrine. Thus it requires us to accept, or at any rate seriously to entertain, a range of anti-realist propositions about the status of truth-claims in sundry areas of discourse – mathematics and history among them – where the default assumption is that truth might always surpass our best powers of proof or verification. On Dummett's account, conversely, it can make no sense to posit the existence of truth-values that possess some kind of objective validity quite apart from the question of whether or not we are able to manifest a knowledge of them or to recognise the signs of such knowledge in others through a shared grasp of the relevant criteria for counting them among the class of valid (epistemically warranted statements. Thus mathematicians are mistaken – in the grip of a false metaphysic – if they think that there must be some objective (bivalent) truth-value to the statement 'Goldbach's Conjecture is true' despite their present lack of any formal proof-procedure, their inability to specify what such a procedure might involve, and the fact that it cannot be verified (or falsified) by even the powerful computer program. And historians are likewise deluded if they suppose that there must be some objective truth of the matter with regard to well-formed but unverifiable statements – such as 'George W. Bush misread his autocue six times during the private practice-run for his inaugural speech to Congress' – which belong to Dummett's 'disputed class' of neither-true-nor-false propositions. Quite simply, to repeat, such 'gaps in our knowledge' are also 'gaps in reality' since any claim that there exist certain truths beyond reach of our best means of verification is a claim that of its very nature transcends the limits of humanly attainable knowledge. In his later work Dummett concedes that there are problems with this strict verificationist approach and that one needs to make room for mathematical theorems or historical conjectures which might *in principle* be verified or falsified given some conceivable advance in our state of knowledge (Dummett 1991). Yet he still draws the line at admitting any version of the basic realist argument that truth is epistemically unconstrained, that is, that it might always turn out to elude even our most advanced, sophisticated, or maximally well-informed means of ascertainment.

Indeed Dummett is quite frank in avowing that among the chief motives for anti-realism is a refusal to accept such limits on the scope of human understanding or knowledge. What the realist regards as an outlook of due humility with regard to our inherently restricted scope of knowledge or powers of comprehension the anti-realist takes as a straightforward affront to the principle that truth cannot possibly transcend the limits of warranted assertibility. Thus:

> [r]ealism about the past entails that there are numerous true propositions forever in principle unknowable. The effects of a past event may simply dissipate...To the realist, this is just part of the human condition; the anti-realist feels unknowability in principle to be intolerable and prefers to view our evidence for and memory of the past to be constitutive of it. For him, there cannot be a past fact no evidence for which exists to be discovered, because it is the existence of such evidence that would make it a fact, if it were one. (Dummett 1991: 7)

This seems to me an extraordinary statement and none the less so for its representing a position that has gained a respectable following among many philosophers who would count themselves very much a part of the analytic mainstream. No doubt one can make the case – with some support from Dummett's more cautious formulations – that he is not so much committed to anti-realism in its full-strength doctrinal form as devoted to exploring its implications in different areas of discourse with the aim of discovering just how far (or in just which areas) the case can plausibly be made. Still it is clear enough to any reader of Dummett's work that he *is* so committed, occasional misgivings aside, and that his stance amounts to a firm repudiation – on logico-metaphysical grounds – of the very idea that there might exist objective truth-values (whether with regard to mathematical statements or assertions of historical fact) that lie beyond the reach of verification.

What is all the more remarkable is that Dummett is led – even, on his own account, logically forced – to this extreme sceptical conclusion by a line of reasoning that claims to represent the only possible answer to scepticism in its other, more familiar guise. Thus the anti-realist standardly maintains that it is realism which has created all the trouble (the so-called 'problem of knowledge') since it entails the existence of objective truth-values which might always, in principle, transcend our current or future-best means of epistemic grasp. As Michael Williams puts it: 'if the world is an objective world, statements about how things appear must be logically unconnected with statements about how they are; this lack of connection is what familiar thought-experiments dramatically illustrate' (Williams 1996: 56). And indeed there is a sense – an ultimate sense – in which the sceptic will always and inevitably have the last word if once he succeeds in shifting discussion onto ground where the realist agrees to accept such a view of truth as epistemically or evidentially constrained. However this is a concession too far for anyone who espouses the realist position that truth-values are *not* thus constrained since they pertain to the way things stand (or once stood) with respect to mathematical or historical reality and not to any state of human knowledge, no matter how advanced or refined. Thus, as Williams nicely remarks, '[t]he sceptic's fallacy is that he takes the discovery that, in the study, knowledge of the world is impossible for the discovery, in the study, that knowledge is impossible generally' (Williams 1996: 53). And the realist will most likely wish to go further by asserting that even here there is a certain equivocation between 'knowledge = justified true belief' (where 'justified' is taken objectively as a matter of truth to the way things stand in reality) and the epistemic view which likewise endorses that classical account but which defines truth in terms of evidential or epistemic warrant.

Hence – as I have said – the marked tendency among RD theorists to start out from what is basically an anti-realist agenda and then suggest various detailed refinements in order to placate the realist opposition, or convince them that in fact they have nothing to lose through the turn to best judge-ment (or idealised rational acceptability) as a substitute for objective truth. More than that, they stand to gain a good deal in the way of intellectual credibility if this means that scepticism can no longer get a hold since truth is brought back within the compass of knowledge and knowledge thus saved from the predicament described by Williams, namely, that 'statements about how things appear must be logically unconnected with statements about how they are'. Yet the realist will again be quick to point out that this supposed benefit is dearly bought in so far as it tailors its concept of truth to the scope and limits of human knowledge, even when conceived as a matter of optimised epistemic warrant. Any such concession can only strike the realist as a veritable Trojan horse which opens the way to renewed scepticism by offering the semblance of an adequate solution to the problem of know-ledge while in fact undermining the realist case at its very foundations.

What this amounts to, in effect, is just another version – albeit less overt or more hedged around with qualifying clauses – of the attitude that Dummett describes in the above-cited passage, that is, the anti-realist's refusal to accept that 'there are numerous true propositions forever in principle unknowable'. Where the RD theorist will typically dissent is at the point where Dummett goes on from this expression of a certain philosophical (perhaps temperamental) mind-set to put forward a doctrine with large revisionist claims on our most basic concepts of knowledge, truth, and reality. Thus if 'the anti-realist feels unknowability in principle to be intolerable and prefers to view our evidence for and memory of the past to be constitutive of it', the RD theorist will find something equally disturbing – even 'intolerable' – about the notion that historical truths are evidentially constrained to the point where what occurred or did not occur can be thought of as entirely dependent upon (or constituted by) our best sources of evidence.

And she will doubtless be yet more disturbed by the idea that any truth-value attaching to statements in mathematics, logic, or the formal sciences must likewise be regarded as requiring our possession of some adequate proof-procedure or, at least, our capacity to recognise and grasp such a proof should one turn up. This is why the chief effort of RD theory has been to elaborate a range of third-way alternatives – such as Miller's 'humanised platonism' – whereby to avoid grasping either horn of what must surely (they think) be a false dilemma (Miller 1998). Yet those alternatives must still leave the realist wholly unimpressed since they yield crucial ground at just the point where an objective (alethic) conception of truth gives way to an epistemic conception which accepts the force of that dilemma and the need to resolve it by adopting some duly provisoed compromise solution. Either that or they reduce – as on one plausible reading of Miller's and other such proposals – to a species of empty (tautological) claim according to which best judgement or optimised response *cannot but* coincide with truth objectively construed.

My point is that analytic philosophy over the past half-century and more has been hooked on certain issues which recur over and again in various guises and which – to put it bluntly – resemble a kind of deep-laid neurotic repetition complex. The primal scene (at risk of overdoing this Freudian analogy) is one that looms from its early period and whose chief episodes include Russellian logical atomism, Vienna-school logical positivism, and the logical empiricist doctrines of Carnap, Tarski, and others. On the one hand what those movements most strikingly embodied was a confident belief in their own ability to define what should count as a genuine philosophic problem and to work at producing a constructive solution through various kinds of applied logical and epistemo-critical procedure. On the other, what they have now come to represent – after so many failures to achieve that aim and after various determined assaults from sceptics like Quine – is a legacy that weighs so heavily on current thinking as to block any prospect of moving the debate onto new ground. To be sure there are those who have claimed to achieve such a break by acknowledging the force of Quine's criticisms but then suggesting some alternative way forward. Among the latter – as I have said – are Davidson's truth-based (Tarskian) semantics for overcoming the Quinean problem of radical translation, McDowell's revisionist reading of Kant as a source of epistemological guidance, and Crispin Wright's version of the RD case for evaluating different areas of discourse in respect of their relative positions on a scale from 'cognitive command', *via* 'superassertibility', to straightforward reliance on the verdict of accredited best opinion. Yet these proposals all have one thing in common, namely their assumption that issues of truth cannot be adequately addressed except by way of an epistemic or – in Davidson's case – a logico-semantic approach that avoids any notion of statements as possessing a truth-value entirely independent of our best knowledge or means of verification. That is to say, they inherit the basic agenda handed down from logical empiricism, whatever the various refinements introduced by way of response to those sceptical challenges thrown up in subsequent debate.

VI

Of course some commentators, Rorty among them, have taken this to show that analytic philosophy has run out of steam – arrived at a stage of terminal exhaustion – and that there is simply no point in continuing to discuss such outworn topics as truth, knowledge, or realism (Rorty 1989, 1998). Rather we should 'change the subject' and give up the deluded idea that philosophy is in the business of providing constructive solutions to problems that lie within its own area of special expertise. That idea was just a product of the old epistemological paradigm espoused by thinkers from Plato to Descartes and Kant, along with the latter-day 'linguistic turn' in its more technical (i.e., distinctively analytic) forms (Rorty 1980). So it is time for philosophy to come back in from the professional cold and reassume its role as one more voice in the 'cultural conversation of mankind'. It will then have no ambition to get things right according to certain agreed-upon standards of 'rigour' and 'truth' but will aim – as should every discipline from the natural to the social and human sciences – to change the current conversational rules by inventing new metaphors, narratives, or preferred modes of self-description. What it *won't* any longer be tempted to suppose is that any one such language might finally succeed in limning the ultimate nature of reality or capturing the 'logical structure of the world'. For the upshot of pushing right through with the linguistic turn – that is to say, beyond the point where analytic philosophy wished to hold the line – is to accept that *no* language could ever be more than a passing expression of those various contingent values, interests, and priorities that happen to accord with some particular stage of the evolving cultural story. Moreover this lesson is reinforced, Rorty thinks, by the way that analytic philosophy has gone since its founding doctrines received their comeuppance at the hands of Quine and throughout the whole history of subsequent attempts – such as those of Davidson, Putnam, McDowell, and others – to redeem some vestige of its early promise.

So if philosophy has any kind of future then it is one in which philosophers willingly renounce their delusions of epistemological grandeur and acknowledge the commonality of interests that brings them out on a level with the poets, novelists, literary critics, ethnographers, cultural historians, and Kuhnian 'revolutionary' scientists. On this view there is no difference – ultimately speaking – between what is achieved by some mould-breaking advance in molecular biology or subatomic physics and what is achieved when a strong-revisionist interpreter comes up with some new reading of Milton or a new slant on historical events (Rorty 1991: 79–92). To suppose otherwise is merely to reveal one's adherence to a bygone 'normal' paradigm based on such surely obsolete notions as the existence of a language-independent reality (complete with natural kinds, properties, causal powers etc.) and a top-down conception of the 'unity of science' which keeps all the disciplines firmly in their place. (On the latter, see Carnap 1995; Causey 1977; also – for some strongly dissenting views – Cartwright 1999; Dupré 1995; Galison and Stump [eds] 1996.) Indeed we should do well to invert this orthodox scale of priorities and accept that since interpretation goes 'all the way down' therefore the scientists have more to learn from the literary critics and creative redescribers than the latter are likely to pick up through a misplaced reverence for scientific truth and method.

In short, there is nothing in the nature of things or in the nature of those various disciplines that could justify the standard division of labour and require our deference to expert opinion on this or that specialist topic. What should take its place in the postmodern-pragmatist culture of Rorty's envisioning is a readiness to cast such notions aside and embrace the full range of creative possibilities opened up by the linguistic turn. For there is always the chance that some fresh-minted metaphor from a field such as literary criticism might revolutionise the discourse of molecular biology, or again, that medical science might just be transformed through an encounter with the kinds of 'thick' narrative description practised by certain ethnographers or postmodernist (i.e., sceptically inclined) historians. Thus the sole difference between 'texts' and 'lumps' is a difference in how inventively we are able to describe them rather than a difference in their essential natures, properties, or – least of all – the proper (duly certified) sorts of expertise that it takes to interpret a text or to analyse a lump. Take your lump to a gifted psychoanalyst rather than a chemist, biologist, or oncologist and you might get a description that changes your whole way of thinking about lumps. Take your text to one of these latter and you might, albeit more improbably, pick up any number of bright new ideas about the scope for creative reinterpretation. At any rate there is nothing about texts or lumps – no intrinsic difference of kind – that could stand in the way of your so doing or make it a downright crazy choice of specialist consultant.

That Rorty's position is itself downright crazy is an argument that does not very often get aired but which should strike anyone with the least grasp of scientific (not to mention common sense and practical) realities. As concerns lumps – or certain types of lump – it is a position that consorts all too readily with that strain of ostrich-like wishful thinking which Russell diagnosed in the Jamesian variant of American pragmatism and whose manifestations range all the way from Christian Science to Hollywood romance and the idea that 'positive thinking' can effect a cure to otherwise incurable forms of malignant disease (James 1907, 1909; Russell 1999). As concerns philosophy it comes across clearly in Rorty's attitude of postmodern-pragmatist disdain for old-fashioned realist talk of natural kinds and their various constitutive properties, structures, or causal powers. Such talk is just a throwback, he thinks, to the quaintly animistic habit of thought which supposed that the gods might somehow be placated by chanting the right words (Rorty 1991: 80). On the contrary, this charge comes back like a boomerang if one considers what Rorty's recommendation amounts to in terms of advice to a cancer patient with the choice between seeking expert medical attention and trusting to the power of positive thought as an alternative means of recovery. However my point is not so much to belabour Rorty's position as to remark – once again – on the curious way that an argument of so extravagant (even preposterous) a character can find its place and be treated to a great deal of serious discussion among philosophers in the broad analytic community (see for instance Brandom [ed.] 2000; Festenstein and Thompson [eds] 2001; Malachowski [ed.] 2002). Nor, for that matter, has Rorty managed to achieve such a radical break with the mainstream analytic tradition that he no longer feels any need to engage those philosophers on their own elective ground. Thus his recent work has a habit of constantly circling back to issues in epistemology and the more technical branches of philosophy of language which he professes to have left far behind but which can still be seen to exert a well-nigh compulsive grip on his thinking (Rorty 1991, 1998). That is to say, his own ambivalence in this regard is matched by his critics' curious propensity to vacillate between a strongly dissenting (at times scandalised) response to his 'end-of-philosophy' pronouncements and a readiness to grant his work the favour of detailed exegesis and critique very much in the normal analytic mode.

What I think this shows – as so often throughout the history of post-Quinean debate – is the way that analytic philosophy has stretched itself around a range of heterodox claims that appear to reject its most basic precepts of method and conceptual rigour yet which it none the less manages to take on board since their seeming radicality counts as such only on terms that the tradition has laid down in advance. Thus it is not hard to see how Rorty's blithely dismissive take on the agenda of his ex-colleagues in the analytic enterprise is one that represents just a further stage in the sequence of strong-revisionist proposals that started out with Quine's radical critique of the logical empiricist programme and have since become something like the stock-in-trade of philosophy in its 'post-analytic' mode. Yet they have all displayed a kind of residual attachment to just those problems that characterised logical empiricism and which continue to exercise the critics and revisionists despite their regular claim to have shifted the entire debate onto different ground. Thus, in Quine's case, it is only by attacking the two 'last dogmas' of Carnap-style logical empiricism – that is, the analytic/synthetic distinction and the idea of a one-to-one correspondence between statements and empirically verifiable matters of fact – that he can put forward his drastic counter-proposal for a full-fledged holistic theory of truth and a thoroughly naturalised epistemology (Quine 1961, 1969). Moreover, there is a sense in which Quine's argument falls prey to an objection just as powerful as that which plagued the exponents of logical positivism, that is, their failure to come up with any statement of the verification principle that would meet its own requirements for counting as a meaningful (and not empirically vacuous) claim (Parkinson [ed.] 1976). For Quine the equivalent problem arises if one adopts his holistic approach and then asks by what standard of empirical warrant or rational acceptability we are to judge the various, often very striking and carefully formulated statements that carry the burden of his argument in 'Two Dogmas of Empiricism'. Thus it provides yet another striking example of the way that even such heterodox proposals – like Rorty's after him – are soon drawn back into the orbit of certain preoccupying topics and issues which continue to exercise a strong hold despite repeated assertions to the contrary.

I started out by citing Austin's quip about philosophers' typical habit of equivocation between 'the bit where you say it' and 'the bit where you take it back'. What I have tried to describe in the course of this chapter is the similar pattern of alternating phases through which analytic philosophy has moved – or by which its various debates have been marked – over the past half-century and more. On the face of it that pattern has involved a constant swing between the advancement of certain extraordinary theses that are taken to constitute a strong challenge to prevalent modes of thought and the normalising trend by which these soon become accepted as part of philo-sophy's standard agenda for resolving a manageable range of well-defined problems. However this distinction very quickly begins to blur – as with Austin's attempt to beat the bounds between ordinary language and its vari-ous deviant, non-standard, or 'extraordinary' mutants – when one examines the kinds of position adopted by some philosophers well within the fold of analytic respectability. Thus few proposals could be more deviant with respect to our normal way of thinking than Dummett's case for the non-existence of objective (recognition-transcendent) truth-values or Kripke's Wittgenstein-derived sceptical idea that standards of correctness in arithmetical rule-following are fixed solely by communal assent (Dummett 1978; Kripke 1982; also Miller and Wright [eds] 2002). Yet in each case they have spawned a huge volume of analytic commentary where philosophers express a good range of conflicting views but where all seem agreed on the basic conviction that these are genuine (philosophically deep) issues and should therefore count among the core topics of informed analytic debate.

Whence – as I have said – the emergence of other, more moderate or middle-ground approaches (like that of the RD theorists) which seek to accommodate some aspects of the sceptic's case while not giving up on a viable, that is, duly qualified or 'humanised' version of realism in this or that area of discourse. All the same this proposal can be seen to work out as a distinctly skewed compromise solution that yields far more to the sceptic or the anti-realist than to anyone who takes an opposing view (Norris 2002b). Nor indeed should we expect otherwise, given the extent to which analytic philosophy has inherited a certain predominant agenda which inclines it toward an epistemic rather than an alethic (objectivist) conception of truth. Of course this is not to deny that some philosophers whose work belongs squarely within the analytic tradition have put up a strong defence of alethic realism and done so, moreover, in terms that reject the kinds of dilemma foisted upon the realist by sceptical arguments which take for granted the epistemic view that truth cannot possibly transcend the limits of optimised response or best judgement (see for instance Alston 1996; Devitt 1997; Katz 1998; Soames 1999). Thus they are wholly unimpressed by the epistemic theorist's claim to show that one can *either* have objective truth *or* humanly attainable knowledge but surely not both unless at the cost of downright self-contradiction. This idea that 'nothing works' in philosophy of mathematics – or in any other field where similar issues arise – can only strike the realist as a downright perversion of philosophical intelligence brought about by the failure to distinguish questions of objective truth from questions of know-ledge, certainty, or epistemic warrant.

VII

I have argued here that a great deal of the history of analytic philosophy can best be understood as a sequence of fairly minor variations on debates that started out in the wake of logical atomism and which have subsequently managed to set the terms for what counts as a relevant or properly informed contribution. When Rorty claims that his kind of postmodern-pragmatist outlook is the end of the road this tradition has been travelling at least since Quine, he is right to that extent but wrong to conclude that no other options exist, or that realism has somehow been discredited along with the various programmes that have attempted to formulate some scaled-down ('empirically adequate' or epistemically acceptable) version of the realist claim. What drops out of sight on the Rortian account – as likewise in other, less provocative renditions of the epistemic case – is the sheer unlikelihood that truth should just happen to be tailored to the scope of present-best or even best-attainable human knowledge. Hence the chronic oscillation between, on the one hand, exorbitant claims that can pass themselves off as nothing more than common sense wisdom (Rorty) or as the upshot of rigorously conse-quent logical reasoning (Dummett) and, on the other, an 'ordinary' discourse which resists such conclusions but fails to provide any adequate alternative approach. To the extent that analytic philosophy is defined in terms of this particular agenda then it does invite the charge of being stuck in a degenerating research-programme, that is, one that has managed to protract its tenure only at the cost of maintaining an ever more elaborate protective belt of provisos and qualifications (Lakatos 1977). Thus – to speak plainly – there is a great deal of current analytic writing that is concerned not so much with substantive philosophical issues as with wiredrawn differences of view or minor technicalities of idiom. In this respect it is strongly reminiscent of that late phase in the defence of Ptolemaic astronomy which has often served (for scientific realists) as a cautionary instance of the strategies adopted by rearguard proponents of a false theory in the face of recalcitrant evidence.

Given time one could press this analogy further through a detailed comparison with the way that theory was sustained by adducing an ever more complex and ad hoc apparatus of epicycles designed to head off any possible objection on empirical or theoretical grounds. Moreover, one could show that the same technique is implicitly endorsed by a wide range of latter-day positions in epistemology and philosophy of science. Chief among them – as I have argued – are Quine's radically holistic approach and the kindred line of argument that runs from Kuhnian paradigm-relativism to Rorty's strong-descriptivist conception of truth as what is currently and contingently 'good in the way of belief'. For good measure one can add a whole range of purported compromise solutions such as van Fraassen's idea of 'constructive empiri-cism' with its attempt to block sceptical arguments by adjusting the limits of empirical warrant to those of technologically unaided human observation (van Fraassen 1980, 1989). In this case the epicycles come in through van Fraassen's need to render the theory plausible by constantly redefining what should count as a legitimate extension of human perceptual powers, as for instance through his decree that optical telescopes or microscopes fall within the class of acceptable prosthetic devices while radio telescopes and electron microscopes must be taken to fall outside it. Yet this discounts all the surely overwhelming evidence to date that progress has most often occurred through successive refinements of observational technology that allow scientists to advance beyond the inherently restricted (anthropocentric) notion of common sense perceptual warrant. That is to say, it entails the odd claim that if astronauts could just get close enough to observe the planets of some remote star through their space-ship window – perhaps with the aid of an optical telescope – then this would qualify as an empirically adequate observation but not if they were situated farther off and deployed some sophisticated high-resolution device that was able to correct for perceptual errors or distortions. And of course the same applies to objects in the microphysical domain – such as atoms and electrons – where van Fraassen is likewise committed to the view that since their existence can only be maintained through theoretical conjecture plus the use of advanced observational technology therefore we had much better treat them as useful (instrumentally convenient) posits. Otherwise – he argues – scientists and philosophers of science are exceeding their empirical remit and yielding unnecessary hostages to sceptical fortune.

However this amounts to no more than an ingenious update on Machian-positivist and old-style verificationist arguments, with the further liability of having to ignore (or to argue away) all the impressive advances in scientific knowledge brought about by those new technologies. (For further discussion, see Norris 1997c: 167–95, 196–217; also Churchland and Hooker [eds] 1985.)

Besides, van Fraassen's argument ends up by endorsing a version of the surely untenable thesis that 'man is the measure', or that the existence of entities depends upon their falling within a certain range of humanly perceptible magnitude, velocity, distance from point of observation, and so forth. Thus it fails to acknowledge a central truth about the history of science: that among the chief hallmarks of scientific progress to date is precisely the willingness to doubt, challenge, or reject the supposed self-evidence of the senses. Had this not been the case then astronomy would still be stuck at the stage of saving empirical (Ptolemaic) appearances by introducing all manner of epicyclic adjustments while chemistry would still be working with a version of pre-Daltonian theory and physics with an Aristotelian conception of matter seeking out its natural place in the cosmological order of the elements. What I wish to emphasise, again, is the extent to which this and other recent proposals for defeating or outflanking the sceptical threat have taken it for granted that realism is no answer since any claim that truth may transcend our best powers of verification is such as to place an insuperable gulf between knower and known or between our best current theories and whatever they purport to describe or explain. Hence the logical positivists' desire to close that gap by adopting a phenomenalist (sense-data based) conception of scientific knowledge, one that would prevent it from opening up in the first place. Hence also – as I have argued – the continuing effort by various thinkers of an anti-realist or 'constructive empiricist' persuasion to achieve the same end while avoiding all the well-known problems with logical positivism, among them its failure to produce a workable (non-self-refuting) statement of the verification principle and, more to the point in this context, its commitment to a form of methodological solipsism.

What these all have in common – along with response-dispositional approaches – is the fixed idea that objective or alethic realism cannot hold up under pressure of sceptical doubt. In which case, it is thought, any adequate answer to the sceptic must adopt some version of the standard argument for renouncing objectivist truth in favour of empirical or epistemic warrant. Then again, the specification can always be stretched so as to encompass such limit-point epistemic notions as 'truth at the end of enquiry' and idealised rational acceptability', or Wright's 'superassertibility' and 'cognitive command' (Putnam 1981; Wright 1992). However these proposals in the end come down to just a series of further variations on the line of anti-sceptical but also anti-realist argument that has typified such a broad swathe of movements in mainstream analytic philosophy. It seems to me that one can reasonably view this debate as having imposed a restrictive agenda and even a certain programmatic limit on the range of duly nuanced, qualified, or provisoed standpoints that philosophers are able to adopt in keeping with that same agenda. However this is not to take the Rortian path and urge that we should simply opt out of the whole analytic enterprise so as to leave the field open for some welcome new turn in the cultural conversation.

Indeed, as I have argued, it is largely on account of Rorty's own obsession with this particular set of epistemological issues that he has arrived at so sweeping a negative diagnosis and so vague an idea of what the wished-for 'post-philosophical' culture might look like. That is to say, he assumes – like others of a broadly pragmatist persuasion – that if truth-talk is to possess the least degree of credibility then it must go by way of those issues and at some stage confront the choice between trundling along in the old analytic ruts and switching to the surely more attractive view that 'truth' is whatever we make of it by the best, most creative or socially acceptable descriptions to hand.

Thus Rorty is altogether dismissive of other approaches within the analytic tradition – realist approaches of various kinds – which strike him as simply missing the point, that is, that we can have no conceivable access to reality except in so far as it reaches us under some description or other. Yet this is once again to adopt an epistemic approach (one with its ultimate source in Kant) and to think that by showing how *that* approach runs up against certain intractable problems one has also shown how *any* form of realism must fall prey to the same kinds of terminal aporia. In which case – Rorty concludes – it is the merest of delusions for alethic realists or for advocates of the causal theory of reference like Kripke and early Putnam to claim that their alternatives to the Frege–Russell descriptivist tradition can somehow get philosophy off the sceptical-relativist hook (Kripke 1980; Putnam 1975; also Schwartz [ed.] 1977; Wiggins 1980). And from here it is but a short step to the full-fledged linguistic constructivist view which in principle accepts no limits on the scope for redescribing reality in terms that accord with what presently counts as 'good in the way of belief'.

It seems to me that Rorty's postmodern pragmatism is the end of one road that analytic philosophy has been travelling from logical empiricism, *via* Quine's 'Two Dogmas', to the current range of middle-ground positions staked out by the RD theorists and thinkers like Wright. Where these efforts most strikingly betray their lineage is in finding such difficulty – and such need for complex epicyclic manoeuvring – with respect to the basic realist idea that truth might always transcend the limits of best opinion or epistemic warrant. This is the most extraordinary feature of much that passes for business-as-usual among philosophers who take the Dummettian anti-realist challenge as setting the terms for informed debate across a range of topic-areas from epistemology and philosophy of mathematics to ethics, historiography, and the social sciences. What it fails to acknowledge – in keeping with this whole entrenched philosophical mind-set – is the fact that one can have *both* an objectivist (alethic) conception of truth *and* an acceptance that our means of finding it out will always be subject to various contingent epistemic constraints. These latter may have to do with our limited perceptual faculties, lack of the required technological resources, restricted access to the relevant information-sources, or inability to follow mathematical proofs or logical arguments beyond a certain stage of formal complication. But there is no reason – anti-realist prejudice apart – to suppose that such constraints carry across from the limits of our knowledge at any given time to the truth-value of well-formed statements concerning objects or events in their topic-domain.

Thus Dummett is merely pushing this line of argument to its logical conclusion when he asserts that any 'gaps in our knowledge' must also be construed as 'gaps in reality' (Dummett 1978). On the contrary: we can have no grasp of what it *means* for there to be such gaps in our knowledge unless those gaps have to do with truths which obtain independently of us and our present or even our future-best-possible epistemic state. That is to say, these are not 'truth-value gaps' (as Dummett maintains) but matters concerning which we are simply not in a position to decide one way or the other, lacking the necessary evidence or means of ascertainment. Thus anti-realism trades on a curious double strategy whereby, on the one hand, truth is confined to the limits of humanly achievable knowledge while, on the other, nothing is allowed to count as knowledge unless it meets the requirements of a certain restrictive (i.e., epistemically constrained) conception of truth. What drops completely out of the picture is the alternative alethic conception according to which it is a straightforward fallacy to suppose that truth could ever be a function of epistemic warrant. This is, I take it, the default position not only for hard-line philosophical realists but also for those who want to make reasonable working sense of how genuine discoveries come about – or how our knowledge progressively approximates to truth – in fields such as science, mathematics, and history. That it is now a source of such deep-laid perplexity – to the point where some have managed to persuade themselves that 'nothing works' (philosophically speaking) in the case of mathematics – is an odd reflection on the way that much analytic philosophy has boxed itself into a sceptical corner of its own elaborate devising. My chief hope for this book is that it may have opened up some alternative prospects and thus (albeit in a sense very different from that intended by Wittgenstein) managed to release a few flies from the conceptual fly-bottle.

References

Achinstein, Peter and Stephen F. Barker (eds) (1969). *The Legacy of Logical Positivism: Studies in the Philosophy of Science*. Baltimore: Johns Hopkins University Press.

Alston, William P. (1996). *A Realist Theory of Truth*. Ithaca, N.Y.: Cornell University Press.

Austin, J.L. (1961). *Philosophical Papers*. Oxford: Oxford University Press.

——(1963). *How To Do Things With Words*. Oxford: Oxford University Press.

Ayer, A.J. (ed.) (1959). *Logical Positivism*. New York: Free Press.

Benacerraf, Paul (1983). 'What numbers could not be', in Benacerraf and Putnam (eds). pp. 272–94.

Benacerraf, Paul and Hilary Putnam (eds) (1983). *The Philosophy of Mathematics: Selected Essays*, 2nd edn. Cambridge: Cambridge University Press.

Blackburn, Simon and Keith Simmons (eds) (1999). *Truth*. Oxford: Oxford University Press.

Brandom, Robert B. (ed.) (2000). *Rorty and his Critics*. Oxford: Blackwell.

Carnap, Rudolf (1967). *The Logical Structure of the World: Pseudoproblems in Philosophy*, trans. R.A. George. London: Routledge & Kegan Paul.

——(1995). *The Unity of Science*, trans. M. Black. Bristol: Thoemmes Press.

Cartwright, Nancy (1999). *The Dappled World: A Study of the Boundaries of Science*. Cambridge: Cambridge University Press.

Causey, Robert L. (1977). *Unity of Science*. Dordrecht: D. Reidel.

Churchland, Paul and C.M. Hooker (eds) (1985). *Images of Sciences: Essays on Realism and Empiricism, with a reply from Bas C. van Fraassen*. Chicago: University of Chicago Press.

Davidson, Donald (1984). 'On the very idea of a conceptual scheme', in *Inquiries into Truth and Interpretation*. Oxford: Oxford University Press. pp. 183–98.

——(1990). 'The structure and content of truth'. *Journal of Philosophy* 87: 279–328.

——(2001). *Subjective, Intersubjective, Objective*. Oxford: Clarendon Press.

Derrida, Jacques (1977a). 'Signature event context'. *Glyph* Vol. 1. Baltimore: Johns Hopkins University Press. pp. 171–97.

——(1977b). 'Limited Inc abc'. *Glyph* Vol. 2. Baltimore: Johns Hopkins University Press. pp. 75–176.

——(1989). *Limited Inc*, 2nd edn (ed.) Gerald Graff. Evanston, Ill.: Northwestern University Press.

Devitt, Michael (1997). *Realism and Truth*, 2nd edn. Princeton: Princeton University Press.

Divers, John and Alex Miller (1999). 'Arithmetical platonism: reliability and judgement-dependence', *Philosophical Studies* 95: 277–310.

Dummett, Michael (1978). *Truth and Other Enigmas*. London: Duckworth.

——(1991). *The Logical Basis of Metaphysics*. London: Duckworth.

Dupré, John (1995). *The Disorder of Things: Metaphysical Foundations of the Disunity of Science*. Cambridge, Mass.: Harvard University Press.

Festenstein, Matthew and Simon Thompson (eds) (2001). *Richard Rorty: Critical Dialogues*. Cambridge: Polity Press.

Fodor, Jerry and Ernest LePore (1991). *Holism: A Shopper's Guide*. Oxford: Blackwell.

Frege, Gottlob (1952). 'On sense and reference', in P.T. Geach and M. Black (eds), *Selections from the Philosophical Writings of Gottlob Frege*. Oxford: Blackwell. pp. 56–78.

Galison, Peter and David J. Stump (eds) (1996). *The Disunity of Science: Boundaries, Contexts, and Power*. Stanford, Ca.: Stanford University Press.

Haldane, J. and Wright, C. (eds) (1993). *Realism, Representation and Projection*. Oxford: Oxford University Press.

Hanfling, Oswald (ed.) (1981). *Essential Readings in Logical Positivism*. Oxford: Blackwell.

Harding, Sandra G. (ed.) (1976). *Can Theories be Refuted? Essays on the Duhem-Quine Thesis*. Dordrecht: D. Reidel.

Hart, W.D. (ed.) (1996). *The Philosophy of Mathematics*. Oxford: Oxford University Press.

Hylton, Peter (1990). *Russell, Idealism, and the Emergence of Analytic Philosophy*. Oxford: Clarendon Press.

James, William (1907). *Pragmatism: A New Name for Some Old Ways of Thinking*. New York: Longmans.

——(1909). *The Meaning of Truth*. New York: Longmans.

Johnston, Mark (1992). 'How to speak of the colours', *Philosophical Studies* 68: 221–63.

——(1993). 'Objectivity refigured: pragmatism without verificationism', in Haldane and Wright (eds). pp. 85–130.

Kant, Immanuel (1964). *Critique of Pure Reason*, trans. Norman Kemp Smith. London: Macmillan.

Katz, Jerrold J. (1998). *Realistic Rationalism*. Cambridge, Mass.: MIT Press.

Kim, Jaegwon (1993). *Supervenience and Mind*. Cambridge: Cambridge University Press.

Kirk, Robert (1986). *Translation Determined*. Oxford: Clarendon Press.

——(1999). *Relativism and Reality: A Contemporary Introduction*. London: Routledge.

Kripke, Saul (1980). *Naming and Necessity*. Oxford: Blackwell.

——(1982). *Wittgenstein on Rules and Private Language*. Oxford: Blackwell.

Kuhn, Thomas S. (1970). *The Structure of Scientific Revolutions*, 2nd edn. Chicago: University of Chicago Press.

Lakatos, Imre (1977). *The Methodology of Scientific Research Programmes* (ed.) J. Worrall and G. Currie. Cambridge: Cambridge University Press.

Lakatos, Imre and Alan Musgrave (eds) (1970). *Criticism and the Growth of Knowledge*. Cambridge: Cambridge University Press.

Locke, John (1969). *An Essay Concerning Human Understanding* (ed.) A.S. Pringle-Pattison. Oxford: Oxford University Press.

Luntley, Michael (1988). *Language, Logic and Experience: The Case for Anti-Realism*. London: Duckworth.

Malachowski, Alan (ed.) (2002). *Richard Rorty* (4 vols). London: Sage.

McDowell, John (1994). *Mind and World*. Cambridge, Mass.: Harvard University Press.

Miller, Alex (1998). 'Rule-following, response-dependence, and McDowell's debate with anti-realism', *European Review of Philosophy* 3: 175–97.

Miller, Alex and Crispin Wright (eds) (2002). *Rule-Following and Meaning*. Chesham: Acumen.

Norris, Christopher (1988). 'Reading Donald Davidson: truth, meaning and right interpretation', in *Deconstruction and the Interests of Theory*. London: Pinter. pp. 59–83.

——(1997a). *Resources of Realism: Prospects for 'Post-Analytic' Philosophy*. London: Macmillan.

——(1997b). *New Idols of the Cave: On the Limits of Anti-Realism*. Manchester: Manchester University Press.

——(1997c). *Against Relativism: Deconstruction, Critical Theory, and Philosophy of Science*. Oxford: Blackwell.

——(2000). *Minding the Gap: Epistemology and Philosophy of Science in the Two Traditions*. Amherst, Mass.: University of Massachusetts Press.

——(2002a). *Hilary Putnam: Realism, Reason, and the Uses of Uncertainty*. Manchester: Manchester University Press.

——(2002b). *Truth Matters: Realism, Anti-Realism and Response-Dependence*. Edinburgh: Edinburgh University Press.

Parkinson, G.H.R. (ed.) (1976). *The Theory of Meaning*. Oxford: Oxford University Press.

Pettit, Philip (1991). 'Realism and response-dependence', *Mind* **100**: 597–626.

——(1992). *The Common Mind: An Essay on Psychology, Society, and Politics*. Oxford: Oxford University Press.

Plato (1977). *Euthyphro, Apology of Socrates, and Crito* (ed.) John Burnet. Oxford: Clarendon Press.

Powell, Mark (1998). 'Realism or response-dependence?', *European Review of Philosophy* 3: 1–13.

Putnam, Hilary (1975). 'The meaning of meaning', in *Mind, Language and Reality*. Cambridge: Cambridge University Press. pp. 215–71.

——(1981). *Reason, Truth and History*. Cambridge: Cambridge University Press.

——(1990). *Realism With a Human Face*. Cambridge, Mass.: Harvard University Press.

——(1992). *Renewing Philosophy*. Cambridge, Mass.: Harvard University Press.

——(1995). *Pragmatism: An Open Question*. Oxford: Blackwell.

Quine, W.V. (1961). 'Two dogmas of empiricism', in *From a Logical Point of View*, 2nd edn. Cambridge, Mass.: Harvard University Press. pp. 20–46.

Railton, Peter (1998). 'Red, bitter, good', *European Review of Philosophy* 3: 67–84.

Rorty, Richard (ed.) (1967). *The Linguistic Turn: Recent Essays in Philosophical Method*. Chicago: University of Chicago Press.

——(1980). *Philosophy and the Mirror of Nature*. Oxford: Blackwell.

——(1982). *Consequences of Pragmatism*. Brighton: Harvester.

——(1989). *Contingency, Irony, and Solidarity*. Cambridge: Cambridge University Press.

——(1991). *Objectivity, Relativism, and Truth*. Cambridge: Cambridge University Press.

——(1998). *Truth and Progress*. Cambridge: Cambridge University Press.

Russell, Bertrand (1905). 'On denoting', *Mind* **14**: 479–93.

——(1986). *The Philosophy of Logical Atomism and Other Essays* (ed.) J.G. Slater. London: Allen & Unwin.

——(1993). *Our Knowledge of the External World as a Field for Scientific Method in Philosophy*. London: Routledge.

——(1999). 'William James's conception of truth', in Blackburn and Simmons (eds). pp. 69–82.

Ryle, Gilbert (1954). *Dilemmas*. Cambridge: Cambridge University Press.

——(1963). *The Concept of Mind*. Harmondsworth: Penguin.

Schwartz, Stephen (ed.) (1977). *Naming, Necessity, and Natural Kinds*. Ithaca, N.Y.: Cornell University Press.

Searle, John R. (1969). *Speech Acts: An Essay in the Philosophy of Language*. Cambridge: Cambridge University Press.

——(1977). 'Reiterating the differences: a reply to Derrida'. *Glyph*, Vol. 1. Baltimore: Johns Hopkins University Press. pp. 198–208.

Soames, Scott (1999). *Understanding Truth*. Oxford: Oxford University Press.

Tarski, Alfred (1956). 'The concept of truth in formalised languages', in *Logic, Semantics and Metamathematics*, trans. J.H. Woodger. Oxford: Oxford University Press. pp. 152–278.

Tennant, Neil (1987). *Anti-Realism and Logic*. Oxford: Clarendon Press.

van Fraassen, Bas C. (1980). *The Scientific Image*. Oxford: Clarendon Press.

——(1989). *Laws and Symmetry*. Oxford: Clarendon Press.

Wedgwood, Ralph (1998). 'The essence of response-dependence', *European Review of Philosophy* 3: 31–54.

Wiggins, David (1980). *Sameness and Substance*. Oxford: Blackwell.

Williams, Michael (1996). *Unnatural Doubts: Epistemological Realism and the Basis of Scepticism*. Princeton, N.J.: Princeton University Press.

Wittgenstein, Ludwig (1953). *Philosophical Investigations*, trans. G.E.M. Anscombe. Oxford: Blackwell.

Wright, Crispin (1988a). 'Moral values, projection, and secondary qualities'. *Proceedings of the Aristotelian Society*, Supplementary Vol. 62: 1–26.

——(1988b). 'Euthyphronism and the physicality of colour', *European Review of Philosophy* 3: 15–30.

——(1992). *Truth and Objectivity*. Cambridge, Mass.: Harvard University Press.

Index